THE
BABY WHISPERER
SOLVES ALL YOUR
PROBLEMS

(BY TEACHING YOU HOW TO
ASK THE RIGHT QUESTIONS)

THE
BABY WHISPERER
SOLVES ALL YOUR
PROBLEMS

(BY TEACHING YOU HOW TO
ASK THE RIGHT QUESTIONS)

Sleeping, Feeding, and Behavior—
Beyond the Basics from
Infancy Through Toddlerhood

TRACY HOGG
WITH MELINDA BLAU

ATRIA BOOKS
New York London Toronto Sydney

ATRIA
BOOKS

1230 Avenue of the Americas
New York, NY 10020

ISBN: 0-7434-8893-8

First Atria Books hardcover edition January 2005

Designed by Nancy Singer Olaguera

10 9 8 7 6 5 4 3 2 1

649
HOGG

To Sara and Sophie, my loving daughters (TH), and

To Henry, my sweet grandson (MB), and

All the other babies and toddlers who allow us to love them

and to be less than perfect

ACKNOWLEDGMENTS

I first want to thank the parents of all "my" babies and toddlers for their stories, their cooperation, and their continued input on my website.

I'd like to thank especially Melinda Blau, and Henry, not only for turning out to be an Angel baby but for being our special mascot. Never let it be said that he was a guinea pig.

Finally, thanks to my family and devoted friends, especially my Nan, whose love, guidance, and strength continue to amaze me daily.

—*Tracy Hogg*
Los Angeles, California

When I stepped off an airplane to meet Tracy Hogg in Los Angeles for the first time in the fall of 1999, she drove me to a modest house in the Valley, where a bedraggled young mother met us at the door and literally thrust a screaming three-week-old into Tracy's arms. "My nipples are killing me. I don't know what to do," she said, tears running down her cheeks. "He wants to breast-feed every hour or two." Tracy held the baby close to her cheek, cooing "shh . . . shh . . . shh" into his ear, and within seconds, he was quiet. She then turned to the young woman and said, "Okay, here's what your baby is telling you."

I have witnessed dozens of similar scenes over these last five years in which Tracy sweeps into a household, tunes in to the baby or toddler, and manages to get right to the heart of the problem. It has been a delight and a constant source of amazement to watch Tracy's work, to analyze how to put it on paper, and to get to know her in the process. Thank you Tracy, for inviting me into your universe and for allowing me to be your voice. Three books later, we've become friends, and I've become a pretty proficient baby whisperer myself—just in time to try it out on Henry.

This book would not have been possible without the sanity and savvy of Eileen Cope of Lowenstein Literary Associates, our intrepid agent, who once again shepherded us from proposal to finished book; and Barbara

Lowenstein, who is always in the wings, guiding, cuing, sometimes pushing us all to do better.

I am indebted as well to our editor at Atria Books, Tracy Behar, who shared our vision for this book and made it better, and to Wendy Walker and Brooke Stetson, who helped keep us on track.

Always last but never least, I appreciate my extended family of relatives and friends, who are there for me throughout it all. You know who you are.

—Melinda Blau
Northampton, Massachusetts

CONTENTS

FROM BABY WHISPERING TO PROBLEM SOLVING

My Most Important Secret

Becoming Ms. Fix It

Dearest mums and dads, babies and toddlers, it is with both joy and humility that I offer what in many ways is my most important baby-whispering secret: how to solve any problem. I have always been proud of my ability to help parents understand and care for their young children and feel honored whenever a family asks me into its life. It's a very intimate and rewarding experience. At the same time, being an author has also given me a public face. Since I published my first two books in 2001 and 2002, I've had a series of adventures and surprises that go beyond anything I could have imagined as a girl in Yorkshire. Besides my usual private consultations, I've been on the radio and the telly. I've traveled around the country and the world and met some of the most wonderful parents and children who've opened their homes and hearts to me. I've spoken to thousands more via my website, reading and responding to their email and joining them in my chat rooms.

But don't worry. Despite my newfound worldliness, I'm still the same old me, still down there slogging away in the trenches. In a way, though, I *have* changed a bit: No longer am I just the Baby Whisperer. I'm now Ms. Fix It, too. And it's all because of you.

In my travels, on my website, and in my email in-box, I've gotten many letters of thanks and confirmation from mums and dads who have followed my advice. But I've also been inundated with requests for help from those of you who bought my first book too late. Maybe you're trying to get your baby on a structured routine, as I suggest, but you're not sure whether the same principles apply to eight-month-olds as to newborns. Maybe you're confused about why your child isn't doing what other children are doing. Or maybe you're faced with a deeply entrenched sleep problem, feeding difficulty, or behavior issue—or, poor dear, all of the above. Whatever the dilemma, your anguished refrain is almost always the same: "Where do I begin, Tracy—what do I do first?" You also wonder why some of the strategies I suggest don't seem to work with *your* baby (see pages 7–12).

I've been fielding such questions for several years now and consulted on some of the most difficult cases I've ever seen: a three-month-old twin who had such bad reflux that he could barely keep a meal down and never slept longer than twenty minutes, day or night; a nineteen-month-old who wouldn't eat solid food because she awoke almost every hour to breast-feed; a nine-month-old whose separation anxiety was so severe her mother literally couldn't put her down; a two-year-old head-banger whose tantrums were so frequent his parents were afraid to leave the house. It was through solving problems such as these that I became known as Ms. Fix It—and why I now know that I must help you go beyond the basic strategies I laid out in my earlier books.

In this book, then, I want to take your hand, ease your fears, and show you how to empower yourself as a parent. I want to teach you what I've learned from a lifetime of baby whispering as well as answer the questions you've asked me. I want to teach you how to think like me. Of course, even though I might try to list all the problems you might encounter, every young child and every family is slightly different. So when parents come to me with a particular challenge, to assess what's really going on in that household and with that baby or toddler, I always ask at least one, if not a string of questions, both about the child and about what parents have done so far in response to their situation. Then I can come up with a proper plan of action. My goal is to help you understand my thought process and get you in the habit of asking questions for yourself. In time, you, too, will not only be a baby whisperer but an ace problem solver—a Mr. or Ms. Fix It in your own right. As you read on, I want you to remember this important point:

> **A problem is nothing more than an issue that needs to be addressed or a situation calling for a creative solution. Ask the right questions, and you'll come up with the right answers.**

Tuning In

If you've read my earlier books, then you already know that baby whispering begins by observing, respecting, and communicating with your baby. It means that you see your child for who she *really* is—her personality and her particular quirks (no insult intended, ducky; we all have them)—and you tailor your parenting strategies accordingly.

I've been told that I'm one of the few baby experts who takes the child's point of view. Well, *someone* has to, don't you think? I've had new parents look at me like I'm crazy when I introduce myself to their four-day-old baby. And parents of older children positively gape at me when I "translate" the mournful cries of their eight-month-old who has suddenly been banished from the parents' bed because *they*—her parents—suddenly decided that enough was enough: "Hey, Mum and Dad, this was your idea in the first place. I'm crying now because I don't even know what a crib is, no less how to fall asleep without two big warm bodies next to me."

I also translate "banguage" (baby language) for parents because it helps them remember that the little being in their arms or the toddler tearing around the room also has feelings and opinions. In other words, it's not just a matter of what we grownups want. How often have I witnessed a scene like this: A mother says to her little boy, "Now Billy, you don't want Adam's truck." Poor little Billy doesn't talk yet, but if he did I'd bet he'd say, "Sure I do, Mum. Why else do you think I grabbed the bloody truck away from Adam in the first place?" But Mum doesn't listen to him. She either takes the truck out of Billy's hand or tries to coax him into relinquishing it willingly. "Be a good lad and give it back to him." Well, at that point I can almost count the seconds 'til meltdown!

Don't get me wrong, I'm not saying that just because Billy wants the truck he should be allowed to bully Adam—far from it. I hate bullies, but believe me it won't be Billy's fault if he turns into one (more about that in chapter 8). What I am saying is that we need to listen to our children, *even when they say things we don't want to hear.*

The same skills that I teach parents of infants—observing body language, listening to cries, slowing down so that you can really figure out what's going on—those skills are just as important as your baby grows into a toddler and beyond. (Let us not forget that teens are actually toddlers in big bodies, so we'd be wise to learn our lessons early.) Throughout this book, I'll remind you of some of the techniques I've developed to help you tune in and take your time. Those of you who know me undoubtedly recall my love of acronyms, such as E.A.S.Y. (**E**at, **A**ctivity, **S**leep, and time for **Y**ou) and S.L.O.W. (**S**top, **L**isten, **O**bserve, and figure out **W**hat's Up) from the first book, and H.E.L.P. (**H**old yourself back, **E**ncourage exploration, **L**imit, and **P**raise) from the second, to name a few.

I don't come up with these things just to be clever. Nor do I think that coining a series of expressions or acronyms makes child-rearing a snap. I know firsthand that parenting is anything but "E.A.S.Y." It's particularly hard for new parents to know which end is up, especially sleep-starved new mums, but all parents need help. I'm just trying to give you tools to use when you might not have your wits about you. So, for example, the acronym E.A.S.Y. (the subject of chapter 1) helps you remember the sequence of a daily structured routine.

I also know that life just gets more complicated as babies become toddlers and as the family grows. My goal is to keep your baby on track and your own life on an even keel—or at least as even as it can be with young children underfoot. In the midst of a tussle with your child or children, it's easy to forget good advice and lapse into old patterns. I mean, how clearheaded can you be when your baby is screaming at the top of her lungs because her two-year-old brother, who is smiling proudly, decided that baby sister's head was as good a place as any to test out his new Magic Marker? I can't be in each of your homes, but if you have my handy little acronyms in your head, maybe it will seem like I'm standing next to you, reminding you what to do.

I've been told by countless parents that, in fact, my acronyms do help them to stay focused and to remember various baby-whispering strategies—at least in most situations. So here's another one for your parental bag of tricks: "P.C."

Be a "P.C." Parent

No, I don't mean *politically correct*. (Not to worry: The Baby Whisperer isn't planning to run for Congress!) Rather, a P.C. parent is *patient* and *conscious,* two qualities that will serve you well no matter how old your child is. Invariably, when I meet parents who are beset by a particular problem, usually one of the Big Three—sleep, eating, or behavior—my prescription always involves one, if not both, of these elements. But it's not just problems that require P.C. parenting; so do everyday interactions. Playtime, a trip to the supermarket, being with other children, and a host of other daily occurrences are enhanced by Mum or Dad having a P.C. mind-set.

No parent is P.C. all the time, but the more we do it, the more it becomes a natural way of acting. We get better with practice. Throughout this book, I'll remind you to be P.C., but here let me explain each letter:

Patience. It takes patience to parent well, because it's a hard, seemingly endless road, one that requires a long-term perspective. Today's Big Problem becomes a distant memory a month from now, but we tend to forget that when we're living through it. I've seen it happen time and again, luv: parents who in the heat of the moment take what seems like an easier road, only to find out later that it leads them to a dangerous dead end. That's how "accidental parenting" begins (more about that later). For instance, I worked with a mum recently who kept comforting her baby with a breast-feed only to find that at fifteen months the child had no idea how to fall asleep on her own and was demanding Mummy's breast four to six times a night. The poor, dear, utterly exhausted mother claimed she was ready to wean her baby, but wanting something isn't enough. You have to have the patience to weather the transition period.

Having a child can be messy and disorderly, too. Therefore, you also need patience (and internal fortitude) to tolerate at least the clutter, spills, and finger marks. Parents who don't will find it harder to get through their child's firsts. What toddler manages to drink from a real cup without first spilling pints of liquid onto the floor? Eventually, only a drizzle slips out the side of his mouth and then finally he gets most of it down, but it doesn't happen overnight, and it certainly doesn't happen without setbacks along the way. Allowing your child to master table skills, to learn how to pour or to wash himself, to let him walk around a living room filled with lots of no-nos—all of these things require parents' patience.

Parents who lack this important quality can unwittingly create obsessive behaviors even in very young children. Tara, a two-year-old I met in my travels, had obviously learned her lessons well from her ultra-neat mother, Cynthia. Walking into this mum's house, it was hard to tell a toddler lived there. And no wonder. Cynthia hovered constantly and followed her daughter around with a damp cloth, wiping her face, mopping up her spills, putting toys back into the toy box the moment Tara dropped them. Well, Tara was already a chip off the old block: "duhtee" was one of her first words. That might have been cute if it weren't for the fact that Tara was afraid to venture very far on her own and cried if other kids touched her. An extreme case, you say. Perhaps, but we do our little ones an injustice when we don't allow them to do what kids do: get a little dirty and get into a little mischief every now and then. A wonderful P.C. mum I met told me she regularly had "Pig Night" with her children, a dinner without utensils. And here's a surprising irony: When we actually give our kids permission to go wild, they often don't stray as far as you think they will.

Patience is particularly critical when you're trying to change bad habits. Naturally, the older the child, the longer it takes. Regardless of age, though, you must accept that change takes time—you can't rush the process. But I will tell you this: It's easier to be patient now and to take the time to teach your children and tell them what you expect. After all, who would you rather ask to clean up after himself, a two-year-old or a teenager?

Consciousness. Consciousness of who your child is should begin the moment she takes her first breath outside the womb. Always be aware of *your child's* perspective. I mean this both figuratively and literally: Squat down to your child's eye level. See what the world looks like from her vantage point. Say you take your child to church for the first time. Crouch down; imagine the view from the infant seat or stroller. Take a whiff of the air. Imagine what incense or candles feel like to a baby's sensitive nose. Listen. How loud is the din of the crowd, the singing of the choir, the rumbling of the organ? Might it be a bit much for Baby's ears? I'm not saying you should stay away from new places. On the contrary, it's good to expose children to new sights, sounds, and people. But if your infant repeatedly cries in unfamiliar settings, as a conscious parent you'll know that she's telling you: "It's too much. Please go slower" or "Try this with me in another month." Consciousness lets you tune in and, in time, allows you to get to know your child and trust your instincts about her.

Consciousness is also a matter of thinking things through before you do them and planning ahead. Don't wait for disaster to strike, especially if you've been there before. For instance, if, after several play dates, you see that your child and your best friend's child are constantly at war and the morning always ends in tears, arrange a play date with a different child—even if you don't fancy that child's mum quite as much. A play date is a *play* date. Instead of forcing your little one to be with a child he doesn't particularly like or get along with, when you want to go out for "a jaw" with your best friend, get a baby-sitter.

Consciousness means paying attention to the things you say and what you do with and to your child—and being consistent. Inconsistencies confuse children. So if one day you say, "No eating in the living room," and the next night you ignore your son as he chows down a bag of chips on the couch, your words will eventually mean nothing. He'll tune you out, and who can blame him?

Finally, consciousness is just that: being awake and being there for your child. I am pained when I see babies' or very young children's cries ignored. Crying is the first language children speak. By turning our backs on them, we're saying, "You don't matter." Eventually, unattended babies stop crying altogether, and they also stop thriving. I've seen parents allow children to cry in the name of toughening them up ("I don't want him to get spoiled" or "A little crying will do him good"). And I've seen mothers throw up their hands and say, "Her sister needs me—she'll just have to wait." But then she makes the baby wait, and wait, and wait. *There is no good reason for ignoring a child.*

Our children need us to be there and to be strong and wise for them, to show them the way. We are their best teachers, and for the first three years, their only teachers. We owe it to them to be P.C. parents—so that they can develop the best in themselves.

But Why Doesn't It Work?

"Why doesn't it work?" is by far one of the most common questions parents ask. Whether a mum is trying get her infant to sleep more than two hours at a time or her seven-month-old to eat solid food or her toddler to stop hitting other kids, I often hear the old "yes, but" response. "Yes, I know you told me I have to wake her during the day in order for her to sleep at night, but . . ." "Yes, I know you told me it will take time, but . . ."

"Yes, I know you said I have to take him out of the room when he begins to get aggressive, but . . ." You get the point, I'm sure.

My baby whispering techniques *do work*. I've used them myself with thousands of babies, and I've taught them to parents all over the globe. I'm no miracle worker. I just know my stuff, and I've got experience on my side. Granted, I know that some babies are more challenging than others—just like adults. Also, some periods of development, like when your child is teething or about to turn two, can be a bit hard on parents, as are unexpected illnesses (yours or your child's). But almost any problem can be solved by going back to the basics. When problems persist, it's usually because of something the parents have done, or because of their attitude. That may sound harsh, but remember that I'm an advocate for your *baby*. So if you're reading this book because you want to change a bad pattern and restore harmony to your family, and nothing seems to be working—not even my suggestions—really ask yourself if one of the following applies to you. If you identify with any of these statements, you'll need to change *your* behavior or mind-set if you want to use my baby-whispering strategies.

You're following your child, rather than establishing a routine. If you've read my first book, you know that I'm a firm believer in a structured routine. (If you haven't, I'll bring you up to speed in the first chapter, which is all about E.A.S.Y.) You start, ideally, from the day you bring your little bundle home from the hospital. Of course, if you didn't start then, you can also introduce a routine at eight weeks, or three months, or even later. But lots of parents have trouble with this, and the older the baby, the more trouble they have. And that's when I hear from them, in a desperate phone call or an email like this:

> I'm a first time mother with Sofia, my 8½-week-old baby. I'm having problems setting a routine for her, as she is so inconsistent. What worries me is her erratic feeding and sleeping patterns. Please advise.

That's a classic case of following the baby. Little Sofia is not inconsistent—she's a baby. What do babies know? They just got here. I'd bet the mother is inconsistent, because she's following her 8½-week-old daughter—and what does an infant know about eating or sleeping? Only what we teach them. This mum says she's trying to institute a routine, but she's really not taking charge. (I talk about what she should do in chapter 1.) Maintaining a routine is equally important with older babies and toddlers. We're there to guide our children, not to follow them. We set their dinner hours, their bedtimes.

You've been doing accidental parenting. As my Nan always told me, *start as you mean to go on.* Unfortunately, in the heat of the moment parents sometimes do *anything* to make their baby stop crying or to get a toddler to calm down. Often, the "anything" turns into a bad habit that they later have to break—and that's accidental parenting. For example, when ten-week-old Tommy can't fall asleep because Mum's missed his sleep window—the optimal time to put him down for a nap—his mother starts walking and rocking and jiggling him. And what do you know? It works. Tommy falls asleep in her arms. The next day when he fusses a bit in the crib at nap time, she also picks him up in the name of soothing him. She herself may be comforted by this ritual, too—feeling that sweet little baby cuddled on her chest is delicious. But three months later, if not sooner, I guarantee you that Tommy's mum will be desperate, wondering why her son "hates his crib" or "refuses to go to sleep unless I rock him." And it's not Tommy's fault. Mum has accidentally caused her son to associate rocking and the warmth of her own body with going to sleep. Now he thinks that's normal. He can't send himself off to Dreamland without her help, and he doesn't like his crib because no one has taught him how to be comfortable in it.

You're not reading your child's cues. A mum will call me in desperation: "He used to be on schedule, and now he's not. How do I get him back on track?" When I hear any version of that phrase, *used to be and now is not,* it not only means that the parents are letting the baby take over, it usually means they're paying more attention to the clock (or their own needs) than the baby himself (more on this on page 20). They're not reading his body language, tuning in to his cries. Even as babies begin to acquire language, it's important to observe them. For example, a child prone to aggression doesn't just walk into a room and start hitting his playmates. He gradually heats up and finally erupts. A wise parent learns to look for the signs and redirect his energy before the explosion.

You're not factoring in that young children change constantly. I also hear the "used to be" phrase when parents don't realize that it's time to make a shift. A four-month-old who is on a routine designed for his first three months (see chapter 1) will become cranky. A robust six-month-old who was formerly a good sleeper might start waking at night unless his parents start him on solid foods. The truth is that the only constant in the job of parenting is change (more on this in chapter 10).

You're looking for an easy fix. The older a child is, the harder it is to break a bad habit caused by accidental parenting, whether it's waking in the night and demanding a feed, or refusing to sit in a high chair for a proper meal. But many parents are looking for magic. For example, Elaine had consulted me about getting her breast-fed baby to take a bottle but later insisted that my strategy hadn't worked. The first question I always ask is, "How long have you been doing it?" Elaine admitted, "I tried it for the morning feed, but then I gave up." Why did she quit so soon? She was expecting instant results. I reminded her of the "P" in P.C.: Be patient.

You're not really committed to change. Elaine's other problem was that she wasn't willing to go the distance. "But I was afraid Zed would starve if I held out" was the reason she gave me. But there was more to the story, as there often is: She said she wanted her husband to be able to feed five-month-old Zed but really didn't want to give up that exclusive domain. If you're trying to solve a problem, you have to want it solved—and have the determination and stamina to see it through to the end. Make a plan and *stick with it.* Don't go back to your old way and don't keep trying different techniques. If you stay with one solution, it *will* work . . . as long as you keep at it. Be persistent. I can't stress often enough: *You have to be as consistent with the new way as you were with the old.* Clearly, some children's temperament makes them more resistant to change than others (see chapter 2); but almost all balk when we change their routine (adults do, too!). Still, if we stick with it and don't keep changing the rules, children get used to the new way.

Parents sometimes delude themselves. They will insist that they've been trying a particular technique for two weeks—let's say my pickup/put-down method or P.U./P.D. (see chapter 6)—and say that it's not working. I know that can't be true, because after a week or less, P.U./P.D. works with any baby, no matter what his temperament. And sure enough, when I really question them, I find out that yes, they tried P.U./P.D. for three or four days, and it worked, but a few days later, when he woke up at 3 A.M., they didn't follow through with the original plan. Exasperated, they tried something else instead. "We decided to let him cry—some people recommend that." I don't; it makes a baby feel abandoned. The poor lad is then not only confused because they changed the rules on him, he's frightened.

If you're not going to see something through, don't do it. If you can't do it on your own, enlist backup people—your husband, your mother or mother-in-law, a good friend. Otherwise, you just put him through the torture of crying his heart out and eventually you take him into your bed (more on this in chapters 5 through 7).

You're trying something that doesn't work for your family or your personality. When I suggest a structured routine or one of my strategies for breaking a bad pattern, I usually can tell whether it will work better for Mum or Dad—one's more of a disciplinarian, the other a softie or, worse, a victim of the "poor-baby" syndrome (see page 247). Some mothers (or fathers) will tip their hand by saying to me, "I don't want her to cry." The fact is, I'm not about forcing a baby to be or do anything, and I don't believe in allowing babies to cry it out. I don't believe in banishing toddlers to a solitary time-out, no matter how short the duration. Children need adults' help, and we have to be there to give it to them, and especially when you're trying to undo the effects of accidental parenting, it's hard work. If you're not comfortable doing a particular technique, either don't do it, or find ways to bolster yourself, by having the stronger parent take over for a bit, or enlisting your mother or mother-in-law or a good friend to help.

It ain't broke—and you don't really need to fix it. Recently I got an email from the parents of a four-month-old: "My baby is sleeping through the night but he's only taking twenty-four ounces. In your book it says he should be taking thirty-two to thirty-six ounces. How can I get the extra ounces in him?" How many mothers would give their right arm to have a baby sleeping through the night! Her so-called problem was that her baby didn't fit my book. He might have a smaller-than-average build. Not everyone grows up in a family of Shaq O'Neals! If his weight wasn't a concern to her pediatrician, my advice was to slow down and just observe her son. Maybe in a couple of more weeks he might start waking in the night—and that would be a sign that maybe she needed to give him more food during the day, but for now, nothing was wrong.

You have unrealistic expectations. Some parents are unrealistic about what it means to have a *child*. Often, they're very successful in their work, good leaders, smart and creative, and they view the transition to parenthood as another major life transition, which it clearly is. But it's also a very different passage because it brings with it a huge responsibility: caring for another human being. Once you become a parent, you can't return to your old life as if nothing had changed. Babies *do* sometimes need to feed in the night. Toddlers can't be managed with the same efficiency you apply to projects at work. Children are not little machines you can program. They require care, constant vigilance, and lots of loving time. Even if you have help, *you* need to know your child, and that takes time and energy. Also, keep in mind that whatever stage your child is in right now—good or bad—will pass. In fact, as we say in the last chapter, just when you think you've got it, everything changes.

About This Book . . .
and the Developmental Olympics

This book is a response to your requests. You've asked for further clarification of strategies you're confused about and solutions to a wide variety of problems. In addition, many of you have requested specific age guidelines. Those of you who've read my earlier books know that I'm not a big fan of age charts and never have been. Babies' challenges can't be sorted into neat piles. Of course, it's true that babies and toddlers *generally* reach certain milestones at designated times, but there's usually nothing wrong with those who don't. Still, in response to your request for greater clarity and specifics, here I have broken down my advice and tailored various techniques according to age groupings—birth to six weeks, six weeks to four months, four to six months, six to nine months, nine months to a year, one year to two, two years to three. My intention is to give you a better understanding of how your child thinks and sees the world. I don't necessarily cover all of the age categories in every chapter—it depends on what we're discussing. For example, in chapter 1, which deals with E.A.S.Y., I cover only the first five months because that's when parents have questions about routine, whereas in chapter 4, which is about toddler eating, I start at six months, which is when we begin to introduce solid food.

You'll notice that the age spans are quite broad. That's to allow for variations among children. Furthermore, I don't want my readers to enter into what I call the "developmental Olympics," comparing one child's progress or problems with another child's, or to become anxious if their little boy or girl doesn't fit a particular age profile. Too many times, I've witnessed play groups composed of mothers whose babies were all born around the same time. Many actually met on the maternity ward or in childbirth classes. The mums sit there chatting, but I can see them observing each other's babies, comparing and wondering. If a mum docsn't actually *say* something out loud, I can almost hear her thinking, *Why is my Claire, who is only two weeks younger than Emmanuel, smaller than he is? And look at Emmanuel, trying to pull himself up—why isn't Claire doing that yet?* First of all, in the life of a three-month-old, two weeks mean a lot—it's one-sixth of her life! Second, reading age charts in general raises parents' expectations. Third, children have different strengths and abilities. Claire might walk later than Emmanuel (or not—it's too early to tell), but she also might talk earlier.

I urge you to read *all* the stages, because earlier problems can persist— it's not uncommon to see a two-month-old concern crop up at five or six months. Besides, your child might be more advanced in a particular area, so it's a good idea to get a sense of what might lie ahead.

I also believe that there are "prime times"—the best ages to teach a particular skill, like sleeping through the night, or to introduce a new element into your child's life, say, giving a bottle to your breast-fed baby or having her sit in a high chair. Particularly as children move into toddlerhood, if you don't start things at optimal times, you're likely to have a power struggle on your hands. You've got to plan ahead. If you haven't already made toddler tasks, such as dressing and toilet training, into a game or a pleasant experience, your child is more likely to balk at the new experience.

Where We Go from Here

We look at a broad range of issues in this book, as I've tried to include all of the problems you encounter, which doesn't lend itself to a tidy formula. All chapters focus on problems, but each chapter is different, structured in a way that will help you go beyond the basics and understand the way I look at various parenting challenges.

In each chapter, you'll find lots of special features: myths about parenting, checklists, boxes, and sidebars that sum up important bits of information, and real-life examples—stories from the trenches. In all of the case studies and when I've reprinted emails and website postings, names and identifying details have been changed. I've tried to zero in on the most common concerns that parents have and then share with you the kinds of questions I typically ask to find out what's really going on. Like a troubleshooter who goes into a company to analyze why it's not running smoothly, I have to figure out who the players are, how they act, and what happened before the particular difficulty observed. I then have to suggest a different way of doing things, which will result in a different outcome than the one they've been getting. By letting you in on the way *I* think about babies' and toddlers' difficulties and how *I* come up with a plan, you can become the troubleshooter in your own family. As I said earlier, my goal is to get you to think the way I do, so that you can solve problems on your own.

> Throughout this book, the questions I ask will be set in boldface type—**like this**—so that they pop out at you.

Throughout this book, I've tried to present an equal number of references to boys and girls. This wasn't possible, however, when it came to mothers and fathers, because most of my emails, website postings, and calls are from mothers, and that imbalance is represented in these pages. Dad, if you're reading this book, I didn't intentionally slight you. I recognize that (thankfully) many fathers are hands-on nowadays, and around 20 percent of you are even at-home. I hope that someday because of you we'll not say that fathers don't read parenting books!

You can read this book cover to cover, or just look up the problems you're concerned about and go from there. However, if you haven't read my earlier books, I strongly recommend that you at least read through chapters 1 and 2, which review my basic philosophy of child care and also help you analyze why problems crop up at various ages. Chapters 3 through 10 focus in depth on the three areas that most concern parents: eating, sleeping, and behavior.

Many of you have told me that what you appreciate even more than my good advice is my sense of humor. I promise plenty of that in this book, too. After all, luv, if we can't remember to laugh and don't remember to cherish the special moments of calm and connection (even when they don't last longer than five minutes at a time), then parenting, which is hard to begin with, will feel way too overwhelming.

You might be surprised by some of my suggestions and might not believe they'll work, but I have lots of examples to demonstrate how successfully they've been applied in other families. So why not at least try them with yours?

ONE

E.A.S.Y. ISN'T NECESSARILY EASY (BUT IT WORKS!)

Getting Your Baby on a Structured Routine

The Gift of E.A.S.Y.

You probably have a routine in the morning. You get up at roughly the same time, maybe you shower first or have your coffee, or perhaps you immediately hop on the treadmill or take your pup out for a brisk walk. Whatever you do, it's probably pretty much the same every morning. If by chance something interrupts that routine, it can throw off your whole day. And I'll bet there are other routines in your day as well. You're used to having your dinnertime at a certain hour. You probably have particular rituals at the end of the day, too, like spooning with your favorite pillow (or partner!) in anticipation of a good night's sleep. But let's say your dinner hour changes or you have to sleep in a bed away from home. Isn't it unsettling and don't you feel disoriented when you wake?

Naturally, people vary in their need for structure. At one end of the continuum are those whose entire days are predictable. At the other end are free spirits who tend to fly by the seat of their pants. But even "flyers" usually have some sort of dependable rituals during their day. Why? Because human beings, like most animals, thrive when they know how and when their needs are going to be met and know what's coming next. We all like some degree of certainty in our lives.

Well, so do babies and young children. When a new mum brings her baby home from the hospital, I suggest a structured routine straightaway. I call it "E.A.S.Y.," an acronym that stands for a predictable sequence of events that pretty much mirrors how adults live their lives, albeit in shorter chunks: **E**at, have some **A**ctivity, and go to **S**leep, which leaves a bit of time for **Y**ou. It is *not* a schedule, because you cannot fit a baby into a clock. It's a routine that gives the day structure and makes family life consistent, which is important because all of us, children and adults, as well as babies and toddlers, thrive on predictability. Everyone benefits: Baby knows what's coming next. Siblings, if there are any, get more time with Mum and Dad—and they get to have less harried parents who have time for themselves as well.

I was actually *doing* E.A.S.Y. long before I named it. When I first started caring for newborns and young babies more than twenty years ago, a structured routine just seemed to make sense. Babies need us to show them the ropes—and to keep it up. The most effective learning comes with repetition. I also explained the importance of a structured routine to the parents I worked with, so that they could carry on after I'd left. I cautioned them to always make sure that their baby had some kind of activity after a feed instead of going right to sleep, so that their little one wouldn't associate eating with sleeping. Because "my" babies' lives were so predictable and calm, most of them were good eaters, they learned to play independently for increasingly longer periods, and they could get themselves to sleep without sucking on a bottle or breast or being rocked by their parents. As many of those babies grew into toddlers and preschoolers, I stayed in touch with their parents, who informed me that not only were their children thriving in their daily routines, they were also confident in themselves and trusted that their parents would be there if they needed them. The parents themselves learned early on to tune in to their child's cues by carefully observing their body language and listening to their cries. Because they could "read" their child, they felt better equipped to deal with any bumps in the road.

By the time I was ready to write my first book, my coauthor and I came up with "E.A.S.Y.," a simple acronym designed to help parents remember the order of my structured routine. Eat, activity, sleep—it's the natural course of life—and then, as a bonus, time for you. With E.A.S.Y., you don't follow the baby; *you* take charge. You observe him carefully, tune in to his cues, but *you* take the lead, gently encouraging him to follow what you know will make him thrive: eating, appropriate levels of activity, and a good sleep afterward. You are your baby's guide. You set the pace.

E.A.S.Y. gives parents, especially first-timers, the confidence to know that they understand their baby, because they more quickly learn to distinguish their baby's cries. As one mum wrote to me, "My husband and I and our six-month-old, Lily, are considered an enigma among my peers in our childbirth education class due to our sleep-filled nights and very pleasant baby." She goes on to say that they put Lily on E.A.S.Y. when she was ten weeks old. As a result, Mum says, "We understand her cues and have a routine—not a schedule—that makes our life predictable, manageable, and fun."

I've seen it time and again. Parents who establish my E.A.S.Y. routine quickly get better at figuring out what their baby needs and wants at a particular time of day. Let's say you've fed your infant (the E), and she's been up for fifteen minutes (the A—activity), and then she starts to get a bit fussy. Chances are, she's ready for sleep (the S). Conversely, if she's been napping for an hour (S), while you (the Y) hopefully have been stealing a little downtime for yourself, when she wakes, there's no guesswork involved. Even if she's not crying (if she's under six weeks, though, she probably is), it's a pretty safe bet that she's hungry. And so the E.A.S.Y. cycle begins again.

Why Go E.A.S.Y.?

E.A.S.Y. is a sensible way to get you and your child through the day. It is composed of repetitive cycles of each letter. The E, A, and S are interrelated—changes in one usually affect the other two. Although your baby will transform over the coming months as she grows, the order in which each letter occurs does not:

Eat. Your baby's day starts with a feed, which goes from all-liquid to liquids and solids at six months. You're less likely to overfeed or underfeed a baby who's on a routine.

Activity. Infants entertain themselves by cooing and gooing at their caretakers and staring at the wavy lines on the dining room wallpaper. But as your baby develops she will interact more with her environment and move about. A structured routine helps prevent babies from becoming overstimulated.

Sleep. Sleep helps your baby grow. Also, good naps during the day will make her go for longer stretches at night, because one needs to be relaxed in order to sleep well.

Your time. If your baby isn't on a structured routine, every day will be different and unpredictable. Not only will she be miserable, you'll barely have a moment for yourself.

Write It Down!

Parents who actually chart their baby's day *by writing everything down* have less trouble sticking to a routine or establishing it for the first time.

They also are better observers. Writing things down, even though it seems tedious at the moment (goodness knows, you have lots of other things to do!), will give you a much better perspective. You'll see patterns more readily, and see how sleep and eating and activity are interrelated. On days that your baby feeds better, I'd just bet that he's less cranky during his awake time and sleeps better, too.

When E.A.S.Y. Seems Hard

In preparing to write this book, I pored over the case files of thousands of babies I've worked with, as well as questions I received from parents who have recently contacted me via phone, email, or through my website. My goal was to identify the stumbling blocks that typically occur when well-meaning and committed parents try to establish a structured routine. Most parents' queries are not about routines. Instead, their questions tend to focus on one of the letters of E.A.S.Y. They might ask, "Why are my baby's feeds so short?" (the E), "Why is he cranky and uninterested in his toys?" (the A), or "Why does she wake up several times during the night?" (the S). In this book I deal with a whole range of questions like those and offer lots of suggestions for dealing with specific problems—all of chapters 3 and 4 are devoted to eating issues, and chapters 5 through 7 to sleep. But we also have to look at how the three areas are *interrelated*, which is what this chapter is about. Eating affects sleep and activity; activity affects eating and sleeping; sleep affects activity and eating—and all of them will naturally affect you. Without a predictable routine, everything in a baby's life can go haywire—sometimes all at once. The solution is almost always E.A.S.Y.

Parents tell me, though, that E.A.S.Y. isn't necessarily easy. Here's a portion of a letter from Cathy, mother of one-month-old Carl and twenty-two-month-old Natalie. It captures the confusion and several of the difficulties parents seem to experience:

> My older daughter, Natalie, sleeps very well (seven to seven, puts herself to sleep, naps well). I can't remember how we got her there and need some sample routines to use as guidance for Carl, starting now and covering the next several months. He is breast-fed and I fear I inadvertently keep nursing him to sleep, and I sometimes confuse tired/hungry/gas pain. I need to have a general structure to

follow to help me keep track of where I should be with him, since his sister demands a lot of attention when she is awake! Tracy's [first] book talks in general terms about amounts of time on E/A/S, but I'm finding it difficult to relate that to the hours in the day and night.

Cathy was ahead of the game in one respect. She at least realized that her problem was inconsistency and her inability to read Carl's cues. She suspected, quite accurately, that the solution is a routine. And like many parents who have read about E.A.S.Y., all she needed was a bit of reassurance and further clarification. It didn't take her long to get on track after we spoke, as Carl was only a month old, young enough to adapt quickly to a new routine. Also, when I found out he weighed seven pounds at birth, I knew he wouldn't have any trouble going two-and-a-half to three hours between feeds (more on that later). As soon as Mum had her son on E.A.S.Y., she was better able to anticipate his needs. (See a sample routine for a four-week-old on page 25.)

All babies thrive on routine, but some adapt more rapidly and readily than others because of their basic temperament. Cathy's first child, Natalie, who is now a toddler, was an extremely easygoing and adaptable infant—I call them Angel babies. That would explain why Natalie napped and slept so well and also why Cathy can't remember how she got her there. But little Carl was a more sensitive type of child, what I call a Touchy baby, who even at a month old could be thrown off by a too bright light or Mum holding his head slightly lower than usual when she fed him. As I detail in chapter 2, temperament affects how a baby reacts to virtually everything in his life. Some babies need a little more quiet while they're eating, less stimulating activities, or a darker room to sleep in. Otherwise, they become overstimulated and *will* resist a routine.

With babies under four months old, problems also can occur because the parents don't realize that E.A.S.Y. has to be adapted to accommodate a special birth condition, like prematurity (see sidebar, page 27) or jaundice (sidebar, page 28), or their particular infant's weight (pages 27–29). Also, some parents misunderstand how to apply E.A.S.Y. For instance, they take "every three

> ## E.A.S.Y.—
> ### Your *Daytime* Routine
>
> E.A.S.Y. does *not* apply in the night. When you bathe your baby and put him to bed, make sure he has lots of diaper cream on his bottom. Don't wake your baby up to do an activity. If he wakes from hunger, you feed him, but send him right back to sleep. Don't even change his diaper unless you've heard him poop or (in bottle-fed babies) smelled it.

hours" literally and wonder how their baby will ever learn to sleep through the night if they wake her for feeds and what kind of activity should be done in the middle of the night. (None—you let them sleep; see sidebar, page 19.)

Parents also have problems with E.A.S.Y. when they think "schedule" and focus more on reading the clock than reading their babies' signals. A structured routine is *not* the same thing as a schedule. This bears repeating: *You can't fit a baby into a clock.* If you do, then both mother and baby become frustrated. Merle, a mother from Oklahoma, wrote to me in desperation after she had "tried unsuccessfully to do the E.A.S.Y. schedule." Straightaway, my antenna went up because Merle used the word *schedule,* which I never do. "It seems every day we are at a different time schedule," she wrote. "I know I am doing something wrong, but what?"

A *structured routine* is not the same thing as a schedule. A schedule is about time slots whereas E.A.S.Y. is about keeping up the same daily pattern—eating, activity, and sleeping—and repeating that pattern every day. We're not trying to control children, we're *guiding* them. The way humans learn—or other species, for that matter—is by doing something over and over, which is what a structured routine reinforces.

Like Merle, some parents misinterpret what I mean by "routine," often because they tend to live by schedules themselves. So, when I write down a *suggested* three-hour routine for a baby who's under four months—say 7, 10, 1, 4, 7, and 10—a schedule-driven mum sees the time slots as written in stone. She panics because one day her baby naps at 10:15 and the next day at 10:30. But you can't put a baby on a clock, especially in the first six weeks. Sometimes you'll have a day when you're on track and everything goes smoothly and other days not. If you're busy watching the clock, instead of your baby, you'll miss important signals (like the first yawn in a six-week-old or eye-rubbing in a six-month-old, which means that your little one is getting sleepy—more on the sleep window, page 181). Then you have an overtired baby on your hands who can't get himself to sleep and who of course resists the routine, because it goes against his physical needs.

The most important aspect of E.A.S.Y. is to read your child's signs—of hunger, of fatigue, of overstimulation—which is more important than any time slot. So if one day, he's hungry a little earlier, or seems tired before it's "time" to put him down, don't let the clock threaten you. Let your common sense take over. And believe me, ducky, the better you get at interpreting your baby's cries and body language, the better you'll be at guiding him and at clearing whatever obstacles get in the way.

The E.A.S.Y. Log

When parents come home from the hospital and start E.A.S.Y., I usually suggest that they keep a log, like the one below (you can also download it from my website), so that they keep track of exactly what their baby is eating and doing, how long she's sleeping, and also what the mum is doing for herself. For babies over four months, you might want to adapt this chart, excluding the "bowel movement" and "urination" columns.

Eat						Activity		Sleep	You
At what time?	How much (if bottle-fed) or how long (if on the breast)?	On right breast?	On left breast?	Bowel movements	Urination	What and how long?	Bath (A.M. or P.M.?)	How long?	Rest? Errands? Insights? Comments?

Getting Started: Guidelines for Different Ages

Establishing a routine for the first time gets a bit harder as the baby grows, especially if you've *never* had structure. And because my first book concentrates mainly on the first four months of E.A.S.Y., some parents of older children find themselves at sea. At least half of my queries come from parents who have either tried another, less structured method, such as "on demand" feeding, or followed a different type of routine and found it lacking. Then they discover E.A.S.Y., and they wonder how to get started.

E.A.S.Y. *is* different with older babies, and on pages 39–46, I lay out a day-by-day plan that works with babies four months or older. Granted, babies' challenges don't necessarily fall into neat categories. As I explained in the Introduction, I have found that certain concerns seem to crop up in particular age groupings. In this review of E.A.S.Y., I will focus on:

Birth to six weeks

Six weeks to four months

Four to six months

Six to nine months

Nine months and beyond

I will offer you an overall description of each stage, plus a list of the most common complaints and their probable causes. Even where the complaints seem to center on a feeding or sleeping issue, at least part of the solution always involves establishing a structured routine if you don't have one, or tweaking the routine your baby is already on. The numbers in parentheses in the "probable cause" column indicate the pages in other chapters where you'll find

---

How Babies Develop

You baby will progress from being a totally dependent being to a little person who's more in control of his body. His routine will be affected by his growth and development, which happens from head to toe in this general order:

Birth to 3 months: From the head and shoulders up, including his mouth, enabling him to hold and lift his head and sit with support.

3 to 6 months: From the waist up, including the torso, shoulders, head, hands, enabling him to roll front to back, reach and grasp, and sit almost unaided.

6 months to a year: From the legs up, which includes the muscles and coordination that will enable him to sit unaided, roll back to front, stand upright, cruise, crawl, finally at around a year or later, walk.

more detailed explanations about what to do (so as not to repeat the information).

No matter how old your baby is, it's a good idea to read through all the sections, because as I will remind you repeatedly, *you can't base strategies solely on age*. Children, like grownups, are *individuals*. With a six-month-old baby, we sometimes see the same issues that crop up with a three-month-old baby, especially if the child has never had a routine. (Besides, if I don't constantly reinforce this point, I'll get letters from parents when this book is published, saying, "But my baby is four months old and she's not doing what you described . . .")

The First Six Weeks: Adjustment Time

The first six weeks is the ideal time to start E.A.S.Y., which generally starts out as a three-hour plan. Your baby eats, plays after his feeds, you then set the scene for good napping. You rest while he rests, and when he wakes up, the cycle starts again. But the first six weeks is also a time of huge adjustment. Your baby once lived in a cozy, climate-controlled place where he ate twenty-four/seven and dined in the seclusion of your uterus, and now he's been thrust into a noisy home with people bustling about. He is expected to get his nourishment from a nipple—yours or a bottle's. Life is dramatically different for you, too. Especially if you're a first-timer, you are often just as confused as Baby! And if it's your second or third baby, you probably have his siblings underfoot, complaining about that crying blob who's suddenly monopolizing everyone's time.

The baby doesn't have much control over anything at this point except his mouth, which he uses to suckle and to communicate. His existence is all about eating and suckling and crying. Crying is his voice, his only voice. The average baby cries somewhere between one and five hours out of twenty-four. And to most new parents, every minute feels like five. (I know, because I've asked parents to close their eyes while I played a two-minute tape of a crying baby. Then I asked them how long they thought they had been listening. The majority thought it was two to three times longer!)

We should never ignore a baby's cries or, in my opinion, let him cry it out! Instead, we always have to try to figure out what he's telling us. When the parents of young infants have problems with E.A.S.Y. it's usually because they're misreading their baby's cries. It's understandable: Here's this little stranger in your midst whose only language is crying, a

The Crying Questions

When a six-week or younger baby cries, it's always easier to determine what she wants if you know where she is in her day. Ask yourself:

Is it time for a feed? (hunger)

Is her diaper wet or soiled? (discomfort or cold)

Has she been sitting in the same place or position without a change of scene? (boredom)

Has she been up for more than 30 minutes? (overtired)

Has she had lots of company or has there been a lot of activity in your household? (overstimulated)

Is she grimacing and pulling her legs up? (gas)

Is she crying inconsolably during or as much as an hour after feeds? (reflux)

Is she spitting up? (reflux)

Is her room too hot or cold, or is she under- or overdressed? (body temperature)

lingo you don't speak. It's hard for you—a foreigner—to understand what he means at first.

Crying often peaks at six weeks, by which time observant parents have usually learned the language. Paying close attention to the baby's movement, they often act before the crying starts. But they also know what a hungry cry sounds like—a slight cough-like noise in the back of the throat, short to begin with and then as a more steady waa, waa, waa rhythm—compared to an over-tired cry, which begins with three short wails, followed by a hard cry, then two short breaths and a longer, even louder cry. They also know *their particular baby*—after all, some are less vocal about their hunger than others. While some infants only fuss slightly and "root" or curl the sides of their tongue, others become absolutely frantic with the first hunger pang.

If you put your baby on E.A.S.Y. straightaway, I guarantee you'll learn her cues more quickly and be better able to determine why she's crying. Looking at your daily chart will help. Let's say, for instance, that she fed at 7 A.M. If she starts crying ten or fifteen minutes afterward, and you can't calm her down, you can be fairly certain it's *not* hunger. More likely, it's a digestive issue (see pages 109–115), and you know you have to do something that will calm her—not give her more food, which would only make her more uncomfortable. On page 26, you will find the common complaints.

A Typical E.A.S.Y. Day for a 4-Week-Old

E	7:00	Feed.
A	7:45	Diaper change; some playing and talking; watch cues for sleepiness.
S	8:15	Swaddle and lay your baby in the crib. It may take him 15–20 minutes to fall asleep for his 1st morning nap.
Y	8:30	You nap when he naps.
E	10:00	Feed.
A	10:45	See 7:45 above.
S	11:15	2nd morning nap.
Y	11:30	Y nap or at least relax.
E	1:00	Feed.
A	1:45	See 7:45 above.
S	2:15	Afternoon nap.
Y	2:30	Y nap or at least relax.
E	4:00	Feed.
A	4:45	See 7:45 above.
S	5:15	Catnap for 40–50 minutes to give him enough rest to handle his bath.
Y	5:30	Do something nice for yourself.
E	6:00	1st cluster feed.
A	7:00	Bath, into jammies, lullaby or other bedtime ritual.
S	7:30	Another catnap.
Y	7:30	You eat dinner.
E	8:00	2nd cluster feed.
A		None.
S		Put him right back to bed.
Y		Enjoy your short evening!
E	10–11	Dream feed and cross your fingers 'til morning!

NOTE: Whether a baby is breast- or bottle-fed, I advise the above routine—allowing for variations in times—until 4 months old. The "A" time will be shorter for younger babies, and get progressively longer for older ones. I also recommend turning the two "cluster feeds" into one (at around 5:30 or 6) by 8 weeks. Continue the dream feed until 7 months—unless he's a great sleeper and makes it through on his own. (Cluster feeds and dream feeds are explained on pages 93–94.)

COMMON COMPLAINTS	PROBABLE CAUSES
I can't get my baby to conform to a three-hour routine. I can't get her to do even twenty minutes of activity time.	If your baby weighs less than 6½ pounds at birth, she may *need* to eat every two hours at first (see "E.A.S.Y. by the Pound," page 29). Don't try to keep her awake for activities.
My baby often falls asleep during feeds and seems hungry an hour later.	This is common to certain types of infants—premies, jaundiced, low birthweight, and some simply sleepy babies. You might have to feed more often and definitely have to work at keeping him awake for his feeds (99–100). If breast-fed, the cause could be improper latch-on, or mum's milk supply (101–109).
My baby wants to eat every two hours.	If your baby weighs 6½ pounds or more, he may not be eating efficiently. Watch out that he doesn't turn into a "snacker" (98). If breast-fed, the cause could be improper latch-on, or mum's milk supply (101–109).
My baby is rooting all the time and I keep thinking he's hungry, but he only takes a little bit at each feed.	Your baby may not be getting enough suckling time, so he's using the bottle or breast as a pacifier (100). He may be turning into a snacker (98). Check your milk supply by doing a yield (104).
My baby doesn't take regular naps.	He may be overstimulated by too much activity (201–204). Or you are not persevering with swaddling him and laying him down awake (181–186).
My baby is a great napper, but she's up frequently at night.	Your baby has switched night for day and her daytime sleep is robbing her nighttime sleep (177–179).
I never know what my baby wants when he's crying.	Your baby may be a Touchy or Grumpy type (see chapter 2) or have a physical problem, such as gas, reflux, or colic (109–115). But whatever the cause, you and he will do better if he's on E.A.S.Y.

E.A.S.Y. by the Pound

When the parent of a baby under six weeks has trouble with E.A.S.Y. I ask: **Did you have a full-term pregnancy?** Even if she says "yes," I ask: **What was your baby's birthweight?** E.A.S.Y. was designed for an *average weight* newborn—6½ to eight pounds—babies who generally can last three hours between feeds. If your baby weighs more or less, we have to adjust accordingly. As the "E.A.S.Y. by the Pound" chart on page 29 indicates, with an average-weight baby, feeds generally last twenty-five to forty minutes (depending on whether they're breast- or bottle-fed and whether the baby chows down or grazes at a more leisurely pace). Activity time (which includes a nappy change) is thirty to forty-five minutes. Sleep, allowing fifteen minutes or so for the baby to drop off, is 1½ to two hours. Such a baby would be fed at, say, 7, 10, 1, 4, and 7 during the day, as well as 9 and 11 in the evening (a strategy that helps eliminate the 2 A.M. feed; see "Tanking Up," pages 93 and 195). These are *suggested* times only. If your baby wakes up for his lunchtime feed at 12:30 instead of 1:00, feed him.

Babies who weigh more than average at birth—say eight to ten pounds—often feed a little more efficiently and take in more food at each feed. There's more weight on them, but you'd still keep them on the above three-hour routine. Age and weight are different things—a baby may weigh eight pounds or more, but developmentally he's still a newborn who needs to eat every three hours. I love to work with those babies, because I can get them to sleep longer stretches at night within the first two weeks.

However, some babies, because they're either premature or just smaller babies, weigh *less* at birth. They're not ready for the three-hour E.A.S.Y. plan. When parents bring them home

---

Special Circumstances: Premature Births

Most hospitals put premies on a two-hour routine until they reach five pounds, the minimum weight at which a baby is allowed to be taken home. That's good news for parents, because it means that premies are already accustomed to the structure by the time they come home. But because their tiny internal systems are so small and not quite developed, premies are also more prone to other problems, among them reflux (baby heartburn, pages 111–114) and jaundice (see sidebar, page 28). Also, premies by definition are more fragile. Even more than low-birthweight babies, they tend to fall asleep on the job, so you have to be extra vigilant at waking them up for feeds. And you have to really protect their sleep by creating womb-like conditions: Swaddle them and let them sleep in a quiet, warm, darkened room. Remember that they're not supposed to be here yet, and they want, and need, to sleep.

from the hospital and try to put them on an E.A.S.Y. routine, the usual complaint is, "I can't get her to do even twenty minutes of activity time" or "She falls asleep during feeds." They want to know how to keep her awake. Simple. *You don't*—at least not for activities. If you do, you'll over-stimulate her, and she'll start to cry. As soon as you calm her down, she'll probably be hungry again, because she's been crying, which uses up energy. And then you'll be utterly confused about her cries. Is she hungry? Tired? Gassy?

At night, smaller babies can only last four hours max at first, so they generally have to feed at least two times a night in the first six weeks. But if they go only three hours at a time, that's okay, too. They need the food. The fact is, you want little babies to eat and sleep a lot in the beginning, because you want them to get fat. Think of baby pigs who eat, snort 'round a bit, and then go back to sleep. All baby animals do that, because they need to gain weight and conserve energy.

If your baby is less than 6½ pounds, put her on a *two-hour* eating schedule at first: Feed for thirty or forty minutes, reduce the activity time to only five or ten minutes, and then let her go to sleep for an hour and half. When she's up, don't expect her to coo and goo at you—and keep stimulation to a minimum. By being fed every two hours and getting the sleep time she needs to grow, she will definitely gain weight. As your baby starts to put weight on, she will probably last longer between feeds, and you'll be able to keep her up a little longer, gradually extending her activity time. Where she could only sustain ten minutes up when she was first born, when she's 6½ pounds, she can stay up for twenty minutes and by seven pounds as long as forty-five minutes. While she's putting on the weight, you'll gradually lengthen the two-hour routine, so that by 6½ or seven pounds, she'll be on the three-hour E.A.S.Y. plan.

Special Circumstances: Jaundice

Just as birthweight changes how we introduce E.A.S.Y., so does jaundice, a condition in which the baby's bilirubin—the orange-yellow pigment of bile—doesn't get eliminated. Everything turns yellow—skin, eyes, palms of the hands, and bottoms of the feet. The liver is like a car engine that hasn't quite cranked up, and it takes a few days to get it going. In the meantime, your baby will be very tired and want to sleep a lot. Don't be fooled into thinking you have a "good sleeper" on your hands. Instead of letting her sleep, wake her every two hours, so that she gets the nourishment she needs to flush the jaundice out of her system. The condition usually goes away in 3 or 4 days—slightly longer in breast-fed babies than formula-fed babies. You'll know everything's fine when her skin regains its pinkish hue and, lastly, the yellow disappears from the eyes.

E.A.S.Y. by the Pound: The First Three Months

This chart shows how birthweight affects your baby's routine. (After 4 months, even most low-weight babies can last 4 hours between feeds.) You'll have to do the math here. Note the time your baby usually wakes up, and write down *approximate times* based on your baby's weight and the information in the "how often" column. Allow for variation—it's not the time slot that matters as much as predictability and order. "How long" tells you what to expect for each letter; "how often" refers to each new repetition of the E.A.S.Y. cycle.

To simplify, I've left out the "Y"—time for **You**. If your baby weighs more than 8 pounds, you'll be getting your nighttimes back a lot sooner than parents with smaller babies. If your baby weighs less than 6½ pounds, you won't have much time for yourself, especially in the first 6 weeks. But hang in there—this phase is over when your baby weighs 7 pounds, and then it gets even better as your baby starts learning to amuse herself, because you'll also have time to putter about when she's awake.

Weight	5 – 6½ Pounds		6½ – 8 Pounds		Over 8 Pounds	
	How long	How often	How long	How often	How long	How often
Eat	30–40 minutes	Routine repeats every 2 hours during the day, until baby weighs 6½ lb., at which point you can switch to an every-3-hour plan. At first these babies can only go 4 hours at night without eating.	25–40 minutes	Routine repeats every 2 ½–3 hours (for babies on the lower end of average) during the day; 4- to 5-hour stretches at night in the first 6 weeks, by which time you should be working at cutting out the 1 or 2 A.M. feed.	25–35 minutes	Routine repeats every 3 hours during the day. By 6 weeks, these babies can generally cut out the 1 or 2 A.M. feed and will do a 5- or 6-hour stretch from 11 to 4 or 5 A.M.
Activity	5–10 minutes at first; 20 minutes at 6½ lb., gradually extend time to 45 when they are around 7 lb.		20–45 minutes (includes diapering, dressing, and, once a day, a bath)		20–45 minutes (includes diapering, dressing, and, once a day, a bath)	
Sleep	1¼–1½ hours		1½–2 hours		1½–2 hours	

Six Weeks to Four Months: Unexpected Wake-Ups

Compared to the first six weeks at home—the classic postpartum period—during the next 2½ months or so, everyone starts to be on a more even keel. You're more confident, and, we hope, a little less harried. Your baby has put some weight on—even low-weight babies have often caught up by now—and is less likely to fall asleep during her feeds. Her feeds are still every three hours during the day, stretching a bit longer, though, as we get closer to the four-month mark (at which point they'll be every four hours; see the next section, page 33). She is able to sustain longer activity periods and is probably sleeping for longer stretches at night, too, say from 11 P.M. to 5 or 6 A.M. Her crying, which probably peaked around six weeks, now slowly starts to decline somewhat over the next 2½ months.

Here are the complaints I generally hear at this stage:

COMMON COMPLAINTS	PROBABLE CAUSES
I can't get my baby to sleep more than three or four hours during the night.	She may not be getting enough food during the day, and you also might need to "tank her up" before bedtime (pages 93–94 and 195).
My baby *was* sleeping for five or six hours during the night, but now she's waking up more frequently, but always at different times.	Your baby is probably having a growth spurt (115–119 and 197–199) and needs more food during the day.
I can't get my baby to nap for more than ½ hour or 45 minutes.	You're probably misreading his cues and either not getting him to bed when he first shows signs of fatigue (181), or you're going in too soon when he first stirs, which doesn't give him a chance to go back to sleep on his own (189–190).
My baby wakes up at the same hour every night but never takes more than a few ounces when I try to feed him.	Habitual waking is almost never about hunger. Your baby is probably waking out of habit (191–192).

As you can see, the problem that usually presents in babies this age is a sudden, inexplicable (to the parents, at least) departure from the "S" part of their routine. Day *and* night sleeping can be erratic and trying—especially if a baby isn't on a structured routine. The parents wonder if they'll ever get any sleep themselves. Some night waking is naturally due to hunger—babies wake up when their tummies are empty—but that's not always the case. Depending on what the parents do in response to their baby's night waking and nap problems, their well-intentioned actions can lay the seeds of accidental parenting.

Say your baby awoke one night and you calmed her by giving her your breast or a bottle. It worked like a charm, and so now you think, *Mmmm, this is a good strategy.* Your baby liked it, too. But you're inadvertently teaching her that she needs to suckle in order to get back to sleep. Believe me, when she is six months old, much heavier, and still wants to feed several times a night, you're going to regret that quick fix. (You're lucky if you catch it by then—I've counseled several parents whose babies are nearly two, and they're still waking up several times a night for a comforting nip at Mum's breast!)

Have You Gone Back to Work?

During the first three to six months, many mothers go back to a former job or begin to leave the house to work part-time. Some need to, some want to. Either way, change can cause glitches in the E.A.S.Y. routine.

Was your baby used to the routine before you went back to work? A good rule of thumb is never to make too many changes at once. If you know you're going back to work, institute E.A.S.Y. at least one month before you do. If you've already gone back, you might have to take a two-week leave to get things on an even keel.

Who takes care of the baby in your absence? Does your caretaker understand the importance of a routine, and is he or she sticking to it? Is your baby's behavior different at day care or with the caretaker in your own home than when he is with you? E.A.S.Y. doesn't work if people don't stick to it. You may not know whether your nanny or day care provider is following the routine you specify—except when your baby seems out of sorts when you pick her up. On the other hand, that person can also do a *better* job of keeping your baby on a routine. Some parents, especially when guilt kicks in, let the structure slip—as in, "Oh, let's keep her up a little so I get to spend time with her."

How much is Dad involved? If you are trying to make changes in your baby's routine, how much are you prepared to *allow* him to be involved? I find that some mothers tell me they want a plan but don't actually carry it through, whereas their partner, perhaps the one who's home less, is better at sticking with it.

Have any *other* big changes happened in your household? Babies are sentient beings. They tune in to their surroundings in ways we don't yet understand. We know, for example, babies of depressed mothers tend to cry more themselves. So a job change, a move, a new pet, illness in the family—anything that disrupts the household equilibrium—can also disrupt your baby's routine.

Four to Six Months: "4/4" and the Beginnings of Accidental Parenting

Your baby's awareness is heightened now, and she interacts more with the world around her than she did a few months ago. Remember that babies develop from the head down, gaining control first over their mouths, then the neck and spine, arms and hands, and, finally, legs and feet (see sidebar, page 22). At this stage, your baby can hold up her head easily and is beginning to grasp at things. She is learning to, or already can, roll over. She can sit up fairly straight with your help, so her perspective is changing, too. She's more aware of patterns and routine. She has grown increasingly better at distinguishing where sounds come from and figuring out cause and effect, so she's much more engaged with toys that move and react to her touch. She has a better memory, too.

Because of these strides in development, your baby's daily routine naturally has to change, too—hence, my "4/4" rule of thumb, which stands for "four months/four-hour E.A.S.Y." Most babies are ready at this point to switch from a three- to four-hour routine. It makes sense: Your baby can play for increasingly longer periods during the day and sleep longer stretches at night. Whereas she used to wake up in the morning because she wanted a feed, most of the time now she wakes because of habit—her own internal clock—and not necessarily hunger. Left on their own, many babies wake somewhere between 4 and 6 A.M., talk to themselves and play a bit, and then go back to sleep. That is, if their parents don't rush in, which is how accidental parenting usually starts.

Your baby is probably a more efficient eater, too, so draining a bottle or breast may take only around twenty to thirty minutes. Including a diaper change, then, the E is forty-five minutes at most. But the A is different: Now she can stay up a lot longer, typically another hour and thirty minutes at four months, two hours by six. Many kids have a two-hour nap in the morning, but even if your baby wakes up after $1\frac{1}{2}$ hours, she can usually stay up the extra half hour while you're getting her ready for her next feed. Around two or two-thirty, she'll want another nap, usually $1\frac{1}{2}$ hours long.

On the next page is a side-by-side glance to show how E.A.S.Y. changes when your baby is four months old. You can cut one feed because she's taking in more at each feed, consolidate three naps into two naps (keeping the late afternoon catnap in either case), and thereby extend your baby's waking hours. (If you have trouble getting your baby to transition from a three- to a four-hour routine, you'll find a detailed plan for this transition on pages 39–46.)

3-hour E.A.S.Y.	4-hour E.A.S.Y.
E: 7:00 wake up and feed	E: 7:00 wake up and feed
A: 7:30 or 7:45 (depending on how long feed takes)	A: 7:30
S: 8:30 (1½ hour nap)	S: 9:00 (for 1½–2 hour nap)
Y: Your choice	Y: Your choice
E: 10:00	E: 11:00
A: 10:30 or 10:45	A: 11:30
S: 11:30 (1½ hours nap)	S: 1:00 (1½–2 hours)
Y: Your choice	Y: Your choice
E: 1:00	E: 3:00
A: 1:30 or 1:45	A: 3:30
S: 2:30 (1½ hours nap)	S: 5:00 or 6:00 or somewhere in between: cat-nap
Y: Your choice	Y: Your choice
E: 4:00 feed	E: 7:00 (cluster feed at 7:00 and 9:00, only if going through a growth spurt)
S: 5:00 or 6:00 or somewhere in between: cat-nap (approximately 40 minutes) to get Baby through the next feed and bath	A: bath
E: 7:00 (cluster feed at 7:00 and 9:00 if going through a growth spurt)	S: 7:30 bedtime
A: bath	Y: The evening is yours!
S: 7:30 bedtime	E: 11:00 dream feed (until 7 or 8 months, or whenever solid food is firmly established)
Y: The evening is yours!	
E: 10:00 or 11:00 dream feed	

The above are ideal days. Your baby won't necessarily conform exactly to these times. Her routine can be affected by weight—a smaller baby might only be able to do a 3½-hour routine at four months but will usually catch up by five, or, at most, six months—and temperamental differences, as some babies are better sleepers than others and some take less time to chow down. Your child might even veer from her own schedule fifteen minutes here and there. One day she'll have a shorter nap in the morning and a longer one in the afternoon, or she'll alternate between the two. The important consideration is that you stick to the eat/activity/sleep pattern (now at four-hour intervals).

Not surprisingly, many of the complaints that I hear most often at this stage have to do with problems in the routine:

COMMON COMPLAINTS	PROBABLE CAUSES
My baby finishes her feeds so quickly, I'm afraid she's not getting enough to eat. It also throws off her routine.	The E may not be a problem at all—some babies are quite efficient eaters by now. As I explained above, you may be trying to keep your child on an E.A.S.Y. plan meant for a younger child—every three hours instead of four (see pages 39–46 to learn how to make the transition).
My baby never eats or sleeps at the same time.	Some variation in your daily routine is normal. But if he's snacking and catnapping—both the result of accidental parenting—he's never getting a good meal or a good sleep. He needs to be on a structured routine suitable for a four-month-old (pages 39–46).
My baby is still waking up frequently every night, and I never know whether or not to feed him.	If it's erratic waking, he's hungry and needs more food during the day (195–200); if it's habitual waking, you have accidentally reinforced a bad habit (pages 191–192). You also might have him on a three- instead of four-hour routine.
My baby makes it through the night but wakes up at five and wants to play.	You might be responding too early to his normal early morning sounds and have inadvertently taught him that it's a good idea to wake up so early (pages 189–190).
I can't get my baby to nap for more than a half hour or forty-five minutes—or she refuses to nap at all.	She may be overstimulated before naptime (pages 249–252), or this is the result of a lack of, or improper, routine (pages 224–230)—or both.

In addition to the above, we also see a continuation of challenges that weren't dealt with earlier. Those seeds of accidental parenting planted earlier now begin to flower in the form of both eating and sleeping problems (so don't forget to read the previous section, "Six Weeks to Four Months," if you've skipped it). The parents find themselves faced with multiple problems and can't see clearly through the chaos. In some cases, it's because they didn't tailor E.A.S.Y. to their child's more advanced development. They didn't realize that they had to go from feeding every three hours to every four, that wake-up times are longer, or that naps are just as important as nighttime sleep. In others, it's because of the parents' inconsistency. They've gathered conflicting advice from books, friends, from the internet or the telly and have been trying this strategy or that, constantly changing the rules on their baby, hoping that *something* will work. Additionally, Mum may have returned to work full- or part-time (see page 32). That and other types of household change can disrupt a baby's routine. Whatever the circumstances, the problem is usually worse at this age because it has been going on longer and, in many cases, because the baby has never been on a routine at all. Indeed, I always ask parents of children four months (and older) one key question: **Has your baby *ever* been on a structured routine?** If the answer is "no," or even "she once was," I tell them that they have to begin with E.A.S.Y. At the end of this chapter, pages 39–46, I give you a step-by-step plan for helping your baby make that transition.

Six to Nine Months: Riding Out the Inconsistencies

The E.A.S.Y. plan is a different ball game now, although we're still looking at a four-hour routine—and I hear many of the same problems I see in slightly younger babies. But by six months, there's a major growth spurt, too. It's the prime time to introduce solid food, and, by seven months or so, to cut out the dream feed (page 123). Mealtimes are a little longer—and a lot messier—as your baby gets to try a whole new way of eating. Parents have lots of questions and concerns about solid food intake (which I answer in chapter 4). You can't blame them: In the beginning, babies are like eating machines, but at around eight months your baby's metabolism starts to change. She often becomes leaner, losing her baby fat, which has been put on to give her the strength to move around. At this stage it's more important to gauge her diet by quality not quantity.

Now, too, the early evening catnap disappears, and most babies are down to two naps a day—ideally, each one lasting one to two hours. Napping is *not* a favorite pastime of babies at this stage. As one mum of a seven-month-old put it, "I think it is because Seth is aware of the world now, and can move around more so he doesn't want to sleep. He wants to see *everything*!" True enough, as physical development now takes center stage. Your baby can hold himself upright—by eight months he'll be able to sit on his own—and he is becoming more coordinated as well. He'll be a lot more independent, especially if you've nurtured this skill by allowing him to play on his own.

The common complaints at this stage are pretty much the same as we saw at four to six months—except of course, habits are more deeply entrenched and a bit harder to change. Eating issues and sleep disturbances that could be tweaked in a few days at earlier stages now can be very intractable, but never impossible to correct. Now problems are just going to take a little longer to solve.

Otherwise, the biggest issue that crops up at this point is inconsistency. Some days your baby will take a long nap in the morning, other days it happens in the afternoon, and still other days it seems he's decided to drop one of his naps altogether. One day she'll eat with gusto, and the next she'd rather skip meals. Some mums roll with these ups and downs, and others want to tear their hair out. The key to survival is twofold: If he doesn't stick to a routine, at least you can. Also, you have to remember that truism of parenting: *Just when you think you've got it, everything changes* (see chapter 10). As the mother of a seven-month-old (who'd had her baby on E.A.S.Y. from the time she brought him home from the hospital) remarked, "The one thing I have learned is that practically every baby who is on this routine is different—you really do just have to do what suits you both."

When I read some postings on my website, it's quite clear to me that one mum's nightmare often seems like an ideal situation to another. On one of the E.A.S.Y. message boards, a Canadian mother was complaining because her eight-month-old daughter had "gone *way* off." She explained that the little girl wakes at 7, breast-feeds, eats cereal and fruit at 8, has a bottle at 11 and sleeps until 1:30, at which time she eats vegetables and fruits. She has a bottle at 3:30, eats dinner (cereal, veggies, and fruit) at 5:30, a final bottle at 7:30, and goes to sleep at about 8:30. The mother's problem: Her baby was taking only one nap a day. "I have lost control of the situation," she exclaims and begs other mothers on the site, "I need some help over here!!!!"

I had to read that posting twice because, for the life of me, I couldn't see a *problem*. Yes, her baby was getting older, able to stay awake for longer periods. But she was eating well and sleeping a solid $10\frac{1}{2}$ hours a night and taking a $2\frac{1}{2}$-hour nap during the day. I thought to myself, *Some mums would give their hind teeth to be in your shoes.* The fact is, because babies nine months and older can stay up for longer stretches without sleeping, it is possible for them to start skipping the morning nap altogether and take one long nap in the afternoon—for as long as three hours. They eat, play, eat again, play some more, and then go to sleep. In other words, "E.A.S.Y." becomes "E.A.E.A.S.Y." Dropping a nap can be a momentary glitch, or it can mean that your baby might be able to get by on one nap a day. If your baby seems grumpy on only one nap, you can introduce another nap or extend too-short naps by using the P.U./P.D. (pages 249–252).

I also get a lot of queries on my website from parents of babies this age who have tried E.A.S.Y. or another type of routine when their child was younger. This is the age that they decide to try again. Here is a typical posting:

> When my baby was 2 months, I tried to put her on E.A.S.Y., but the sleep part was so difficult, and the nursing was so often I gave up. Now that she is older I would like to try it again, but I would like to see sample schedules of other babies too.

Just for fun, I looked on the website for postings of mothers with babies between six and nine months old to compare their E.A.S.Y. routines. Putting them side by side, a surprisingly similar pattern emerges that looks pretty much like this:

7	Wake up and feed
7:30	Activity
9 or 9:30	Morning nap
11:15	Breast or bottle (the snack)
11:30	Activity
1	Lunch (solids)

1:30	Activity
2 or 2:30	Afternoon nap
4	Breast or bottle (snack)
4:15	Activity
5:30 or 6	Dinner (solids)
7	Activity, including bath and then the nighttime routine, which consists of a bottle or breast, book, and tuck in

While the above is typical, there are of course many variations on that theme: Some babies are still getting up at 5 at this age, having a pacifier or an extra bottle. Some nap far less than the ideal hour and a half or two, or take only one nap, which can make the "A" period that follows a very cranky and trying affair for their parents. And, sadly, some children are still waking several times a night, even at this age. So it's not just the daytime we have to look at. As I will keep drumming into your head, *E.A.S.Y. is not about time slots.*

E.A.S.Y. after Nine Months

Sometime between nine months and a year, your baby will be able to go five hours between feeds. He'll be eating three meals a day, just like everyone else in the family, and have two snacks to tide him over. He can be on the go for 2½ to three hours, and, usually around eighteen months—earlier in some children, later in others—get by on one big nap in the afternoon. We're not technically following E.A.S.Y. at this point, more likely he's on E.A.E.A.S.Y., but it's still a structured routine. Every day may not be exactly the same, but the elements of predictability and repetition are still there.

Starting E.A.S.Y. at Four Months or Older

If your baby is four months or older, and she's *never* had a routine, it's time to put her on one. The process is different from that of younger babies for three important reasons:

1. *It's a four-hour routine.* Sometimes parents don't realize they have to adjust the routine to their child's more advanced development. Their baby is eating more efficiently and sustaining ever-increasing periods of activity but they're still feeding her every three hours—in effect, they're trying to turn back the clock. For example, Diane and Bob's six-month-old Harry was suddenly starting to wake at night, seemingly hungry. Well-meaning parents that they are, they fed him at night. And knowing he needed more food during the day, instead of feeding him every four hours, they started feeding him every three hours as they had done when he was younger, reasoning, quite correctly, that he was having a growth spurt. But that's a solution for a three-month-old, not a six-month-old, who should be eating every four hours *and* sleeping through the night. (They need to feed him *more* at each feed, which I explain in chapter 3, pages 120–122.)

2. *We use my "pick-up/put-down method" (P.U./P.D.) to make changes.* With babies over four months old, sleep difficulties are invariably part of the reason why it's impossible to sustain a daily routine, if not the entire problem. This is when I introduce beleaguered and skeptical parents to P.U./P.D., a technique I rarely advise for younger babies (a detailed description of this key sleep strategy is the subject of chapter 6).

3. *Establishing a structured routine over four months is almost always complicated by accidental parenting.* Because parents have already tried other methods, or a medley of methods, their baby is confused. And in most cases, the baby has already gotten into a bad habit, such as falling asleep on the breast or waking repeatedly during the night. Therefore, putting an older baby on E.A.S.Y. invariably involves more commitment and work, a bit of sacrifice, and a great deal of consistency. Bear in mind that it took at least four months for those bad habits to develop. It won't take nearly that long to get rid of them *if you stick with the plan.* The older the baby, obviously, the harder it will be to change his routine, especially if he's still waking at night and is not used to any type of structure in his day.

Because babies are individuals, and because what happens inside each of their homes is different, too, I need to find out exactly what the parents have been doing so that I can tailor my strategies accordingly. If you've read thus far, you should already be anticipating the kinds of questions I'd ask parents whose baby has never had a routine:

REGARDING THE E: **How often are you feeding your baby? How long are his feeds? How many ounces of formula or breast milk is he eating during the day? If he's close to the six-month mark, have you also introduced solid food?** Although it's only a guideline, see how your baby measures up on the "E.A.S.Y. by the Pound" (page 29) and "Feeding 101" (page 95) charts. If he's eating every three hours or less, that's inappropriate for a four-months or older child. If his feeds are too short, he might be a snacker; if too long, he may be using you as a pacifier. Also, babies who aren't on a routine by four months often eat too little during the day and get up at night for additional feeds. Particularly if they're over six months, they often need more sustenance than a liquid diet provides. You might want to read chapter 3 as well before introducing E.A.S.Y.

REGARDING THE A: **Is he more alert than ever? Is he starting to roll over? What kinds of activities does your child do during the day—play on a mat, attend a Mommy and Me group, sit in front of the TV?** It's sometimes harder to establish a schedule with a more active baby, especially if he's never had one. You also have to make sure that you're not doing too much with your baby, which would make it hard for him to calm down for naps and bedtime and disrupt his eating as well.

REGARDING THE S: **Is he sleeping through at least six hours in the night—which he should be by four months—or does he still wake for a feed? What time does he get up in the morning, and do you go right in to him or allow him to play independently in his crib? Does he nap well, and for how long? Do you put him in his crib for naps, or do you just allow him to get exhausted and sleep wherever he passes out?** The S questions help gauge whether you've been allowing your baby to learn how to self-soothe and get to sleep on his own, whether you've taken charge of his sleeping, or let him lead you. The latter, obviously, leads to problems.

REGARDING THE Y: **Have you been under more stress than usual? Have you been ill? Depressed? Do you have support from your partner, your family, your friends?** It takes stamina and dedication to establish a routine if your life has been chaotic. If you're not up to speed, make sure that you nurture your adult needs first. It's almost impossible to minister to a baby, if it feels like *you* need to be taken care of. If you don't have support, get some. Having someone else by your side to give you a break is great, but even a shoulder to cry on is better than nothing.

The thing to keep in mind when introducing a routine for the first time is that there are rarely overnight miracles—three days, a week, even two, but never overnight. When ushering in any new regime to a baby of any age, you're going to get resistance. I've counseled enough parents to know that some of you out there really do expect magic. You may *say* you want your baby on the E.A.S.Y. routine, but to do so, you have to take certain actions. You have to be the monitor and guide, at least until your baby gets on track. Especially if your baby hasn't ever had a routine, you may have to forfeit something for a few weeks—your own time. Many parents resist that notion, like the mum who assured me she'd "do anything" to get her baby on E.A.S.Y., all the while firing off a barrage of questions: "Do I have to stay home every day in order to get him on a routine? Or can I go out with him and have him take naps in the car seat? If I have to stay home, will I ever get out of the house with my son? Please help me."

Have some perspective, luv! Once your baby gets used to the E.A.S.Y. routine, you don't have to feel like a prisoner. Fit your errands into your baby's time. You might feed the baby and then his A time will be riding in the car with you and doing errands. Or you might do a feed and activity at home, and let your baby sleep in the car seat or stroller. (Your baby may not nap as long, though, if he's the type who wakes up when the car engine turns off; more about routine busters on page 179.)

However, when you're first trying to establish a routine, the *ideal* would be for you *and* your partner to stay at home for a fortnight (two weeks) to give your child a chance to get used to a new routine, a week at the least. *You must make the time to make the change.* During this critical introductory phase, see to it that his feeds, his activities, and his sleep times happen in a familiar environment. Just two weeks, mind you, not the rest of your life. Yes, you might have to put up with a little extra crankiness, even crying, while your baby adjusts to the change. The first few days will be especially tough because you've already programmed this baby in a different way and now you have to *undo* the old patterns. But if you hang in there, E.A.S.Y. *will* work. Like the old saying goes, "It works if you work it."

Think of it this way: When you first go on holiday, you're not in holiday mode. It takes a few days for you to switch gears, leaving thoughts of your job and other responsibilities behind. It's the same for babies. Their minds are fixed on the old regime. When you try to change things, your baby is going to say (with his cries), "What the hell are you doing? We don't do it this way! I'm screaming as loud as I can, but you're not listening!"

The good news is that babies' memories are relatively small. If you're as consistent with the new way as you have been with the old, he'll eventually get used to it. And after a few really tough days or weeks, you'll find that it is better—no more erratic feeds, no waking up in the middle of the night, no frustrating days when you don't understand what he wants.

I always suggest that parents set aside at least five days to introduce E.A.S.Y. (see sidebar below for age-specific estimates). One of them should take the week off if possible. As you read through the plan, you might be surprised to see that I tell you to follow the suggested times pretty rigidly, whereas I have repeatedly told you *not* to go by a clock. For the purpose of this retraining period *only*, you have to be somewhat of a clock-watcher and far more inflexible than I would usually recommend. Once your baby is on a structured routine, it won't matter if you veer half an hour one way or the other. But at first, try to stick to the times I advise.

The Plan

Days One and Two. Don't intervene at this point; just observe for two solid days. Pay attention to everything. Reread the questions I ask (page 41), and try to analyze the effects of having no routine. Make note of feeding times, length of naps, bedtimes, and so on.

On the evening of Day Two, in preparation for Day Three, you must go to sleep when your baby does, and do the same thing each successive night as well. You're going to need to be rested to withstand the next few days (or longer). Ideally, since you're planning to stay at home for this week, you can also nap when he naps. Most things in your life can be put off for a bit. You might be in for a rough few days, but they will be worth how smashing your baby *and* you will feel when he's on a routine.

Day Three: The day officially starts at 7 A.M. If he's asleep, wake him—even if he usually sleeps 'til 9. If your child gets up at 5, do

---

Starting E.A.S.Y.: What Am I in For?

These are estimates; some babies take less or more time.

Four to nine months: Although babies take significant strides during this period, most require 2 days of observing and 3–7 days of reprogramming their day and night.

Nine months to a year: 2 days of observing, 2 days of screaming while you're trying to reprogram their day and night, 2 days of "Oh, God, we cracked it," and on the 5th day you might feel like you're back at Square One. See it through and by the end of the 2nd week, you'll be home free.

P.U./P.D. (pages 221–224) to try to get him back to sleep. If he's used to rising so early, and especially if you normally take him out and play with him at that hour, he's going to protest. You might end up doing P.U./P.D. for an hour or more, because he's adamant about getting up. Do *not* take him into your bed, a mistake a lot of parents make when their babies wake so early.

Take him out of his crib and feed him. Follow this with an activity time. A four-month-old can usually sustain $1\frac{1}{4}$- to $1\frac{1}{2}$-hour play period; a six-month-old, as long as two hours; a nine-month-old, two to three hours. Your child should be somewhere in that range. Some parents insist, "My baby won't stay up that long," and to them I say, do whatever you can to keep her up—a fan dance if necessary. Sing songs, make funny faces, keep her upright with lots of whistles and bangs.

Following the four-hour E.A.S.Y. routine on page 34, start to put your baby down for her morning nap around twenty minutes before you actually want her to sleep, say around 8:15. If you're unbelievably fortunate and have an adaptable baby, she'll do the usual twenty minutes of settling in and then nap for an hour and a half or two. However, most babies who have never had a routine resist going down, so you will have to do P.U./P.D. to send her off to sleep. If you're committed and you're doing it correctly—putting her back down the second she stops fussing—after twenty to forty minutes she'll eventually go to sleep. Yes, some babies take longer; I myself have had to do it for an hour or hour and a half, using up almost all the baby's "S" time. But remember that old saying, "It's darkest just before the dawn." The method takes resolve and patience and a bit of faith as well: It does work.

If you've had to do P.U./P.D., expect her to stay asleep for only forty minutes (remember you've spent almost that much time getting her down). If she wakes up earlier, go back in and do P.U./P.D. You might think this is crazy. If she's had forty minutes' sleep and nap time is supposed to be $1\frac{1}{2}$ hours, you might have to spend forty minutes getting her back to sleep and then she has only ten minutes left. Trust me: You're changing her routine and this is how you do it. Even if she's slept for only ten minutes, wake her up at 11 in time for her feed, so you don't get off track.

It's a Myth

Catnaps Ruin Sleep

Many babies between 4 and 6 months take a 30- to 40-minute catnap in the late afternoon, even as late as 5. Parents worry that the extra nap will ruin nighttime sleep. It's just the opposite: The more rest your baby gets in the day, the better she will sleep at night.

After you feed her, do an activity, and, again, go into her room at around 12:40, twenty minutes before it's time for her 1 P.M. nap. This time, it might only take her twenty minutes to get to sleep. If she doesn't sleep at least an hour and a quarter, do P.U./P.D. again. She also might sleep longer, but be sure to wake her up by 3 when it's time for the E.

The day will be pretty exhausting for both of you. So she might be extra tired in the afternoon. After she has a feed and does an activity, watch for signs of sleepiness. If she's yawning, let her have a forty-minute catnap somewhere between 5 and 6. If not and she's playing happily, put her to bed at 6 or 6:30, instead of 7. If she wakes up at 9, do P.U./P.D. again. Give her a dream feed between 10 and 11 (dream-feeding is explained in great detail on pages 93–94 and 195–196).

There's a good chance she'll get up at 1 or 2 A.M. You do P.U./P.D. again. You could be there for an hour and a half, just to get her to sleep for three hours straight. Do it all night if you have to, until 7 A.M., at which point you're into Day Four.

Day Four. Even if she's sleeping at 7, and you're utterly exhausted, wake her up.

You will go through the same process as on Day Three, but now instead of P.U./P.D. taking forty-five minutes or an hour, it will probably take only a half hour. She probably will sleep longer, too. We're aiming for naps of an hour and a half each at least. But use your judgment. If she has been asleep an hour and fifteen minutes and seems happy when she wakes, get her up. On the other hand if she has slept only an hour, you had better do P.U./P.D. again, because most babies regress quickly once they are accustomed to shorter naps. Remember to let her have that five o'clock nap if she's tired.

Day Five. By Day Five you should have smooth sailing. Maybe you'll have to do P.U./P.D. a bit, but it will take far less time now. With a six-month-old, it may take seven days altogether—two for observing, five for this turnaround process. With a nine-month-old, it could take up to two weeks (that's the worse case I've seen) because the baby is so deeply entrenched in his own routine that when you try to change him to yours, he'll be much more intractable than a younger baby.

The stumbling block is that parents are afraid it's going to last for-ever. After devoting four days to changing five-month-old Sam's routine, Veronica, his mum, expressed wonder at the fact that she and her hus-band could now have a leisurely glass of wine after dinner, unafraid that their son would disturb their evening. "I can't believe it took us such a short time." I say to every mum as I said to Veronica, "It worked because you were as consistent in the new way as you were in the old way." I also warned her that sometimes, especially with little boys (whom I've noticed, and gender research also indicates, tend to be the more fragile sleepers), a baby will do fine for a week and then regress and start waking in the middle of the night again or taking too short naps. When this happens, many parents mistakenly think that my plan failed. But you have to be as consistent in the structure as you were with the chaos. If you have a regression, go back to doing P.U./P.D. I guarantee that because your baby has already experienced it, the technique will take less time whenever you have to reapply it.

Routine is key. I will keep reminding you of the importance of E.A.S.Y. throughout this book. I give it so much time and attention, because a lack of structure and consistency is often at the heart of the most common child-rearing challenges. That is not to say that eating, sleeping, and behavior problems (which I discuss in greater detail in chapters 3 through 8) won't crop up even if you're on a good routine. Still, it's a lot easier to come up with solutions if you already have structure in your day.

TWO

EVEN BABIES HAVE EMOTIONS

Gauging Moods in the First Year

Visiting an Old Friend

Eight-month-old Trevor is lying on his back playing happily on a mat in the living room, while his mum, Serena, and I chat, mostly about how big Trevor has gotten and what a difference six months makes. I first met the two of them when Trevor was a day old. At the time, my job was getting Serena and Trevor off to a good start with breast-feeding. Putting Trevor onto the E.A.S.Y. routine straightaway was relatively simple because he was what I call a Textbook baby, a child who is fairly easy and who does pretty much whatever the books describe for particular ages (more on Textbook and other types of babies, pages 53–61). Over the next six months, Trevor reached each of the predictable physical and mental mile-stones right on time. And as this little vignette illustrates, his emotional life was proceeding on course as well.

As Serena and I talk, Trevor amuses himself with the toys hanging over his play mat. Ten minutes go by, and he starts making little "nyeh, nyeh" noises—not quite cries, but enough to let his mum know he needs a change of scene. "Oh, you're getting a little bored, honey?" Serena says, as if she's reading her child's mind. (She's actually just reading his signs.) "Let me just sit you over here." Trevor looks up at his mum, happy for the attention and, after being relocated, is just as content to play with a different toy. Serena and I pick up our conversation while Trevor, sitting nearby, curiously experiments with the crunchy sounds emanating from the brightly colored ball in his lap.

Serena asks if I'd like some tea, an offer that I, English to bone, can never refuse. There's nothing like a good "cuppa," as we call it. Serena gets up to head toward the kitchen, and just as she reaches the doorway, Trevor starts to wail. "This is what I mean," she says, referring to the real reason Serena called. "Suddenly it's as if his whole world revolves around me. I can't leave a room without his getting upset," she adds, almost apologetically.

Starting between seven and nine months, a baby's world does revolve around the beloved person who takes care of him most of the time—usually Mum. Most babies develop a fear of Mum leaving, some in only minor degrees, while others take it quite hard. Here, too, Trevor is right on time. But this little story isn't just about separation anxiety (which I discuss in greater detail on pages 80–83). It's about the bigger phenomenon of which separation anxiety is only a small part: your child's emotional life.

My Baby Has an Emotional Life?

Many parents are surprised when I talk about emotional milestones in the first year. They keep track of what their babies eat and how much they sleep, and parents are aware of, and sometimes worry about, their children reaching various physical and intellectual plateaus. But they seem less aware of, and consequently less interested in, their babies' emotional fitness, those skills that help them manage their moods, have empathy for others, and become social beings who can develop and maintain good relationships. Emotional fitness is not something parents should take for granted—it has to be taught. *And we have to start early.*

Training your baby to be emotionally fit is just as important as teaching him how to go to sleep, monitoring his diet, fostering his physical achievements, or enriching his mind. We're talking about your child's moods and behavior, his "emotional intelligence," to use a term popularized by psychologist Dan Goleman in his 1995 book of the same name. Goleman's book summed up research spanning the last several decades, during which time scientists have been exploring the many types of "intelligence," not just the kind that produces academic whizzes. And of all the types, numerous studies have proven, emotional intelligence is perhaps the most important, the foundation on which every other ability and skill is built. But you needn't scan the research or be a psychologist to realize how true that is. Just look around you. Think of the adults you know. Haven't you ever known someone whose intelligence is off the charts but who can't hold a job because he has "emotional problems"? Aren't there talented artists or brilliant scientists who don't know how to relate to other people?

Hold on, Tracy, you might be saying to yourself just now as you look across the room at your infant, be he six weeks, four months, or eight months. You undoubtedly want to ask me, "Isn't it a little early to be thinking about my baby's *emotions*?"

Absolutely not. You can't start too early. At birth, your baby displayed his emotions starting with that first loud wail in the delivery room. His emotional development—how he reacts to events, his general mood, his ability to self-regulate and to withstand frustration, his activity level, how excited he gets and how easy he is to soothe, his sociability, his reaction to new situations—will proceed as surely as his physical and mental development.

How Babies Feel

Babies' emotional lives, just like ours, are regulated by the limbic system, a small part of the brain that's also known as the "emotional brain." Don't worry, ducky, I'm not going to give you an anatomy lesson here. To be honest, detailed scientific explanations make my eyes cross! All you need to know is that by the time she was born, your baby had about half of the brain circuitry she needed to begin to experience emotions. Because the limbic system develops from the bottom up, the first thing to mature is her lower limbic structures. This lower part of her brain includes the almond-shaped amygdala, which is like action central for one's emotions. The amygdala alerts other parts of the brain that there's something worth reacting to. In other words, it's responsible for generating raw emotion— the spontaneous fight-or-flight reaction in the brain that makes the pulse race and the adrenaline flow. The upper limbic system begins to develop somewhere between four and six months, which is when the conscious mind becomes aware of emotions. Although your child's brain continues to mature well into her teens, let's consider what happens in just the first year (in chapter 8, we look at the toddler years and beyond):

Under four months. Even when your baby is a wee little thing, her primitive brain is in control. Emotions at birth are spontaneous and somewhat uncontrollable—such as a grimace in response to a gas pain. But within a few weeks, she will smile and also begin to imitate you, and that's a sign that she is already tuning in to *your* emotional style. She will cry to show discomfort or fatigue and smile, gurgle, and coo when she's happy or excited. She will begin to hold your gaze longer and longer, develop a social smile, and make a simple but important association: If I cry I get picked up. She begins then to realize that with cries and facial expressions she can get you to react to and meet her needs. When you respond to her she learns to trust, when you smile and mimic her she learns to engage.

Remember, luv, that crying is your baby's only means of expressing her emotions and needs. When your baby cries, it doesn't mean you're a bad parent. It is merely her way of saying, "I want your help, because I'm too little to do it for myself." Crying, which sounds rather ambiguous to a new parent, is most intense in the first six to eight weeks. It may take you a few weeks, but you'll soon learn the difference between hungry, bored, overtired, and pain cries. You'll become more adept at reading those cues if you also tune in to her body language. And, as I explained in chapter 1, all the better if she's on a routine, in which case time of day and where she is in her routine will tell you a lot about her emotions.

But for all her charm and utterly captivating qualities, for all her crying and complaining, scientists suspect that your baby isn't actually feeling her emotions *inside* at first. In one experiment with two- and three-day-old babies, the testers administered small tastes of vinegar water or sugar water. The babies' facial expressions clearly indicated distaste (wrinkled nose, squinted eyes, protruded tongue) or enjoyment (open mouth, raised eyebrows). But by using brain-scanning devices, the researchers could see that there was very little activity in the limbic cortex, the area of the brain where emotions are actually *felt*.

It may be comforting to know that when your baby cries, her wails are reflexive, and she won't remember the pain. That doesn't mean that I advocate letting a baby "cry it out." No, indeed. That goes against my philosophy of care. Quite the contrary, I believe that as long as you respond to your baby and heed her "voice," no lasting damage will be done by her crying. For that reason, too, I often recommend pacifiers for infants (see page 199) because they allow a baby to self-soothe, a key emotional skill. But the most important factor is *your* response to your baby's crying. Studies have shown that when parents are adept at interpreting and responding to various cries, their babies shift more smoothly into what researchers call "non-crying communication," which happens somewhere between twelve and sixteen weeks. By then most babies have settled down and spend less of their day crying. They're also easier to read and soothe.

Between four and eight months. When the upper limbic system kicks in, your baby's brain takes a giant leap forward. He will start to recognize familiar faces, places, and objects and become much more interactive with his environment, even enjoying the company of other children. He'll notice the family pet. Depending on your baby's temperament, which I discuss later, there's usually more joy and laughter at this point than distress and tears. You can see that he is starting to *feel* and to communicate those emotions in his facial expressions and his babbling, not just his crying.

Your baby's emotional life is more complex now. Some children begin to show rudimentary signs of being able to control their emotions this early. For example, if your baby goes down for a nap, fusses and talks to himself for a bit, sucks on his pacifier or cuddles with a favorite toy or blanket until he falls asleep on his own, he has already started to learn how to comfort himself and calm down. This tends to happen earlier with even-tempered babies, but self-soothing, like other emotional skills, is learned. Just as you hold your baby's hands to help him walk, you can help him take his first emotional steps, too.

Even if your baby doesn't seem to be in control of his feelings, he is probably easier to soothe now. The mere sight of you and the sound of your voice can be enough to calm him. He might cry out of boredom when left too long in one position or place, or display anger when a toy is taken away or when he's moved from one position to the next. With some infants you see escalating signs of stubbornness as well. A six-month-old might scream and pull his fists into his chest. He's already capable of manipulation, too. He can flirt with adults to get their attention, watch a face to see whether the person responds to his whimpering, and appear almost smug when he is finally picked up.

Your baby will become even more of a social and emotional presence, too. He'll let you know his preferences for food, for activities, and for people. He'll start to imitate not just sounds but the inflection in your voice. He'll squirm more in confined places, and might even balk at the mere prospect of being strapped into his stroller or high chair. Although he doesn't actually play with them, he'll be more interested in other babies now. Depending on his temperament, he may be frightened of more active children or of strangers. By burying his head in your shoulder (or crying) he's telling you, "Get me out of here." He's not only feeling his feelings (if you've been responsive thus far), he's expecting something to be done about them.

Eight months to a year. Babies of this age feel more and understand more than they can communicate, but if you watch your little one carefully you can see those little wheels spinning and the emotions—negative and positive—ebbing and flowing throughout her day. She's a real presence in your household and delights in your company. You can call her from across the room and she'll turn as if to say, "What's up?" She has a new sense of herself. She probably loves you to hold up a mirror—she'll smile at, pat, or kiss her own image. She also has a deeper connection with you and other close caretakers and might be reticent around strangers, burying her head in your shoulder until she's ready to warm up.

She knows the difference between children and adults. She's a great mimic. And she has a better memory, because that part of her brain, the hippocampus, is almost fully formed between seven and ten months. The good news is that she remembers various people in her life and the books that you read her. The bad news is that if you change her routine now, she'll have a very emotional reaction to anything new. Also, some children get frustrated because their communication skills lag behind their mental activities, and they can't express what they need. They may become aggressive or self-destructive at this age (head-banging, for example). Whining is common now, too, and not something you want to encourage.

It's quite apparent that by the end of the first year, your baby already has a rich emotional life. But babies don't come into this world knowing how to handle frustration, how to soothe themselves, or how to share with others, all of which are part of developing emotional competence. We have to *consciously* teach them. Some parents wait too long, by which time bad habits, like chronic tantrums, are more difficult to break. Others, unaware of the ways in which their own behavior teaches just the opposite of what they're trying to achieve, tend to take the road of least resistance. They give in and figure, "What's the big deal?" That's the beginning of accidental parenting.

Think of Pavlov's dog, which salivated every time the scientist rang a

> ## What Do You Want?
>
> The "banguage" (baby language) stage can be frustrating for parent and child. It's always a good idea to ask your child to *show* you what he needs. However, having a routine takes a lot of guesswork out of the process. If he is banging angrily on the refrigerator door and it has been four hours since breakfast, he's probably hungry!

bell, because it had heard that bell each time it was fed. Babies are like that, too. They quickly associate your response with their actions. So if you laugh today when your frustrated nine-month-old dumps over his bowl of Cheerios on the floor because he's bored and doesn't want to eat any more, I promise you that tomorrow he'll do it again, looking for the same laugh. The second time he does it, you undoubtedly will not find it funny. Or, let's say you're trying to get your one-year-old to wash his hands but as you lead him to the sink, he starts to cry. You say to yourself, *Oh, what the hell—we won't wash hands today.* You may not make the connection, but in a day or two when you're in the checkout line of the supermarket and he reaches for those strategically placed candies, and you say, "no," he already has a trick that he knows will make you give in. He'll cry and when that doesn't work, he'll cry a little louder until you finally relent.

Helping your baby develop emotional competence is as important as encouraging his first attempts at crawling or his first words. Indeed, how you respond to your baby's whines and other feeling states will determine to some extent what kind of emotions you can expect in toddlerhood. But don't wait for a full-blown tantrum to be convinced. Keep in mind my Nan's saying, *start as you mean to go on.* In other words, don't let bad habits develop in the first place. I realize that's easier said than done. Some babies are more of a challenge than others, but all are teachable. The trick is to know your baby so that you can tailor your strategies to his needs. Below, we look at the delicate balance between temperament and teaching.

Nature: Your Child's Temperament

Every baby's emotional makeup is predetermined, at least in part, by his biology—genes and brain chemistry. You can look at your own family tree to see how temperament is passed on from one generation to the next like some kind of emotional virus. Haven't you found yourself saying that your baby is "as mellow as I am" or "as shy as his Dad"? Or perhaps your mother has said, "Gretchen's aggressive behavior reminds me of your grandfather Al" or "Davy is as grumpy as Aunt Sue." Clearly, baby temperament is inborn—that's the *nature* part of the equation. But there's more to the story. By studying identical twins, who have exactly the same genes but rarely the same personalities by the time they reach adulthood, scientists conclude that environment—*nurture*—is equally influential. So let's look at the role of both nature and nurture.

Nannies, day care workers, pediatricians, and others who've seen as many infants as I have, agree that babies are different *at birth*. Some are sensitive and cry more than others, some are barely affected with what's going on around them. Some seem to greet the world with open arms, some cast a suspicious eye on their environment.

In my first book, I introduced five broad temperamental types: *Angel, Textbook, Touchy, Spirited,* and *Grumpy*. Some practitioners and researchers who have classified infants cite three or four types while others say there are as many as nine. Or they view babies through a particular lens, such as their adaptability or their activity level. They also use different names to distinguish the types. But the bottom line is one on which most observers agree: Temperament—which is sometimes referred to as "personality," "nature," or "disposition"—is the raw material that babies possess when they come into the world. Temperament affects how they eat, sleep, and react to the world around them.

Temperament is a fact of life. In order to work *with* your baby's temperament, you have to really understand it. Rifling through my mental filing cabinet, I've come up with five children, who exemplify each type, and given them pseudonyms that begin with the same first letter: Alicia *(Angel),* Trevor *(Textbook),* Tara *(Touchy),* Samuel *(Spirited),* and Gabriella *(Grumpy).* What follows is a thumbnail description of each child. Admittedly, some types are easier to handle than others. (In the next section, I also look specifically at how the five types differ throughout the day and how their moods affect them—and you.) Keep in mind that the portraits highlight *dominant* qualities and behavior. You may recognize your child in a particular category or you may feel she's a cross between two of them:

Angel. Alicia, now four, is just what her label implies: a dream child, one who easily adapts to her environment and to whatever changes you throw her way. As a baby, she rarely cried and when she did, it was never hard to read her cues. Her mum hardly remembers her terrible twos—in short, she is rarely hard to deal with because her predominant emotional style is easygoing and even-tempered. (Not surprisingly, some researchers have called this the "easy" type.) It's not that she never gets upset, but when she does, it doesn't take much to distract or calm her. As a baby she was never rattled by loud noises or bright lights. She has always been very portable, too. Her mum could go from store to store in the mall, for example, without worrying about a meltdown. From the time she was a wee infant, Alicia was a good sleeper. At bedtime, you simply laid her in her crib and she'd happily drift off with her pacifier, needing almost no other encouragement. In the morning, she babbled to her stuffed animals until someone came in. She adapted easily to a big-girl bed when she was eighteen months. Even as a baby, she was a social being, smiling at whoever came her way. To this day, she fits in easily when confronted with new situations, play groups, or other social settings. Even when her baby brother came along last year, Alicia took the change in stride. She loves being Mum's little helper.

Textbook. Seven-month-old Trevor, whom you met at the opening of this chapter, has reached every milestone like clockwork. He had a growth spurt at six weeks, slept through the night by three months, rolled over by five, sat up at seven, and I'll just bet that when he's a year old, he'll be walking. Because he's so predictable, his mother has no trouble reading his cues. For the most part, he has a mellow temperament, but he also has his cranky periods—just like the books describe. However, it's a relatively simple matter to calm and reassure him. As long as his mother introduces new things slowly and gradually—a good rule of thumb with any baby—Trevor goes with the flow. All his firsts thus far, like his first bath, his first taste of solid food, his first day at day care, have been pretty uneventful. It takes Trevor twenty minutes to fall asleep for a nap or nighttime sleep—the "average" time for a baby—and if he's restless, he responds well to an extra pat and a reassuring "shush-shush" in his ear. From the time he was eight weeks old, Trevor could amuse himself with his own fingers or a simple toy, and every month since then he has become a little more independent, playing on his own for increasingly longer periods. Because he's only seven months, he doesn't yet "play" with other babies, but he's not frightened to be around them. He's fairly good in new places—his mum has already taken him on a cross-country trip to see his grandparents. When he got home, it took him a few days to reorient himself, but that's normal for any baby who travels through different time zones.

Touchy. Tara, now two, weighed only six pounds at birth, slightly below average, and was also ultrasensitive from the beginning. By three months old, she had put on weight, but emotionally she was high-strung and easily excitable. She flinched at noises, blinked and turned her head away in bright light. She cried often and for no apparent reason. During her first few months, her parents had to swaddle her and make sure that her room was warm enough and dark enough for her to sleep. The slightest noises disturbed her and it was hard for her to get back to sleep. Everything new to Tara has to be introduced extremely slowly and very gradually. A great deal of research has been done on babies like Tara. Labeled as "inhibited" and "highly reactive," they represent around 15 percent of all children. Studies indicate that their internal systems are in fact different from other children's. Because they possess more of the stress hormones cortisol and norepinephrine, which activate the fight-or-flight mechanism, they actually *experience* fear and other feelings more intensely. Tara fits the profile. Shy of strangers as a baby, she'd tuck her head into Mum's shoulder. As a toddler, she is bashful, fearful, and cautious. She tends to clutch her mother in any new situation. At play group, she's getting a little more comfortable with the children, a carefully selected group of mellow kids, but it's still hard for her mum to leave the room. With help, Tara comes out of her shell, but it takes lots of time and patience on her parents' part. Tara is great at puzzles and games that require concentration, a trait that will probably carry over once she starts school. Touchy children often become quite good students, perhaps because they find the solitary work more manageable than running about with their classmates in the schoolyard.

Spirited. Four-year-old Samuel is a fraternal twin. People who know his brother and him differentiate Sam as the "wilder one." Even his birth foretold his nature: A sonogram prior to delivery showed his brother in the lower position, but Sam somehow managed to squeeze his way past Alexander to emerge first. He's been doing that ever since. He is aggressive and very vocal. As a baby and toddler, his loud screams always let his parents know, "I need you . . . now!" In social situations, such as family gatherings or play groups, he jumps right into the middle of the action. Sam always wants whatever toy his brother, or another child, is playing with. He loves stimulation and is drawn to anything that bangs, pops, or flashes. He's never been a good sleeper and even at four still has to be coaxed into bed at night. He eats well, and is a sturdy chap, but he can't sit at a table for very long. Sam climbs incessantly and heedlessly. Not surprisingly, he often gets into dangerous situations. He sometimes bites or pushes other children. And he throws fits when his parents don't give him what he wants, or don't do it fast enough. An estimated 15 percent of children are like Sam. Researchers refer to them as "aggressive" or "uninhibited," as "high activity" children or "high reactors." If Spirited children sound like they're challenging, they are. But properly handled they are also born leaders. They can become captains of sports teams in high school, and as adults, explorers and entrepreneurs who are fearless about plunging ahead where others have dared not go. The hard part is getting them to channel that wonderful energy.

Grumpy. Gabriella seems like she's got a chip on her shoulder, and she's only three. As a baby, it was hard to make her smile. Dressing and diapering her has always been a challenge. She tended, even as a baby, to go stiff on the changing table and then become fidgety and irritable. In her early months, she hated being swaddled and would cry angrily for a long time whenever her parents tried. Luckily her parents got her onto a routine as soon as she came home from the hospital, but whenever they veered slightly from it, Gabriella loudly voiced her displeasure. Feeding has been difficult all along, too. She was a breast-fed baby, but getting her to latch on and stay with it took a lot of work on Mum's part. Mum quit at six months because it was just too hard. Gabriella was also slow to adapt to solid food and even today is not a great eater. She gets impatient if food isn't presented the moment she's ready for it and exactly the way she likes it. She's a quirky eater, preferring certain foods over all others and sticking with them no matter how much her parents coax her. She is social when she wants to be, but she tends to hold back to assess each new situation. In truth, she prefers to play on her own and tends to resent other children being in her space. When I look into Gabriella's eyes, I see an old soul—it's as if she's been here before and she's not so happy about being back. But Gabriella is also a character; she has a mind of her own and isn't afraid to use it. Grumpy children teach their parents patience. They're also good at maintaining their own boundaries. You simply can't push them, a trait that later on makes them persevere with problems. As children and adults they tend to be very independent and good at taking care of and amusing themselves.

Everyday Moments: The Five Types

Temperament is a key factor in how your baby or toddler gets through the day. The following thumbnail descriptions and information come from years of observing babies. I give this to you only as a guide, not because your baby *should* be acting a certain way.

ANGEL

EATING: They're generally good eaters as babies; if given a chance, they're open to trying new (solid) foods.

ACTIVITIES: Moderately active; they play independently from babyhood on. These babies have a high tolerance for change; they're very portable. They're also very social, like to interact, and are good at sharing, unless overwhelmed by another child's aggressiveness.

SLEEP: Go down easily and independently; sleep long stretches by six weeks. After four months will take a good two-hour nap in the morning, 1½-hour nap in the afternoon, and until around eight months, a forty-minute catnap in the early evening.

MOOD: Usually easygoing and upbeat and not extremely reactive to stimulation or change. Their moods are steady and predictable. Parents find them easy to read because their emotional signs are so apparent. Hence, hunger is not often mistaken for fatigue.

HOW THEY'RE OFTEN DESCRIBED: Good as gold. Didn't even know I had a baby in the house. I could have five children like him. We were really lucky.

TEXTBOOK

EATING: Very similar to Angel babies, although solid foods may have to be introduced more slowly.

ACTIVITIES: Moderately active. Since they do everything on time, it's easy to choose appropriate-level toys. Some are real doers; others hang back a bit.

SLEEP: They usually need the full twenty minutes—the typical time it takes a baby to drift from tiredness to settling into sleep. If particularly overstimulated, they may need a bit more calming from a parent.

MOOD: Similar to Angel babies, they're low reactors—fairly unflappable, as long as someone pays attention to their signs of hunger, sleep, overstimulation, and so on.

HOW THEY'RE OFTEN DESCRIBED: She's right on time with everything. She's mellow unless she needs something. A low maintenance child.

TOUCHY

EATING: Tend to get easily frustrated, and anything can upset their desire to eat—flow, body position, conditions in the room. If breast-fed, may have trouble latching on and difficulty getting a sucking rhythm. Will balk at any kind of change or if you talk too loud. Refuse solids at first— you have to be persistent.

ACTIVITIES: Very cautious about new toys, new situations, new people, and need a lot of support in such instances, or when going through any kind of transition. They tend to have low-activity levels, and need to be encouraged to participate. They're usually less sensitive in the morning and better at one-on-one play than groups. Avoid afternoon play dates.

SLEEP: Extremely important to swaddle and block out stimulation. If you miss their "sleep window," these babies get so overtired that it takes at least twice as long to get them to sleep. They tend to go back to sleep in midmorning for a long stretch and only catnap in the afternoon.

MOOD: They're sometimes cranky in the delivery room, where the bright lights seem to overwhelm them. They are highly irritable, very reactive to and easily upset by external stimulation.

HOW THEY'RE OFTEN DESCRIBED: A real crybaby. The slightest thing sets him off. He's not good with other people. He always ends up in my lap or clinging to my leg.

SPIRITED

EATING: Very similar to Angel baby in the eating department, but breast-feeders can get impatient. If Mum's letdown is too slow, he'll bob off the breasts as if to say, "Hey, what gives?" Sometimes, you need to give a supplement with a bottle until the milk really gets flowing.

ACTIVITIES: High energy, feisty, and very active. They are ready to jump into almost any situation, and exercise little impulse control or caution when they do. They are highly reactive and can be aggressive with peers. Because they're usually more cooperative in the morning, avoid afternoon play groups so they can wind down.

SLEEP: As babies, they hate being swaddled, but you absolutely need to block out any visual stimulation. They tend to be resistant to naps or nighttime rituals, because they don't want to miss anything. If you're lucky, even though they sleep less in the morning, it will be followed by a long afternoon nap, which is key to a good night's sleep for these kids.

MOOD: When they want something, they want it *now*! Opinionated, very vocal, and often stubborn, their moods are mercurial, going quickly from happy to sad and back again. They love the action but also tend to *overdo it*, which can lead to a meltdown. Tantrums are hard to stop once they get going. Transitions can be tough, too.

HOW THEY'RE OFTEN DESCRIBED: A handful. Always into something. I don't have the energy to keep up with her. She's fearless.

GRUMPY

EATING: They're very impatient. If breast-fed, they don't like to wait for Mum's letdown; they sometimes do better if bottle-fed. However, in both cases, feeds can take a long time, which tends to overtire them. They don't adapt easily to solids and when they finally do, they tend to insist on the same foods over and over.

ACTIVITIES: They're on the low end of the activity continuum, preferring to play by themselves and to use their eyes and ears more than their bodies. If they're engaged with a toy or an activity, they hate to be interrupted and find it hard to end one thing and start another.

SLEEP: Sleep doesn't come easily to these babies. They often get overtired because they're so resistant, and then they tend to fuss themselves to sleep. These children also tend to be catnappers, sleeping in only forty-minute stretches, which sets off a vicious cycle (see pages 249–252).

MOOD: As we say in Yorkshire, these babies are often "on the fuss." Like a simmering pot that you have to watch to make sure it doesn't boil over, you have to keep an eye on their emotional signs. The slightest variation from routine can set them off: a missed nap, a stimulating activity, too much company. Without a routine, their lives are in turmoil, and eventually they take over your life.

HOW THEY'RE OFTEN DESCRIBED: What a sourpuss. He seems to prefer playing on his own. I feel like I'm always waiting for his next meltdown. He always has to have his way.

Nurture: How Parents Override Temperament

Temperament is not a life sentence. Although Nature provides what babies come in with, children's experience—the nurture they get, starting in infancy—has just as much of an impact. In other words, your baby's emotional life is determined both by her temperament, which shows itself as early as a few days after birth, and her life history—events, experiences, and most important, the people who care for her. Parents can have a beneficial effect on children's temperament, or just the opposite, because their young brains are still moldable. We know this because a number of studies have shown that parents' behavior can actually modify the wiring in a baby's brain. For instance, even within their first year, babies of depressed mothers become more irritable and withdrawn and are less apt to smile than babies of nondepressed mothers. Likewise, the limbic systems of abused babies are different from nonabused babies.

Those are extreme examples of the ways in which we know that temperament can be affected by environment. This plasticity of the brain can also work in more subtle ways as well. I've seen Touchy babies grow out of their shyness to become poised, sociable teenagers. I've watched Grumpy children grow up and find a special niche for themselves. And I know lots of Spirited kids who go on to be responsible leaders instead of troublemakers. But the reverse is true, too. Any type of child, no matter how good her innate disposition, is at risk if parents don't heed her needs and wants. An Angel can become a grouch, a Textbook toddler can turn into a terror.

I get emails all the time that begin with the line, "My child used to be an Angel baby . . ." So what happens? Well, consider the sad saga of Yancy, a healthy eight-pound baby at birth. His mum, Amanda, is an entertainment lawyer in her late thirties. Like many women of today, Amanda pursued a career out of college and was so focused on becoming a partner, her twenties and thirties were all about work. After achieving that dream and claiming some of the biggest stars in Hollywood as her clients, she met Matt, a fellow attorney. After they married, both knew they wanted children "someday" and so when Amanda found herself pregnant at thirty-seven, she put any ambivalence aside and said, "I guess it's now or never."

Amanda applied the same keen managerial skills to her baby "project" as she did to the cases she handled for her firm. By the time Yancy was born, she had the nursery well appointed and the cupboard filled with formula and bottles. She had planned to breast-feed but wanted the flexibility . . . just in case. She intended to return to work after a six-week leave of absence.

Luckily, Yancy was the kind of baby who cooperated. "Good as gold," was the phrase most often heard around the house in those early days. He slept well, ate well, and was a generally happy little boy. When Amanda returned to her job as planned, she breast-fed Yancy in the morning, had the nanny give Yancy formula during the day, and breast-fed him again when she came home from the office. But when he was around three months old, Amanda was beside herself. "I don't know what happened," she told me tearfully over the phone one day. "He's not sleeping as well as he used to. He used to last from eleven to six, but now he's waking up two or three times a night. I've had to go back to breast-feeding him at night, because he seems hungry, and he won't take a bottle from me. So now I'm exhausted and he's just plain off."

Because Amanda had gone back to work so quickly, she felt guilty about not spending more time with her son. Rather than keep him on the consistent routine he'd been on since birth, she had instructed the nanny to keep him up later so that she could spend time with him when she got home and do his last feed. Most nights, instead of going down at seven, he was up until eight or nine o'clock. Whereas they had been cluster feeding him and giving him a dream feed, those tanking-up strategies had fallen by the wayside as his routine began to change. His nighttime sleep was fitful, because he went to bed overtired. And when he woke throughout the night, Amanda reached for the nearest solution—her breast—because she couldn't figure out what else to do. What started out as a quick fix turned into a full-blown case of accidental parenting. Suddenly her Angel baby was more like a Grumpy baby, because he was crying inconsolably. He *was* "off"—off his routine. Once she started nursing him at night, Yancy came to expect it. During the day, when she was at work, he started refusing the bottle, too. He was holding out for his mum's breast. (Some babies actually go on hunger strikes; see the box on page 129.)

Because Yancy's essential disposition was so mellow, it wasn't hard to get him back on a good routine. Amanda agreed to come home early from the office for at least two weeks, so we could undo the fallout of her accidental parenting. Because he was waking erratically, I suspected that Yancy was probably going through a growth spurt. Rather than have him expect his meals at night, though, I wanted to increase his calories during the day, so we added an ounce to each of his daytime bottles and went back to cluster feeding at 5 and 7 and a dream feed at 11. We moved Yancy's bedtime back to 7. We also made sure that he wasn't allowed to nap more than a total of 2½ hours in the day, so that it didn't rob his nighttime sleep.

The first night was a bit hellish, because I had made Amanda promise not to feed Yancy when he woke. I explained that by increasing his calories as we did, Yancy went to bed with more in his tummy than usual, and he wouldn't starve. He woke up three times, and each time Amanda used a pacifier and my shush-pat method (page 184) to calm him. No one got much sleep that night. But the second night, after a day of good feeds and good naps, Yancy woke only once, and instead of it taking forty-five minutes to send him back to sleep, it took ten. The third night, he slept through and what do you know? Matt and Amanda's Angel baby was back, and calm returned to their household.

Of course, just as parents can "ruin" a good baby's temperament, the reverse is happily true. We can do a great deal to help our children overcome shyness, channel aggressiveness, learn how to exert self-control, and become more willing to engage in social situations. For example, Betty knew, and accepted, that Ilana, her third child, was a cross between Touchy and Grumpy. When Ilana let out her first scream in the delivery room, I looked at her mum and said, "I think we have a Grumpy baby on our hands." I've been at enough deliveries and taken enough babies home to know the differences are there at birth: Touchy *and* Grumpy babies act as if they don't want to be born.

As Ilana grew, her temperament lived up to my early prophecy. She was a shy, often churlish child who could have a meltdown at any minute. Betty, who had experience with her other children, could see that Ilana might never be a cheery, happy-go-lucky kid. But instead of focusing on what wasn't or trying to change her baby's nature, Betty worked with who

Ilana really was. She kept her on a good routine, protected her sleep times, and paid careful attention to her emotional ups and downs. She never forced her to smile at strangers or coaxed her into an activity. She didn't worry about the fact that Ilana was always the last to try new things, or sometimes didn't try them at all. She saw that Ilana was also creative and bright and tried to foster those qualities. She played lots of fantasy games with her, read to her constantly, and, as a result, Ilana developed an astoundingly large vocabulary. Betty's patience paid off. With people she knew, Ilana could be very talkative, as long as you gave her a chance to warm up.

Ilana is about to go off to kindergarten. She is still on the inhibited end of the personality continuum, but in the right environment she comes out of her shell. Luckily for her, her mum also takes steps to make her daughter's path a little smoother. Betty has already had a talk with Ilana's new teacher, alerting her to the kinds of approaches that work well with her child. Because Betty knows who her child is, she also expects that the first week or so in her new class might be a big adjustment for Ilana. But with such a caring and observant mum in her corner, I'm sure Ilana will be fine.

I've seen countless other examples of parents whose patience and consciousness have helped override temperament that might have been problematic in other families. Even before Katha was born, for example, her mum, Lillian, knew that she had a very active and assertive little girl on her hands. In utero, Katha kicked incessantly, as if to send a message to her mum: "Here I am and you'd better get ready." Once in the world, Katha did not disappoint. She was a typical Spirited baby who demanded her mum's breast and cried immediately if it took too long for the milk to start flowing. Seemingly more interested in being awake than sleeping—she might miss something—Katha resisted going to bed and usually managed to get out of her swaddle. Fortunately, Lil put Katha on a good routine from Day One. As her little spitfire grew into toddlerhood, she made sure that Katha, who walked at nine months, had ample opportunity to put her energy to good use in the morning. They spent lots of time outdoors, admittedly easier in sunny southern California. In the afternoon, they did quiet activities because Lil knew how hard it was for Katha to wind down. It was particularly challenging when Katha's little sister arrived on the scene. Not surprisingly, Katha did not like to share Mum's attention. But Lillian made special "big girl" places for Katha in the house ("where the baby isn't allowed") and made sure that she spent one-on-one time with her energetic older daughter. Today, at five, Katha is still a bold and adventurous child but also polite and fairly well-behaved because her parents have always reined her in and limited her behavior when she was unable to control herself. Katha is also a precocious athlete—the result no doubt of all the climbing and ball playing her mum encouraged. Lillian had no illusions that her firstborn would grow out of her temperament. Instead, she worked with her nature, a strategy I suggest that all parents adopt.

Why Some Parents Can't See

Children like Katha are innately more of a challenge than others, but all children do better with "P.C." parents like Lillian who understand and accept their child's nature and who tailor their day and, when needed, discipline accordingly. That's the ideal of course. But parents are not always able to, and in some cases don't want to, see what's right in front of them.

When they first bring their little one home, parents' vision is sometimes obscured by their expectations. Almost every pregnant couple, as well as parents contemplating a second or third child, have preconceived notions of who that child will be and what he or she will be capable of doing. Usually our fantasies reflect who we are. So the athlete imagines herself out on the soccer field or hitting tennis balls with her child. The hard-driving lawyer thinks about how smart his kid is going to be, where he's going to go to school, and what great discussions the two of them will have.

Very often, however, our real children don't come close to the ones parents see in their daydreams. They might have imagined an angelic child but when reality hits there's a squirming, screaming little devil, interrupting dinner, waking them up at night. In such cases, I remind them, "You have a baby. Babies cry. It's the only way they can communicate." Even an Angel or Textbook baby needs adjustment time, and it doesn't happen in a few days.

As your baby gets older and certain emotional traits become more apparent—grumpiness, sensitivity, feistiness—it's also bound to remind you of yourself or your partner or your Great Aunt Tillie. So let's say you have a Spirited baby. If you are a go-getter and feel positive about high-energy people, you might boast about it: "My Charlie is as assertive as I am." But if you're somewhat overwhelmed by, or fearful of, the exact set of traits that are characteristic of Spirited children, you're likely to have just the opposite response: "Oh, I hope Charlie doesn't turn out to be as aggressive as his dad. I'm afraid he'll turn into a bully." Of course, we're bound to see family traits reemerge in our children, but we don't have a crystal ball. Even if your child *reminds* you of a part of yourself or your partner that you'd rather not see repeat itself, or of a relative you don't like, you have no idea how he will actually turn out. *He is a different person, with different influences, and a path all his own.* And most important, if you teach your Spirited child how to manage his emotions and to channel his energy, he doesn't have to become a bully.

The trouble with fears or fantasies is that when we act on them and not on what we see in front of us, the real-life child suffers. So one of the first orders of baby whispering is:

> **Look at the child you have, rather than at the fantasy of the one**
>
> **you *wanted* to have.**

Grace, a very shy woman herself, called me because she was concerned about Mack's "stranger anxiety." On the phone she explained that her seven-month-old was turning out to be "just like me" at that age. But when I met seven-month-old Mack, I saw a Textbook baby who was a little skittish about new people. Given a few moments to adjust, he was happily sitting on my lap. "I can't believe he's sitting on your lap," said Grace, her mouth wide open in surprise. "He never goes to anyone else."

After asking Grace to honestly look at her own behavior, the truth came out: Grace never *allowed* Mack to get close to anyone else. She hovered over her son constantly, keeping everyone away because she believed she was the only one who understood how painful it was to be so sensitive. In her mind, she was the only one who could protect him and knew how to handle him. Even Dad was being pushed out of the picture. To make matters worse, Grace did what many worried parents do: She voiced her concerns in Mack's presence.

Oh, but you say, Mack was just a *baby*. He doesn't really understand what Grace means when she says "He never goes to anyone else." Codswallop! Babies learn from listening and watching. Even researchers aren't sure exactly when understanding really kicks in. But we do know babies pick up on their caretakers' feelings and we do know that they understand long before they start to talk. So who are we to assume that those little ears aren't taking it all in? When Mack hears, "He never goes to anyone else," it tells him that no one else is safe.

Another common pitfall that occurs when parents don't respect a child's emotional makeup is that they sometimes try to force her to conform. This happens frequently as babies become more independent. This posting from my website is a great example:

> My Chloe hates being held. As soon as I pick her up she's struggling to get down on the floor to explore. She's perfected her crawling technique now so she always wants to try it out. Sometimes I wish she would cuddle me or at least sit on my lap and listen to a song or look at a book but she's just not interested. She's definitely not a "clingy baby," quite the opposite. She's very independent and wants to do her own thing. Anyone got an independent baby who hates being held?

I would guess that Chloe is between nine and eleven months old. She is obviously a Spirited baby. The problem is that whereas Spirited babies don't mind some snuggling when they're younger, as soon as they can move out on their own, cuddling feels too restrictive. This mum has to accept that *her* child will not be content to sit and watch from her mother's lap the way some of her friends' babies do. She might be aching for the closeness, and maybe she can catch a few minutes of it at a time when her Spirited child will be more receptive, before bedtime when Chloe winds down and is ready for a story. But in the meantime she has to recognize what her child is capable of, especially when she's actively engaged in exploring the world.

A Tennessee mother had a similar problem with her Touchy baby, who was only five weeks old when she wrote to me: "My husband and I are very sociable and like to go to friends' houses. Keith did not do well when we did that. We even had him in our friend's nursery trying to calm him and he would not stop crying. Any suggestions?" Well, luv, maybe your son is too young to deal with such a big day. It's "big" from his point of view: a car ride and then spending the evening in a strange house with all those big people cooing and gooing at him all night. It's unfortunate and limiting at times, but you have to accept that that's who he is, at least for now. He's only five weeks old, for goodness' sake. Give the boy a little time to adjust. Then gradually work with him; nurture and develop his strengths and focus on positive traits that you want to enforce. Still, some children are just more sociable than others and always will be.

Certain types of parents also take their children's disposition personally, and then *their* emotions get thrown into the mix as well. I can remember Dora calling me because whenever she tried to hold Evan, a Grumpy baby, he slapped her. Dora took the slap as a rejection and she felt hurt. Some days when that happened, Dora, who was herself quite sensitive, longed even more to hug her little boy, but some days she felt like slapping back at the little ingrate (who was only seven months old, mind you).

"How do I discipline him?" she asked. The fact is, children lack the brain development at seven months to understand cause and effect. Evan's slap was his way of saying, "Let me down." I'm not saying that Dora should just let the slap go. She needs to restrain his hand and say "We don't hit," but she can't expect him to really "get" it for another six months (more about this in chapter 8).

Goodness of Fit

Evan and Dora's story is not unusual. Parents' understanding of their children's emotional life is often thwarted when their baby's temperament clashes with their own emotional style. In the case of Chloe's mother, for example, the mother sounded a bit needy herself, and her desire for physical closeness overpowered her ability to see who Chloe really was. The fact is, you, dear reader, as well as every other parent reading this book, have a temperamental style all your own. You were a baby once yourself and fit into one of the five categories I described earlier, or perhaps you were a blend of two or more. An array of experiences have influenced you since then, but your temperament—your emotional style—is still a factor in how you relate to people and situations.

Stella Chess and Alexander Thomas, two renowned psychiatrists who were pioneers in the research on babies' temperament as far back as 1956, coined the term "goodness of fit" to describe the degree to which parents and babies were compatible. In other words, healthy development is not just about your baby's temperament; it's also about your demands and expectations—whether you see your baby for who she really is and can adapt your strategies to fit her needs, not just yours. Although I don't have any hard research based on the following parent types, my experience with thousands of parents has given me a pretty good idea of what happens when a parent with a particular emotional style interacts with each of the baby types:

Confident parents are easygoing and calm, so they're a good fit with all of the baby types. When they first have a child, they tend to roll with the changes in their life and with the ups and downs of parenthood. They're fairly carefree about the job—"naturals" who trust their intuition and are very good at reading their baby's cues. Because they're usually pretty laid-back and patient, they do well with Grumpy babies, are willing to take the extra time that Touchy babies need, and have the stamina and creativity to raise Spirited kids. Confident parents tend to think the best of everyone, and so they look for the best in their child. Though they have their own opinion about various parenting practices, they're very open to new ideas, and they're quick to recognize when they're attributing their own motives to something their baby is doing.

By-the-book parents do everything quite literally . . . "by the book." Sometimes, they open themselves up to a lot of frustration, because they expect their baby not to deviate from the norm. When problems arise, these are parents who search wildly in books and magazines and on the internet to find their exact situation and a recipe for correcting it. They come onto my website complaining because their baby will not do this or that. They try to get their baby to conform to what's typical—not necessarily because it's good for the baby but because it's "normal." The ideal baby for these parents is a Textbook baby who reaches milestones right on time. They do well with Angel babies, too, because they're such adaptable children. But because Textbook parents want so desperately to keep to a schedule, they may miss the baby's signs. So it's not a great fit for a Touchy baby who is ultrasensitive, or a Spirited baby who is anything but a conformist. By-the-book parents run themselves in circles, trying various schedules and strategies, depending on which book or expert they're following today. Probably the worst fit is with a Grumpy baby, who will get even more upset with each new change. By-the-book parents' strength lies in their ability to research and deal with problems. They are extremely open to suggestions.

High-strung parents are sensitive themselves. They may be shy, so it's hard for them to reach out to other parents for company and support.

High-strung mums often get weepy and feel incompetent in the early days of motherhood. High-strung dads are afraid to hold the baby. With an Angel or Textbook baby, they are usually okay, although if the baby is having a bad day, as all babies sometimes do, they think they must have done something to cause it. They have a low tolerance for noise and are very bothered by crying, so a Touchy or Grumpy baby is rarely a good fit. They're likely to feel frustrated and weepy much of the time. If they have a Grumpy baby, they're likely to take her moods personally. I've had parents say to me, "He never smiles because he hates us." High-strung parents tend to be overwhelmed most of all by a Spirited baby, who quickly learns that he's in charge. Their sensitivity has a positive side as well: They are extremely tuned in.

Go-getter parents are always on the move, always involved in a project. Go-getter parents can't sit still; they may have trouble with the fact that a baby slows them down and may even have quick tempers. Go-getter parents tend to resist advice. Though many call me to ask what to do, if I give them a plan, they're likely to come back with a series of "Yes, but . . ." statements and "What if . . ." questions. As they tend to schlepp their baby everywhere, Go-getter parents could even wear out an even-tempered Angel or a Textbook baby or worse, make them insecure in all the chaos. In the process, they often miss what's in front of them: the joy in having such a child most other parents would be grateful for. Go-getter parents might get angry at a Touchy baby, feel affronted by a Grumpy baby's bad humor or lack of adaptability, and lock horns with a Spirited baby. They tend to be somewhat rigid and to favor the extremes, like having a baby cry it out rather than taking a gradual, more compassionate approach to sleep difficulties. They are very rigid, driven by their own needs, and therefore tend to see everything in black or white. They don't do well with E.A.S.Y., because when they hear "routine," they think *schedule.* On the other hand, these are very creative parents who expose their children to a wide variety of experiences and encourage them to try new things and take risks.

Headstrong parents seem to think they know it all and get upset when their baby doesn't respond as they think she should. They're very opinionated and often stubborn, and it's often hard for them to compromise. These parents are always moaning and complaining. Even if they have an Angel or Textbook baby, they find and focus on the one thing their baby doesn't do or, in their minds, is doing wrong. Headstrong parents find it hard to tolerate a Touchy baby's crying. They don't like the bother of having to constantly calm down or chase after a Spirited baby. And they resent that their Grumpy baby is so stubborn and that he doesn't smile very much, perhaps because it reminds them of their own nature. In short, these parents find a way to criticize and carp no matter what kind of baby they have. To make matters worse, they bad-mouth their babies and complain to others when the children are within earshot, and in doing so, these parents make their little ones turn into what they keep telling them they are. The good thing about Headstrong parents is that they have a lot of staying power. Once they recognize a problem, they're open to suggestion, and are willing to follow through, even when the going gets hard.

Bear in mind that the above emotional styles are composites taken to the extreme. No one fits any category exactly; most of us see pieces of ourselves in each one. But if we're honest, we know who we are most of the time. Also, I'm not implying that parents aren't allowed to make mistakes. Parents are only human. Their needs are always simmering beneath the surface, and they have lives and interests outside their children (and that's a good thing). My purpose in showing you the possible "poorness of fit" scenarios is that this will heighten your awareness and make you a bit more conscious about how your style might affect your child's emotional fitness. Sadly, when parents are unable to see through the veil of their own self-interest, and when their demands and expectations are not compatible with their child's temperament and abilities, their attitude can seriously hamper a child's emotional fitness, particularly the development of trust.

Trust: The Key to Emotional Fitness

Your baby's emotional life is initially expressed as pure emotion, mostly through his different types of cries and his interactions with you; these are his first experiences of communication and contact, his growing attachment to you. By cooing and gooing at you, your baby is actually trying to relate and have a conversation to keep you engaged and connected (scientists call this "proto conversation"). But it takes two to keep the social and emotional dance going, which is why your response is critical. When you smile back at his smiles and his babbling or comfort his mournful cries, he knows you're there for him, and it is the beginning of trust. Seen through this lens, you can understand why crying is a good thing: It means your baby expects that you'll respond. Conversely, a number of studies have shown that neglected babies eventually stop crying. It's useless to cry if no one comes to comfort you or meet your needs.

Trust lays the groundwork for your baby's emotional fitness in the coming years, her ability to understand her emotions, her self-control, her respect for other people's feelings. And because emotions can enhance or inhibit your child's intellect and her special gifts, trust is also the foundation of learning and social skills. Several long-term studies have shown that children who have formative relationships they can count on not only have few behavior problems in school, they also have confidence in themselves, develop a sense of curiosity about the world, and are motivated to explore it (because they feel safe knowing that you're there to catch them if they fall). They are also better able to interact with peers and adults than children who lack strong early bonds, because their first relationships have shown them that others can be relied on.

Trust-building begins with understanding and accepting your baby's temperament. Every child's threshold and emotional reaction is bound to be different. Given a new situation, for instance, an Angel, Textbook, or Spirited baby is more likely to adapt quickly, where a Touchy or Grumpy baby might get upset. Spirited, Grumpy, and Touchy babies wear their emotions on their sleeve and let you know loudly and clearly what they're feeling. Angel and Textbook babies need relatively little to calm them, but Touchy, Spirited, and Grumpy babies sometimes seems inconsolable. However your baby's emotions manifest themselves, never try to push her to feel something different ("Oh, there's nothing to be afraid of") or in some way cajole her "out of herself"—a common and telling expression I often hear parents use. What's really happening is that the parents are uncomfortable with their child's intense emotion so they try to talk her out of it.

Instead of negating a child's feeling—even an infant's—*describe* the emotion ("Oh, Sweetie, you must be tired, that's why you're crying"). Don't worry about whether your baby understands; eventually she will. Equally important, you then tailor your response to what *she* needs at the moment—with a Touchy baby you'd swaddle her up and put her down, but not with a Spirited or Grumpy baby because they hate the feeling of confinement. With each emotional moment, and each appropriate response, you build up a reservoir of trust.

All babies need you to respond to their cries and meet their needs, but Touchy, Spirited, and Grumpy babies in particular are more challenging than others. Here's what you need to remember about each of these three types:

Touchy. Protect her space. Look at her environment, and try to imagine the world through her sensitive eyes, ears, and skin. Any kind of sensory stimulation—an itchy label, a loud TV, a glaring overhead light—can send her over the edge. Give her lots of support in new situations, but try not to hover, because that might reinforce her fears. Explain everything you're about to do—from diapering to getting ready for a ride in the car—even if you don't think she understands. Reassure her in new situations that you're there for her. But let her take the lead; sometimes your Touchy child will surprise you. Socialize with only one or two (easygoing) children at first.

Spirited. Don't expect him to sit still for very long. Even as babies, these kids need to change positions and scenes more often than other babies. Provide lots of opportunities for active play and safe exploration but take care not to allow him to be overstimulated. Remember that when he's overtired, his emotions are more likely to overwhelm him. Watch for signs of overload and try to avoid tantrums, which are most difficult to stop with Spirited babies. If distraction isn't effective when he gets close to the edge of a meltdown, remove him from the scene until he calms down. Make sure that relatives and other caregivers understand and accept his intensity.

Grumpy. Accept the fact that she might not smile or laugh as much as other babies. Present opportunities that allow her to use her eyes and ears, not just her body. Hold back when she's playing, and let her choose which toys she wants to play with. She may get frustrated or angry with toys or situations that are unfamiliar. Take care in transitions. If she's playing and it's time for a nap, warn her ("It's almost time to put the toys away") and then allow her a few minutes to acclimate to the idea. Start to socialize with only one or two children at first.

Breaking the Bond of Trust

One afternoon, I was invited to watch a play group, because the mothers who had only recently decided to meet twice a week were concerned that their children "didn't seem to get along." The three mothers, Martha, Paula, and

Sandy, were good friends, and their sons, Brad, Charlie, and Anthony, were all between ten and twelve months old. The babies, of course, didn't really "play" with each other. Rather, they amused themselves while their mums talked. Groups such as these are mini-laboratories for me, for they allow me to observe how children interact and how their mothers deal with them.

Brad, a Touchy ten-month-old, didn't want to join the other kids, a "problem" his mother had already told me about. He kept whining and putting his hands up to Martha, obviously wanting to be in her lap. The more Martha tried to talk him out of his feelings ("Come on, Brad. You like Charlie and Anthony. Look how nicely they're playing"), the louder her little boy whined. Hoping that he would eventually give up and join the other two boys, Martha then tried to tune him out. She went back to chatting with the other mothers. But none of her strategies worked. Brad kept whining and eventually started crying. Martha finally took him onto her lap but by then he was inconsolable.

Across the room, Charlie, a Spirited child, was wound up with excitement, racing from toy to toy. Finally spotting a ball that he absolutely had to have, Charlie tried to wrench it from Anthony, who held on for dear life. Finally, Charlie shoved Anthony, who then tipped over backward and joined Brad's crying chorus. As Sandy swept her son into her arms to comfort him, she shot an unmistakable look at the other women: *not again*.

Paula, Charlie's Mum, was mortified. She had clearly been here before. She tried to scoop Charlie into her arms, but he would have none of it. The more she tried to restrain him, the louder he screamed in protest and the more he tried to squirm out of her arms. Paula was also trying to reason with her son, but Charlie had tuned her out.

Talk about trust-breaking! First of all, pushing

Trust-Busters

Here are the most common mistakes parents make with babies (and older children) that can shatter trust.

✓ Not honoring—or worse, negating—a child's feelings ("You love doggies. Stop crying").

✓ Forcing a baby or toddler to eat when she's full ("Just a little bit more").

✓ Cajoling a child into changing his mind ("Come on now, Becky brought Billy here for you two to play").

✓ Not communicating. (Even before your baby talks, you should be having a running dialogue with her.)

✓ Introducing new situations, such as a play group, without warning and then assuming your baby or toddler will be okay.

✓ Sneaking out of the house to avoid a scene (when you're leaving for work or going out for the evening).

✓ Saying one thing ("You can't have candy") and doing another (caving in when he cries).

Brad into a crowd of children (to a baby like Brad, three feels like a roomful) was like throwing a child who can't swim into a pool. And trying to restrain or talk sense to a Spirited baby, an overstimulated one at that, was like spitting on a wildfire!

What could each of these mothers have done to deal with the situation and, at the same time, build trust instead of tearing it down? As I explained to Martha, she first should have realized—even before she arrived—that Brad's "problem" wasn't going to magically go away. She should have acknowledged and reassured her son ("It's okay honey, you don't have to play till you're ready"). She needed to allow him to sit on her lap *until he was ready*. I'm not saying she shouldn't have coaxed him a little. But rather than pushing or ignoring him, as she had done, she should have gently encouraged him to join. She could have gotten down on the floor with him, perhaps pointing out a toy that she knew he liked to play with. Even if she was afraid it was going to take him six months to join the fray, she needed to let him go at his own pace.

I told Paula, too, that she should have planned ahead. Knowing that Charlie was very active and prone to excitability, the moment she noticed him starting to get a little wild, she should have stepped in. The warning signs of a meltdown usually start with a child talking louder, his arms and legs flailing, and whining. Rather than letting Charlie's emotions get the best of him, she should have taken him out of the room earlier to give him a chance to calm down and in that way possibly avoid a scene all together. Once a meltdown begins, especially with a Spirited child, there's no point trying to reason with him or restrain him. I stressed that taking him out of the room was not a punishment—it was a way of helping him manage his emotions. At this age, when babies' brains are unable to compute cause and effect, we can't expect to talk sense into them! If instead Paula had removed him from the room, gently taking him by the hand instead of restraining him, she could have said, "Let's go into the bedroom, and I'll read you a story. You can come back and play with the other children when you feel a little calmer."

No Solo Time-Outs!

Never leave an emotional baby (or toddler) on his own. Babies can't manage their own emotions, so we have to help them. If your baby is crying, hitting, flailing, or in any other way out of control, a change of scene is almost always helpful, especially if other children are around. That gets him out of the center of the action and distracts him, which is one of the most effective ways of diffusing a baby's emotions. Always explain to him what he's feeling, even if you don't think he understands. He might not understand you today, but eventually he will.

In time and at his own pace, Touchy Brad may become braver, more outgoing, and eventually learn to interact with others—but only if he feels secure and comfortable to begin with. Spirited Charlie can learn that it's not okay to bully other kids, but not unless he's reined in when he's out of control. Charlie will have to be several months older to really understand what "calming down" means, but he's not too young to start learning. Martha and Paula have to be a safety net for each of their boys, not police officers. Even when children are too young to regulate their own reactions, they feel safer when their mothers step in to help them handle themselves. They see that Mum can be counted on when a situation is fearful or overwhelming.

Most important, I told the three women, especially Martha and Paula, that they need to learn from this experience—what triggers their children's emotional reactions and what calms them. Next time, hopefully, they'll step in *before* either boy has a meltdown. The most important lesson, though, is that they cannot get into their child's emotions. They have to see them through it and explain it for them, without getting into the drama and becoming reactive themselves.

Instead of meeting in the afternoon, they also might consider seeing each other in the morning after nap time, when the children are more likely to be well rested, and also meeting once a week instead of twice, which is a lot for babies under a year. Additionally, even though the moth-

---

Oh, the Dreaded Doctor's Office!

Many babies start crying the minute they reach the pediatrician's door. And who can blame them. They associate the place with being stripped naked in a too-bright room and then getting stuck by a needle! Don't be one of those mothers who apologizes when her baby screams at the sight of the doctor: "Oh he's not usually like this. He really likes you." Such lies negate a baby's feelings. A better approach would be:

- Try to have a few appointments before the first inoculation.

- Be honest: "I know you don't like it here, but I'm staying with you."

- Ask the nurse when the doctor will be in to examine your baby, and undress him at the last minute. Hold him until the doctor actually comes in.

- Stand at your baby's head when the doctor is examining her and talk to her.

- If it's time for a shot, don't say, "Oh, what a nasty doctor." But do tell the truth: "We have to do this because we don't want you to get sick."

- Don't be afraid to change pediatricians if you feel as if the doctor is treating your child like an object—doesn't talk to him and fails to make eye contact.

ers themselves are good friends, they have to pay attention to their kids' chemistry and ask themselves, "Is this really the best social situation for my child?" Charlie may calm down, but his basic nature might be too overwhelming for a baby like Brad in the meantime. Even for Anthony, who is a Textbook child, it might not be the best mix. Granted, holding the group in the morning might be a calming influence on Charlie, who isn't at his best in the afternoon. But for his sake, too, a group with more active kids might be better—say, one that meets at a gymnasium or in a park. He won't be the only Spirited one in that case, and that kind of setting will allow him to run off some of that excess energy.

Twelve Trust-Building Tips

In chapter 8, I cover how parents can help toddlers and older children avoid what I call "runaway emotions," feelings that get the better of them and can override all their positive traits and talents. However, emotional fitness, which enables a child to understand his emotions and be able to manage them, begins with a secure attachment. Trust-building starts in infancy in a dozen different ways:

1. *Tune in.* Interpret his cries and body language so that you understand why he's crying and, therefore, what his "mood" is about. If your baby is crying, ask yourself, "Do I know who my baby is?" Is she highly active, sensitive, moody, quick to cry, in foul moods a lot of the time? Is this reaction unusual for her? If you can't describe your baby's emotional core, then you're not paying enough attention to her signals, and it also might mean she's not getting her needs met.

2. *Put your baby on the E.A.S.Y. plan (see chapter 1).* All babies thrive when life is predictable and calm, but a structured routine is especially important for Touchy, Spirited, and Grumpy types. Have predictable rituals for everyday transitions—mealtimes, nap and bedtimes, bath, putting away toys—so that your baby knows what to expect.

3. *Talk with your baby, not just to her.* I like to think of it as having a running *dialogue*, rather than a one-way conversation. Make eye contact whenever you're talking to your baby, no matter how young she is. Even though she won't answer back for several months, a year, or

more, she's taking it all in and "talking" back to you with her cooing and her cries.

4. ***Respect your baby's physical space.*** Even if you think he doesn't understand your words, always explain what you're about to do. For example, when you're about to put on a new diaper, say, "I'm going to lift your legs now and put a new diaper on." When you're going for a walk, "We're going to the park now, so I have to get your warm winter coat on." Especially when you go to the pediatrician, tell him what's happening and reassure him: "Dr. Schneck needs to examine you now. I'll be right here with you." (See sidebar, page 76, "Oh, the Dreaded Doctor's Office!")

5. ***Never ignore your baby's cries, and start to label her feelings long before you think she understands them.*** She is trying to tell you something about the way she feels. You can get her acquainted with the language of emotions early by giving her words to go with the various cries ("You're hungry—you haven't eaten for three hours" or "You're just tired and trying to get to sleep").

6. ***Let your baby's emotions guide your actions.*** For example, if every time you turn on the mobile over your Touchy baby's head, she starts to cry, she's telling you, "That's too much." Let her look at it without the music.

7. ***Figure out what methods calm*** **your** ***baby.*** While swaddling is a great technique for most babies, Grumpy and Spirited types only become more excitable when confined. Likewise, where the shush-pat method (page 184) usually helps a baby get to sleep, a Touchy baby might find it too intrusive. Distraction works well with almost any type, but a Spirited, Grumpy, or Touchy baby might have to be removed from a too-stimulating situation in order to calm down.

8. ***Take steps to make sure your baby is eating well, right from the start.*** If you're having trouble breast-feeding and the advice in this book doesn't help, contact a lactation specialist immediately. Suffering through a mum's learning phase can make an Angel or Textbook baby disagreeable, but it's particularly upsetting to Touchy, Spirited, and Grumpy types.

9. ***Keep to his nap and bed times.*** A baby who gets enough sleep is emotionally better able to cope with whatever comes his way. Especially if

yours is a Touchy baby, put the crib in a safe, quiet place, and darken the room for naps.

10. ***Don't hover; let your baby explore and enjoy her independence.*** Think of my H.E.L.P. acronym (see sidebar this page) when you watch your baby at play. Look at what she likes to do and respect her pace. If she wants to crawl back in your lap, let her. A Touchy or Grumpy baby is more likely to venture out on her own if she knows you're there to reassure her when she needs it.

11. ***Plan activities at times when your baby is at her best.*** Overtiring or overstimulating a baby almost guarantees runaway emotions. Factor in temperament and time of day when making plans to do errands, visit relatives, or see other mothers. Don't schedule a Mommy and Me group too close to nap time. Especially with older babies who are able to bang and push and move around, you might not want to pair a Touchy baby with a Spirited one.

12. ***Make sure anyone else who cares for your baby understands and accepts his temperament.*** If you're hiring someone to care for your baby, spend a few days with the caretaker so that you see how your baby reacts to her. You might love a nanny, but you can't expect your baby to take to a new person without a period of adjustment (see "Stranger Anxiety," page 388).

H.E.L.P. Your Baby Thrive

Parenting always means walking a fine line between being there to keep a child safe and letting her go so that she can explore. To remind parents of this balance, I suggest "H.E.L.P."

Hold back: Don't jump in immediately. Take a few minutes to figure out why your baby is crying, or why he's clinging onto you for dear life.

Encourage exploration: Let your baby or toddler discover on his own the wonder of his fingers, or the new toy you've just placed in his crib. Your baby will tell you when he needs you to step in.

Limit: You probably know how much is too much for your baby. Limit the amount of stimulation, the time she's up, the number of toys that surround her, and the choices she's given. Step in before she's on overload.

Praise: Start when she's a baby to praise her efforts, not the results ("Good job getting your arm into your jacket"). Don't overpraise, however. (He is *not* "the smartest boy in the world," no matter how bright you think he is!) Appropriate praise not only nurtures your child's sense of self-worth, it is also a motivator.

Prolonged Separation Anxiety: When Attachment Leads to Insecurity

Instilling trust and tuning in to your baby's needs are vital skills. But many parents confuse sensitivity with hypervigilance, especially those who come to me because their babies have separation problems. When I ask about a typical day, it becomes clear to me that they believe being a good parent means they must carry their baby all the time, let her sleep in their bed, and never, ever allow her to cry. They respond immediately to every gurgle and squeak, without waiting to see if it's just a normal baby noise, or a call of distress. When they're not carrying their babies, they're hovering over them. They can't leave the room without their baby having a meltdown, and by the time they call me, they've lost sleep, freedom, and friends. All the same, they rationalize what's going on by saying, "But we believe in attachment parenting," as if they're talking about a religion.

Granted, babies need to feel connected and safe, to learn how to tune in to their own feelings and how to read other people's facial expressions. But this diffuse notion of attachment parenting sometimes gets out of hand. Babies feel attached when they're understood. You could keep your baby in your arms for every waking hour, let her fall asleep on your chest, and share your bed with her until she's a teenager. But if you don't recognize her uniqueness, tune in to her, and give her what she needs, no amount of holding or coddling is going to make her feel secure. Research bears this out: Babies with smothering mums are actually less securely attached than those whose mothers respond in a timely but not overbearing way.

We see this most dramatically somewhere between seven and nine months, a time when almost every child has *normal separation anxiety*. She's at a point in her development when her memory enables her to grasp how important her mother is, but her brain has not matured enough to realize that when Mum leaves, it doesn't mean she's gone forever. With the right kind of reassurance delivered in an upbeat tone of voice ("Hey, it's okay—I'm right here") as well as a little patience on the parents' part, normal separation anxiety goes away in a month or two.

But consider what happens to a child whose parents are overattentive and constantly hovering. The baby is never allowed to be frustrated and has never been taught to soothe himself. He doesn't learn to play independently because his parents believe it's their job to entertain him. When he begins to experience normal separation anxiety, and cries for his parents, they rush to his rescue, unwittingly reinforcing his fears. They say fretfully, "I'm right here. I'm right here," in a tone of voice that mirrors the baby's panic. If this goes on for more than a week or two, it probably will turn into what I call *prolonged separation anxiety.*

One of the most dramatic examples of this phenomenon was Tia, a nine-month-old in England whose mother was desperate for help, and when I met this family I could see why. In all my years of helping parents, this was the most serious case of prolonged separation anxiety I'd ever seen. To say that Tia was clingy is an understatement. "From the moment I wake up," Belinda explained, "I have to carry her around. She'll play by herself for two or three minutes at most. And if I don't pick her up, she'll scream to the point of hurting herself or getting sick." Belinda was reminded of the time she was driving back from Grandma's house. Tia, feeling bereft because she was in a car seat and not in her mum's arms, began to cry. Belinda tried to comfort her, but Tia's cries only got louder. "I decided I couldn't keep stopping the car. But when we got home, she had vomited all over herself."

With the help of several of her women friends, Belinda had made feeble attempts at leaving the room while a friend held Tia. Even a two-minute absence sent her daughter into wails of hysteria. Invariably, although her friends were there to support her, Belinda caved in and resorted to her usual remedy: "As soon as I pick her up, she turns it off like a faucet."

To complicate matters, Tia was still waking up throughout the night; waking only twice was considered a "good night" in this household. Martin, who for the last six months had made attempts to share the burden with his wife, couldn't console Tia, who only wanted Belinda. During the day, with Tia constantly in her arms or screaming when she wasn't, Belinda was not only exhausted, it was also impossible for her to get anything done, much less spend meaningful time with Jasmine, Tia's three-year-old sister. And forget couple time. Belinda and Martin barely had a peaceful or private moment with each other.

Within moments of talking to Belinda and watching her interact with Tia, I could see that Belinda was accidentally reinforcing Tia's worst fears each time she swooped down and "rescued" Tia from her tears. By picking her up so much, she was telling Tia: "You're right: There is something to be afraid of down there." There was also the sleep problem to contend with, but we had to tackle Tia's severe separation issues first.

I told Belinda to put Tia down but to continue talking to her while she was standing at the sink doing her chores. And, if she had to leave the room, to call out so that Tia could hear her voice. I had to also make sure that Belinda didn't continue to use her poor-baby tone of voice. She was to master a tone of cheerful reassurance instead: "There, there, Tia. I haven't gone anywhere." When Tia did cry for her, I instructed her to get down on her hands and knees to Tia's eye level, rather than picking her up. She could comfort her and cuddle her, as long as it didn't involve holding. This was another way of telling Tia, "You're okay, I'm right here." Once Tia began to calm down, Belinda was to distract her with a toy or a song—anything to make her forget her fear.

I told them I'd be back in six days. They called me back in three. My suggestions didn't seem to be working. Belinda was more exhausted than ever, and quickly ran out of ideas for distracting Tia. Jasmine, feeling even more neglected, was starting to have tantrums, which was her way of snagging a bit of Mum's attention. On my second visit, even though Belinda and Martin didn't see much progress, I could see that Tia was doing a little better, especially in the living room. But in the kitchen, where Belinda did many of her household chores, Tia was still pretty miserable. I realized what the difference was: In the living room, Tia played on the rug surrounded by lots of toys—multiple distractions—whereas in the kitchen she sat in a bouncy exercise saucer. It was much harder for Belinda to distract her daughter in the saucer, because Tia was already bored with its cranks, pulleys, and other gadgets, which she no longer found particularly amusing. Also, Tia felt confined. She not only had to be separated from her mum—albeit by no more than six feet—she couldn't move.

My suggestion was to get her a large play mat for the kitchen and bring in some of Tia's favorite toys. Mum also found a new activity station for her, with piano keys and push buttons that Tia loved. The novelty made it easier to distract Tia. And now even if Mum refused to pick her up, Tia could at least crawl closer to her. Slowly, Tia's attention span got longer, and her ability to play independently increased as well.

We still had to work on the sleep problem. Tia had never been a "good sleeper," and like many mums Belinda had taken the path of least resistance for months, by allowing her baby to fall asleep on her chest. Now it was the only way Tia could get to sleep. When she was sure Tia was fast asleep, Belinda would very slowly get up and transfer her to the crib, which was . . . guess where? In her parents' bedroom, of course. So now you have this child who's afraid of Mummy leaving her during the day waking up in the middle of the night in her crib. Her little baby mind is saying, *How'd I get here? Where's Mum and that comfy chest of hers? I'll bet she's never coming back.*

We put Tia's crib back into her own room, and to get Dad back into the picture, I taught him how to do "pick up/put down" (pages 221–224). When Martin did P.U./P.D., I instructed him to keep telling his daughter, "It's okay, you're just going to sleep." It took a few nights of crying and lots of persistence, but Martin hung in there.

After a few days of reassuring Tia, teaching her how to fall asleep independently, and helping her get through the night in her own bed (more about all of that in chapter 6), Tia was waking only once a night and sometimes, to her parents' amazement, she slept through. Her morning and afternoon naps were better, too. Now that she wasn't overtired, the separation issues were far less severe as well.

A month later, it was like visiting another family. Because Belinda wasn't pacifying Tia twenty-four/seven, she could spend more time with Jasmine. Martin, who once felt helpless, was now part of a parenting *team*. Even better, he was finally getting to know his younger daughter.

Comfort and Distract

If your baby is between 7 and 9 months old and suddenly starts whining when you leave the room, or having problems with naps or nighttime sleep, it may be the beginnings of normal separation anxiety. It happens to lots of babies when they first realize that their mums are separate from them. Normal separation anxiety doesn't have to turn into prolonged separation anxiety if you:

✓ Get down to your child's level when he is upset and comfort him with your words and hugs, but not by picking him up.

✓ Respond to your baby's cries in a relaxed upbeat manner.

✓ Watch your tone of voice—don't mirror his panic.

✓ Once your baby calms down a bit, distract him.

✓ *Never* resort to a controlled crying approach (sometimes referred to as "Ferberizing") to solve sleep problems. It breaks a baby's trust and tells him that he was right after all: You did abandon him.

✓ Play peekaboo with him, so that he gets to see that even though you go away for a minute, you come back.

✓ Walk around the block to allow him to experience short periods in your absence.

✓ When you leave the house, have your partner or childcare provider take him to the door and wave good-bye. He might scream for the whole time—that's normal if he's become dependent on you. But you have to build up trust.

Playing Independently:
A Cornerstone of Emotional Fitness

Parents often ask me, "How do I amuse my child?" To young children, the world itself is a wonder. Children by nature are rarely "bored," unless parents inadvertently teach them to depend on adults for their amusement. Given the overload of toys nowadays that shake, rattle, vibrate, whistle, sing, and talk to them, I see more overstimulated babies than bored ones. Still, it's important to strike a balance: Make sure that your child gets the proper level and type of stimulation but also build in periods of calm and times to decompress. Eventually, your child will know when he's overdoing it or is too tired to play—an important aspect of emotional fitness—but in the beginning, you have to guide him.

To enable your child to develop the emotional muscle it takes to play on her own, you have to walk a fine line between helping and hovering. You want to create an atmosphere at home where there are opportunities for her to safely explore and experiment, and at the same time, you need to be careful not to slip into the role of Director of Amusements. Following are some age-related guidelines to help you walk that line.

Newborn to six weeks. At this young age, feeding and sleeping are all you should expect from your baby—it's all he can handle. While you're feeding, talk softly to keep him awake. Try to keep him up for fifteen minutes after a feed, so that he learns to delineate eating and sleep periods. Don't start freaking out if he starts falling asleep. Some babies can only stay awake for five minutes at first, but they eventually extend their awake time. As for toys, he mainly wants to see your face and other people's. A big "activity" can be a visit with Granny or simply your walking around and showing him things in the house or outdoors. Talk to him as if he understands every word: "See, this is the chicken I'm going to make for dinner tonight." "Look at the beautiful tree outside." Save those adorable picture books you were given at your shower. Instead, position him near a window, so he can look outside, or put him in his crib to watch his mobile.

Six to twelve weeks. By now your little one can play on her own for fifteen minutes or more but be careful not to overstimulate her. For instance, don't lay her under a Gymini for more than ten or fifteen minutes. She'll love to sit in an infant seat, but don't use that darn vibrating feature; just let her sit and observe her surroundings without being shaken, rattled, or rolled. And don't put her in front of the telly, which is *way* too stimulating. Take her with you when do laundry or cook or sit at your desk reading email, and let her sit near you. Continue the practice of talking to her; explain what you're up to, and acknowledge her presence as well. ("So what are *you* doing? I can see you're getting a little tired.") Plant the seeds early that rest is a good thing.

Three to six months. If you haven't been *over*involved with him, you now have a baby who has an hour and twenty minutes or so of awake time (including feeding). He should be able to play on his own for fifteen or twenty minutes, and then he'll start getting fussy. At that point, he's getting close to needing a nap, so it's a good idea to allow him to wind down in his crib. If he can't play on his own by now, it usually means that you've done a form of accidental parenting, making him dependent on you for stimulation. This will not only inhibit your freedom, it also robs your child of independence and can ultimately cause him to feel insecure.

Continue to avoid overstimulation. Now is the time when you—as well as his grandparents and aunts and Nelly next door—will delight in his responsiveness. Grandma smiles and makes funny faces, and before you know it, he starts smiling and laughing, too. But all of a sudden, he's in tears. He's trying to say, "Please leave me alone now or put me to bed. I've seen enough of Granny's tonsils!" He's got more control over his torso, is able to control his head and coordinate his arms, so that instead of just lying under his Gymini, he's reaching out for things. But his new physical assertiveness has a downside: He might try to eat his own hand and gag on it, or pull his own ears, or scratch himself. All babies poke themselves. But parents tend to panic. They rush in, swoop the baby up so fast that not only does the poke hurt, his parents have also frightened him by picking him up so fast. To him, it seems like he's gone from Ground Zero to the Empire State Building at the speed of light. So don't fall prey to the "poor baby" syndrome (see page 247). Instead, acknowledge the pain but make light of it. "Silly goose! I bet that hurts—ouch!"

Six to nine months. Your baby can stay up for around two hours now, including her feed. She should be able to amuse herself for a half hour or more, but change her position—say, from the infant seat to lying on her back under a mobile in her crib. When she's able to sit up, put her in an exercise saucer. She likes to manipulate objects. She will also put everything into her mouth, including the dog's head. Now is the best time for you to bring out the picture books, recite nursery rhymes, and sing songs like "The Wheels on the Bus" and "The Eeensy Weensy Spider."

This is the age when children first see a connection between their own behavior and a subsequent chain of events and when bad patterns are easily reinforced. When parents tell me that their child of six to nine months cries to be picked up after five or ten minutes of activity, I say, "Well, don't pick her up." Otherwise you're teaching her that when I make this noise, Mum picks me up. It's not that your child is thinking, *Oh, I know how to wrap Mum around my little pinky.* She's not consciously manipulating you . . . at least not yet. Instead of rushing to pick her up, sit next to her and reassure her, "Hey, hey, hey, it's okay. I'm right here. You can play on your own." Distract her with a squeaky toy or a jack-in-the-box.

I'd also remind you to make sure that she's not crying because she's tired or because *too much* is going on around her—the vacuum, other siblings, the television, the play station, as well as her own toys. If the former, put her down. If the latter, take her into her own room. If she doesn't have her own room, make a safe area in the living room or your bedroom that she can retreat to when she becomes overstimulated. Another way to calm her down is to walk her outside and talk to her gently ("Look at the trees, look at how pretty they are"). No matter what the weather, take her out into the fresh air. In the winter, don't even bother with a jacket—just wrap her in a blanket.

Now social life should begin. Even though children don't really "play" together at this age, it's a good time to start a morning play group. Granted, many American mothers leave the hospital as members of a "mom's group," or they join one when their baby is weeks old, but those groups are for mother more than baby. Children love to observe each other, and the exposure is good for them. Don't expect your child to share or be social, though. That comes later.

Nine to twelve months. Your child should be very independent by now, able to play nicely on his own for *at least* forty-five minutes and also able to tackle more complex tasks. His ability to learn will seem to take a giant leap. He can put rings on a post or shove a block into a hole. Water play and sand play are wonderful outlets now, too. Big boxes and huge throw pillows make for great fun, as do pots and pans. The more your child plays independently, the more he will be willing to be on his own and trust that you're there in the wings, and that if you're out of sight, at least you will come back. At this age, children have no concept of time, so once they're secure it doesn't matter whether you're gone for five minutes or five hours.

When a mother tells me, "He won't play on his own" or "He makes me sit with him, and I can't get my housework done" or "He won't let me go near another baby," I immediately suspect a case of accidental parenting that probably started months earlier. Baby cried; Mum picked him up immediately instead of encouraging him to play on his own. In essence, the mother has always been in the child's face and never really allowed him to develop the skills of independence. She might not have involved him in a play group, so he hasn't been outside the safe realm of his family and is afraid of other children. Or it could be that Mum works and, feeling ambivalent about leaving her child with anyone else, has unwittingly set up the situation. She *acts* guilty when she leaves and says things like "Sorry, dear. Mummy has to go to work. Will you miss me?"

If your child has reached age one, and still can't play by herself, enroll her in a small play group. It's also time to start weeding out the baby toys. Children don't like to play with toys once they've mastered them. A child who is bored with her toys is more likely to be dependent upon a grown-up for amusement. If your child is still having separation anxiety, gently pry yourself away and take steps toward making her more independent (see "Comfort and Distract," page 83). Also look at your own attitudes. When you leave her in someone else's care, do you present Dad, the nanny, or Grandma as a fun and capable person, or do you somehow give your child the impression that other adults are inferior substitutes? It might make you feel important to be The One in your child's eyes, but you'll both pay for it (emotionally) in the long run.

Remember, too, that playing is serious business for babies. The seeds of learning grow out of emotional fitness. They are planted in infancy, and as you gradually increase your child's independent playtime, you are also honing his emotional skills—his ability to amuse himself, to explore without fear, to experiment. Play teaches young children how to manipulate objects. Through play, they learn cause and effect. They learn how to learn, too: to tolerate the frustration of not being able to get something to work the first time they try it, to be patient, and to practice a task over and over. If you encourage your child and then stand back and watch her become aware of the world, she will become an adventurer and a scientist, a child who is able to play on her own and who never says to you, "I'm bored."

THREE

YOUR BABY'S LIQUID DIET

Feeding Issues in the First Six Months

Food, Glorious Food!

In the first six months of your baby's life, the "E" in E.A.S.Y. refers to her liquid diet—breast milk, formula, or a combination of the two. It's kind of a no-brainer to say that food is important to your baby. We all know that every living creature needs to eat in order to survive. So it's not surprising that eating concerns are second only to sleep when I rifle through my call records, emails, and the postings on my website. And if you've read this far, you also know that sleep problems can be related to eating issues as well—and vice versa. A well-rested baby eats better; a properly fed baby sleeps better.

If you're one of the lucky ones, your child got off to a good start from the first few days of life. Babies are little eating machines at first, they're feeding all the time. Typically, most babies plateau out and start to take less liquid at around six months. Some parents will say to me, "She used to eat every three hours," or "My baby used to take thirty-six ounces and now takes only twenty-four or twenty-six." Well, luv, she's growing up! With growth also comes a change in routine. Remember, the 4/4 rule of thumb is that at four months the "E" in E.A.S.Y. switches to every four hours during the day (see page 33).

Both breast- and bottle-feeding mums voice similar concerns (especially at the beginning): How do I know if my baby is getting enough to eat? How often do I feed her? How can I tell if she's hungry? How much

Freedom of Choice

The way mothers feed is a matter of *choice*. Though I support any woman who wants to breast-feed and believe in the benefits of breast milk, I'm an even bigger believer in a mum making a careful, informed—and guilt-free—decision about how to feed rather than trying to do something that makes her unhappy or even frustrated. Some mums can't breast-feed because of diabetes, antidepressant use, and other physical reasons. With others, it's a matter of not *wanting* to. Breast-feeding doesn't fit with their temperament, or it's too stressful or a logistical nightmare given their particular situation. Still others have had a bad experience with their first baby and don't want to try again. Whatever their reason, that's fine. Formula nowadays has all the nutrients a baby needs.

That said, breast-feeding is most assuredly in fashion. A 2001 survey done by *Pediatrics* magazine showed that 70 percent of all new mothers breast-feed when they leave the hospital. Around half stop by six months; others nurse for a year or more. (On page 108, I also discuss why I think it's a good idea to do both—bottle- and breast-feeding.)

is enough? If she seems hungry an hour after she's eaten, what does that mean? Will I confuse her if I breast-feed *and* give her a bottle? Why does she cry after feeds? What's the difference between colic and gas and reflux—and how do I tell whether my baby has any of them? This chapter is the place to find the answers to these and other feeding questions. Here (and in the next four chapters), you'll see many of the same common complaints I introduced in chapter 1. But now I'll teach you how to troubleshoot and figure out what's wrong. Then I'll give you lots of strategies and tips about what to do.

Is My Baby Eating Enough? What's *Normal*?

Everyone wants specifics—how much should a baby eat and for how long? See "Feeding 101" on page 95, a chart that will take you through the first nine months, by which time your baby should be eating a variety of solid foods (see chapter 4) in addition to his liquid diet.

When you first bring your baby home, the "E" in E.A.S.Y. often involves a lot of experimenting, sometimes two steps forward and one step back. If you're bottle-feeding, you might have to try a different-shaped nipple or a smaller one to see which is best suited to your baby's mouth. Or, if your baby is smaller and seems to be sputtering or choking at feeds, you might have to switch to a slow-release nipple—one in which he controls the flow, not gravity. If you're breast-feeding, you will have to make sure that your baby is latched-on properly and that your milk is coming in. Regardless of how you do it, though, feeding an infant can be a challenge.

The overriding concern of new mums is, "Is my baby getting enough to eat?" One surefire way to find out is to look at weight gain. In England, we send mums home with a scale and suggest that they weigh their baby every three days. A half to two ounces a day is the typical range of weight gain. But if your baby gains only a quarter of an ounce, she might still be fine—just a small baby. It's always a good idea to check with your pediatrician (and to look for the kinds of danger signals listed in the sidebar on this page).

With older babies, weight gain can be a tricky matter. If you consult a growth chart, or your pediatrician refers to one, remember that they're designed for average children. Some babies are just bigger, some smaller. The old growth charts, originally designed in the fifties, were based on formula-fed babies, so don't be alarmed if your breast-fed baby doesn't measure up. Breast-fed babies often don't gain as much as formula-fed babies, at least in the first six weeks. Depending on the mother's health and diet—say she doesn't eat enough carbs, which makes her breast milk higher in fat—her breast milk may not be as fattening as formula, which consistently delivers the same nutritional value. Also, if your baby starts out less than six pounds, he'll follow a lower-weight curve than a baby who weighs more.

As I explained in chapter 1, smaller babies

When to Worry About Your Newborn's Weight

Weigh your baby if you're concerned, but not every day. It's normal for a baby to lose up to 10% of her body weight in the first two weeks, because she's had a steady flow of food from you through her umbilical cord. Now she has to depend on an outside source—you—to feed her. However, you should seek the advice of a pediatrician and, if you're breast-feeding, a lactation consultant if your baby . . .

. . . loses more than 10% of her birth weight

. . . doesn't gain her birth weight back within two weeks

. . . stays at her birth weight for two weeks (classic "failure to thrive") naturally consume less and in the beginning have to eat more often. Review the "E.A.S.Y. by the Pound" chart on page 29 to make sure that you take birth weight into account and don't have unrealistic expectations about your baby's consumption. Babies who are premature or weigh less than 6½ pounds simply don't have the capacity to eat a lot at a feed—their little tummies can't hold enough. They have to eat every two hours. To give yourself a *visual* understanding of this, fill a plastic bag with water to equal the amount of breast milk or formula your baby usually takes, probably an ounce or two. Hold the bag next to your baby's tummy. It's easy to see that there's just no room in there to accommodate larger feeds. Don't expect her to eat like a seven-pound baby.

Of course, no matter what your baby's birthweight was, with each new day she will increase her capacity. You also have to factor in her developmental growth and activity. So don't go comparing your one-month-old with your sister's four-month-old!

Remember that the chart is only a *rough guideline.* On any given day, other factors affect your baby's appetite, such as a poor night's sleep or too much stimulation. Babies are like us: On some days we're hungrier than others, so we eat more. On some days we eat less—for example, if we're tired or just out of sorts. On these "off" days, your baby will probably eat less, too. On the other hand, if he's in the midst of a growth spurt (page 115), the first of which usually happens at six to eight weeks, your baby might eat more. Also, the ages are approximate and the particular groupings are somewhat arbitrary. Even with babies that are full term, one six-week-old might be more like an eight-week-old and another more like a four-week-old.

Consider this posting from my website. The italicized comments in brackets are mine!

My son, Harry, is six weeks and is 11 pounds, 4 ounces. He has been wanting to eat six ounces of formula every three hours. I have been told that it is way too much. *[By whom, I wonder—her friends, Nellie next door, the check-out lady at the supermarket? Notice she* doesn't *mention her pediatrician.]* They say the max should be 32 ounces, not taking weight into consideration. *[How can you not take a baby's weight into consideration?]* He is maxing out at around 38–40 ounces. We don't know what to do to help Harry interpret his need for food vs. his need to pacify himself.

This is a very smart mum who's listening too much to other people's advice instead of her own inner baby whisperer. She's right to be concerned about not pacifying her son with food, but she needs to tune in to her baby, not her friends. To me, thirty-eight to forty ounces doesn't sound like too much for a big baby. I don't know what he weighed at birth, but I'd guess he's around the seventy-fifth percentile, according to universal growth charts. He's only taking an extra six or eight ounces over what someone told her he's "supposed" to take. That's only around 20 percent more, and he's got the body to handle it. And it's not like he's snacking (see box, page 98)—he lasts three hours between feeds. He might even start taking eight ounces as he gets closer to eight weeks. He also might be a baby who needs solid food a little earlier (see box, page 144). I say to this mum, "You and your son are doing just fine—stop listening to other people!"

The bottom line is: Look at *your baby*. We always want to look at the individual, not the norm. Books and charts (including the one on page 95) are based on averages. I'm afraid mums sometimes get so hung up on numbers, and other people's opinions, that it sometimes drowns out their common sense. There are so many exceptions to the rule—babies who eat slower or faster than the norm, babies who eat more or less. Some children are heftier, some more slight. So if a baby seems very hungry, he's lasting three hours between feeds, and he's in the seventy-fifth percentile as far as weight goes, doesn't it make sense to simply feed him more? I would go so far as to say that there's no such thing as feeding a baby *too much* if he's going three or four hours between feeds. By knowing your baby, tuning in to his cues, learning what is developmentally typical, and then using common sense to gauge where your baby stands, you'll probably know what's best. Trust yourself!

Tanking Up

One way of insuring that your baby eats enough is to increase his intake during the day, before 11 P.M. By "tanking up," as I call this strategy, you get more food into his tummy, which, in turn, enables him to sleep through longer stretches at night. Tanking up is also great for growth spurts, those two- or three-day periods when your baby eats more than usual (see pages 115–119).

Tanking up consists of two parts: *Cluster feeding*, which is done at two-hour intervals in the early evening, at 5 and 7 or 6 and 8; and *the dream feed,* which is given somewhere between 10 and 11 (depending on how late you or your partner can stay up). With the dream feed, you literally feed your baby in his sleep. You don't talk to him, or put the lights on. It's easier to do with a bottle, because you just wiggle the nipple into his mouth and that will activate the sucking reflex. It's a little more challenging if you breast-feed. Before you give him your breast, stroke his bottom lip with your pinky or a pacifier to get his sucking reflex started. Either way, at the end of the dream feed, your baby will be so relaxed you can put him down without burping.

I recommend tanking up as soon as your baby comes home from the hospital, but you can start using both strategies any time during the first eight weeks and the dream feed until seven or eight months (by which time your baby is drinking between six and eight ounces per feed and getting a fair amount of solid food). Some infants are harder to tank up than others. They might take early evening feeds but not take a dream feed. If that describes your baby, and you have to choose one, *concentrate on the dream feed only.* Don't bother clustering. For example, you feed your baby at 6, give her a bath and do the bedtime routine, and top her off at 7—she'll probably only take a few ounces. Then at 10 or 11 (if you're normally up that late, or if your partner is) try to give her a dream feed—never later than 11. But don't give up after one or two nights. It's unrealistic to think you can change a baby's habit in less than three days, and for some infants it takes as long as a week. There are no miracles here, but persistence usually pays off.

Feeding 101

This feeding chart is designed for a baby who weighs 6–6½ lbs. or more at birth. If you're breast-feeding, it also assumes that you haven't had any kind of problems with latch-on or milk supply, and that the baby doesn't have any kind of digestive, anatomical, or neurological problems. If your baby was premature, you can still use the chart as a reference, but adjust according to his *developmental* age. So, for example, if your baby was due January 1, but arrived December 1 instead, consider him a newborn when he is one month old. Or, if he weighed less at birth, just go by his weight, not his age.

Age	If bottle-feeding, how much?	If breast-feeding, how long?	How often?	Comments
The 1st 3 days	2 oz. every 2 hours (between 16 and 18 oz. total)	1st day: 5 minutes each breast	All day, whenever baby wants	Breast-feeding mothers need to feed more often to get the milk flowing, which usually happens in the 1st 3 days; on Day 4 switch to single side feeds (see page 102).
		2nd day: 10 minutes each breast	Every 2 hours	
		3rd day: 15 minutes each breast	Every 2½ hours	
Up to 6 weeks	2–5 oz. per feed (7 or 8 feeds per day—typical range is 18–24 oz. total)	Up to 45 minutes	Every 2½–3 hours during the day; cluster feed in the early evening (pages 93–94). Your baby should be able to go 4–5 hours during the night, depending on weight and temperament.	At first, bottle-fed babies can go longer between feeds than breast-fed babies; it usually evens out at 3–4 weeks, if the mother hasn't had any problems with latch-on or milk supply.
6 weeks–4 months	4–6 oz. (6 feeds plus dream feed; typical range is 24–32 oz.)	Up to 30 minutes	Every 3–3½ hours; by 16 weeks should be able to go 6–8 hours during the night. Don't continue cluster feeding past 8 weeks.	Your goal should be to extend the time between feedings during the day, so that at 4 months, your baby lasts around 4 hours between feeds. But if he's in a growth spurt, and you're breast-feeding, you may need to "tank up" (page 93) and/or go back to the 3-hour routine.

Feeding 101 (continued)

Age	If bottle-feeding, how much?	If breast-feeding, how long?	How often?	Comments
4–6 months	5–8 oz. per feed (5 feeds plus the dream feed—typical range is 26–38 oz.)	Up to 20 minutes	Every 4 hours; should be able to go 10 hours during the night.	Between 4 and 6 months, some babies' appetite is affected by teething and their newfound mobility, so don't be alarmed if your baby eats less.
6–9 months	5 feeds a day, including solids. Typical range of liquid intake is 32–48 oz. As you introduce solids, liquid consumption declines by the same number of ounces—e.g., a baby who once took 40 oz. of liquid now takes 15 oz. of solids and 25 of liquid. *Note: 2 T. of solid = 1 oz. of liquid; 2 T. of solid fruit or veggie mashed = ¼ of a 4-oz. jar, if not making your own*	Give food first and then the bottle or 10 minutes on breast. They gulp liquids down quite quickly at this age, so that in 10 minutes they can take in more than they used to in half an hour.	A typical routine: 7:00—liquid (5–8 oz., bottle or breast) 8:30—solids "breakfast" 11:00—liquid 12:30—solids "lunch" 3:00—liquid 5:30—solids "dinner" 7:30—breast or bottle before bed	Some babies have early difficulties adapting to solid foods. Your baby may get a runny nose, red cheeks, sore bottom, and possibly diarrhea, which could indicate a food allergy; check with your pediatrician. Drooling doesn't necessarily mean teething. Drooling starts around 4 months when the saliva glands develop and become mature. When you introduce solids (see chapter 4), your baby's liquid intake declines. For every 2 oz. of solids, deduct 2 oz. of liquid from every feed.

The First Six Weeks: Food-Management Issues

Even if your baby is putting on weight, other food issues can develop during the first six weeks. Here are the most common complaints at this stage:

My baby falls asleep during feeds and seems hungry an hour later.

My baby wants to eat every two hours.

My baby is rooting all the time and I keep thinking he's hungry, but he only takes a little bit at each feed.

My baby cries during feeds or shortly thereafter.

These are what I call food-management problems, issues that are usually resolved by making sure that your baby is on a structured routine that's appropriate for her birthweight. It's also important for you to learn the difference between hunger cues and other kinds of cries, so that you can get your baby to take full feeds instead of "snacking" (see below). Even more important, if your baby has some kind of problem like reflux, gas, or colic, by tuning in you're less likely to overfeed her, which will only make her problem worse.

Easy enough for me who has seen literally thousands of babies, but a lot harder for new sleep-deprived parents! To help you figure what's going on with your baby and what to do about it, here are the kinds of troubleshooting questions I ask my clients, followed by detailed strategies to correct the problem:

What was your baby's birthweight? I always factor in a baby's birthweight, as well as any other extenuating circumstances during or right after delivery. If your baby was premature or had a low birthweight or another health problem, he probably needs to feed every two hours. On the other hand, if he weighed over 6½ pounds at birth, and he's not lasting more than two hours between feeds, something else is going on. Either he's not getting enough at each feed or he's pacifying instead of eating, and he's on his way to becoming a "snacker"—a baby who eats little bits at a time but never really has a full feed (see the box, page 98).

Bottle-Feeders: Read the Directions!

I've known mums who put extra formula into their baby's bottle, hoping to fatten them up or give a double dose of nutrition. So, instead of one scoop to 2 oz. of water, they put in two. Formula is very precise. If you use less liquid, your baby can become dehydrated or constipated, so follow the directions.

Is Your Baby a Snacker?

Babies can develop a kind of eating pattern in which they never have a good solid meal but just take in little bits at a time.

How it can happen: If the baby isn't on a structured routine, the parents confuse their baby's need to suckle with hunger. Instead of giving her a pacifier between meals, they give her the breast or a bottle. This starts in the first 6 weeks but can continue for months as the baby gets in the habit of snacking.

How you know: Your baby is 6½ lb. or more but doesn't last more than 2½–3 hours between feeds, *or* she never takes more than a few ounces of bottle or 10 minutes of breast at each feed.

What to do: If breast-feeding, check for a proper latch-on and do a yield (see page 104) just to rule out those problems. And make sure that you feed from only one side at a time, which ensures that your baby gets to the richer hind milk (page 103). If your baby starts crying after 2 hours, use a pacifier to hold her off—just 10 minutes the first day, 15 the second, so she lasts a bit longer between feeds. By doing this, you'll also increase your milk supply. If it's impossible to hold her off, just give her a smaller snack—less time on the breast, or an oz. less of the bottle—and then she'll make that up at the next feed. It may take 3 or 4 days, but if you're consistent, she'll become a feeder . . . especially if you catch it in the first 6 weeks.

Are you bottle- or breast-feeding? With bottle-feeding, there's less guesswork involved than with breast-feeding, because you can actually *see* what your baby takes in. If she's 6½ pounds or more and drinks two to five ounces of formula, but still seems hungry an hour after a feed, you're misreading her cries for hunger. In all likelihood, she really just needs to suckle. Give her a pacifier instead. If she still seems hungry, she might not be getting enough at each feed.

If you're breast-feeding, you must gauge how much your baby is consuming by factoring in *how long* a feed takes. Most infants up to six weeks old will nurse at least fifteen or twenty minutes at each feed—any less and they're probably snacking. But you also have to make sure that your baby is latched on properly, and that your milk supply is adequate. (For detailed help with breast-feeding, see pages 101–109.)

How often do you feed your baby? Average-size and bigger babies need to eat every 2½ to three hours in the beginning, no less, no longer—

not even the bigger babies. (I also like to tank up at the evening feeds; see page 93.)

If you're like the mum who complains, "My baby is hungry every hour," your feeds may be too short (see below) or your baby isn't getting enough to eat at each feed, so you have to give her more. If you're bottle-feeding, the solution is simple: Add an ounce to each of your baby's feeds. If you're breast-feeding, it may be that your baby needs more milk than you're producing or that the baby isn't latched on properly and therefore isn't getting much out of your breast. This can also cause your breasts to produce less milk over a two- or three-week period. When babies feed for only ten minutes at a time, your body will think that you don't need to make as much milk, so your supply will continue to diminish and eventually dry up (see pages 101–107 for more about milk supply). It's also possible that your baby is going through a growth spurt, but that doesn't usually happen in the first six weeks (see pages 115–119).

How long does a feed usually last? During the first six to eight weeks, an average-weight baby's feedings take twenty to forty minutes. So if, for example, he starts a feed at 10, by 10:45 it's over, and by 11:15 he should be down and sleeping for 1½ hours. Although bottle-fed babies can fall asleep on the job, too, once they weigh 6½ pounds or more, they're less likely to pass out during a feed than a breast-fed baby. Breast-fed babies tend to get sleepy around ten minutes into a feed because they've had a slug of the "quencher," the fore part of the milk which is rich in oxytocin, a hormone that acts like a sleeping pill (see the sidebar on page 103, "If Breast Milk Were Labeled . . ."). Premature and jaundiced babies also tend to fall asleep before finishing a feed. In both cases, the babies absolutely need to sleep, but they need to be wakened for feeds as well.

Falling asleep on the job every now and then isn't the end of the world. But if the sleepy-baby pattern continues for more than three feeds, you might be accidentally turning your baby into a snacker. Also, if a baby learns to associate suckling with sleep, it will be harder to teach him to fall asleep on his own. And then it becomes difficult, if not impossible, to establish any kind of routine. (See pages 106–107 for more on how this vicious cycle progresses with breast-fed babies.)

Try to keep your baby up after a feed, even for as little as five minutes. You might rouse her by gently rolling her palm (never tickle her feet) or putting her in an upright position (like a baby doll, her eyes will pop open!). You can also lay her down on the changing table, change her diaper, or just talk to her for a few minutes. When you lay her down, do circular motions with her arms and bicycle her legs as well. Spend only ten to fifteen minutes trying to wake her, by which time the oxytocin should have made its way through her system. After that, consider her into the "S" part of E.A.S.Y. And try again at the next feed. Be persistent. We have to teach babies to eat efficiently.

The problem here is often the parents have mixed feelings about waking their baby. They'll say, "Oh, she's tired, we need to let her sleep. She was up all night, poor little thing." And why do you think she was up all night, demanding to be fed? Because she's catching up on the food she wasn't getting during the day. If you let the pattern persist, you're training her to snack, not eat, and when she's four months old, you'll be wondering if you'll ever get her to sleep through the night.

Between feeds, are you giving your baby suckling time? Babies need suckling time, especially in the first three months, so this question helps me analyze whether a baby is getting enough of it. I know lots of mums out there who don't "believe" in pacifiers. I certainly cringe when I see a two-year-old walking around with one. But we're talking about *babies* now. Using a pacifier (page 199) prevents your baby from sucking endlessly on you (or a bottle). So try one between feeds. It's a way to gradually stretch the times between feeds, so your baby doesn't become a snacker. It's also useful for breast-feeding babies who tend to empty the breast and then continue lolling over feeds because they want more sucking time.

Does your baby cry a lot after meals or at least within the hour? A hungry infant stops crying when he's fed. He's told you what he needs— food—and you've given it to him. Infants who cry during or shortly after feeds aren't crying because they're still hungry. Something else is going on. First, rule out problems in your own body like a poor milk supply or blocked duct, which would frustrate your baby's attempt to suck. If that's fine, it probably means your baby is in pain and has gas or esophageal reflux, the technical term for baby heartburn (see pages 111–114).

How long is your baby's activity period? Remember that we're talking about babies six weeks and under. The "A" after the "E" isn't going to be a game of catch. Some infants, especially small ones, can only stay up five or ten minutes after a feed. Consider the case of three-week-old Lauren, who weighed six pounds at birth, just a tad under average: "We have been trying the E.A.S.Y. routine with her for a few days now," her concerned parents wrote. "Here is our dilemma: She is done eating from the breast in ten minutes, we do an activity for thirty minutes, at which point she starts to become overstimulated, and then we move on to sleep. She only naps for twenty to thirty minutes. At this point it has only been 1½ hours, too early to eat again on the E.A.S.Y. routine. What do we do with her during this time?"

Test your own baby-whispering skills on that one. You can see from reading above that little Lauren is not taking a real feed. Because Lauren's mum is breast-feeding, I'd also want to find out if she's producing enough milk. So I'd also do a yield (see page 104) to see how much she's taking from each breast. Also, a thirty-minute activity is far too long for a small three-week-old. Is it any wonder that she's overstimulated? She naps only for twenty or thirty minutes because she's hungry. Think of it in adult terms: If I eat only a slice of bread and butter, and then run on the tread-mill and take a nap, you can be sure I'm going to wake up hungry. The same thing is happening with Lauren—she's not eating enough to sustain her activity and can't take a meaningful nap because her tummy's empty. Her parents have to go back to Square One, extending Lauren's feeds and shortening her awake time. Then she's likely to eat better and take longer naps during the day to boot.

Breast-Feeders' Alert: How to Avoid (or Correct) Poor Latch-on and Low Milk Supply

A woman's body is a miraculous creation. If you're healthy, when you're pregnant, it gets revved up to produce milk, and when your baby is born, all the mechanisms are in place to feed her what she needs. It's a natural process, but not every woman or baby necessarily takes to it immediately, despite what some of those gung-ho breast-feeding books tell you. Plenty of women have difficulties. Even those who work with a lactation con-sultant in the hospital sometimes have trouble once they come home. You're not wrong or bad if you need help.

When new mums come to me with so-called breast-feeding prob-lems during the first six weeks—the official "postpartum" period when everyone is adjusting (the baby to the world, the new mum to the baby)—it usually boils down to either a *poor latch-on* in which the baby's mouth is not positioned in a way that allows her to get the most milk, or an *insuffi-cient milk supply*. These two problems can, of course, be related. When a baby latches on properly, and begins to suckle, the body sends a message to the mother's brain: "This baby is hungry. Get busy and produce more milk." Obviously, if that message isn't getting through, you'll have an insufficient milk supply.

As my Feeding 101 chart (page 95) indicates, the first few days are different for breast-fed babies, because Mum's breasts first secrete colostrum (see sidebar, page 103) until her milk comes in. To get the maximum benefit of colostrum you feed *all day* on the first day, five minutes on each side. The second day, you feed every two hours, ten minutes on each side, and the third every $2\frac{1}{2}$ hours, fifteen to twenty minutes on each side. When your baby takes in colostrum she has to use a lot of energy to suck it in. It's so thick, it's like forcing honey through a pin hole. It can be especially hard for babies who weigh less than six pounds. But this frequent suckling is critical at first, because the faster your milk comes in, the less chance you'll get engorged.

Once your milk comes in, do single-side feeding. In other words, don't switch to the other breast until you've emptied the one. Some experts will tell you to switch sides after ten minutes, but I don't agree. Look at the sidebar to see why. Breast milk has three parts. If you left a bottle of it standing on your counter for a half hour, you'd see a watery liquid sink to the bottom, a bluish white liquid in the middle, and a thick yellowish creamy substance on top. The watery part—the quencher—comes out during the first ten minutes of a feed. So, if you switch sides after ten minutes, you're not only going to put your baby to sleep, you're giving her a double dose of quencher and none of the nutritious, creamier parts that follow the quencher. In my opinion, babies whose mums switch sides get a lot of the "soup" course, but never make it to the rich dessert. Those are often the babies who seem hungry an hour after a feed and turn into snackers. These babies can develop digestive problems as well, because the fore milk is also rich in lactose, too much of which can cause tummy aches.

Make sure your baby is latching on properly. Buy yourself a box of those little round elastoplasts—you call them Band-Aids. They're around $\frac{1}{2}$ to $\frac{3}{4}$ inch in diameter, and they look like the bull's-eyes you'd use in target practice, which is what I'm suggesting here.

Which Side Next?

A mum writes, "I have trouble remembering which side I nursed on. What can I do?"

What sleep-deprived mum doesn't forget? Use a safety pin on your shirt or nursing bra as a marker. I also suggest keeping a log in the beginning, writing down which breast and how long each feed takes. That way, if you have problems, you'll have a clearer picture of what's going on.

Before you do a feed, place one an inch above your nipple, and one an inch below—these are your "targets." Prop your baby up on a firm pillow or "boppie" –a specially designed breast-feeding cushion—and lay him in the fold of your arm level with your breast, so he doesn't have to strain his neck. Place your thumb on the top target and your forefinger on the bottom one, and squeeze. Then, gently take your baby's head and thrust the nipple into his mouth. To make sure that your baby is latched on correctly, watch yourself in the mirror or ask your partner, your mum (even if she never breast-fed), or a good friend to observe how your baby's lips grasp on to your nipple. This is what to look for: Make sure your baby's mouth is wide and positioned squarely on the nipple. The baby's lips will form a tight flange around the nipple and areola. If the baby is not latched on properly, his bottom lip might be tucked in. Or, the baby might be on top of your nipple, rather than full on. If your fingers aren't on the targets, an inch above and below your nipple, that would prevent your baby from getting the full nipple into his mouth.

The surest sign of an improper latch-on is in *your* body. I've seen so many a mother go through absolute agony— sore, even bleeding, nipples. She thinks, *Oh, I'm doing this for the baby.* She is probably trying to be the best mother in the world, but the sad truth is, her baby isn't being fed correctly. If breast-feeding doesn't *feel* right, trust your body's signals. A little soreness in your nipple in the first two or three days is normal, but if discomfort lasts longer or get worse, something probably *is* wrong. If it pinches or it hurts when your baby suckles, she isn't latched on correctly. If your nipple develops a blister, your

---

If Breast Milk Were Labeled . . .

When you buy formula, you know just what's in it by reading the label. But breast milk changes as your baby does. Here are its components:

Colostrum: For the first 3 or 4 days, your baby will be nourished by colostrum, a thick, yellowish substance that's like a power bar. In it are all the antibodies your child needs to stay healthy.

Quencher: Once your milk starts to come in, the first 5–10 minutes consists of a watery substance that's high in lactose and slakes your baby's thirst. It's also rich in oxytocin, which acts like a sleeping pill—and is the reason why babies (and mums) sometimes fall asleep 10 minutes into a feed.

Fore milk: The next 5–10 minutes, a high-protein liquid comes through. It's good for bones and brain development.

Hind milk: 15–18 minutes later comes the fat-rich cream of breast milk. High in calories and thick, it helps your baby gain weight.

hands are in the wrong position. If you physically feel sick—fever, chills, night sweats—and have any kind of pain or swelling in your breasts, those are all signs of problems, such as engorgement or a blocked duct, which could lead to mastitis, or inflammation of the mammary gland. If you have a fever or are otherwise symptomatic longer than a week, seek the help of a physician. It is probably also worth your while to call in a lactation consultant as well, to help you get a proper latch-on.

If your baby weighed less than six pounds at birth, feed more frequently, even after the first four days. Milk supply problems are common with small infants, because your body is designed to sustain a 6½-pound or larger baby. When the baby doesn't suck as strongly or take in as much milk as a larger baby would, the mum's body reacts accordingly and reduces her milk supply. The remedy is to feed every two hours, which not only keeps the baby's weight up, but also keeps Mum's milk flowing. In extreme cases, such as with premies, full-term babies under five pounds, or babies who are kept in the hospital for some other health reason, I also tell the mother to pump between feeds just to keep the baby's milk supply going (see sidebar this page). It's hard work for the mum, but worth it if she intends to breast-feed.

If you're worried about supply, do a yield to find out how much you're producing. When a mum is not sure whether her baby is snacking or whether she's not producing enough milk, I suggest doing what I call a "yield," which is something we did back on the farm in Yorkshire. Once a

---

How to Increase Your Milk Supply

The key is to stimulate the sinuses in your breast, either by pump or by your baby's mouth:

No pump method: If you don't want to pump, put your baby on your breast every 2 hours for a few days, and that will get your milk flowing. By latching on, the baby stimulates the sinuses, which sends a signal to the brain: Produce milk. Your baby will then be able to go 2½–3 hours between feeds, because he's getting the proper amount to eat. If feeds don't automatically extend within the next 4 days, make sure he's not becoming a snacker (see page 98).

Pumping method: Pump straight after feeding or wait for an hour after the baby is fed and then pump. If your baby is feeding every 2 hours, it might seem strange to pump afterward, but by pumping you empty the reservoir completely. At the next feed your baby's suckling will then signal your body to produce more milk, rather than his drinking from the reservoir left over from a prior feed.

Either way, after 3 days, your milk supply should increase.

day, fifteen minutes before a feed, pump your breasts and see how much comes out. Let's say it's two ounces—you can figure that your baby would probably have gotten three ounces out of you. (Physical suckling is more efficient than any pump.) Then, give her that breast milk in a bottle. If you haven't introduced a bottle yet, you can give your breast milk by a syringe or pipette. You could also put your baby on your breast, let him empty the rest, and then give him whatever milk you pumped.

Make sure you get enough sleep and eat well. One advantage of formula over breast milk is that its content is always the same. What you see is what you always get. Breast milk changes as a result of the mother's lifestyle. Too little sleep can deplete your supply or even reduce the caloric value of your breast milk. Obviously, so can diet. You have to double your intake of liquid—drink sixteen glasses of water or an equivalent beverage a day. You will need to eat an extra 500 calories—50 percent from carbs, 25 to 30 percent each from fats and proteins—added to your daily intake in order to replenish the energy that your body is using to manufacture and dispense breast milk. Factor in your age, normal weight, and height, too. You may need more or less than the averages. Consult your obstetrician or a nutritionist if you're in doubt. Recently, I got a call from thirty-five-year-old Maria, a new mum who was wondering why her eight-week-old baby, who'd started out on a good solid three-hour routine, was now going back to eating every 1½ hours. As it turned out, the problem was Mum's no-carb diet. She also exercised for two hours a day. When I told her that her breast milk was probably depleted, she wanted some quick "tips" for increasing her supply. But, I explained, that wasn't all she needed. Her lifestyle was too active for a nursing mum. Even if she had taken steps to increase her supply, she still needed to rest more and add carbs back into her diet so as to improve the *quality* of her breast milk as well.

Supplement with formula if you have to. I had a client, Patricia, whose doctor told her that little Andrew wasn't gaining weight, and he was also sleepy and unresponsive. The doctor didn't inquire about Patricia's milk, though, so we did a yield (see page 104). When she pumped, only one ounce came out. Patricia was very upset. "But I want to breast-feed him," she insisted. Well, no matter—she *had* to supplement his feeds with formula, at least until her milk supply increased. We added formula to Andrew's liquid diet and put her on a pump, even though she didn't want to. Within a week, Patricia's milk supply was increasing, so we were able to feed Andrew less formula and more breast milk. By the second week, she was back to breast-feeding, although at my suggestion, she continued giving him pumped breast milk in a bottle so that Dad would be able to feed him, too. (That's a suggestion I always make; see page 108.)

IMPORTANT REMINDER: Some mums who pump like to "stockpile" their breast milk "just in case." Unless you're going into surgery and you physically won't be around to feed your baby, don't pump more than an extra 3 days' worth. As your baby grows and changes, the content of your breast milk changes, too. Last month's breast milk may not be suited for this month's baby!

Be wary if feeds regularly take less than ten or fifteen minutes. When a breast-feeding mum tells me, "My six-week-old only has ten-minute feeds," a red flag goes up in my brain. But before I jump to any conclusions, I first rule out improper latch-on or poor milk supply by asking the mum: **Have you taken a yield to see how much breast milk you're actually producing? Are your nipples sore? Are you getting engorged?** "Yes" to either the second or third question might indicate that her baby isn't latched on properly. She's grinning and bearing it, but she probably has blocked ducts. I might then recommend a lactation consultant, or pay a call myself.

But here's where I've seen a lot of breast-feeding mums go wrong in the first six weeks: They don't leave the baby on long enough to get a full feed. With a very young baby, especially a small one, you can get into serious problems if this pattern is allowed to persist. Take Yasmin, the mother of four-week-old Lincoln. She called me because Lincoln was having all sorts of problems. He wasn't gaining weight, his longest naps were forty-five minutes—most were twenty or twenty-five—and, needless to say, Yasmin couldn't even begin to figure out how to get Lincoln on a structured routine. "I feel like I'm on a bucking bronco, Tracy, and I'm going to fall off at any minute. I have no control."

I spent the morning with Yasmin, whom I instructed to go on about her routine as if I wasn't there. Her problem was apparent to me within the first hour. Ten minutes or so into his feed, Lincoln's eyes started closing. Yasmin, assuming that the feed was over and that her little boy was into the "S" part of the routine, put him down. She didn't realize that

Lincoln had taken in only fore milk; he couldn't have gotten to the fatty hind milk, which starts flowing around fifteen minutes into a feed. Instead, he was in a kind of oxytocin-induced coma! Ten minutes later, he woke up. Not only had the oxytocin made its way out of his system, but also he had barely enough in his stomach to sustain him. It was as if all he had eaten was a glass of skim milk. Then, Yasmin wondered aloud, "Well, I've just fed you—what's wrong?" So, she went through the ritual of checking the diaper, swaddling him, and trying to get him back to sleep by patting and shushing him. But Lincoln continued to cry, and twenty or thirty minutes later was still crying. Why? Because he was hungry. Yasmin tried to calm him down by pacing and rocking a bit. But after twenty or thirty minutes of crying, any young baby will be so exhausted, no matter what you do, that he will fall back to sleep, which is exactly what Lincoln did. But—and this is what was driving his mum crazy—he didn't *stay* asleep. Sure enough, twenty minutes or so later, Lincoln was up again, and his poor mum hadn't a clue about what to do next.

"Well I only fed him an hour ago, and he should be going three hours or at least two and a half," she moaned. "Tracy, you have to help me." I retraced her actions for her and explained that the problem occurred because she didn't realize that Lincoln wasn't taking full feeds. Once she understood what was happening and resolved to use my wake-up techniques (see pages 99–100) to rouse Lincoln when he nodded off during a feed, Lincoln was eating proper meals, gaining weight, and, of course, sleeping better as well.

The moral of this story is to pay attention to the length of feeds. But I also have to remind you—once again—that all babies are different. Some babies are efficient eaters right from the start. For example, Sue in Michigan wrote:

> My DD is three weeks old and feeds for about five minutes (from each side) at a time. She feeds about every three hours or so, but I've been told she should be feeding for at least 10 minutes. Any advice on how long she should be feeding for?

Your darling daughter could be an efficient feeder, Sue. I've seen a range, from lollygaggers who need to be on the breast for forty-five minutes to children like this little one who just gulp it down. The key here is that she's lasting three hours between feeds, which tells me she's not snacking. Unless

Baby Whisperer's Best Advice: Breast *and* Bottle!

I always tell mums who breast-feed to introduce their baby to a bottle as well. I recommend starting as soon as your baby has latched on correctly, and you've established a good flow, which for most mums is around 2 or 3 weeks. Then give a bottle at least once a day. Make it a ritual—say Dad gives the bedtime bottle or Grandma the bottle in the afternoon. At this point your baby is still quite adaptable. Now I know that my suggestion flies in the face of others' advice. Some mums are advised to breast-feed exclusively, or to at least wait until the baby is 6 months old before giving a bottle. They are warned not to start earlier because of so-called nipple confusion or because their own milk might dry up. Codswallop! I've never had either of those problems with my babies.

Besides, it isn't just a matter of your baby's health. You also have to factor in your own needs and your lifestyle. Some mums are happy to breast-feed exclusively—and you may be one of them—but at least think ahead. Here are some critical questions to ask yourself. If you answer yes to any of them, consider introducing a bottle in the first few weeks. (If you've already missed that window, see "From Breast to Bottle" on pages 125–129.)

Would you like someone else to be able to feed your baby—Dad, Grandma, a nanny? A baby who takes breast and bottle gives Mum a break and, just as important, can be fed by others. Then they get an opportunity to cuddle, talk to, and bond with the baby, too.

Are you planning to go back to work or work part-time before your baby is a year old? If you're going back to work, and baby is not used to both breast and bottle, you risk a hunger strike (see box, page 129).

Are you're planning to put your baby in day care before he's a year old? Most facilities won't take a baby who can't be bottle-fed.

Now that you've started breast-feeding, are you sure you want to continue? I get countless emails from mums asking "permission" to stop breast-feeding after a certain point, be it 6 weeks, 3 months, or 6 months. But there's no magic date, no optimal time to wean a baby. Whenever *you* decide to quit, it will be a smoother transition if your baby is already used to a bottle.

Do you plan to breast-feed for a year or less? You *don't* want to start introducing a bottle at 8 or 10 months for the first time. If you do you're likely to run into a resistant baby.

her weight were unusually low, we'd have to assume she's taking enough food to sustain her. (I would suggest, though, that Sue stop switching breasts; see page 102.)

Needless to say, the first six weeks are critical for all babies, but it can be especially tricky if you're breast-feeding. Although these problems can continue or crop up later, it's now that you want to try to get it right.

Painful Feeds: Gastric Distress

Babies don't come out as full human beings—sometimes their digestive systems need a little more time to develop. The worst thing about any gastrointestinal problem is that it sets in motion a series of events and emotions that only make the problem worse and more difficult to deal with. Mum and Dad often feel helpless and inept because they can't figure out the problem. They start questioning their own skills; that inse-

---

The Crying Game

To determine why a baby is in distress, I ask specific questions about crying. Of course, it's only one piece of information. I also need to ask birthweight, eating patterns, activities, sleeping habits—to rule out hunger, tiredness, overstimulation, or, more likely, a combination of the three.

When does he usually cry? If he cries after feeds, it's probably gas or reflux. If he cries like clockwork at the same time every day, it could be colic (if the other 2 conditions have been ruled out). If his crying is erratic and random, it might be his temperament—certain types of babies cry more than others.

What does his body look like when he cries? If he pulls his feet up to his chest, it's probably gas. If he goes rigid and arches his back, it could be reflux, but it also could be his way of shutting out the world.

What comforts him when he cries? If burping him or bicycling his legs eases his crying, you probably helped him pass a gas bubble. If sitting him upright—say in a car seat or a swing—does the trick, it could be reflux. Motion, the sound of running water, the vacuum might distract a baby who has colic, but more often there's very little one can do to console a colicky baby.

curity, in turn, affects their behavior. They become tense, and while feeding are worried and anxious.

When parents tell me that their baby is "crying all the time," the first thing I suspect is some kind of gastric problem: gas, reflux (baby heartburn), or colic (as opposed to either of the first two conditions, which are sometimes mistaken for colic). Infants' digestive systems are very immature. They've been fed intravenously for nine months, and now they have to feed independently, so the first six weeks can be a tottering time.

Gas, reflux, and colic are all different conditions, but it can be extremely confusing for new parents to differentiate between the three. Making matters worse, pediatricians sometime use the umbrella term "colic" to describe all three, among other reasons because even researchers don't agree on what colic is. The following should help you understand as much as anyone knows:

GAS

WHAT IT IS: Air that your baby swallows during feeding. Some babies like the sensation of swallowing, so they'll gulp air even when they're not eating. Gas can be very painful to a baby, just as it is to an adult. When that air gets trapped in the intestine, it causes pain, because there's no way for the body to it break down. Your baby just has to eliminate it by passing gas or burping.

WHAT TO LOOK FOR: Think of your own body and recall what it feels like to have gas. Your baby will probably bring his legs up to his chest. He'll scrunch up his face. There will also be a definite pitch and tone to his cry—it's an intermittent crying and he'll look like he's panting—as if he's about to belch. He might also roll his eyes and wear an expression (between cries) that almost looks like a smile (which is why Grandma often insists that Baby's first smile is "really" just gas).

WHAT TO DO: When you burp your baby, rub upward on his left side (the soft part under his left rib is where his stomach is) using the heel of your palm. If that doesn't work, pick him up with his arms dangling over your shoulder and legs straight down. This gives the air a direct path. Rub upward, as if you're smoothing a piece of wallpaper to get the air bubble out. You can also help your baby expel the gas by laying him on his back, pulling up his legs, and doing a gentle bicycling motion. Another way to encourage him to pass gas is to hold him against you and pat his bottom, which gives him a sense of where to push. To relieve the soreness in his tummy, lay him across your forearm, face down, and put gentle pressure on his tummy with your palm. Wrapping a makeshift cummerbund around his middle by folding a receiving blanket into a four-inch band and tucking it in snugly around his middle can also accomplish the same thing. Just make sure it's not too tight.

REFLUX

WHAT IT IS: Baby heartburn, sometimes accompanied by vomiting. In extreme cases, there can be complications and the baby can regurgitate blood-tinged liquid. Heartburn is extremely painful in adults, and worse for babies because they don't know what is happening. When your baby eats, food goes into the mouth and down the esophagus. If the digestive system is working properly, the sphincter—the muscle that opens and closes the stomach—allows the food to drop in and keeps it there. If the gastrointestinal tract is fully developed, there's a rhythmic pattern of swallowing, and then the sphincter opening and closing as it should. But with reflux, the sphincter is immature and doesn't close properly after opening. The food doesn't stay down and, to make it worse, stomach acid comes up with it, burning your baby's esophagus.

WHAT TO LOOK FOR: One or two episodes of spitting up should not alarm you. All babies have reflux at one time or another, especially after eating. Some have it more often, and some infants are simply more sensitive to digestive issues. When I suspect reflux I first ask: **Was he breach? Did he have the cord wrapped around his neck during delivery? Was he premature? Was he jaundiced? Was he a low-birthweight baby? Did Mum have a C-section? Have any of the adults or other children in the family had reflux?** A yes to any of those questions points to a higher chance of reflux.

If she has reflux, your baby will have trouble getting through her feeds. She might splutter and choke, because her sphincter has stayed shut, making it impossible for her to get food down in the first place. Or, she might spit up or even projectile-vomit a few minutes after eating, because the sphincter didn't close once the food went down. Sometimes you'll also see a watery cottage-cheese spit-up as long as an hour after a

---

It's a Myth

It's not reflux if the baby isn't spitting up.

The old-fashioned diagnosis for reflux included constant spitting up and/or projectile vomiting. But we now know that some babies have the pain and the problem without those symptoms. Because of this confusion, reflux can still be misdiagnosed as colic. Many pediatricians nowadays are as likely to suggest reflux as colic, but some old-school doctors automatically say "colic" when a baby's crying has no apparent reason (see "colic," page 114). Others contend that reflux is one type of colic. That might explain why some cases of colic "magically" disappear at around four months. By then, the immature sphincter muscle starts to strengthen—the more it's used, the stronger it gets—and the baby finds it easier to eat and digest.

---

feed, because the stomach is in spasm and whatever is on top comes back up through the esophagus. She might have explosive poops. Like a gassy baby, she might also gulp air, but with reflux the gulp is accompanied by a little squeaky noise. Reflux babies are often hard to burp. Another key sign is that the only way they feel comfortable is when they're sitting up or are held upright on a shoulder. Any attempts to lay them down result in bouts of hysterical crying, which is why a red flag goes off in my brain when a parent tells me, "He's happiest when sitting in the swing" or "He'll only go to sleep in his car seat."

The vicious cycle with esophageal reflux is that the more tense a baby is and the more crying he does, the more likely it is that he'll have a spasm and that the acid will come up his esophagus and make him even more uncomfortable. You try every trick in the book and nothing calms him. Chances are, you're trying the wrong tricks. You may tend to jiggle him up and down to comfort him, which only helps the acid move up the esophagus. Or you'll think, "The problem is that he needs to burp," so you pat his back, which also pushes the acid up through his undeveloped sphincter. You might attribute his crying and his discomfort to this or that—usually colic or gas—without realizing he has heartburn, which requires a very specific kind of management. You get confused and abandon your routine because you're having trouble reading his cues. Meanwhile, your baby is exhausted. He gets hungry again from all that crying (which takes a lot of energy), so you try to feed him again. But before you know it, he's uncomfortable, maybe spitting up, and the cycle continues.

WHAT TO DO: If your pediatrician says it's colic, get a second opinion from a pediatric gastroenterologist, especially if the adults in your family or other children have gastrointestinal problems. Reflux runs in families. Often a health history and thorough examination is enough to diagnose the problem. Most babies are diagnosed without lab tests. In extreme cases or if your doctor thinks there might be complications from your child's reflux, various tests may be performed—X-ray with a barium swallow, ultrasound, endoscopy, esophageal pH study. The specialist will determine if your baby has reflux, gauge its severity, and can usually estimate how long your baby's reflux will last. She will also give you medications and guidelines to manage it.

The most common treatment for reflux is medication: baby antacids and relaxants. That part is in the doctor's hands. But there are also things you can do besides taking him for rides in the car or getting him addicted to that darn mechanical swing:

Elevate the crib mattress. Raise it to a 45-degree angle by using a baby wedge or a couple of books—anything, as long as the head is higher. Babies with reflux do best when propped up and swaddled.

Do not pat your baby when burping him. If you pat you'll make him vomit or he'll start crying, which starts the vicious cycle. Rather, gently rub in a circular motion on the left side of his back. The reason to rub is that if you pat his back, which is where his esophagus is, it irritates an already inflamed area. Rub upward with baby's arm straight over your shoulder so there's a clear passage up the esophagus. If after three minutes, he doesn't burp, stop burping him. If there's air in there, he'll start being fussy. Gently lift him forward and the air will probably come out.

Pay attention to feeds. Avoid overfeeding your baby or feeding him too quickly (which is more likely to happen on a bottle). If a bottle-feeding takes less than twenty minutes, the hole in the nipple may be too large. Switch to a slow-release nipple. If he starts fussing after a feed, use a pacifier to calm him rather than feed again, which will only make him more distressed.

Don't rush to give him solid food. Some experts suggest giving solid food earlier than six months when a baby has reflux, but I disagree (see "Solid Advice, page 142). If you fill his tummy too much, it will give him even worse heartburn. He'll stop feeding if he has pain.

Try to stay calm yourself. Reflux tends get better at around eight months, when the sphincter is more mature and your baby is eating more solid foods. Most babies outgrow reflux in the first year; the most severe cases can continue through age two, but they're definitely in the minority. With those serious cases, you just have to accept that your baby isn't going to conform to a normal eating pattern—at least not for now. In the meantime, take the steps you can to make him comfortable and know that at some point he will outgrow it.

COLIC

WHAT IT IS: Not even doctors agree about what colic is or how to define it. Most consider it a complex clustering of symptoms characterized by loud, excessive, and inconsolable crying, which seems to be accompanied by pain and irritability. Some see it as an umbrella that covers: *digestive problems* (allergies to food, gas, or reflux), *neurological problems* (hypersensitivity or highly reactive temperament), and *unfavorable environmental conditions* (nervous or neglectful parents, tension in the home). Babies diagnosed with colic can have any—or all—of these conditions, but not all will necessarily have true colic. Some pediatricians still use the old 3/3/3 rule: three nonstop hours of crying, three days a week, for three consecutive weeks, which statistically adds up to about 20 percent of all babies. Pediatrician and colic researcher Barry Lester, author of *For Crying Out Loud,* calls colic "a disorder of crying." He puts it simply: "Something is making that kid cry in an unusual way and whatever it is, it also impacts on the rest of the family." Lester agrees that only about 10 percent have true colic—severe bouts of loud crying that last for several hours at a time, often at the same time of day every day and with no apparent reason. First-born infants seem to be affected with colic more often than later children. It usually begins within ten days to three weeks after birth, and lasts until three or four months of age, at which time it generally disappears on its own.

WHAT TO LOOK FOR: When a mother suspects that her baby is "colicky," I first rule out gas and reflux. Even if they are considered subsets of colic, at least you can take steps to alleviate them, which we can't say about colic. One important difference between colic and reflux is that despite their crying, colicky babies put on weight, whereas many babies with reflux lose weight. Also, with reflux, your baby will tend to arch backward during a crying spell; with gas, he pulls his legs up; and both spells typically occur within an hour or less of the last feed whereas colic isn't necessarily related to feeds. Some studies now suggest that colic has nothing to do with stomach pain at all (even though the word *colic* comes from the Greek word for colon). Instead, it's caused by a baby´s inability to console himself when dealing with all the things that bombard his senses.

WHAT TO DO: The trouble is, all babies cry. They cry when they're hungry or upset or when you change their routine. I've helped "cure" so-called colicky babies by putting them on a structured routine, teaching the parents how to tune in to the baby's cues, modifying feeding techniques if necessary (changing nipples if the baby is bottle-fed or the position of the baby's body during feeds, changing the way the baby is burped), and ruling out food allergies (changing formulas). But in those cases, we obviously weren't dealing with true colic.

Your pediatrician might prescribe a mild sedative (knock-out drops), advise you to avoid overstimulating your baby, or suggest various tricks of the trade like running water, the vacuum, or your hair dryer to distract your baby. Some will also suggest breast-feeding more frequently, which I categorically *don't* recommend, because if the problem is in your baby's gastric system, overfeeding makes it worse. Whatever the suggestions, remember that true colic has no "cure." You pretty much have to ride it out. Some parents are better equipped than others to do this. If you're anything but a "Confident" parent (see pages 68–71), a colicky baby might be a bad fit. In that case, call in the reserves. Get all the help you can. Take lots of breaks so that you don't get to the breaking point yourself.

Six Weeks to Four Months: Growth Spurts

Now many of the early feeding wrinkles are ironed out. Your baby is probably a bit more consistent, eating and sleeping better—unless of course she's plagued by gastrointestinal problems or she's very sensitive to her environment. In that case, hopefully you've learned to accept her temperament and are more tuned in to her cues by now. You also know the best way of feeding her and keeping her comfortable after meals, and you're using your common sense to make life a little easier for her. At this stage, I get variations on the following two complaints:

> *I can't get my baby to sleep more than three or four hours during the night.*
>
> *My baby was sleeping for five or six hours during the night but now she's waking up more frequently, but always at different times.*

Parents *think* they're calling me about a sleeping issue, but to their surprise, both problems are related to food at this stage. By eight weeks, many babies—*my* babies—are sleeping at least five hours through the night, if not six. Naturally, it also depends on birthweight and temperament, but after six weeks, we should at least be moving in that direction, encouraging them to sleep a good stretch at night. And with babies who have already started to sleep longer stretches, night-waking is commonly due to a *growth spurt—a period, typically lasting a day or two, when your baby's body demands more food.* The ol' Baby Whisperer has a few little tricks up her sleeve just for either situation.

If your baby is average-sized or heavier and has *never* been able to get to sleep more than three or four hours, I first ask, **How many naps and for how long is your baby sleeping during the day?** It could be that her daytime naps are robbing her nighttime sleep (an issue I cover on pages 177–178, where I advise you to never let your baby sleep for more than two hours at a time during the day). But if her naps aren't too long and she still can't put more than three or four hours together at night, it probably means she needs to be eating more food during the day and to have a full tummy when you put her to bed. If you haven't already done so, I would suggest tanking up (see page 93 and 195).

In the second situation, where a baby has been sleeping through for five or six hours and now starts waking at different times, it usually means that she's going through a growth spurt. Growth spurts happen for the first time between six and eight weeks and recur thereafter about once a month or every six weeks. The one at five or six months is usually a signal that it's time to introduce solid food.

Growth spurts can occur earlier in bigger babies, which can be confusing. A mum will call and say, "My baby is four months old, he's eighteen pounds, and he's eating eight ounces at every feed, but he's still waking up once or twice in the night. I'm not supposed to give him solid food in the night." In that case, you have to use your judgment. You can't give him more liquid and he obviously needs more to sustain him.

Growth spurts in breast-feeding babies shouldn't be confused with improper latch-on or a problem with mum's milk supply, both of which also cause night-waking but usually happen earlier than six weeks. The question that helps me determine whether a baby is having a growth spurt is: **Does she wake at the same hour every night, or is her waking pattern erratic?** If it's erratic, it's usually a growth spurt. This email illustrates a typical scenario:

I've just started my seven-week-old Olivia on E.A.S.Y., which she has taken to really well. But since we've started, her sleeping schedule at night has become more erratic. Before she would wake up at 2:45. But lately she seems to have no consistency despite her eating and sleeping at relatively the same time during the day. We have kept a log and we can't really find anything that we are doing differently each night that would cause her to sometimes wake up at 1 and other times not until 4:30. Is there anything we can do to promote her to sleep until at least 2:45 like she used to?

In a case like Olivia's, I knew it was definitely a growth spurt, because she had been a pretty good eater and sleeper all along, and her parents seem to have instinctually had her on a routine. Another real tip-off was that although she usually woke at 2:45 A.M., her mum noted, "since we've started, her sleeping schedule at night has become *more erratic* [emphasis mine]." Because her waking happened to coincide with the parents' putting Olivia on E.A.S.Y., they naturally assumed her sudden sleep disturbances had something to do with the new routine. But in reality, their baby is just hungry. And the reason Mum and Dad can't figure out anything *they* are doing is that this is about what Olivia's body is doing!

Let's say that we're talking about a baby who's never slept well. She still wakes up twice a night. She, too, might be going through a growth spurt, but she also could be getting into a very bad sleep pattern, and Mum and Dad reinforce it by feeding her when she wakes. So how do you know the difference? One clue is the waking pattern: Generally, habitual wakers get up at almost the same time every night—you can almost set a clock by them. Babies who wake erratically are usually hungry. But the best clue is food intake: When Mum tries to feed her, if she's having a growth spurt, she will take a full feed because her body needs the extra food. If she doesn't take more than a few ounces, it's pretty conclusive evidence that we're dealing with a bad sleeping pattern, not a hungry baby (see pages 191–192 for more on habitual waking).

The prescription for a growth spurt is always the same: Increase food during the day and, if you haven't already started doing so, add a dream feed at night. With bottle-fed babies, we increase by one ounce the amount of formula you give during the day. With breast-fed babies, it's a little trickier, because you increase the feed *time* rather than the amount.

So if your baby is on a three-hour routine, bump it up a bit to every 2½ hours. With an older baby who's on a "4/4" routine (page 33), you have to go back to feeding every three or 3½ hours. Some mums find this advice confusing, like Joanie, a mother in Florida, who told me, "That feels like we're going backward. I finally got him on a four-hour routine." I explained that this is just a *temporary* measure. By feeding more often, she was letting her body know that it had to manufacture more milk for four-month-old Matthew, and in a few days, she would be producing enough milk to satisfy his new needs.

Growth spurts can disrupt your baby's routine at bedtime, during the middle of the night, or when you put them down for a nap. Even parents who are aware that growth spurts periodically occur may not realize that the so-called sleep issue or a bad case of crib-phobia is really about food. One mother, whose son David was six weeks old, had been working with the E.A.S.Y. method for three days. The first two days, she wrote, "worked like a charm. We followed the routine, and I was so proud that he was able to fall asleep in the crib consistently (with the help of a pacifier). However, today (the third day), he has been crying pretty hard from the moment we enter his bedroom and begin our routine before his nap. He also has been eating more frequently since last night, and I suspect he's in a growth spurt. Can this resistence to his bedroom be related to a growth spurt?"

Absolutely. Little David is saying (through his tears), "I don't want to go to sleep. I want more food. So feed me." If he isn't fed, he'll start to associate hunger with his bedroom. Babies are primal creatures, but they also very quickly learn by association. If you were sent to your room before you finished your dinner, there's a good chance you wouldn't want to go to your room, either! You'd see it as a bad place.

If your baby is resistant to the dream feed, you also might want to reevaluate how you're feeding him during the day One little lad I cared for, Christian, was nine weeks old at the time, and no matter how hard his mum and I tried, he wouldn't take that 11 P.M. feed. For weeks, Mum had been feeding him at 5 and 8 and then trying to feed him again at 11, which was only three hours later. Chris was almost nine pounds at that point, so it wasn't surprising that he wasn't hungry at 11. But then he woke up at 1 A.M. starving. We decided to adjust his earlier feeds. We only gave him two ounces at 5 P.M. instead of the seven ounces he usually

---

Spotlight in the Trenches

Dream Feeding Too Late

Janet called me because her son was waking up at 4:30 or 5 every morning. "But I'm doing a dream feed," she insisted. The problem was, she was feeding four-month-old Kevin between midnight and 1 A.M. At his age and for his size (he was 8 lb. at birth), he should have been sleeping at least 5, if not 6, hours during the night. But because Janet was unwittingly disrupting his sleep with a too-late dream feed, he slept fitfully. After all, babies' sleep patterns are affected just like ours would be if we are disturbed or overtired. If we're kept up, we don't sleep soundly and are more likely to toss and turn. Then to make matters worse, Janet fed him when he woke in the wee hours of the morning, which only reinforced his waking *habit*. (Remember: Waking up like clockwork is a pattern; waking sporadically is hunger.) I suggested that she gradually move the dream feed to 10 or 10:30, but stop feeding him when he wakes (see more about how to do this in chapter 5, pages 198–199). Also, she was to give him a little more food during the day by adding an oz. to each of his daytime bottles.

---

took, and moved the 8 P.M. feed back an hour, to 7 P.M., and only gave him six ounces instead of his usual eight. In other words, we took away seven ounces altogether from his evening feeds. He had an activity afterward—his bath—and by the time he was massaged, swaddled, and put to bed, he was pretty tired. Then we took the dream feed to 11, which meant that now there were four hours between his early evening feeds and lo and behold—Chris took a full eight ounces at 11. At that point, we also figured he needed more food during the day, so we upped his feeds an ounce per bottle. Thereafter, he lasted through the night from the dream feed to a 6:30 A.M. wake-up.

Remember that a dream feed should never be later than 11. Otherwise, you're cutting into the night, which we're trying to avoid, because a feed at night means the baby will eat that much less during the day, and he'll get into the habit of waking at night from hunger. That's backward. We don't want to start a baby on a routine that we'd do with a six-week-old.

Four to Six Months: A More Grown-Up Eater

This is a stage of relative calm in the eating department—that is, if you've got your baby on a structured routine. If not, you're probably still experiencing some of the problems that come up at earlier stages, except now they're harder to manage. She'll still cry for her meals, but, depending on her temperament (and how you respond to her), your baby will probably have a less desperate tone. Some babies will even play on their own in the morning, rather than wake their parents with a "Feed me!" wail.

These are the concerns that are often thrown at me at this stage. They might seem different from one another, but all three are solved by establishing or tweaking a routine and helping parents see that their little one is growing and changing.

> *My baby never eats at the same time of day.*

> *My baby finishes her feeds so quickly, I'm afraid she's not getting enough to eat. It also throws her off schedule.*

> *My baby doesn't seem interested in eating anymore. Mealtimes have become a chore.*

I'll bet you can guess the first question I ask when a client comes to me with any of the above concerns: **Is your baby on a structured routine?** If the answer is "no"—and it usually is when parents say their baby never eats at the same time every day—you can't blame eating problems on the baby. It's the adults who have to get their act together. Of course, *some* variation in your daily routine is normal. But if your baby is always eating at random all the time, I'll just bet he never gets a good sleep either. He needs to be on a structured routine. (See "Starting E.A.S.Y. at Four Months or Older," pages 39–46.)

If a client insists that her baby *has* been on a routine, my next question is: **How long does your baby go between feeds?** If she's feeding every two hours, I know it's a snacking problem, because no four-month-old or older baby needs to eat that often. That was little Maura's problem. At almost five months old, she was still feeding every two hours, even through the night. A friend had suggested putting cereal in Maura's bottle "to help her get through the night"—an old wives' tale if I ever heard one (see "It's a Myth," page 143). As Maura had never had solids, all that did was constipate her, and she still woke up looking for her mum's breast. Instead, I advised her parents, Jessica and Bill, to tank Maura up at 6, 8, 10, and then *not* feed her at night—no matter what. After all, Maura was not an infant. She was an older baby whose parents had accidentally taught her how to snack. The first night, she naturally woke up screaming several times between 10 and 5, but Jessica and Bill didn't cave in. Dad used my pick-up/put-down method (chapter 6) to get Maura back to sleep each time. But it was a hard night for the three of them, especially Mum, who thought she was starving her baby. Jessica could tell the difference in the morning, though, because for the first time in a long time (maybe ever) Maura took a full half-hour feed at 5 A.M. For the rest of the day, Maura ate pretty efficiently every four hours, too. The second night was a little better. Maura woke up twice, Dad put her back to sleep each time, and the next morning she lasted until six. She's been on track ever since. I suggested that her parents keep her on the dream feed until six months, when they make the transition to solid food.

If a baby at this stage is still feeding every three hours, she might not be snacking, but I suspect that the parents are trying to keep her on an eating plan that's meant for a younger child. They need to lengthen the feeds to every four hours. You have to do it gradually, though. It's unfair to make a baby this young suddenly wait an hour more between feeds. So, you extend it by fifteen minutes a day over a four-day period. The good thing about this age group, though, is that they're easier to hold off. They can be amused with toys and silly faces, or a walk in the park, not just a pacifier, which is what you'd have to use with a younger infant to delay a feeding.

In a similar vein, parents who are worried that their baby is finishing his feeds "too quickly" also may be forgetting that their baby is growing up. Babies become more efficient eaters at this age. So your baby may be getting plenty to eat but it just takes him less time to down it. This, of course, depends on whether he's taking breast milk, which we measure in time, or formula, which is measured in ounces.

If he's on formula, it's a simple matter to gauge whether he's getting enough to eat, because you can actually measure in ounces what he's drinking. Keep track for a few days. He should be taking between five and eight ounces per feed, *every four hours.* Including a dream feed at night, he will therefore be taking a total of twenty-six to thirty-eight ounces per day.

Too Skinny—or Just More Active?

Often, when babies become more mobile, they also become less interested in eating. Many also start to slim out from the increased activity. As the baby fat starts disappearing, they begin to look more like toddlers. Depending on your child's physique, which she's inherited from you, her cute little Buddha belly may be less obvious. As long as she's healthy, don't sweat it. If you're worried, check with your pediatrician.

If he is a breast-fed baby, feeds at this stage should only take around twenty minutes, because he's now able to chug-a-lug in that short time the same five or six ounces of breast milk that once took him forty-five minutes to finish. If you want to be sure, though, do a yield (pages 104–105). By now, milk supply is not usually a problem.

In either case, if your baby is nearing the six-month mark, it's time to introduce solids as well, because as your baby begins to really move about, he needs more than just liquid to sustain his activities (see chapter 4).

As for the baby who "doesn't seem interested" in feeds anymore, I'm afraid that just goes with the territory. Between four and six months, babies take a developmental leap forward. Your baby is more curious and more mobile at this stage. Although she may be an efficient eater, sitting still for a feed is boring compared to all the new wonders of the world that surround her. Once, a breast or bottle was all your baby needed to be content. Perhaps she glanced at the little mobile over the crib during a feed, but all that is old hat by now. She can turn her head and reach for things, so eating is not necessarily a high priority. You may even have a week or two when she's absolutely uncooperative and impossible. Take some proactive steps. Feed her in an area relatively free of distractions. Tuck her little arm in under you, so she doesn't start fiddling. If your baby is very active, you can half-swaddle her to cut down on the squirming. Put a brightly colored piece of cloth that has decorations on it over your shoulder so your baby has something novel to look at. Sometimes, I have to admit, the best you can do is ride it out—and watch in awe at what a little person your baby is becoming.

Six to Nine Months and Beyond: The Perils of Accidental Parenting

Talk about giant steps! Now your baby is about to enter the real world, at least when it comes to food. Well, almost. Even though some food concerns at this stage are centered on her liquid intake—many of them prob-

How Do I Stop the Dream Feeds?

The process of cutting out the dream feed—usually around 7 months—has to be done in 3-day increments, to insure that your baby makes up during the day what you're taking away at night:

Day 1: Add 1 ounce to the 1st feed of the day, and take away 1 ounce from the dream feed that night. If you're breast-feeding, go back to clustering so that you get more calories in. Give the dream feed (now 1 ounce less) half an hour earlier, at 10:30 instead of 11.

Day 4: Add one ounce to the first feed, one to the second, and take away two ounces from the dream feed. Give the dream feed (two ounces less) at 10.

Day 7: Add one ounce to the first feed, one to the second, one to the third, take away three ounces from the dream feed, and give it at 9:30.

Days 10 (dream feed at 9 P.M.), *14* (8:30), *17* (8), and *20* (7:30): By continuing every 3 days to add ounces during the day and take away the same amount from the dream feed, you will end up doing a feed at 7:30 with only a few ounces.

lems that weren't dealt with successfully at earlier stages—the spotlight now is on Big People Food. No more living solely on a liquid diet. Now she's going to learn how to chow down mush and then little pieces and finally all the foods you eat. (You'll find everything you need to know about that transition in the next chapter.)

I also suggest cutting out the dream feed at around seven months (see box above), as your baby starts to get solid food in him. If you continue to give it, you're working against the introduction of solid food, because for every ounce of extra liquid your baby takes, he won't be hungry for an ounce of solid food. However, as the box indicates, when you cut out the dream feed, you have to add the same number of ounces to the day feed. If you don't, your baby will wake up at night.

The other most common concerns at this stage are:

My baby still wakes up hungry at night.

I'm trying to get my baby on a bottle, but she's having none of it.

My baby uses a sippy cup but she won't drink milk out of it, only water or orange juice.

Like many problems that crop up after the six-month mark, these are most likely the result of accidental parenting. The parents didn't start as they meant to go on. Or, they just didn't think it through.

Take the first one: When a baby is still waking up for food at six months or—heaven knows I've seen it as old as nineteen months—it's because parents have responded to earlier episodes of night-waking with a feed, even though the baby only took a few ounces. As I noted earlier, when babies night-wake at different times, it's usually hunger. By six months, I rarely see this, except during growth spurts or when it's time to introduce solids. But when they wake up like clockwork, it's usually about accidental parenting. It's not hard to turn a six-month or older baby into a snacker if he starts waking up in the middle of the night and you give him a bottle or breast. In these cases, where children are inadvertently taught to snack throughout the night, which naturally affects their appetite during the day, it's really a sleeping issue, not a food problem. Instead of feeding them, you have to hold them off by using my pick-up/put-down method (see chapter 6). The good news? It takes less time with older babies to change this habit because they have enough fat on their bodies to last between feeds.

The second and third complaints are also due to accidental parenting. As you know, I suggest that parents introduce a bottle as early as two weeks (see box, page 108). For any number of reasons—the advice of their friends, something they read—some think that's "too early." Then three, six, or ten months later, I get frantic calls like this: "I'm a prisoner, because no one else can feed her" or "I have to go back to work in a week and I'm afraid she'll starve" or "My husband thinks our baby hates him because she screams if he tries to give her a bottle." This is what my Nan has in mind when she says start as you mean to go on. By not taking a few moments to ask herself, "Mmmm . . . what do I want my life to look like in few months? Am I willing to be the *only* person in the household—in the world—to feed this baby until she graduates to a sippy cup?" a new mum could be setting herself up for a big problem down the road.

It's the same with making the transition to a sippy cup. This is a common scenario: A mum will introduce her baby to this more grown-up form of drinking by giving him something other than breast milk or formula. Often it's juice, because she figures that he'll be more willing to drink the sweet, strange-tasting liquid from a cup than boring old milk. Some use water, too, because they're worried about adding too much sugar to Baby's diet (I agree). Well, babies are like Pavlov's dogs. So after a few months of tasting that "other" liquid, when Mum tries to give him milk instead, he makes a face that means, "Hey, Mum, what gives? This isn't supposed to be in *here*." And he categorically refuses to drink it. (See page 132 for what to do.)

If you're reading this book before you went too far down either of those side roads, great. Let other mothers know about the pitfalls. If not, read on. You may be in for a struggle, but all is not lost.

From Breast to Bottle: The First Steps of Weaning

There are two factors that influence what happens when you try to introduce a bottle: your baby's reaction and yours, the impact on both your mind and body. You might want to introduce a bottle because you're ready to wean your baby entirely, or because you want to make your life easier by replacing one or more breast-feeding sessions with bottle-feeds. Either way, you've got both factors to contend with. The older your baby, the harder it will be for you to get her used to a bottle in the first place if she's been exclusively on the breast. But with older babies it also will be easier for your body to adapt to the change, because your milk will dry up more quickly (see box, page 126). At the same time, though, a lot of mums have a strong emotional reaction to reducing the number of breast-feeds and, especially, to quitting altogether.

So let's take the baby first. The procedure is the same for one who's never had a bottle as it is for one who had one several months earlier and now seems to have forgotten how to drink from one. I get tons of emails and calls from mums who have struggled with both problems. Here's a posting from my website:

> Hi, I am mum to a six-month baby boy. Does anyone have advice on introducing the bottle? I don't want to stop nursing but I need a break. He will not entertain a bottle, we have been trying for the last twelve weeks. I have tried almost everything, cups, bottles, breast milk, formula, etc.

Twelve weeks! That's a lot of coaxing and cajoling and frustration—yours and your baby's. Obviously, this mum is not in a hurry. Imagine if

Winding Down Breast-Feeding

How Does Mum Do It?

Whether they want to quit altogether or just wind down, many mothers are worried about how their breasts will feel when they first skip a feed. The plan below assumes that your baby is willing to take a bottle and that you want to continue breast-feeding only twice a day, in the morning and after work. If you want to quit altogether, just keep eliminating feeds. Your body will cooperate, but you have to help it along.

Pump instead of skipping feeds. To avoid becoming engorged, for the next 12 days, continue to put your baby on your breasts in the morning and whenever you want to give the 2nd feed. During the day, pump when you'd normally feed him. Pump 15 minutes per session for the 1st 3 days. On the 4th through 6th days, pump only 10 minutes; on the 7th through 9th, 5 minutes; and on the 10th through 12th days, only 2 to 3 minutes. By then, your breasts will fill only before the 2 feeds, and you won't need to continue pumping.

Wear a tight bra between feeds. A snug sports bra helps your body reabsorb the milk.

Do 3 to 5 sets of overarm exercises daily. Act as if you're throwing a ball. This also aids reabsorption. If necessary, take Tylenol every 4 to 6 hours for pain. Engorgement is rare when a baby is 8 months or older; milk production stops more quickly than at, say, 3 months.

she had to go back to work, as many do! For example, I remember Bart's mum, Gail, who breast-fed her son for the first three months and then called me: "I am going back to work in three weeks and would ideally like to breast-feed in the morning, late afternoon, and evening and then use bottles of formula for the other feedings."

Regardless of whether you're switching to a bottle and plan never to breast-feed again or you want to do only a few feeds a day, my advice is make sure you're ready, stay the course, and steel yourself for a bumpy day or two. Of course, if your baby is six months or older, you might consider going straight to a sippy cup and skip the bottle. But if you decide to go ahead . . .

Find a type of nipple that most closely resembles your own. Some gung-ho breast-feeding experts warn of "nipple confusion" and use it as a reason

---

Too Old for a Bottle?

Mothers are often advised to get rid of the bottle by a year or 18 months at the latest, but I think 2 is plenty of time. It's not the end of the world if your baby takes a few minutes at bedtime with his bottle to snuggle up in Mum or Dad's lap.

Left to their own devices, many toddlers give up their bottles voluntarily by 2. When they want to hang on longer it's usually because they've been allowed to use a bottle as a pacifier—for instance, Mum gives it to him as a quick fix to shut him up at the mall, or Dad shoves it into his mouth to avoid a meltdown in front of company. Or the parents may use a bottle to send him off to naps or nighttime sleep. Some parents leave a bottle in the child's crib, hoping to grab an extra hour of sleep, which is not only habit-forming, it's dangerous. The child could choke. Also, when a child is allowed to nurse a bottle all day, he fills up on liquid and often eats less food.

If your child is 2 or older and is still walking around with a bottle, it's time to intervene:

- Make some ground rules about the bottle—only at bedtime, or only in the bedroom.
- Bring snacks with you, instead of relying on the bottle for sustenance, and deal with tantrums differently (see chapter 8).
- Make the bottle less attractive. Cut a slit in the nipple, about ¼–⅜-inch across. Wait 4 days and then cut a slit the other way, so you'll have an X. After another week, cut first 2 and then all 4 of the triangles. Eventually, you'll have a big square opening and your child will lose interest altogether.

---

not to give a bottle before three or six months of age (depending on which book you read). If anything, babies can be confused by *flow*, not the nipple itself. Pick a type and if your baby takes to it, don't keep switching nipples. It's enough for her to adapt to a bottle; she doesn't need you to experiment with nipples, too—*unless* she starts choking, sputtering, or gagging. If so, buy the slow-release type of nipple, which is specially designed to respond to her suckling actions, as opposed to the standard types, which drip into her mouth even when she stops sucking.

Start with the first bottle of your baby's day, when she's hungriest. I don't agree with people who suggest starting when your baby isn't very hungry. What's her incentive to accept the bottle if not hunger? Expect to be anxious yourself, and expect that your baby is going to be resistant and ill at ease, too.

Never force the bottle. Look at it from the baby's point of view. Imagine what it is like after several months of sucking on warm, human flesh to taste a cold rubber nipple for the first time. To make it more enticing (or at least more like your body temperature), run warm water over it. Push it into his mouth gently and jiggle it on his bottom lip, which stimulates the sucking reflex. If he doesn't take it within five minutes, stop, or you'll give him an aversion to it. Wait an hour and try again.

Try every hour the first day. Be persistent. Any mum who says she's been at it for twelve weeks, or even four weeks, is not really keeping at it. More likely, she tries for a day or two—or even a few minutes—and then forgets about it. Then she starts feeling tied down or she's worried about leaving her baby with a sitter. So she tries again. If she doesn't commit to staying with it every day, it's less likely to work.

Let Dad or Grandma, a friend or a nanny give it a try, but only when you're first introducing the bottle. Some babies take bottles from others and absolutely refuse it from their mums. It's a good way to get your baby started, but it's not something you want to foster. The idea of giving a bottle is to have the flexibility. Let's say you're out with your baby and you'd rather not breast-feed. You won't want to have to call Dad or Granny in every time. Once she's accustomed to the bottle, you give it to her, too.

Expect—and be willing to ride out—a hunger strike. If your baby refuses the bottle altogether, don't whip out your breast. I promise, your child won't starve to death, which is what all mums fear. Most babies will take at least an ounce or two after three or four hours of not getting the breast. I've seen babies refuse bottles all day long, holding out 'til Mum comes home, but those are the exceptions (and they don't starve either). If you're persistent, the trauma of introducing a bottle is over within twenty-four hours. Some older babies, usually Grumpy types, can take as long as two or three days.

Thereafter, always give a bottle at least once a day. A common mistake that mothers make is not sticking with at least a once-a-day bottle. Babies will always go back to their original feeding method. So if a baby starts out breast-feeding and, say, his mum had to go to the hospital for a week, and he was bottle-fed during that time, he'd know how to start right in again. Though it's less common, if a baby starts out with a bottle and then Mum decides to breast-feed, that baby will always be comfortable with a bottle as well. But they won't remember the second method

---

Spotlight in the Trenches

Making the Switch

Janna, a television producer I was working with, had been leaving work every day, driving 30 miles in traffic, in order to feed her 7-month-old baby, Justin. She was at her rope's end because now she really wanted to have the flexibility of a bottle. At my suggestion, she gave Justin a feed before she left for work and left a bottle of pumped milk for the nanny to do the midday feed. But Justin refused and went on a hunger strike. Every time Janna called home to see how things were going, she heard Justin crying in the background. "I thought he was starving. I don't think I've every suffered through a day as much as that one." When Janna walked through the door at 4 that day, Justin was still screaming for her breast. She offered him a bottle instead and when he pitched a fit, she told him calmly, "Okay you're not hungry now." By 6, he was willing to take the bottle. Janna called me afterward and said, "I'd like to breast-feed him tonight." "You can't," I stressed, "unless you want another hunger strike on your hands tomorrow." I told her to keep up the bottles for 2 days and after 48 hours, she could resume giving him the bedtime feed.

---

you teach them unless you keep it up. I get mums all the time who tell me, "My baby used to take a bottle but she seems to have forgotten how." Of course, she has—it was a long time ago. In such cases, the mum has to start all over, using the above method to *re*introduce the bottle.

"But My Baby . . .": Mums' Feelings of Loss and Guilt over Weaning

There's one other piece of advice I have about taking steps to begin the weaning process: Make sure you *want* to introduce a bottle. In Janna's case (see box above), for example, her fears about Justin starving were not merely about his physical well-being. She was feeling guilty for causing him to "suffer" and, I would wager, ambivalent about the whole process. Many breast-feeding mums have similar kinds of mixed feelings about giving their babies bottles.

Breast-feeding can be a very emotional experience for the mothers, especially when a mother decides she wants her life back. Nowadays with the big push to breast-feed, many women feel like a Bad Mother with a capital B when they even think about weaning. It's a double whammy: On the one hand they feel guilty and, on the other, when they give it up, they feel a sense of loss.

Looking at my website recently, I came across a series of postings in response to a mother who for nine months had had trouble keeping up her supply and getting her son to nurse. Determined to "make it at least a year," she felt guilty for "wanting a little freedom" and wondered if "anyone ever felt like this?" Poor dear! If she only knew how many other mothers suffer the same feelings. I was pleased to see that the mums who responded to her offered the same kinds of comments I'd have made. Here's a sampling:

> Ultimately, it is your decision. You know what is best for you and your child.

> Nine months is wonderful. It is a major commitment to nurse for any period of time and I commend the mothers who attempt it for even a short amount of time.

> I had a mixed bag of emotions, too. On the one hand, I wanted to continue nursing for as long as possible. On the other, I wanted my freedom and own identity. I wanted to be Rosa and not just Marina's Lactating Mother. When I did wean, I missed our closeness. However, I gained my normal breasts back. I didn't have to worry about leaking. I no longer had to use a bra at night for sleeping. And DH was no longer restricted from that zone!

Breast-feeding is a wonderful experience for some mothers, and I'm all for it. But there comes a time for it to end. Perhaps it will ease your guilt to know that you're not weaning just because you're tired of leaky breasts or pumping at work, but for the sake of your baby's growing up and moving on to the next stage. One mum admitted, "It broke my heart the first time I offered my daughter a bottle—and she took it." Her daughter was off breast milk by nine months. "The anticipation of weaning actually proved to be more traumatic than the actual weaning itself," she concluded. "Once I accepted that bottles were (a) healthy alternatives and (b) not going to replace me, everything just fell into place."

Sippy Cups: I'm a Big Kid Now!

Around the time you start thinking about introducing solid food, you should also think about getting your child used to a sippy cup, so that he can make the transition from sucking his liquids down through a nipple to drinking like the big kids. It, too, is part of allowing your child to grow up, to go from being fed to eating on his own. As I mentioned earlier, some breast-feeding mums go straight from breast to sippy cup. Others introduce a bottle early on, or later, and also give their children a sippy cup at the same time.

When a mother says to me, "I just can't get my child to use a sippy cup," I wonder how hard she's trying, what mistakes she's made in her attempts to teach her child how to use it, and whether she expects overnight results. As always, I ask my questions:

At what age did you first try to introduce it? Even if a baby is on a bottle and breast, at six months, it's important to try out a sippy cup. You can also give her a paper cup or beaker (that's what we Brits call plastic cups), but a sippy cup is better because it has a spout that controls the flow. Your child can hold it herself, too, which promotes her independence. (Never *ever* give a glass to a baby or young child, not even up to four or five years old. I've seen too many children rushed to the emergency room with glass in their lips and tongue.)

How often did you try to give it? You have to give your child three weeks to a month of *daily* practice for him to get used to a sippy cup. It will take longer if you don't give it every day.

Did you try different types? Few babies immediately take to a sippy cup. If yours doesn't like it at first, remember that it's new and foreign to him. There are also so many sippy cups on the market now—some have a spout and others a straw. Breast-feeding babies often do better with a straw type of sippy cup. Regardless of the type you buy first, try one and stick with it for at least a month. Resist switching from one back to the other.

In what position do you hold your baby when giving him a sippy cup? Many parents hand their baby a sippy cup while he is sitting in a high chair or booster seat and expect him to know what to do. Instead, you should sit your baby on your knee, facing outward. Guide his little hands onto the handles and help him pick the cup up to his mouth. Do it gently, and do it at a time when he's in a good mood.

How Much Fluid a Day?

Once your child is on solid food 3 times a day, he should be having at least 16 oz. of milk or formula a day (up to 32 for big babies). Most mums split it up and give a little liquid after meals to wash down food and also offer a thirst-quencher after they've been running around. Don't wean if your child is solely on breast milk until he's mastered a sippy cup or at least is willing to drink from a bottle.

How much—and what kind of—liquid do you put into the cup? Here's where I see a lot of parents go wrong: They put too much liquid into the sippy cup, so it's too heavy for the baby to hold. I'd recommend no more than an ounce of water, pumped milk, or formula to begin with. Avoid juice, because your baby doesn't need the extra sugar. You also risk that she'll always associate the sippy cup with a sweet liquid and refuse all others.

Okay, but you say you've already made that mistake! She's now using a sippy cup like a champ but refuses to drink milk in it. You can't go cold turkey on her—she'll get upset, perhaps start associating the sippy cup with a negative experience, and she might even get dehydrated (especially if she's been weaned from the breast and doesn't take a bottle). Start by offering her two cups of liquid at her meal. In one, have an ounce of the liquid you've been giving her— say juice or water—and in the other pour two ounces of milk. After she has a sip of the water, take that cup away and try to give her the milk. If she refuses, leave it, and try an hour later. Even if she's already proficient, try sitting her on your knee for a drink. As with most things, if you persist, and try to make it a fun, loving experience, instead of seeing it as a skill you have to teach her *immediately*, you're more likely to be successful.

As with weaning, when you see your baby with a sippy cup, you might have mixed feelings, because he looks older. That's okay—most mums do. Just let go and enjoy the journey.

FOUR

FOOD IS MORE THAN NOURISHMENT

Solid Foods and Eating Happily Ever After

The Great Journey from Being Fed to Eating

Babies are amazing creatures. Watching them grow and develop sometimes takes my breath away. Take a moment to appreciate how human infants progress when it comes to eating. (It might help to look at the chart on pages 136–138, which shows how children advance from feeding to eating over the first three years.) At first, your baby is nourished twenty-four/seven in the comfort of your womb. She gets everything she needs from you via the umbilical cord, without worrying about how hard she suckles. And you, Mum, don't have to worry about whether your milk is coming in or whether you're holding the bottle at just the right angle. Your easy ride ends at birth, though, when both of you have to begin to work harder to make sure that she's eating adequate amounts at the right time, and that her tender digestive system isn't overtaxed.

For the first few months after they're born, babies' taste buds aren't developed. Their liquid diet is pretty bland, consisting of formula or breast milk, either of which provides them with all the nutrients they require. This is an amazing time. As I said earlier, newborns are like little piggies—they eat and eat and eat. At no other time in your child's life will she gain weight at this rapid pace. And a good thing, too: If you weighed 150 pounds and were to grow at the same rate as your baby, by the end of twelve months you would weigh around 450 pounds!

It takes a while for the two of you to finally get into a good rhythm, but most parents eventually find that feeding a baby is relatively uncomplicated. Then, at around six months—just as you're beginning to feel comfortable with your baby's liquid diet—it's time to introduce solid foods. Now you have to help your baby make an important developmental transition, from being fed to eating on her own. It doesn't happen overnight, and on the way, you might travel over some rocky terrain. In this chapter, we look at the assorted joys and difficulties this amazing journey involves. Your baby's taste buds will wake up, and she'll experience new sensations in her mouth that will make her life more interesting, and yours, too. If you approach this period with a positive attitude and lots of patience, it can be fun to observe your baby as she experiments with each new food you introduce and makes attempts, however fumbling and inept at first, to feed herself.

In England, we refer to this transition as "weaning," by which we mean getting the child off the breast or bottle and onto solid food. But in the United States, I've been told, "weaning" only refers to getting off the breast or bottle—which may or may not happen around the same time you "introduce" solid food. So here we'll talk about the two as separate processes. They are of course related, because as your baby learns to eat solids, the amount of liquid she consumes will decline.

Weaning and introducing solids are related in another important way: Both are signs that your child is growing up. Again, think about the progression: At first you have to hold your baby to feed her; she eats in an almost horizontal, and quite vulnerable, position. Then, as she gets physically stronger and better coordinated, she can squirm, turn her head, push a breast or bottle away—in short, she can assert herself. By six months, when she can sit up fairly well and is beginning to grab hold of things—a spoon, her bottle, your breast—it becomes obvious that she wants to be more of a partner in this eating thing.

You might welcome these changes, or they might make you sad. Many mums I've met have mixed feelings, or are downright distraught, about weaning. They don't want their babies to grow up "too" quickly. Some wait until nine or ten months to introduce solids, because they don't want to "rush" the process. These are understandable feelings, but those are also the mums who call me when their fifteen-month-old (or even older toddler) seems to have "eating issues." They tell me that their child is still not taking solid food or is a "poor eater." Others are upset because their little one refuses to sit in a high chair or engages in other power struggles at mealtimes. As I'll show you in this chapter, some of these problems go with the territory of toddlerhood. Others come from what I call "food mismanagement"—a particular type of accidental parenting that occurs when parents don't realize that a particular habit warrants correction or don't know what to do about it. But problems also can occur because the parents don't really want to see their baby grow up.

So wake up and smell the formula, luv. You need to let go and let your baby become an independent eater. Granted, she will have to work even harder at getting it right than she did as a tiny infant—and you'll have to have even more patience. But the payoff is having a child who relishes eating, is willing to experiment, and associates food with good feelings.

From Feeding to Eating: The Adventure Continues

This at-a-glance chart shows the progression from feeding to eating, the basics of getting there, and common concerns (beyond the usual, "Is my child eating enough?"). Throughout this chapter, you will find more detailed information about introducing solids and how to resolve problems that come up along the way.

Age	Intake	Suggested Schedule	Common Concerns
Birth to 6 weeks (see page 95 for details)	3 oz. liquid	Every 2 to 3 hours, depending on baby's birth weight	Sleeping during feeds and hungry an hour later. Eating every 2 hours. Lots of rooting, but baby only takes a little bit at each feed. Crying during feeds or shortly thereafter.
6 weeks to 4 months (see page 95 for details)	4–5 oz. liquid	Every 3 to 3½ hours	Waking for nighttime feeds (seemingly a sleep problem, it's cured by proper food management).
4–6 months (see page 96 for details)	6–8 oz. liquid If you start solids this early, place your baby in an infant seat or feed her on your lap, elevating her head. Solids should be finely pureed and almost watery at this age. Restrict solids to pureed pears, apples, and single-grain baby cereals (not wheat), which are easiest to digest. Give 1–2 tsp. before the bottle or breast.	Every 4 hours If you start solids at this age, which I don't normally advise, liquids should still be the mainstay of your baby's diet.	Finishing bottle or breast too quickly—is she getting enough to eat? When to start solid foods? What foods should we try? How will we get our baby to chew? What's the proper way to feed her?

Age	Intake	Suggested Schedule	Common Concerns
6–12 months	Everything will be pureed at first. Start with 1–2 tsp. for the 1st week, only at breakfast; the 2nd week, at breakfast and lunch; and the 3rd week, all 3 meals. You will add a new food every week—always at breakfast—and move the proven foods to lunch and dinner. Give solids when your child is alert and fully awake. If at first she finds it frustrating, take the edge off her hunger with a bit of breast or bottle. Once she gets the hang of things, always give solid foods first. As your baby adjusts and seems able to chew, add foods with some texture. Gradually progress to 1–1½ oz. of solid per meal, more or less depending on her appetite and capacity. Finger foods are added at 9 months or when she can sit on her own. Suggested foods at 6–9 months: mild fruits and veggies (apples, pears, peaches, plums, bananas; squash, sweet potatoes, carrots, green beans, peas); single-grain cereals; brown rice, bagels, chicken, turkey, cooked white fish (like fluke), canned tuna. By 9 months, start finger foods. You can also add pasta, stronger fruits (prunes, kiwi, pink grapefruit) and veggies (avocado, asparagus, zucchini, broccoli; beets, white potatoes, parsnips, spinach, lima beans, eggplant; beef broth, lamb. If you or your partner have allergies, consult with your pediatrician about the introduction of new foods.	It takes 2 months, at most 4, to ease into solids. By 9 months, most babies are eating solids at breakfast (approximately 9 A.M.), lunch (12 or 1 P.M.), and dinner (5–6). Breast or bottle first thing in the morning, between feecs (as a snack), and before bed. By the end of the 1st year, you have gradually cut in half the amount of liquids you give as the amount of solids increases, so that solids are the mainstay of the diet. Your baby will drink between 16 and 32 oz. cf liquid a day, depending on his size. Once he is able to eat finger foods, always start the meal with them and then spoonfeed other foods. At around 9 months, you can start giving light snacks between meals—bagel, crackers, bits of cheese—but be careful not to let him fill up on snacks (see pages 156–158).	What solids to start with and how to introduce them? How much to feed compared with liquids? Having trouble adapting to solid foods (closing his lips so Mum can't even get the spoon in; gagging; choking). Fear of food allergies.

From Feeding to Eating: The Adventure Continues (continued)

Age	Intake	Suggested Schedule	Common Concerns
1–2 years	Foods are no longer pureed; your toddler should be eating lots of finger foods and starting to feed himself. Once every week, you can also start introducing foods that are on my "Proceed with Caution" list, such as dairy products, including yogurt, cheese, and cow's milk (see sidebar, page 153), as well as whole eggs, honey, beef, melon, berries, citrus fruits other than pink grapefruit, lentils, pork, and veal. I'd still be very careful with, even keep away from, nuts, which are hard to digest and easy to choke on, as well as shellfish and chocolate, because they can cause allergies.	Three meals a day; bottle or breast morning and night until your child is completely weaned, usually by 18 months if not sooner. You can give light healthful snacks between meals, as long as it doesn't affect your child's appetite for other foods. Plan at least one of your own meals around your toddler's and pull her high chair up to the table, so she begins to get used to the idea of family dining.	Not eating as much as she used to. Still prefers his bottle to solid foods. Refuses to eat _____ [insert name of a food, like carrots]. Refuses to wear bib. Won't sit in the high chair or tries to climb out. Won't even try to feed herself. Mealtimes are a disaster—and a huge mess. Dumps or drops food.
2–3 years	By 18 months, and certainly by 2, your child should be eating a full range of foods, unless she has developed allergies or any other problems along the way. How much she eats depends on her size and appetite—some kids eat and need less than others. Your child should be eating what the family eats; resist the temptation to prepare a different dinner for her.	Three meals a day, with light snacks between meals. By now your child has very definite likes and dislikes, maybe even a sweet tooth. Resist giving too many snacks between meals, or snacks with little nutritional value or too much sugar. It will affect her intake at meals. For one meal of the day, at least a few days of the week, have family dinners so that your child becomes a social eater as well as a well-nourished human being.	Picky eating—not a "good" eater. Food fads (eats same foods over and over). Quirky "rules" around eating (cries if food breaks, peas and potatoes can't touch, etc.). Eats only snacks. Won't sit at dinner table. Atrocious manners. Throws food. Purposely makes mess. Has tantrums at mealtimes.

Food Management:
Did You Grow Up in a BARN?

Food management—making sure your child gets enough to eat, at the right times, and in the right amounts—is critical from the day he is born. I explained in the last chapter that as early as the first six weeks, food *mis*management can cause erratic eating, crying, and gas and other intestinal problems. Still, most parents find (with a little help) that the early weeks and months are fairly simple once they get into a good routine. When solid foods are added, though, good food management is once again very tricky.

With older children, there are four keys to food management: *Behavior* (your child's), *Attitude* (yours), *Routine,* and *Nourishment.* To my amusement, the first letters spell out the word BARN, as in a question parents often ask children when they're appalled by their table manners: "Did you grow up in a barn?" Come to think of it, you also could turn it into BRAN, a very healthful food. In any case, most of the eating problems I encounter are related to one, if not more, of those elements. I will discuss each factor in greater detail:

Behavior: Every family has a set of values that relate to eating; each has its own definition of what's proper. **When it comes to eating, what do you find acceptable and what won't you allow?** You have to figure out what *your* limits are and convey them—not when your child is a teenager, but *now.* Start when you first put your baby in a high chair. For instance, the Carters are fairly lax about table manners. Their children are never reprimanded if they play with their food, while in the Martini household, they're told to leave the table if they do. And that includes nine-month-old Pedro, who is taken out of the high chair the moment he starts squashing or smearing his food. Mum and Dad view his misbehavior as a sign that he's finished eating and tell him, "No, we do not play with our food. We sit at the table to *eat.*" He may not understand exactly what his parents are saying (or he might), but Pedro will quickly make the association that the high chair is for eating not playing. It's the same with manners. If you believe they're important, as I most certainly do, even before your child is old enough to say "please" and "thank you" and "may I be excused from the table?" you say the words *for* her. Believe me, a child who already understands the rules of behavior at home is a joy to take out to a restaurant. But if at home she's allowed to climb out of her chair or put her feet on the eating tray, what do you expect her to do outside?

Attitude: Children imitate us. If you pick at your food, or if you're always eating on the run, your child might not appreciate food either. Ask yourself, **Is food important to you? Do you care about the meals you serve and relish eating?** If not, there's a good chance that you're less likely to prepare foods in an appetizing way. Maybe you glop everything together, or serve utterly bland food. Or let's say you're always dieting yourself and hypervigilant about what you eat. Maybe you were chubby as a child, even teased because of it. I've seen mothers put babies on a low-fat regimen or worry because their toddler is "eating too many carbs." Both are nutritionally unsound; babies and toddlers have different food requirements from adults. Also, your withholding food or labeling certain foods as "bad" (or particular body types for that matter) can send a message to your child that can later lead to serious eating issues.

Another aspect of attitude is willingness to let children learn from experience. Unfortunately, some parents are impatient and/or reluctant to let their child experiment and get a bit messy while he's learning. If you're always wiping your toddler's mouth, making comments about what a "mess" he's making, your child will very quickly begin to view eating as an unpleasant experience.

Routine: I know you're sick of hearing the word "routine," but here goes: Being consistent about when and where a child eats, rather than eating on the fly, tells your child that not only is eating important, but so is he. Make mealtime a priority, rather than something you squeeze in between phone calls and appointments. And if it's at all possible, have family dinners together at least two nights a week. If your baby is an only child, you're his role model. If he has siblings, all the better—more people to learn from. Be consistent, also, in the words you use. For example, if he goes to grab a slice of bread, you stop him and show him what to say: "Please, may I have that?" If you do it every time, by the time he can say the words himself, he'll know what is expected of him.

Hey, Guys—What's for Dinner?

Recommended Reading

When you get stumped, these three books have great ideas:

☞ *Super Baby Food* by Ruth Yarrow
☞ *Mommy Made and Daddy Too: Home Cooking for a Healthy Baby and Toddler* by Martha and David Kimmel
☞ *Anabel Karmel's Complete Baby and Toddler Meal Planner: 200 Quick and Easy Recipes*

Nourishment: Though we can't influence a child's capacity or appetite (except genetically), *choice* of food is controlled, at least in these early years, by parents. Your child may have particular or even peculiar tastes, but in the end, it's up to you to ensure that he has healthy options. If you're an observant, healthy eater yourself, you'll probably have no trouble figuring out what to give your baby. But if you're not, please educate yourself about good nutrition. And I don't just mean when your child is a baby. When he gets to the point, usually around age two, that he's eating everything you eat, it might seem easier to pull into that fast-food restaurant that gives away free toys and has "happy" meals. But if you do that too often, you might be compromising your child's nutrition. Keeping a food log can be helpful because it will make you more conscious of what you're serving. Talk to your pediatrician. You might also get ideas from friends who are really into food, or go to the library and find books on the subject. In the sidebar on page 140 are three I often recommend.

While proper nutrition is paramount, and B.A.R.N. is a good reminder of the total picture, I also want to stress that your child will have good eating days and days when he couldn't care less about food. He might really love a particular food for a month and then suddenly refuse it. Or he might surprise you and eat something you've been trying to get him to taste for months. But don't insist and please don't get upset when he doesn't eat. Just keep giving him options, as this wise mum did with her nineteen-month-old:

Dexter is happy no matter what I cook or what restaurant we go to. While he doesn't each much quantity-wise at a meal, he will eat just about anything—and I know this is because we have given him all sorts of foods from the very beginning. We never forced him to eat anything, we just offered whatever we were eating and he could choose to eat it or not. One example is broccoli; he hated the jarred baby broccoli, hated it the first twenty times I put it on his plate (he would sometimes try a nibble, sometimes not), then one day he just ate it and now Dexter loves it.

We also don't make a big deal out of eating things. We don't say "good boy for eating your cucumbers," or "if you eat your cabbage you will get a cookie," because that implies that there is something wrong or yucky with it, like it is a chore to be rewarded.

My point is PLEASE . . . offer new foods! You would be amazed what toddlers will take a liking to. Red onions, bell peppers, tofu, hot chunky salsa, Indian food, cabbage, salmon, egg rolls, grainy bread, eggplant, mango, and sushi rolls are all things that DS has eaten in the last few days!

Keep the B.A.R.N. keys—**B**ehavior, **A**ttitude, **R**outine, and **N**ourishment—in mind as you read through the chapter sections that follow. Beginning with the four-to-six-month period, then six months to a year, one to two years, and two to three years, I talk about what typically happens at each stage and the common complaints that crop up. As always, I urge you to read through *all* the sections, as some challenges that happen to a particular child at six months might come up for another child at a year.

Four to Six Months: Getting Ready

Somewhere around four months, many parents start thinking about giving their child solid foods. They don't necessarily view it as a problem at this point, but more as a set of concerns:

When should we start solids?

What foods should we try?

How will we get our baby to chew?

What's the proper way to feed him?

Most of those questions are a matter of readiness. Babies are born with a tongue-thrust reflex that initially helps them latch on to a nipple and suck effectively. When this instinctive protrusion of the tongue disappears, somewhere between four and six months, babies are then able to swallow thick, mushy foods, like cereal and pureed fruits and vegetables. In other societies, parents chew babies' foods for them when they introduce solids. But we're lucky—we have blenders, and can also buy prepared baby foods.

Your baby is probably not ready at four months. I (and many pedia-

---

Solid Advice

Sometimes, pediatricians advocate adding solids for reflux babies, reasoning that heavier foods are more likely stay in the stomach. In such cases, I advise clients to seek the help of a gastroenterologist, who can determine if their baby's intestines are mature enough to handle solid food. Otherwise, the baby might get constipated, and you'll just be exchanging one gastric problem for another.

tricians) believe that it's best to be on the conservative side and start solids around six months. The reason is simple: Before that, babies' digestive systems aren't mature enough to metabolize solid foods. Also, most are not able to sit upright, and it's more challenging for them to take in solids while reclining. Peristalsis, the physical process by which the food moves down the esophagus, is more effective when you're upright. Think of yourself: Wouldn't it be easier to have a scoop of mash (better known in the United States as *mashed potatoes*) if you were sitting in a chair rather than lying down? In addition, allergies are more likely to develop in younger babies, so it makes sense to play it safe.

However, it's okay to start *thinking* about giving solids and watching for signs that your child is getting ready to start solids. Ask yourself these questions:

Does my baby seem hungrier than usual? Unless he's been sick or has been teething (see sidebar, page 158), increased feeds often indicate that a baby needs more than an all-liquid diet supplies. Every day, the average four-to-six-month-old consumes around thirty-two to thirty-six ounces of breast milk or formula. For a large, active baby, especially one whose physical development is proceeding at a rapid pace, liquid alone might not be enough to sustain him. In my experience with average-weight babies, activity becomes a factor at five or six months and not usually before. But if your baby is above average—for example, at four months weighs sixteen or seventeen pounds—he drinks to full capacity at every meal, and still seems to need more nourishment, then it might be time to consider solids.

> **It's a Myth**
>
> No scientific research supports the popular notion that solids help a baby sleep longer. A full tummy does help a baby sleep, but it doesn't have to be full of cereal. Breast milk or formula does the trick without running the risk of digestive problems or allergies.

Does your baby get up in the middle of the night for a bottle? If your baby finishes a full bottle when he wakes, his night-waking is due to hunger. But a four-month-old should not be eating in the middle of the night, so you first have to take steps to stop the night feedings (see Maura's story at the bottom of page 120). Once you've upped her liquid intake *during the day*, if she still seems hungry for more, that might indicate that she needs solids as well.

Has your baby lost his tongue-thrust reflex? The tongue-thrust reflex is apparent when a baby roots, or sticks his tongue out in search for food. This action helps babies suckle in infancy, but tongue-thrusting works against ingesting solid foods. To see where your baby is developmentally, put a spoon into his mouth and watch what he does. If the tongue-thrust reflex hasn't disappeared, his little tongue will automatically push the spoon out. Even when this reflex disappears, your baby will still need time to get used to eating from a spoon. At first, he'll probably try to suck the spoon the way he sucked a nipple.

Does your baby look at you when you're eating as if to say, "Hey, why aren't I getting any of that?" As young as four months, some babies start to notice us eating; most do by the time they're six months. Some even imitate a chewing motion. That's often the time parents decide to take those cues seriously and offer a few teaspoons of mushy food.

Can your baby sit up without support? It's best for a baby to have fairly good control of her neck and back muscles before starting solid food. Start your child out in an infant seat and then progress to a high chair.

Does your baby reach for things and put them in his mouth? Those are precisely the skills he'll need for finger foods.

Spotlight in the Trenches

Solids Before 6 Months?

There are few cases in which I recommend solids as early as 4 months, but one in particular springs to mind: Jack weighed 18 lb. at 4 months, and his parents were large, too—his mum was 5'9" and Dad, 6'5". Jack was wolfing down 8 oz. of formula every 4 hours and had recently started waking in the night, too, always taking a full bottle. Although he was drinking nearly 40 oz. a day, his tummy could only hold so much liquid, and it was obviously not sustaining him. It was clear to me that Jack needed solid food.

I've seen this pattern in other babies, too. But instead of waking in the night, they seem hungry 3 hours after a full feed. Rather than keep a baby on a 3-hour routine, which is not appropriate for a 4-month-old, we introduce solids as we did in Jack's case.

In either instance, if you start your child on solids as early as 4 months, the food has to be finely pureed. Most important, solids should be an add-on, not a replacement for breast milk or formula, as they are with children over 6 months.

Six to Twelve Months: Help! We Need a Solid-Food Consultant!

Most babies are ready to begin eating solids in earnest at this age. Although some will start earlier and some later, six months is the prime time. Because they're more active now, even thirty-two ounces or more of breast milk or formula isn't enough to keep them going. The process will take a few months, but gradually your child will develop a pattern of eating three solid meals a day. He will continue to have breast or bottle feeds in the morning, between meals, and at night. By eight or nine months, you will have introduced several types of foods—cereal, fruit and vegetables, chicken, fish— and your baby should be well on his way to being a good eater of solid foods. By a year, solids will replace half his liquid intake.

At around the same time, your baby's manual dexterity will take a giant leap, too, which means he can coordinate his little fingers and use them like pincers to pick up small objects. His favorite activity might be retrieving pieces of fluff from the carpet. But, ideally, you want to encourage him to use this newfound skill to pick up finger foods instead (see box, page 151).

This six-month period is probably the most exciting and, to some mums, the most frustrating time because it's all about trial and error. Your baby is tasting new foods and learning to chew them—well, at least gum things to death. Once he starts picking up finger foods, he'll need to develop the coordination to find his mouth and actually get food into it. At first, more will end up in his ears and hair, as well as in the little catch-all pocket of his bib or on the floor, which your dog will appreciate. You, in turn, have to be both creative and patient—and quick (to catch flying objects). This might be the time to purchase a sou'wester (you call them slickers) or maybe a rubber fishing suit to at least keep yourself dry!

Kidding aside, this is also the time I typically get calls from confused parents who have a list of questions. As one mother of a seven-month-old remarked, "There are lots of breast-feeding consultants out there, but what my friends and I need now is a solid food consultant." The common concerns that I hear are usually from parents who are anxious about introducing solid food or who seem to be having problems right from the start. Typically, they sound like this:

I don't know where to begin—what food to start with, or how to do it.

How much solid food do I feed now, compared with liquids?

When I look at charts in various books, I'm afraid my child isn't eating enough.

My baby is having trouble adapting to solid foods (the many variations on this include the baby closing his lips so Mum can't even get the spoon in; gagging; choking).

I'm worried about food allergies, which I hear are common in babies who are on solids.

If you hear yourself in any of the above, let me take you by the hand and be your solid food consultant. As usual, we'll start with a series of questions. Answering them can help you see where you need to begin or where you might have to make changes. The important thing to remember is that at this stage, almost everyone has some type of confusion, if not an actual problem. So you're not alone. Also, it's much easier to correct problems now before bad habits—your child's and yours—have a chance to develop.

At what age did you begin to introduce solids? As I stated above, I advise parents to introduce solids at six months. One reason I feel this way is that I often get calls from parents of six-, seven-, or even eight-month olds, who had been started earlier—say at four months. Things went smoothly for a while, but then the baby hit a brick wall and began to refuse solids. Often but not always, this coincides with teething, a cold, or any other vulnerable time in the baby's life. By the time I hear from the parents, they say, "He seemed to be eating fine. We had introduced cereal and some fruits and vegetables. But now he won't touch any solid food." In most of these cases, this is what happened: As the parents introduced solids, they also decreased their baby's suckling time. They pushed him forward too much, too fast. And when a baby is deprived of suckling time in this way, essentially weaning him too early, there's a good chance he'll want to make up for it and demand more of the bottle or breast.

Be patient, and keep offering the solids. Continue to give him the bottle or breast. If you're relaxed about it, his reluctance should last no more than a week to ten days. Never force solid foods, but if he still seems hungry *do not feed him in the night.* Rather, keep offering solids during the day. Don't panic. If he's hungry, he'll eventually try them.

Was your baby premature? If so, even six months might be too early to introduce solids. Remember that her chronological age, counting from the day she was born, is not the same as her developmental age, which determines readiness. So, for example, if she was born two months early, when she's six months old on the calendar, she's actually only four months old developmentally. Another way to look at it is that during the first two months of her life, your baby was supposed to be in the womb, not in the world. Now she needs time to catch up. Although she, like most premies, will probably look like a full-term baby by the time she's eighteen months and certainly by age two, at six months her digestive system might not be ready for solids. Go back to the liquid diet, and at 7½ or eight months, try again.

What is your baby's temperament? Think of how your baby has been with other new circumstances and transitions. Temperament always influences how he reacts to his environment, including how well he adapts to new foods. Modify your introduction of solids accordingly:

Angel babies are generally open to new experiences. Introduce foods gradually and you'll have no problem.

Textbook babies may need a little more time to adapt, but most proceed on schedule.

Touchy babies tend to refuse solids at first. It stands to reason that if these children are sensitive to light and touch, they also need extra time to get used to new sensations in their mouths. You have to go very slowly. Never force them, but be persistent.

Spirited babies tend to be impatient but adventurous. Be sure everything's ready before you put them in the high chair, and watch out for flying objects once they're done.

Grumpy babies don't adapt easily to solids, and they're reluctant to try unfamiliar foods once they do. When they find foods they like, they tend to want them over and over and over.

How long have you been trying to introduce solids? Maybe your baby isn't the problem—it could be that your expectations are too high. Eating solids is not like sucking down a bottle or emptying a breast. Imagine, after having solely breast milk or formula, what it must be like to feel a gloppy mass in your mouth. Some children can take as long as two or three months to get used to the idea of gumming down solids. You have to stay with it and be calm yourself.

What are you feeding your baby? Introducing solid foods is a gradual process of going from very sloppy and runny foods at first to finger foods. For one thing, your baby has been reclining for six months, and now her esophagus has to get used to eating in a different position. I recommend starting with fruit; pears are easy to digest. Some experts also advise cereal as a first food, but I prefer fruit for its nutritional value. Few babies take any kind of solid straightaway. You have to start with one teaspoon and you may have to try many times.

As the "From Feeding to Eating" chart on pages 136–138 illustrates, the process is very slow and gradual. When you start to introduce solids, for the first two weeks, you give only one to two teaspoons of pears at breakfast and at dinner, and you continue to give bottle or breast when your baby wakes up, at lunch, and before bed. Assuming your baby has no adverse reaction, you can introduce a second food, such as squash, again giving the new food at breakfast and moving the pears to dinner. Try out a new vegetable or fruit— sweet potatoes or apple in the third week—in the morning. Now your baby will be eating three new foods. By the fourth week, you can introduce oatmeal and give your baby solids at lunch as well, increasing the amount to three or four teaspoons per meal, more or less depending on your baby's weight and capacity. In the next four weeks, you can add rice or barley cereal, peaches, bananas, carrots, peas, green beans, sweet potatoes, plums.

You can either buy prepared baby foods, or make your own. When you're doing potato and veggies for the whole family, puree them for Junior. Don't glop everything together. Remember that you're trying to help your baby's taste buds blossom. How will he know what he likes if everything is mixed together? That doesn't mean you shouldn't add a bit of applesauce to his cereal to make it more appealing, but I've seen mothers who make chicken and rice and vegetables for the family and pop it all in the blender for the baby. They give the same exact combo to their baby day in and day out. We're feeding a child, not a dog.

If you want to make your own baby food, be sure to ask yourself, "How much time am I willing—and do I need—to invest?" If you don't have the time, don't panic. The mush stage lasts only a few months. It won't harm your baby to have some jarred foods. Moreover, even the big companies are now preparing organic baby foods with fewer additives. It's a simple matter of reading the labels.

If you're one of those parents who worries whether your baby or toddler is getting "enough," set aside a week to keep track. Admittedly, it was easier to figure out her intake on liquids by adding up the number of ounces she drank. But how do you figure what four spoonfuls each of applesauce and oatmeal add up to in nutritional terms? You need to count ounces. If you make your own baby food, freeze the food in ice cube trays, which makes it easy to measure—one cube equals one ounce (see sidebar this stage)—and is more convenient. (If you use the microwave to thaw and reheat food, be careful; always stir and check the temperature before feeding it to your child.) It's easy with store-bought baby food, too. If your baby is eating a whole jar, simply look at the label to see how much she's eaten. If she eats only a half or quarter jar, pay attention to how many spoonfuls she eats and tally that up in ounces.

> ## How Much Solid Food Equals One Ounce of Liquid?
>
> 1 ice cube = 1 oz.
>
> 3 tsp. = 1 T. = ½ oz.
>
> 2 T. = 1 oz.
>
> 1 jar of baby food = 2½, 4, or however many oz. it says on the label.

You can do the same with finger foods. If, for example, you buy a quarter pound of turkey that weighs four ounces, and there are four slices in the package, you know that each slice is one ounce (if there are more slices, each ounce obviously weighs less!). You could compute the weight of cheese and most other finger foods in this way or at least come up with a good guesstimate. Now this might sound like a lot of trouble and even too complicated (if you're bad in math as I am). I mostly suggest this to parents who are worried because their babies have lost more than 15 to 20 percent of their weight (a little weight fluctuation is normal) or have lower than usual energy levels (in which case I also tell them to talk to their pediatrician or to a nutritionist).

The important thing is to give your child a balanced diet of fruits, vegetables, dairy, protein, and whole grains. Remember that we're talking about tiny tummies here. One way to think about portion size is to give one to two tablespoons of food for each year of a child's life—at age one, one to two tablespoons; at age two, two to four; at age three, three to six. A "meal" is usually two or three portions. Your child may eat way less or way more, depending on his size and appetite.

Does your baby reject the spoon? When introducing a spoon, take care to put the food on your baby's lips, just inside her mouth. If you stick the spoon too far in, it might cause her to gag. And one or two instances of this might be enough for your child to associate the spoon with an unpleasant experience. If you want to see how it feels, ask your partner or a friend to feed *you* that way!

If your baby has no problem with the spoon, it won't be long before she tries to grab it out of your hands. Let her. Don't expect her to use it properly at this stage. But even playing with it will help her get ready for feeding herself. Of course, it can be maddening, too, because she'll always want the spoon in *her* hand. That's why I always advise parents to have an arsenal of three or even four spoons on the ready. You feed her with one, allow her to grab it, and then use one in reserve. She'll probably drop a few as well.

Does your baby frequently gag or choke? If you're just starting to introduce solids, it could be because you're putting the spoon in too far (see page 149), putting too much on the spoon, or because you're rushing him—shoveling in another mouthful before he's had a chance to gum down the first. It could also be that the food isn't pureed enough. Whatever the reason, it won't take your baby very long to conclude, "This is no fun. I'd rather have a bottle." Gagging also might be unrelated to your impatience or your feeding technique. Some babies, particularly Touchy types, need more time to get used to the sensation of solids and even more patience on the parents' part (see page 59). If your baby gags or doesn't seem to enjoy his first tastes of solid foods, stop. Try again a few days later. Keep trying, but never force the issue.

If your baby has gotten past that initial stage, and you've started her on finger foods, she still might choke or gag once in a while, especially with an unfamiliar food. You can keep such incidents to a minimum if you don't introduce finger foods too early and if you're careful about what you give her. For example, on my website, one mum wrote:

> Ellie is nearly six months so I am going to start giving her finger food. I was told to give her anything that will turn to mush easily, like small slices of dry toast, or baby rusks [a hard, meringue-like English cracker that gets soft when in liquid].

Well, whoever gave that mother advice was right about the mush part, but a six-month-old is more than likely going to choke on dry toast. First of all, dry toast has crumbs that little Ellie might inhale or catch in her throat. Second, six months is too early for most children to start finger foods. They need to be able to sit up without your help, which is usually not before eight or nine months. And, as I said, it takes babies a month or two of getting used to the feeling of mushy solids in their mouth before attempting different textures. They have to practice pushing the food to the roof of their mouth and squishing it with their tongue until it turns to mush (see the box, page 151).

The Fine Points of Finger Foods

When: At 8 or 9 months or when your baby is able to sit on his own in a high chair.

How: At first, just put the food on the tray of his high chair. He might just smash it and spread it around. That's okay; it's part of the learning experience. Don't pop it in his mouth *for* him—that defeats the purpose. Instead, eat some yourself. Babies imitate us. He will soon get the idea, especially if it's something yummy. Give finger foods first, before you start feeding him. If he doesn't eat them, don't worry about it. Just keep presenting them at the beginning of every meal, and he eventually will.

What: If you're in doubt about what constitutes a good finger food, sample it for yourself first. The food should dissolve easily in your mouth and have no grit, grain, or crumbs on which your baby could choke. Pretend you don't have any teeth and use your tongue to shove the food to the roof of your mouth and with a series of jabs, squash it. Be creative. Even oatmeal (cooked to a slightly stiffer consistency), mashed sweet or regular potatoes, or large-curd cottage cheese can be a finger food. It depends on your tolerance for mess. Ripe fruit is a great finger food, but sometimes it's better to cut it in larger chunks or sticks, because it tends to be slippery. And if you're in a restaurant, bring foods from home, but if your baby looks longingly at what you're eating (and it passes the above test), let him try it. I've seen babies eat all sorts of ethnic foods. The more you allow your child to eat on his own, the more quickly he will learn, and the more he'll enjoy eating. Below are a few other suggestions:

Cheerios, Puffins, or other dense, chunky dry cereals (avoid flakes at first)

Various shapes of pasta (macaroni, rotelli, tortellini)—toss with pureed veggies to add flavor and nutrition

Baby chicken sausages

Sliced pieces of chicken or turkey

Canned tuna or other kinds of cooked fish (left over from *your* dinner)

Avocado chunks

Semisoft cheeses, like string cheese, American cheese, soft cheddar, Baby Bel, Laughing Cow

"Crazy sandwiches"—Cut crust off bread (or make shapes with a cookie cutter) and spread with sugarless jam, hummus, cream cheese, or cottage cheese. You can also grill them.

Bagel, plain or with any of the above spreads

Have you been consistent about giving your baby solid foods, or do you sometimes offer her your breast (or a bottle) because it's convenient, because you enjoy the experience of breast-feeding, or because you feel guilty? If so, you could be inadvertently sabotaging your child's introduction to solids. Given everyone's hectic schedule nowadays, it's certainly easier to whip out your breast or pour formula into a bottle than it is to prepare a meal. Also, as I pointed out in the previous chapter, some breast-feeding mums are reluctant to wean their babies, because they enjoy that special bonding time. Particularly if a mother has gone back to work and feels guilty about leaving her baby, she might try to make it up to the baby by breast-feeding the moment she comes home. Whatever the reason for Mum's inconsistency, the problem is that children learn from repetition and by knowing what to expect. If you give your baby three meals of solid foods on some days, one or two on others, she is going to be confused. And when a child is confused, she will retreat to what she knows and what gives her comfort—suckling.

Spotlight in the Trenches

A Mother's Reluctance to Start Solids

Lisa, a 28-year-old social worker, returned to work when little Jenna was 6 months old. She had a wonderful nanny in place, but felt a bit guilty about leaving her daughter nonetheless. One of the nanny's first suggestions was to start Jenna on solid food. Lisa, who had been breast-feeding her daughter, objected at first. "I think she's too young. Breast milk is better for her and I'm planning to pump and to come home on my lunch hour to do the midday feed." Three weeks later, Jenna started waking up at night for a feed. Lisa complained that the nanny must have been let her "sleep too long" during the day. The nanny explained that the baby's naps were as usual. "But the problem," she added, "is that breast milk isn't enough to sustain her." After speaking to her pediatrician, Lisa gave in and begrudgingly allowed the nanny to start Lisa on solids. Jenna, an Angel baby, took to it right away and within a few weeks was eating several foods—and, no surprise, sleeping through the night. Lisa missed the breast-feeding experience, but she made peace with the loss by continuing to give her baby a feed first thing in the morning and before bed—a special time for the two of them.

After eating, does your baby vomit, develop a rash, have diarrhea or unusually loose stools? If so, what kinds of solids have you introduced and how often? He may be having some type of adverse reaction to a particular food, even an allergy. Although *he* won't make the connection between eating solids and not feeling well, a baby in pain or just feeling under the weather won't be very eager to try new experiences. That's why I always tell parents to go very slowly as they're beginning to introduce solids. Start with *one* food, and one food only. For the first week (or ten days, if your baby is on the sensitive side), give that food at the morning meal. Stick with that one food for a week, after which you can move it up to the midday meal and introduce another new food in the morning. As each new food passes this test, you can combine it with other foods you've introduced.

I always suggest trying new foods in the morning, so that if a problem develops, it's less likely to upset your baby's nighttime sleep—and yours. Also, by isolating foods this way, it's easier to determine the cause of your baby's distress.

Certainly, if you have a Touchy baby, who has a sensitive system, or if allergies run in your family, you ought to be particularly vigilant, because your child might be more prone to allergies. Pediatric allergies have increased dramatically over the last twenty years; experts estimate that between 5 and 8 percent of children have them. *They don't get better by giving the child more of the triggering food—they get worse.* So, keep a good log of the foods you introduce and when. Then if your baby has frequent or serious reactions, you're armed with information when you consult your pediatrician.

Milk

The Big Kid Beverage

At one year, most pediatricians suggest making the transition from breast milk or formula to cow's milk. Go slowly, just as you would with a new solid food, to make sure your baby doesn't have a reaction. Start by replacing the morning feed with whole milk. After a few days to a week (depending on your child's sensitivity), if your child has no reaction—diarrhea, rash, vomiting—then give him milk in the afternoon and finally in the evening. Some people like to introduce cow's milk by mixing it with breast milk or formula. But I'm against mixing because it changes the composition of the breast milk or formula. If your baby has a reaction, how would you know whether it's because of the mixing or the milk itself?

One to Two Years: Food Mismanagement and the Food Olympics

The question "How much should my child be eating?" becomes a bit tricky around the first birthday, both because babies come in all sizes and have different needs and because their rate of growth starts to slow at one year. Their appetites naturally diminish because they don't need quite as much fuel to sustain the incredible growth they accomplished in the first year. As one mother of a one-year-old wrote on my website, "This is what Brittany is eating at the moment—although two weeks ago she was refusing all food, so having an eating schedule is a novelty!!" Brittany's mum was able to laugh at her baby's inconsistency and take it in stride. But many parents panic: "Why isn't my baby eating as much as he used to?" I explain that he's got other fish to fry, and he doesn't need to eat as much. Also, teething in the first year can interfere with eating (see sidebar, page 158). The bottom line is that almost every baby eats less now.

At the same time, your child hopefully will have expanded her repertoire of foods. She should have tasted—and now be able to eat—a variety of solids, including finger foods. Some children just get to that point at a year; others have been eating solids since around nine months. But by a year most are well on their way. Most pediatricians urge parents to introduce cow's milk (see sidebar, page 153) to the diet at one year, as well as many of the "proceed with caution" foods, like eggs and beef, because the likelihood of developing allergies diminishes (unless other family members have them).

Your baby should now be having five feeds a day, three of mostly solids and two of around eight ounces of liquid per feed for a total of sixteen ounces. In other words, half his liquid intake should be replaced by solids. If, however, he is still downing thirty-two ounces of breast milk, formula, or cow's milk (which pediatricians allow at one year), you have to adjust that balance by decreasing the liquid and adding more solid food. If all goes as planned, at around fourteen months, he will begin to develop the coordination needed

---

Proper Fuel = Proper Weight Gain

At your baby's periodic visits, your pediatrician will check his health, weigh him, and make sure his gains are consistent with his age and size. Report any changes in energy level to your doctor. If your child is between one year and 18 months, low energy might indicate that he is not getting enough solids compared to liquids or that he's not eating foods that will fuel him. If he's older, it might mean he's not eating enough protein—foods that would fuel his active lifestyle.

to feed himself, too, a skill that continues to develop (with your help). Of course, things don't always go as planned. Problems at this stage fall into one of two categories: food mismanagement and what I call the "food Olympics," which I explain later in this section (pages 158–163).

Food mismanagement. When a child over one still prefers his bottle to solid foods, it usually indicates some form of food mismanagement, often a throwback to an earlier issue that was never addressed or not fully resolved. Therefore, I pose many of the same questions I ask parents of younger children: **At what age did you begin to introduce solids? What are you feeding your baby? How long have you been trying to introduce solids? Have you been consistent about giving your baby solid foods?**

If you started too early you could be having the backlash reaction I explain on page 146. If you recently started or if you haven't been consistent, you might need nothing more than a little patience to see it through. Although six months is a prime time, your baby might be taking a bit longer to adjust to solids. Just remember that the goal is to replace half the liquid intake with solids. So, add up what your child normally drinks in ounces at breakfast, lunch, and dinner, and then convert it into solids. For instance, if little Dominic usually has a six-ounce bottle at breakfast, the idea is to get him to eat the equivalent in solid food—say two ounces of cereal, two ounces of fruit, and two of baby yogurt (see the sidebar on page 149, for computing amounts).

> ### The Hamster Maneuver
>
> When presented with a food they don't like, some children will hold it in their mouth. This "hamster maneuver," as I call it, is often followed by gagging. If you see the food piling up in your baby's cheeks, tell her to spit it out. Eliminate that food for a week and then try to introduce it again.

Always give your baby solid food *first* at the three main meals of the day. Until he's weaned, which for most children is around eighteen months, his bottle or a breast-feed can be his "snack" between meals. Once he's accustomed to eating solids, you also can offer your baby a sippy cup of water or milk *at* meals to quench his thirst *after* the meal.

Sometimes the problem is not *all* solids but a particular kind of food—say, peaches. If your toddler isn't very adventurous about trying new foods or seems "picky" at this point, and rejects certain foods, it's because children now start showing distinct preferences for certain foods. It also might mean that he just needs a little more time to get used to the new flavors and sensations in his mouth, and that you have to be persistent (but relaxed) about offering unfamiliar foods to him.

Some children are, in fact, picky eaters—they don't like a big variety of foods at this stage and they never will. And some also require less food than other kids. What may seem "normal" for one child is too little or too much for another. If a child doesn't want to eat all his food, allow him. Otherwise he can't learn when he's full. In my experience, if a baby is on a good routine, he'll eat. A picky eater will even try new solids. Just try two teaspoons of a new food—that way, you're at least introducing it to him.

My rule of thumb is to give a new food four days in a row. If your child doesn't eat it, give it a rest and try a week later. If your child doesn't like a huge variety of foods (see "food fads," page 166), don't worry about it—some adults don't either. But I've found that when parents eat lots of different kind of foods themselves and also expose their children to a variety of tastes without forcing the issue, their kids usually end up being fairly adventurous eaters. Also, don't be surprised if your child relishes sweet potatoes for two months and then suddenly doesn't like them. Just go with the flow.

> ### Don't Pry!
>
> Trying to pry a 9- or 11-month-old's mouth open is like trying to get a fish from the jaws of a shark. If your child won't open her mouth for another bite, please, please, assume that she's finished eating and doesn't want any more.

When a child is reluctant to eat solids, I also ask, **Does your baby get up in the middle of the night to nurse or have a bottle?** Liquid intake, especially night feeds, can interfere with a baby's desire to eat solid food (which is why I'm against allowing toddlers to walk around with a bottle). Sadly, I've met countless parents whose one-year or older babies continue to feed at night—in worst cases, *throughout* the night. They wonder why their child won't take solids, but it's not rocket science: If your baby fills up on breast milk or formula, there's no room for solids! It's no mystery that he's not hungry at mealtimes or particularly interested in solids. He's full. Also, by giving your baby a bottle or your breast in the middle of the night, even if he's hungry, you're inadvertently going backward to a twenty-four-hour routine (to cut out night feeds in older babies and toddlers, you have to do P.U./P.D.; see chapter 6).

Does your child eat a lot of snacks? If so, he might be filling himself up between meals. This problem can crop up in the first year or second. It can be a matter of too much snacking or the wrong kind of snacks. I'm not against giving a child a Goldfish cracker now and then, but I do prefer more healthful snacks, like fruits or bits of cheese. Instead of making excuses when your child refuses to eat ("She's tired," "She's having an off day," "She's getting new teeth," "She doesn't usually act like this"), take a proactive stance and eliminate giving so many filling snacks, especially snacks with empty calories.

If you recall, I talked about babies, especially breast-fed babies, becoming "snackers"—doing ten-minute feeds, instead of having full feeds every three to four hours (see box, page 98). Well, the same thing can happen in toddlerhood if a child munches on potato chips or goldfish crackers all day. If your toddler is a snacker instead of a child who eats three solid meals a day, give yourself three days to change her pattern. To get her back on track you have to be prepared to stick to your regular mealtimes and not give her snacks between meals (see box below).

This is not to say that snacks are a bad thing. In fact, for some smaller-built children, they supply more calories than meals (see sidebar, "Good News for Picky Eaters," page 165). Some little tummies need to

---

Snack Attack!

This is a 3-day plan for transforming a toddler from a snacker into an eater:

When your child wakes up in the morning at 7, she'll have a bottle or a feed. At breakfast, around 9, she'll have more of a snack than a full meal—as usual. But today will be different, because when her energy starts flagging at 10:30, instead of giving her crackers or fruit or whatever you usually give her, you'll distract her. Perhaps you'll take her out to play. I guarantee by lunch, she'll eat more, because she's going to be very hungry. If she's really out of sorts, you can make lunch a little earlier, too.

In the afternoon, also skip the usual snack after her nap. If she normally has a bottle when she wakes up, halve the amount you usually give her. Many parents will be concerned when I suggest this. "Doesn't she need the extra food for energy? Aren't I depriving her?" The answer is absolutely not. Remember that we're doing this at most for *3 days*. You're not starving her to death. You're offering her meals when she's supposed to eat them.

Believe me, it will be harder on you than her. Keep your eye on the goal: Wouldn't you prefer to wait an hour and have her eat a whole meal rather than let her continue to be a snacker? If you don't give in again, by the 3rd day—or sooner in most cases—your baby will be eating full meals, not snacking.

eat more often. In such cases, snacks (nutritious ones) are more like small meals. Observe your child's eating patterns. If he has trouble finishing his meal and his weight is in a low percentile, it might be normal for him. Still, it wouldn't hurt to give him more high-calorie snacks, like avocado, cheese, ice cream. Also, talk to your pediatrician about feeding him more often. The right foods, in small amounts, are great energy boosters, as well as great distractions in the supermarkets. Besides, snacks are a way of life once your baby starts to socialize. Every mother brings them. So even if you are conscious of giving your child only the good stuff, the more he socializes, the more he will be exposed to a wide variety of snacks, including junk foods. Bring your own, so that you can control what he eats and also so that your child doesn't go begging to other mothers!

Another question at this stage is, **Do you take his not eating personally?** Under a year, not eating is rarely a matter of willfulness or spite. Babies don't manipulate parents' behavior through eating. So there's usually something else going on, such as teething (see sidebar this page), lack of sleep, illness, or it's simply not an eating day. But over a year, the act of not eating could be a weapon that your toddler has discovered he can use against you. If you have a great deal of anxiety around what he eats, I guarantee that by fifteen months or earlier, he will pick up on your feelings. And knowing that he's expected to perform won't make for a very pleasant eating environment. In such cases, I've seen children refuse to try new foods or refuse to eat altogether.

The food Olympics. Parents' answer to, **Does your child often misbehave at mealtimes?** tells me whether their children are contestants in what I call the "food Olympics." Concerns that fall in this category include issues such as:

Teething: An Appetite Buster

Signs: A child can have any (or all) of these: reddened cheeks, diaper rash, drooling, gnawing on fingers, runny nose, and other signs of a postnasal drip, fever, concentrated urine. You put a bottle or breast in his mouth and he comes off it immediately because his gums are sore. His appetite may diminish because eating is so uncomfortable. If you touch the area, you may feel a bump or see a reddened spot. If you're breast-feeding you might feel the actual tooth coming through.

Duration: Teething happens in 3-day increments—the time leading up to it, the tooth actually breaking through, and the aftermath. The worst 3 days are when the tooth is actually cutting through the gum.

What to Do: Use a prophylactic dose of Motrin, as per the label, and numb the gums with Baby Orajel or another teething salve. Your baby needs to chomp down. He may or may not be willing to suck on a frozen teether, a cold bagel, or a frozen washcloth.

I have to chase my child around the kitchen to get him to eat.

My child won't sit in the high chair, or tries to climb out.

My child won't even try to feed herself.

My child refuses to wear a bib.

My child repeatedly drops food on the floor—or dumps it on his head.

Your child's newfound skills at the dinner table are happening at the same time as she's making huge developmental strides. Many children can walk at this age. Those who can't are at least crawling and climbing. And all are endlessly curious. Eating isn't at the top of most toddlers' lists of fun activity. Who wants to sit in a chair, even for ten minutes, when there's a world out there to explore? And who wants to eat food, when throwing and smearing it are so much more fun? In many households with one- to two-year-olds, mealtimes are trying, if not a disaster—and a huge mess. Parents who have trouble reining in their toddlers at mealtime come to me with concerns that reflect their toddler's growing independence, ability, and as he gets closer to age two, his willfulness. In fact, sometimes a toddler's refusal to try a particular food is more about his need to experiment with control rather than the actual taste of the food. It's often better to back off on the food and avoid the power struggle. (At the next meal, substitute something equally nutritious.)

Even with a one-year-old, you can begin to establish ground rules. I can hear some of you protesting: "But that's too young to teach *rules.*" Not true, my dears. It's *now* that you start, before the terrible twos set in, at which point everything can turn into a power struggle.

Remember my B.A.R.N. acronym—at least the first three letters—as you read about some of the common concerns related to the food Olympics. The "B" represents the various undesirable behaviors that occur at this age, behaviors that will persist if you don't step in now.

The "A"—your attitude—is critical. You'll notice that in each of the statements above describing a parent's concern about their child's behavior, the implication is that *the child* is in charge. The tip-off to me is that Mum or Dad preface their statements by phrase such as, "My child refuses . . ." and "My child won't . . ." Granted, we're entering "terrible" two territory now, but let's not assume that mealtime is in your child's hands. You have to take charge. (The twos don't have to be a nightmare if you do; see chapter 8.)

No Games! No Coaxing!

Some parents make mealtime into playtime, and then wonder why their children act up around food. If you play "airplane," for example, by putting food on a spoon and "flying" it through the air, don't be surprised if your toddler later tries to propel his food *without* the spoon.

Also, children should never be coaxed into eating. They'll eat when they're hungry. They'll eat when food they like is laid out before them. But they won't eat because we trick them into it. When we try to cajole or even force children to eat more, we accidentally cause them to develop negative feelings about eating. And once children see us become upset by their not eating, it doesn't take long for them to realize, "Oh, I can use this as a weapon."

To deal with these problems, to set guidelines, we have to remember to look at the mealtime routine—the "R"—which offers us a way of approaching the problem by actually *doing* things differently. It's important to set up structure and boundaries, particularly before eighteen months, when truly obstinate behavior often starts.

The trick at this stage is to maintain a healthy balance, allowing your child to experiment and knowing what is developmentally realistic to expect from her. For example, if your child balks at wearing a bib, give her a sense that she has a say in the matter. Offer her two bibs and say, "Which one would you like to wear?" On the other hand, if you have to chase your child around the kitchen to get her to eat, you may be giving her too many choices. Instead of *asking*, "Do you want to eat?" as I hear many parents do with toddlers, simply say, "It's time to eat." You don't give kids a choice about eating. You simply say, "It's dinnertime." If they say no, you still sit them at the table. If they're hungry, they'll eat. However, if they then act up in any way, you take them out of the high chair and away from the table. Give them two chances and then wait until the next scheduled mealtime, when they'll definitely be hungry.

To some extent, fidgeting at meals, refusing to get into the high chair, or wanting to stand up in it, is just part of toddler territory, and many of these challenges are almost impossible to avoid. I have noticed, though, that mums who engage in contact and conversation with their children have less trouble in this arena. It helps to keep your child involved with the meal. Try asking her, "Where are the potatoes?" or point out, "The peas are green." Smile, talk to her, tell her what a good job she's doing. When she stops eating, or the moment she looks like she's about to stand up, you take the lead: Immediately take her out of the high chair and say, "Okay, lunch is over. Time to wash our hands."

When a toddler is exceptionally wiggly or seems uncomfortable in his high chair, I suspect that the parents might be asking too much of the child. **Do you put him in the high chair and make him wait until you prepare dinner? If so, how long does he have to wait?** Even five minutes is an eternity for an active toddler. Prepare his meal and get everything ready *before* you put him in the high chair. **Do you leave him in the high chair past his eating time?** If you keep him in his high chair after he's stopped eating, the high chair might start to feel like jail to him. I recently worked with a mum who tried to make her eighteen-month-old sit there until he was finished and—surprise, surprise—her son refused to get into his high chair. What's worse is that he's a poor eater and screams bloody murder whenever anyone tries to hoist him into his high chair.

Then there's the child who refuses to get into his high chair in the first place, and each time, Mum gets exasperated or downright angry. She might battle with him, which will only make him more resistant, or she might give up and try to feed her toddler on the fly. I've seen the latter so many times: a mother chasing her little one around the room wielding a spoonful of porridge that she hopes to get into the little boy's mouth. Mum is asking for trouble. Far better to figure out *why* her child hates his high chair so much and then gently reintroduce him to it. So, I ask, **How old was he when you first put him in?** *Had he been sitting up on his own by then?* If you put a child into a high chair before he's able to sit up on his own for at least twenty minutes, he might get uncomfortable and fatigued. No wonder he has a negative association with the high chair.

It's important to acknowledge a child's reluctance or fears. If your child kicks his feet, arches his back, or squirms to get out the moment you put him in, take him out immediately. Say, "I can see you are not ready to eat just yet." Then try again in fifteen minutes. Sometimes the problem is that parents don't give young children transition rituals—in this case, to go from playing to eating. It's not respectful to whisk a child away from an activity and simply plop him into a high chair. Just as he needs time to adjust to the idea of sleeping (more about the bedtime transition in the next chapter), he needs time to get into the eating mode, too. Use words. ("It's time for lunch! Are you hungry? Let's clean up these blocks and get our hands washed.") Give a few moments for the words to sink in, approach him respectfully, and then do the actions—put the blocks away, and help him wash his hands. Before you actually put him in the high chair, say, "Okay, now I'm going to put you in your high chair."

That's all most children need. But if your child has become almost phobic about the high chair because she has a negative association with it, take a few steps back. Make mealtimes a pleasure again. Start by sitting her on your knee to feed her. Then graduate to a side-by-side situation, using a child-size table or booster seat at the big table. You can try the high chair again after a few weeks of this, but if she still resists, you might have to stick with the booster seat. High chairs have a very short life span anyway—six to ten months. By a year to eighteen months many children prefer a booster chair at the table with the rest of the family.

Making a child part of the family dining experience often goes a long way in promoting not only more cooperative behavior but also toddlers' willingness to eat on their own. If your child seems reluctant to feed herself, examine your own part in the problem: **What is your attitude about her feeding herself? Or, are you rushed at mealtimes? Are you worried about the mess she makes?** It makes me sad to see two-year-olds who are capable of putting food on a fork but their parents are too rushed or too anal to allow them. If you act impatient, constantly clean her up, or wipe the high chair table off *while* she's eating, it won't take her long to realize that this is not fun. Why would she want to feed herself?

It's also a matter of readiness. Therefore, when a parent is concerned about a child not feeding himself, I ask, **What do you mean by "feeding himself"?** You may have to adjust your expectations. Most one-year-olds are capable of feeding themselves with their hands, but not with a spoon. If your child hasn't started hand-feeding, leave finger foods on her tray, and she'll eventually get the idea. Using a spoon or fork is a much more complicated bit of business. Think of what it involves: having the manual dexterity to hold the spoon, slide it under the food, lift it without turning it over, and, finally, get it into her mouth. Most babies can't even start to attempt those maneuvers until around fourteen months. Before that, you can give her a spoon to play with. Even before your baby is able to master a spoon, she will fight to the death to take it away from you. Eventually, she'll put the spoon into her mouth. When you see that, start to fill the spoon for her—ideally, with gloppy oatmeal that sticks to the spoon. Most of it will end up in her hair (and yours!), but you have to give her time to experiment and to miss her mouth entirely. Somewhere between fourteen and eighteen months, she'll start getting the food into her mouth.

Of course, no matter how ready your child is, no matter how relaxed you are, all children, at some point in toddlerhood, decide to wear their cereal or their spaghetti as a hat. When parents are concerned because such antics happen *repeatedly,* I always ask, **Did you laugh the first time your baby did it?** I know that it was a moment in time, and he was absolutely adorable and irresistible. How could you not laugh? The problem is, your reaction delighted him even more than the act of putting the cereal on his head. He thinks, *Wow! That was cool. Mummy really likes when I do that.* So he does it again, except the second, third, and fourth times, you're not so amused. You get increasingly angry, and he gets increasingly confused. *It was funny two days ago when I did it—so how come Mum's not laughing now?*

It's a simple fact: Toddlers like to throw things—the mere act is empowering to a child. He doesn't know the difference between throwing his ball and hurling a hot dog at you. If he's under age one, you don't make a big deal out of it—it's not meant to get your attention—but be clear that you don't find throwing food acceptable. As one mother said to her seven-month-old when he dropped bits of cheese on the floor, "Oh, I guess you want that on the floor."

> ### Break Bread, Not Plates!
>
> We all know enough not to give a toddler a breakable plate. But it also might be a good idea to skip a plate altogether, especially if it keeps ending up on the floor. Another alternative is the type of plastic plate with a suction cup on the bottom. Once your toddler is strong enough (and clever enough) to yank it up, go back to putting food directly on his tray.

If you're lucky, and you haven't yet witnessed the dump-on-the-head act, brace yourself. It's coming. And when it does, try not to laugh. Just say, "No, you can't put food on your head. We eat our food." And then take it away. If, on the other hand, you've already been a great audience for him, make the same kind of statement, but expect that it might take several incidents to change the behavior. If you don't act now, I assure you that in the next stage, from age two to three, you'll be dealing with even worse behavior at the dinner table.

Two to Three Years: Food Fads and Other Annoying Traits

By now your child can eat—and should be eating—just about everything that the grownups eat. He is able to eat at the table, in his high chair or booster seat, and you should be able to take him to restaurants as well. The biggest problems come at around two, when everything and anything can become a power struggle. Your toddler could be terrible or terrific at this point. A lot depends on his nature and how you've handled problems that came up beforehand. Fortunately, though, as your child approaches the third-year mark, things usually become easier.

Common concerns at this point are of two types: poor or weird eating habits and mealtime misbehavior, a continuation of food Olympics issues that weren't nipped at the previous stage. Below we look at both categories:

In the "poor or weird eating habits" category, I often hear:

My child is not a good eater.

My child hardly eats anything.

My child only eats snacks.

My child is on a hunger strike.

My child insists on eating foods in a particular order.

My child eats the same foods over and over and over.

My child can have a meltdown if his peas touch his potatoes.

I always ask parents to clarify what they mean by "a good eater." Is that a child who eats a lot? A child who eats everything? "Good eating," like beauty, is in the eye of the beholder. So if parents are worried about their child's consumption of food, I tell them to look carefully and ask themselves what's really going on.

Is this something new or did he always eat like this? Just as there are all kind of people, temperaments, body shapes, there are all kinds of eaters. Individual differences in temperament, household environment, and attitudes about food all affect kids' eating patterns. Some toddlers eat less than others, just as some are more sensitive to strong tastes or don't like to experiment with new foods. Some children relish food more than others. Some have a smaller build and don't need as much. And some just have more bad eating days than others.

By this age, you should have a pretty good idea about who your child is and what's normal for him. If he's always been a kind of reluctant eater, or eats less than his peers, be realistic about his eating. This is who he is. It's also perfectly normal for a child not to eat as much as he did the day before—he'll probably make up for it the next day. As long as your pediatrician gives him a clean bill of health, leave him to work it out on his own. If you keep offering good food, making mealtimes pleasant, and showing an interest in good food yourself, he'll more likely eat better than if he knows you're having an anxiety attack over every bite he takes. Classic research conducted decades ago by Clara Davis, a pediatrician who studied infants' and toddlers' food preferences, showed that when given a choice, even babies selected exactly what they need for a balanced diet. (You might be interested to know that among the favorite foods cited in those early studies are those your twenty-first-century baby probably likes, too: milk, eggs, bananas, apples, oranges, and oatmeal. The least-liked foods included vegetables, peaches, pineapples, liver, and kidney—no surprises there!)

If your child was a good eater in the past and isn't now, what else is going on? Has he just learned to climb? Is he ill? Teething? Under stress? Any of those factors can make a good eater become less interested in food.

Is eating a social experience for your child? As long as no one is harping on him to "Eat! Eat! Eat!" being at the family dinner table can be a good experience for a reluctant eater. And it's even better when she's given the opportunity to eat with her peers. When you plan play dates, devote part of the time to a snack or light lunch. Surprisingly, even a poor eater becomes more attentive to food when she sees another child eating. (Both occasions are good times to reinforce manners, too.)

Is he really not eating *anything*? Parents tend not to count liquid intake or snacks in between meals. Keep track for a day or two of everything that goes into your child's mouth, and you might be surprised.

Good News for Picky Eaters (and Their Parents)

Studies have found that up to 30% of 4- and 5-year-olds are either picky eaters or children who do not eat a lot. A recent study, done in Finland, concluded that parents have no "reason for serious concern." The researchers polled parents of over 500 children whom they'd been following since age 7 months. In this study, poor eaters were defined as any child who ate too little "often" or "sometimes," according to their parents. At 5, the poor eaters tended to be a little shorter and weigh a little less than other children, but they were also smaller at birth, suggesting that they always needed less food to sustain them. In other words, *for their size,* poor eaters don't really consume less than their peers. One difference did emerge: Poor eaters get more of their calories from snacks than meals, so it's even more important for their parents to make sure there are lots of healthful snacks on hand.

Maybe he's a snacker. If so, he's eating—just not what you give him at mealtimes. You can takes steps to correct that (see box, page 157). Often, a parent will say, "He'll only eat snacks," and I want to say, "Well, who's giving him the snacks—the good fairy?" We have to take responsibility for what our children eat, and pay attention.

Even toddlers who get a good start on solids can sometimes get into what I call "food fads" at this stage. Some eat the same food over and over and over. Others are not only picky eaters, they're peculiar eaters. Both cause parents to worry.

Young children are particularly prone to food fads, both in the behavioral sense and also in their selection of foods. They will select a certain food or a few preferred foods and eat them for a long time, refusing to eat anything else. That's why it is so important that we give children healthy foods; at least the one food your child is getting will be good for her. Remember, too, that once a child has eaten her fill of a particular food, she'll frequently resist eating that food again for a very long time. Sophie, my youngest child, was—and still is—a food fadder. Most of her binges usually lasted no more than ten days. Then she'd eat normally for a while and, just when I thought she was over it, she would adopt another favorite food. Sophie, who is now eighteen, has actually done this her whole life and—come to think of it—the apple doesn't fall far from the tree. I tend to get comfortable with certain foods myself, but I'm a bit old for my mum to worry about it. Maybe fads run in families, though I've never seen a scientific study that proves it!

Quirky behavior around food causes parents even more stress than repetitive eating patterns. Here's a portion of a website posting from a mother—we'll call her Callie—whose 2½-year-old clearly fits the profile. The mum says that although her "wonderful boy," Devon, is "sweet, affectionate, and funny," she's "increasingly frustrated" by his behavior around food.

> Whenever Devon is eating and his food breaks—e.g., a banana or a cereal bar splits into two pieces—he refuses to eat the rest of it. I cannot figure out why this is the case, unless it's just that he sees grown-ups eating things like this and doesn't want it to break. Does anyone else's kid do this or something similarly strange-seeming?

Anyone else? Lots of toddlers in fact. Mothers who responded to her posting told of one kid who had a meltdown if his mother gave him a broken cracker, another who would not eat any "mixed up" dishes, like stews or casseroles, a third who would eat only the top of a slice of toast, not the bottom. Some children insist on eating their food in a particular order—for example, one little boy absolutely had to start every meal with a piece of banana. Or, they have strict rules about what's put before them, that foods can't touch or that they have to be on a certain kind of dish or bowl. The variations are endless and unique. *Why* they happen is anyone's guess. We're human beings, and we all have our eccentricities. Maybe quirky eating habits run in families, too. The only thing I can tell you for sure is that most kids grow out of them . . . eventually.

In the meantime, none of these issues are cause for concern. Indeed, if Callie reacts too strongly or puts too much energy into trying to "fix" Devon's aversion to "broken" foods, she risks making it worse.

The other kind of issues I hear at this age center on mealtime misbehavior, which includes concerns such as:

My child has atrocious manners—what's okay at this age?

My child can't sit still at the dinner table (what I call the "wiggly worm syndrome").

My child throws food when she doesn't want any more or doesn't like it.

My child has tantrums at mealtime—the slightest thing can set her off.

My child purposely makes a mess, like painting the table (or the new baby) with spaghetti sauce.

Many of the behavior problems we see at mealtimes are an extension of similar issues that crop up during the day, but parents notice them more at dinner, especially at a restaurant, where other people witness the scene. To find out whether this is part of a bigger picture, I ask, **Is this behavior new, or has it been going on for a while? If the latter, in what other situations does it happen? What usually prompts it?** More often than not, the behavior is not new. It's the result of accidental parenting: The child acts out, and the parent is either rushed or too embarrassed, and lets it go or gives in to whatever demand the child is making (much more about this overall pattern in chapter 8, which is about "taming toddlers").

So let's say your child is finger-painting the table with spaghetti sauce. What do you do? If you say to yourself, *No big deal—I'll just clean it up,* and you say nothing to your child, by ignoring her misbehavior you're telling her it's okay. But what happens a few weeks later when you're at Grandma's house and she starts "decorating" your mother-in-law's heirloom tablecloth? I'd have to say, it's not your child's fault; it's yours. You have to *teach* her that spaghetti sauce is not for finger-painting. The first time she did it, you should have said, "Food is for eating. You don't play with it. When you're finished eating, you take your plate to the sink."

Suppose instead that your daughter is a bit on the active side and is fond of putting her feet on the table, and tapping out the rhythms of the Barney song. It's a novelty to her, but imagine the same behavior in a restaurant. You'd probably want to duck under the table. Be consistent and persistent. Whatever your child is doing that's unacceptable—feet on the table, fork up her nose, throwing food—be direct and tell her it's wrong: "No, we do not [describe what she's doing] at the dinner table." If she doesn't stop, excuse her from the table. You can invite her back in five minutes and allow her to try again. It's with continuity and persistence that children learn not only what to expect but also what we expect of them.

It's the same with throwing food. It's one thing to see a fourteen-month-old experimenting with motion and throwing; it's best to make light of it (see page 163). But with a two- or three-year-old who's doing it to get a rise out of you, you have to tell him what he did was wrong, and make him clean it up. Let's say you put a plate of chicken in front of your two-year-old, and he lets out a loud "No!" and proceeds to hurl bits of chicken onto the floor. Take the plate away, saying, "No throwing food." Get him out of the chair and try again in five minutes. Give him two chances, and then he doesn't get anything.

This might sound stern, but believe me, children of this age know how to manipulate their parents. I've seen mothers who are like outfielders, catching food on the fly but never telling their children that it's wrong. Instead they say, "Oh, do you want some cheese instead?" And then it turns into a longer-term problem, and you have a thrower on your hands who hurls not only food but toys and other potentially harmful objects (see Bo's story on page 329). You have to take the same steps at every meal until he stops. The problem is, parents lose energy and give in. They just clean up the mess. It's a very common problem, and eventually a serious one, because the parents can't take their child out anywhere. I hate going out to restaurants where you see kids who don't know how to behave. They've crushed up the bread, thrown the food about, and the parents don't seem to care—they let the server clean it up. They're not showing respect for their own mealtimes.

The parents will say, "He's only two—he doesn't know any better." But who is going to teach him to be respectful—and when? Is some magic fairy going to fly in and teach him? No, the parent has to be the teacher and, I suggest, has to start early on (more about this in chapter 8).

Sometimes, misbehavior is solved by parents' paying closer attention to their child's cues. When a parent says his child has tantrums, for example, I ask, **Do you watch for signs that your child is full?** Parents sometimes try to get children to eat "one more bite" even though the kid is whining, turning his head away, kicking his little feet. They keep trying, and eventually they have a meltdown on their hands. Instead, they need to take their child away from the table immediately.

Parents can unwittingly lay the seeds of more serious eating issues later on, so be careful about the unintentional messages you might give your child about food. Pushing her to eat more than her fill doesn't give her an opportunity to control her own body, or to know when she's full. Many overweight adults, who look back on their childhood, recall that they were given a lot of treats and sweets and praised for cleaning their plate. Their parents said things like, "What a good girl you are for finishing your food," and they quickly began to associate eating with parental approval. Especially if you have eating issues yourself, either chronic dieting or food phobias, be sure to acknowledge them and get help, so that you don't pass them on to your child.

To be sure, even if we don't have food issues ourselves, there's a lot of emotional stress associate with feeding. We want our children to be healthy. When they don't eat, we naturally worry. Sometimes we can do something about it, sometimes not. Either way, we parents have to stay in charge. A well-fed baby or toddler is one who plays well and sleeps well. We owe it to our kids to give them the fuel they need and, at the same time, to respect their individual differences, even their idiosyncracies. And just to keep things in perspective, check out "The Toddler Miracle Diet" on the next page. On the days you're worried about how much *your* toddler is eating, read this wonderful bit of humor that has popped up on several internet parenting sites. The anonymous author—who is no doubt the parent of a toddler—suggests that the diet is why most toddlers are so thin!

The Toddler Miracle Diet

Consult Your Physician Before Following This Regimen

DAY ONE

Breakfast:	*1 scrambled egg, 1 piece of toast with grape jelly. Eat 2 bites of egg, using your fingers; dump the rest on the floor. Take 1 bite of toast, then smear the jelly over your face and clothes.*
Lunch	*4 crayons (any color), a handful of potato chips, and a glass of milk (3 sips only, then spill the rest).*
Dinner	*A dry stick, 2 pennies and a nickel, 4 sips of flat Sprite.*
Bedtime snack	*Throw a piece of toast on the kitchen floor.*

DAY TWO

Breakfast	*Pick up stale toast from kitchen floor and eat it. Drink half bottle of vanilla extract or 1 vial of vegetable dye.*
Lunch	*Half tube of "Pulsating Pink" lipstick and a handful of Purina Dog Chow (any flavor). One ice cube, if desired.*
Afternoon snack	*Lick an all-day sucker until sticky, take outside, drop in dirt. Retrieve and continue slurping until it is clean again. Then bring inside and drop on rug.*
Dinner	*A rock or an uncooked bean, which should be thrust up your left nostril. Pour Grape Kool-Aid over mashed potatoes; eat with spoon.*

DAY THREE

Breakfast	*2 pancakes with plenty of syrup, eat 1 with fingers, rub in hair. Glass of milk; drink half, stuff other pancake in glass. After breakfast, pick up yesterday's sucker from rug, lick off fuzz, put it on the cushion of best chair.*
Lunch	*3 matches, peanut butter and jelly sandwich. Spit several bites onto the floor. Pour glass of milk on table and slurp up.*
Dinner	*Dish of ice cream, handful of potato chips, some red punch. Try to laugh some punch through your nose, if possible.*

FINAL DAY

Breakfast	*A quarter tube of toothpaste (any flavor), bit of soap, an olive. Pour a glass of milk over bowl of cornflakes, add a half cup of sugar. Once cereal is soggy, drink milk and feed cereal to dog.*
Lunch	*Eat bread crumbs off kitchen floor and dining room carpet. Find that sucker and finish eating it.*
Dinner	*Drop pieces of spaghetti onto back of dog, insert meatball into ear. Dump pudding into Kool-Aid and suck up with a straw.*

REPEAT DAYS AS NEEDED!

FIVE

TEACHING BABIES HOW TO SLEEP

The First Three Months and the Six Troubleshooting Variables

Sleep Like a Baby?

"I can't get my five-week-old to sleep in her crib."

"My six-week-old resists going down for naps."

"My one-month-old baby is a great napper, but he doesn't sleep at night."

"My baby is three months old and is still waking up throughout the night."

"My ten-week-old won't go to sleep unless he's lying on my chest."

"I watch for the signs and try to put my five-week-old in his crib when he seems tired, but he cries when I lay him down."

"My eight-week-old will only sleep in the car, so we put his car seat in the crib."

Every day, my online mailbox is packed with emails like the ones above, most from parents whose babies are three months old or younger. Their subject lines read "Help!" or "I'm Desperate" or "From a Sleep-Deprived Mom." It's not surprising: Sleep is the Number One issue that plagues parents from the moment they bring their baby home from the hospital. Even the lucky ones, whose babies are naturally good sleepers, wonder, "When will my baby sleep through the night?" Sleep is also the most important issue because all other aspects of baby care revolve around sleep. To sleep is to grow. If you have a tired child, he won't eat or play. He'll be cranky, and prone to digestive problems and other illnesses.

In almost every case of sleep difficulties, parents have the same basic problem: They don't realize that sleep is a set of skills that we have to *teach* babies—how to fall asleep on their own and, when they wake in the middle of the night, how to get back to sleep. And instead of taking the lead in those first three months when they should be laying the groundwork for good sleep habits, they follow the baby and, without realizing it, allow all sorts of bad habits to develop.

Blame it, in part, on a popular misconception about how babies sleep. When an adult says, "I slept like a baby last night," he means he had a great night's sleep—his eyes closed, the night passed uneventfully, and when he woke, he felt refreshed and energetic. What a rare treat! Rare indeed. Most of us twist and turn during the night, get up to go to the bathroom, look at the clock and wonder whether we'll be rested enough for the day ahead. Well, guess what? Babies are the same way. If our language was really accurate, "sleep like a baby" would mean, "I woke up every forty-five minutes." No, babies don't fret about new clients or rehearse a report they have to present the next day, but they have similar sleep patterns. Just like adults, babies go through forty-five-minute cycles, alternating a deep, almost coma-like sleep with lighter REM (rapid eye movement), when the brain is active and we tend to dream. It was once thought that infants didn't dream, but recent research proves that, on average, they actually spend 50 to 66 percent of their sleep time in REM, far more than adults, who average 15 to 20 percent. Thus, babies often wake up throughout the night, just as we do. If no one has taught them how to settle down on their own, they cry, essentially saying, "Come help me, I don't know how to get back to sleep." And if their parents don't know either, that's when the seeds of accidental parenting are planted.

The kinds of sleep issues that crop up in the first three months can be categorized as either *not wanting to go to sleep* (which includes crib resistance) or *not staying asleep*—or both. In the pages that follow, I look at the most common sleep difficulties and their possible causes, and in each case, come up with *a plan,* a course of action that will solve the problem. Granted, each sleep concern is unique in its own way because it pertains to *your* family and *your* baby, so there's no way I could cover all the possibilities, not in one book or ten. Indeed, if there are a million babies, there are a million different scenarios.

But to help you with your problem, I can at least take you beyond the basics and allow you to peek inside my brain. My goal is to help you understand how I assess the various kinds of sleep problems that occur during the first three months, so that you can do your own troubleshooting. (Bear in mind that many of these same issues persist in older babies as well, but are a lot easier to deal with before your baby hits the four-month mark.) My hope is that this extra information will help you see where you might have taken a left turn when you should have stayed straight and help you move your baby forward along the yellow brick road to Dreamland.

The Six Troubleshooting Variables

Sleep problems at any age tend to have multiple causes. They're affected not only by what happens at night, but the entire day. They're influenced as well by the baby's temperament and the parents' behavior. For example, a baby who wakes up repeatedly during the night might be getting too much sleep, eating too little, or having too much activity during the day. At the same time, his frequent night waking could instead—or also—be the result of accidental parenting. Perhaps his mum, desperate for a solution when he's crying at 4 A.M., has taken to breast-feeding him when he wakes. Or maybe she takes him into her bed and lets him sleep there for the rest of the night. He might only be four weeks old, but it doesn't take long for a baby to get used to a particular routine, so he now associates going to sleep with having a nip of Mum's breast or getting into the family bed.

Also, a sleep "problem" tonight might not have the same cause as last night's. Your

> ### "Sleeping Through the Night" in Other Cultures
>
> Sleep practices reflect the culture in which they evolve. We are probably so obsessed with getting babies to sleep through the night because we need to get up the next day and tend to business. We need Baby to cooperate. In other cultures, though, babies are a more integral part of adult life. For example, when a baby is born into the !Kung San, a hunter-gatherer culture from the Kalahari Desert, the young infant is in constant skin-to-skin contact with her mother, sleeping with her at night and being carried continually during the day. The mum breast-feeds her baby small amounts every 15 minutes or so. If the baby fusses, she responds immediately before it turns into an out-and-out cry. Not surprisingly, no one pays much attention to getting the baby to sleep through the night.

Don't Do It Alone!

Sleep deprivation is a parent's problem, not a baby's. Your newborn doesn't care how much sleep he gets at night. He doesn't have to take care of the house or go to the office. As far as he's concerned, there's nothing wrong with a 24-hour day. Especially in the first 6 weeks, get lots of help. Trade off with your partner to make sure the burden of middle-of-the-night feeds doesn't only fall on your shoulders. Don't do trade-off every other night. Each should be "on duty" for 2 nights and off for 2, so that you can really catch up on your sleep. If you're a single mum, ask your own mother or a good friend to pitch in. If no one can sleep over, at least invite them to come a few hours during the day to give you a chance to nap.

baby could wake up because his room is too cold one night, because he's hungry the next, and because he's in pain a few nights later.

You can see what I'm getting at. Figuring out how to solve sleep difficulties is like a puzzle—we have to be like detectives and put the pieces together. Then, we must come up with *a plan*, a course of action.

Making the picture even more complex, the phrase "sleeping through the night" confuses many parents. In fact, sometimes when parents call me I find that the child doesn't actually have a sleep *problem*—rather, her parents expect too much of her too soon. Recently, the mother of a newborn said to me, "I can't get any more than two hours out of her and I'm up at all hours . . . When will she sleep through the night?"

Welcome to parenthood! Sleep deprivation (yours) is just part of your initiation. Another, the mother of an eight-week-old, wrote: "I want him to be asleep by 7—and to get up at 7. What do you suggest?" I suggest *Mum* needs help, not her child.

Let's be realistic: Babies don't actually sleep *through the night* in the early months. In the first six weeks, most wake twice a night—at 2 or 3 A.M. and then at 5 or 6 A.M.—because their stomachs can't hold enough to sustain them longer than that. They also need the calories to grow. We work toward getting rid of that 2 A.M. feed first. Certainly, you should be starting to teach the skills of sleep the moment your baby comes home from the hospital, but you probably won't reach that goal until four to six weeks at best. It depends on your baby's temperament and size, among other factors. But you also have to be realistic. Even when your baby is over six weeks and is able to sleep through a longer stretch, you might still be getting up at 4 or 5 or 6 in the morning at first. To an adult, five or six hours of sleep hardly qualifies as sleeping through the night! There's not much you can do about it, except to go to bed earlier and to remember that these early months will pass fairly quickly.

My goal in this chapter is to help you to be realistic about your baby's capacity for sleep, to understand a variety of sleep scenarios, and to train yourself to think like me. If your baby has a hard time going to sleep or wakes unexpectedly in the middle of the night, consider all the possible causes, observe your baby, and retrace your own steps as well.

To make it all a little less complicated, I've isolated six different variables that can affect sleep during the first three months (see the sidebar below). All six variables are related and sometimes intertwined and can continue to affect your baby's sleep habits well past the four-month mark, into the toddler years, and, sadly, even beyond, so it's a good idea to understand them no matter how old your child is now. Three of the variables have to do with what you've been doing (or not doing) to promote your baby's sleep: lack of routine, inadequate sleep preparation, and accidental parenting. And three have to do with your baby: hunger, overstimulation/overtiredness, and pain/discomfort/illness.

Especially in the middle of the night when adults are at their worst, it's not a simple matter to figure out which of the variables is the culprit—even more so, if there's more than one at work! Even *I,* the Baby Whisperer herself, have to ask a series of questions before I can help a family get on track. Otherwise, I'm fishing in the dark. Then, using their answers, I put together all the clues so I can come up with the cause—or causes—of the sleep disturbance and a plan for teaching the baby to sleep. I'm confident that once you understand the nature of infants' sleep and what can affect it, you'll be as good a detective as I am.

In each of the sections that follow, I explain the six variables, along with a "tip-off" sidebar showing the kinds of complaints I often hear associated with each variable and a plan—what you can do to change the situation. Some of these topics have been dealt with in other chapters—the importance of routine in chapter 1 and recognizing and

---

The Six Troubleshooting Variables

If a baby either resists going to sleep or doesn't stay asleep, it's either because of something the parent is doing (or not doing) or something in the child.

The parents might have

. . . failed to establish a daily routine

. . . set up an inadequate sleep ritual

. . . gotten into accidental parenting

The child might be

. . . hungry

. . . overstimulated or overtired or both

. . . in pain, uncomfortable, or ill

Important User Note

If you're desperate and in need of help for a particular sleep problem, you might want to first skim through the next 31 pages and look at only the "Tip-Off" sidebars that go with each of the variables. (Although I've numbered the variables, they are not in a particular order.) Find the scenario (one or more) that comes closest to what your baby is doing and read about that. However, you'll see that very few tip-offs are associated with only one variable. For instance, when a parent tells me, "My baby refuses to sleep in his crib," I know immediately that some type of accidental parenting has gone on. However, because sleep problems are more often caused by *multiple* variables, most of the tip-offs—like, "doesn't settle down to sleep easily"—are listed more than once. That's why it's important to read through and understand each of the six variables. Consider it a crash course in sleep intervention.

Tip-Off #1

These complaints often indicate that a **lack of routine** is at least in part responsible for your baby's sleep problem:

My baby doesn't settle down to sleep easily.

My baby wakes up every hour at night.

My baby sleeps great during the day but is up all night.

dealing with hunger or pain in chapter 3. Rather than be repetitive, in certain instances I refer to you to the appropriate pages. However, here we look at these subjects again, as each relates to *sleep*.

Variable #1: Lack of Routine

The first question I ask when parents come to me with a sleep problem is usually, **Do you keep track of his feeds, naps, bedtimes, and wake-up times?** If they don't, I suspect that they have never established a structured routine or they've been unable to stick to one.

No routine. Sensible sleep is the "S" in E.A.S.Y. And in the first three months, it's often less a matter of sleep "problems" per se and more about trying to keep your baby on E.A.S.Y. For average-birthweight babies under four months of age, staying on a three-hour routine is an essential key to success. I'm not saying that babies on E.A.S.Y. never have sleep issues—after all, there are five other variables. But babies on a structured routine from Day One are usually off to a good start.

A PLAN: If you're not on a structured routine, reread chapter 1, and commit to giving your baby a predictable sequence of events. Or, you might have to *re*establish E.A.S.Y. if somehow you've gotten off track. Include my "Four S" wind-down ritual (see "winding down," pages 181–186) every time you put him down. Remember that a routine is not the same thing as a schedule. It's about watching your baby, not the clock. One day your baby might go down for a nap at 10 and the next day at 10:15. As long as the sequence is consistent—eating, activity, sleep—and each occurs at more or less at the same time, you'll promote sensible sleep.

The Day-for-Night Dilemma: One of the most common difficulties that arise from lack of routine is switching day for night. When a baby is born, she's on a twenty-four-hour clock and doesn't know the difference between day and night. We have to *teach* her to do that by waking her for her regular feeds. When I hear that a baby is up for a long stretch at night, or wakes frequently, I often suspect that parents haven't been consistent with the daytime routine. Typically, the baby is eight weeks or younger. To find out for sure whether this is a day-for-night problem, I ask, **How many naps a day does she take, and for how long? How much daytime sleep is she getting altogether?** One of the biggest stumbling blocks to sleep training in the early weeks is that parents let their baby sleep more than 5½ hours during the day, which throws the three-hour routine off kilter and causes babies to stay up all night. In essence they've switched day for night. I call it "robbing Peter (nighttime sleep) to pay Paul (daytime sleep)."

A PLAN: If your baby has switched day for night, extend her waking hours during the day. If she sleeps more than two hours during the day, wake her. If you don't and you allow her to sleep through a feed, she's going to have to make up for the lost nutrition at night. And yet, I constantly hear, "But it's cruel to wake a sleeping baby." No, luv, it's not cruel—it's a way of teaching your baby to distinguish day from night. If you're one of those who believes in the old sleeping baby myth, you're going to have to give it up.

Start by keeping track for a few days. If your child is getting more than five hours of continuous sleep in one cycle during the day or two or more three-hour naps, there's a good chance that she's switched day for

---

It's a Myth

Never Wake a Sleeping Baby

Somewhere, at some time in our lives, most of us have heard "Never wake a sleeping baby." Poppycock! Babies come to us with 24-hour internal clocks. They don't know how to sleep; they don't know the difference between night and day. We have to teach them. Waking a baby is not only acceptable, it's imperative at times, because in the end it enables her to get on a structured routine.

night. You therefore have to *re*introduce E.A.S.Y., in this way: Don't allow your baby to sleep longer than forty-five minutes to an hour during the day for the first three days. This will get her out of the long-nap habit and ensure that she gets the calories she needs by regular feeds. To wake her, unswaddle her, pick her up, massage her little hands (not her feet!), and take her out of the bedroom and into an area where there's activity. Sit her upright, a simple trick which (most of the time) will make her eyes pop open. If she's difficult to wake up, that's fine. Just keep trying. Unless she's dead to the world, you'll probably be successful.

Once you've reduced her daytime sleep, your baby will start making up the hours at night and you can gradually—every three days—increase her nap time by fifteen minutes. Never let her sleep for more than 1½ to two hours during the day, which is the proper nap period for babies four months and younger.

The only exception here is a premature (see sidebar, page 179) or small baby. Some small babies take five half-hour naps during the day at first, have only a few minutes of up time in between, and fall back to sleep until the next feed. They're not yet ready to last longer between feeds and you just have to ride it out for a few weeks. However, once your baby has reached his due date, it's important to make sure that you gradually extend his awake time during the day. Here's a typical scenario:

> My five-week premature baby, Randy, who is now five weeks old, has been on your method since about three weeks old, but just this week, he's begun after his midnight feeding to stay awake and fussy until the 3 o'clock feeding. He really does sleep most of the day still, with just 15 minutes here and there awake time. Is he getting his days and nights mixed up? What should I do???? I've been a walking zombie all week!

Mum is right: Randy *is* getting his days and nights mixed up. Although she hasn't given me her baby's daytime routine, she tells me, "He really does sleep most of the day," a sure sign that he's robbing Peter to pay Paul. Because he's only up fifteen minutes at a time, that tells me he's falling asleep during feeds. He also might not be eating efficiently or Mum's milk supply might not be sufficient, either of which could keep him up at night. Even though Randy was premature and developmentally still needs more sleep than a full-term baby (see sidebars, pages 27 and 179), we want to encourage him to sleep at night instead. I don't know his current weight, but I do know that he's reached his due date and, I suspect, is therefore ready for at least a 2½-hour E.A.S.Y. routine during the day. Mum now needs to work at extending his waking time during the day, even if she just gets ten minutes more out of him after each feed. I'd suggest that she work at it for three days to a week, and when she sees he's able to stay awake, she should start increasing his up time to fifteen and then twenty minutes. Eventually, Randy will start robbing Paul (daytime sleep) and pay back to Peter, and thereby sleep better at night. He'll also start putting on weight and increase his tummy's capacity, which will also help him sleep longer stretches through the night.

Routine busters. Sometimes parents veer from their routine with a young baby because of their own needs. **Do you schlepp your baby with you on errands throughout the day?** It's important to keep to your routine during the early months, because you're training your baby to sleep. Consistency is vital.

A PLAN: I'm not saying that you shouldn't ever leave the house. But if your baby is having trouble settling down, it might be because she's not able to go with *your* flow. For at least two weeks, commit to a structured routine, observe her cues, and establish a good sleep ritual. If your child's sleep difficulties begin to diminish or disappear altogether, you know that she needs a bit more consistency than you've been giving her.

If you work out of your home, full- or part-time, sticking to a routine is not solely in your hands. You might find that when you come home from work or when you pick up your baby at day care, she's cranky and out of sorts. **Even though you have a good routine, do**

Premature Babies

Sleep, Sleep, and More Sleep

As I explained in the previous chapter (page 146), if your baby was premature, at this stage his chronological age—counting from the day he was born—is not the same as his developmental age. Premature babies need lots and lots of sleep. In fact, you want the child to be asleep most of the time. Even a 4-week-early premie is still not supposed to be here for the first 4 weeks of his life. So if you're comparing your 8-week-old to your sister's baby, who could go 5- or 6-hour stretches during the night by the time he was 8 weeks, and you're trying to keep him up for 20 minutes of activity time, readjust your expectations. Your baby is different. He has to be on a *2-hour* routine, at least until he reaches your due date, which is when he *should* have arrived. His only "jobs" are eating and sleeping. Your day will consist of feeding him, swaddling, and putting him back to sleep in a quiet, darkened room. When he reaches or is past his due date and weighs at least 6½ pounds, you can put him on a 3-hour routine.

you know for a fact that whoever else is taking care of your child—your mate, Grandma, a nanny, or a day care provider—is following it, too? Did you take the time to explain it? If you have a nanny, stay at home for a week to show her your routine, including your wind-down ritual. If you take your child to a day care provider away from home, spend extra time there to show the person or staff how you handle your baby and what you do at nap times. Give your caretaker a notebook in which she can keep track of your baby's ups and downs. She can take note: "didn't nap well" or "was difficult to feed." Most day care facilities do this anyway—and if yours doesn't or refuses your request to do so, you've picked the wrong day care provider. Whether you have an in-home provider or you drop your child off, pay a surprise visit every now and then. (More events that disrupt your everyday routine in chapter 10, pages 372–374.)

If You Stick to Your Routine . . . Here's What to Expect

The following applies to a healthy baby who has been on E.A.S.Y. from Day 1. Your baby might not conform exactly. It depends on her weight, temperament, and whether you've consistently taken steps to *promote* sensible sleep.

One week:

Day: Feed every 3 hours; 1½ hours of sleep every 3 hours.

Evening: Cluster feed at 5 and 7, dream feed at 11.

Wake up: 4:30 or 5 A.M.

One month:

Day: Feed every 3 hours; 1½ hours of sleep every 3 hours.

Evening: Cluster feed at 5 and 7, dream feed at 11.

Wake up: 5 or 6 A.M.

Four months:

Day: Feed every 4 hours; 3 naps, 1½–2 hours each, plus 45-minute catnap in the late afternoon.

Evening: Dinner at 7, dream feed at 11.

Wake up: 7 A.M.

Variable #2: Inadequate Sleep Ritual

"Going to sleep" is not an event. It's more like a journey that begins with your baby's first yawn and ends with her finally dropping off into a deep sleep. You have to help her get there. To do that, you have to recognize her sleep window and help her wind down.

The sleep window. To promote sleep, you have to recognize when your baby is ready for bed. **Do you know what your baby looks like when she's tired? Do you act on it immediately?** If you miss your baby's sleep window, it's going to be a lot harder to get her to sleep.

A PLAN: Some infants are naturally better sleepers than others—typically, Angel babies and Textbook types. But even those babies need their parents to be observant, because each baby is an individual. So pay attention and figure out what *your baby* does when he's tired. With newborns, who don't have control over anything except their mouths, a yawn is often the biggest clue. But your baby might also fuss (Grumpy babies often do), fidget (Spirited), or make other involuntary movements. Some open their eyes wide (also common in Spirited babies) while others sound like a creaking door and still others squeak. By six weeks, as your baby increasingly gains control over his head, he might also turn away from your face or from a toy, or burrow into your neck when you're carrying him. Whatever his particular signs, the idea is to act immediately. If you miss your baby's sleep window, or try to extend his awake time in the name of getting him to sleep longer (another myth), it's going to be a lot harder to teach him the skills of settling down.

Winding down. Even if you're good at recognizing when your baby is tired, you can't just plop her straight into her crib without giving her a few moments to transition from an activity (even if it's just staring at the wall). **What method have you been using to put her to bed or down for a nap? Do you swaddle**

Take Note!

For parents who have trouble reading their babies, I often suggest a sleep diary. Taking notes helps hone your powers of observation. For 4 days, write down not only when your baby sleeps and for how long, but what you were doing before each sleep period, what your baby was doing, and what he looked like. I promise that you'll see patterns emerge and, if your baby's not a good sleeper, you might even discover why.

her? If she has trouble settling in, do you stay with her? A wind-down ritual—a predictable, repetitive sequence—allows a baby to learn what to expect, and swaddling helps a baby feel cozy and safe. Both act like cues, in essence telling your baby, "It's time to switch gears. We're getting ready for sleep." Starting a wind-down ritual when your baby is very young will not only teach the sleep skills she needs, it will also lay a foundation of trust for the later months when separation anxiety kicks in.

With a child under three months old, preparation for bed or nap time is generally no longer than fifteen minutes. Some mums can just walk in, close the curtains, swaddle, lay their baby down, and the child will coo and babble and what have you and go off to sleep. But it's been my experience that just before they go down, most children need their parents' calming presence in order to make the transition from activity to sleep. And some—typically, Touchy and Spirited types—might need even more.

A PLAN: My "Four S" ritual consists of *Setting the stage* (getting the environment ready for sleep), *Swaddling* (getting your baby ready for sleep), *Sitting* (quietly, without physical stimulation) and, when necessary, doing the *Shush-pat method* (spending an extra few minutes of physical intervention to help a fussy or fidgety baby drop off into a deep sleep).

Setting the stage. Whether it's bedtime or nap time, you set the stage for sleep by removing your baby from a stimulating setting to a more calm one. Go into his room, draw the curtains, and, if you like, put on soft music. You want to make sure the last couple of minutes are quiet, still, and very low-key.

Swaddling. The ancients swaddled their babies. Most primitive cultures swaddle babies. They swaddled your baby in the hospital, and you should continue swaddling at home. It's best if you swaddle her *before* you lay her down in her crib.

What's so great about swaddling? Under the age of three months, babies have no control over their arms or legs. Unlike adults who become lethargic when they're overtired, babies become more hyper—their arms and legs jerk or wave in the air when they're exhausted. And when that happens, the baby doesn't even realize that her limbs are attached to her. As far as she's concerned, those moving objects are part of the environment—they distract and disturb her. In a sense, then, swaddling is another form of removing stimulation from the environment. I recommend swaddling at least up to three or four months, although some babies can go as long as seven or eight months.

Although most mothers are shown the swaddling technique in the hospital, some abandon the idea when they get home. If you dismissed the idea (or didn't pay attention), here's a refresher: Lay flat a receiving blanket (a square one works best) like a diamond. Fold one corner of the diamond down (toward you), to make a nice straight edge. Lay your baby on the blanket, so that his neck is even with the fold and his head is out of the blanket. Place his left arm at a forty-five-degree angle across his chest and bring the right corner of the blanket across your baby's chest and tuck it under the left side of his body. Bring the bottom of the blanket up to cover his outstretched legs. Finally, bring the left corner of the swaddle across his chest and tuck it under his right side. Make it nice and snug. Some parents are fearful of wrapping their baby lest it restrict his breathing or his leg movements, but research has shown that proper swaddling doesn't put infants at risk. Quite the contrary, this ancient practice helps babies sleep more soundly.

> ## "My Baby Hates Swaddling!"
>
> I can't stress how important it is to get in the habit of swaddling your baby. Unfortunately, some parents resist swaddling; they feel it confines the baby. They may be claustrophobic themselves, so they project their own feelings on their child. You might say, "My daughter hates being swaddled—she fights me by waving her arms and legs wildly." But flailing is not a conscious action on your baby's part. Usually it's because she is overtired and/or overstimulated and is having trouble settling down for sleep. By swaddling you'll help her calm herself down. The reason we start to *unswaddle* some babies at around 3 months is that that's the average age when they start to find their fingers. But some babies don't find their fingers until 5 months, or even later! (Yet another reason to know your own baby.)

At a certain point, where you used to be able to swaddle your baby and she'd stay in a nice bundle, now her arms come out and she starts to explore and move around. Sometimes a parent will see this and say, "She doesn't like being swaddled anymore—she struggles to get out." I then ask, **What do you do if she gets out of her swaddle?** One mother—not one of my clients, I assure you—used electrical tape when her baby got out! But more often, the answer is, "I stop swaddling." What Mum and Dad have to do instead is recognize that once a baby becomes more mobile, she *will* move about, swaddled or not. Some babies do this as early as four weeks. They have more control of the neck and arms. If your baby gets out of her swaddle, reswaddle her (without the tape, please). Later, at around four months, you might choose to experiment by leaving one arm out of the swaddle so that she can work at finding her fist or fingers.

Sitting. After your baby is swaddled, sit with him quietly for around five minutes with him in the vertical position. It's best with a young baby to hold him so that his face is tucked into your neck or shoulder, to block out any visual stimulation. Don't rock or jiggle him, and don't pace. I know, I know, that's what most of you do. We see it in the movies, we see our friends doing it, but most of the time side-to-side rocking and jiggling stimulates a baby, rather than calms him down. And if you shake a baby, or move too fast, you can actually startle him. You should feel his little body relax and then maybe jerk a little. That's him trying to descend into a deep sleep. Ideally, you want to put your baby into his crib *before* he sleeps. This is not possible with every baby, but it's a goal you must work toward. As you're about to lay him down, say, "You're going to sleep now. I'll see you when you get up." Give him a kiss, and then put him in his crib. He might or might not understand the words, but he'll definitely get the feeling. If he seems calm, leave the room and allow him to drift off to sleep on his own. Unless he's having problems settling down, *you don't have to wait for him to fall asleep.* If your baby is swaddled and calm, trust that he has the skills to fall asleep on his own. The 2004 *Sleep in America* poll (more about this in chapter 7) conducted by the National Sleep Foundation, proves that independent sleep fosters better sleep. Infants and toddlers who are put to bed awake are more likely to sleep longer hours than babies who are put to bed asleep and three times *less* likely to wake two or three times during the night.

Shush-pat. If your baby is a bit fussy, or he starts crying when you try to lay him down, he is probably ready for sleep but needs *physical intervention* in order to settle. This is the point at which parents first get into accidental parenting. They rock or jiggle or use some kind of prop to calm their baby. But I have another suggestion, the shush-pat method: You simultaneously whisper "shh, shh, shh . . ." into your baby's ear and pat his back. I use this technique on all babies under the age of three months who have trouble settling down on their own. It calms them because at this point in their development, babies cannot hold three thoughts in their minds at once. They can't continue to concentrate on the crying whilst being patted and shushed. So your baby will focus instead on the shush and the pat, and eventually stop crying. But it's critical that you do the shush-pat as follows:

Do this while he's lying in the crib, or, if it doesn't settle him, hold him over your shoulder: Pat him on the center of his back in a steady, rhythmic motion—like the tick-tock, tick-tock of a clock. The patting needs to be quite firm, and you want to be in the center of the back, not on one side or the other, and certainly not as far down as their little bottom, because too far down you're going to be whacking their kidneys.

While you're patting him, put your mouth near his ear, and whisper a slow, fairly loud, "Shh . . . shh . . . shh." Elongate the *shh* sound, so that it comes out more like the whooshing of air or a faucet on full force, not the slow chug-chug of a train. The idea is to convey a feeling of confidence to the child, as if to say, "Hey, I know what I'm doing here." It's important not to be too timid and soft with the pat or the sound. You're not thumping them and you're not yelling; you're just in charge. Also, be careful not to shush directly into your baby's ear, because you don't want to perforate his eardrum. Rather, make sure the shushing goes *past* his ear.

When you sense that his breathing is getting a little deeper and his body is starting to relax, gently lay him down, slightly on his side, so that you can have access to his back. Some parents complain that it's difficult to pat on the back while the baby is lying down, so they'll pat the shoulder or the chest once the baby is in the crib. But I don't think that's as effective. I prefer to lay him on his side and to continue patting on the back. If he's swaddled, it's fairly easy to roll him over, and use a wedge or rolled-up towel to keep him in place. (Place tape around both ends of the towel, securely fastening it so that the towel doesn't unravel. This would be a *good* use of duct tape as long as you don't tape the towels to your baby!) With the wedge or towel positioned on the baby's tummy, I also like to put my other hand on the chest, and then pat on the back. Then you can also bend down to his ear and do the shushing without picking him up. If the room isn't dark enough, you might also have to put your hand over (not on) his eyes to block out visual stimulation.

Once your baby is in his crib, use the skills of patting and shushing to *keep* him in the crib, unless he starts crying. I pat probably seven to ten minutes after the baby has calmed down. Even if he's quiet, I don't stop. I keep it going until I'm fairly sure he has his complete focus on it, and then I start to slow the patting down more and more. Finally, I also stop the shush. If your baby still doesn't settle, continue the shush-pat until he does. If he cries, pick him up again, and do the shush-pat with him on your shoulder. When you put him down again, continue to pat him and see if he starts up again. If he does, pick him up and calm him down *again*.

When he's quiet, step back from the crib and stay a few minutes to see whether he falls into a deep sleep or jolts again to consciousness as some babies do. Remember that it takes a baby twenty minutes to pass through the three stages of sleep—*the window* (the point at which you notice his sleep cues and set the scene), *the zone* (when he gets a glazed look in his eye, by which time you've swaddled him), and *the letting go* (he starts to nod off). The letting go stage is the trickiest—you have to know your baby. If he's the type who jolts into sleep rather fitfully, he needs the extra shush-pat to calm him down.

But what often happens is that you see your baby's eyes shut and think, "Great, he's out." So you stop patting and sneak out of the room, but just as you do, his whole body jolts, his eyes pop open—and lo and behold, he's come back to consciousness. When you leave too soon, you could be in and out every ten minutes for an hour and a half. And each time, you have to start the process again, which takes a full twenty minutes. (If you've got a Touchy, Spirited, or Grumpy baby, who tend to get tired more quickly and often take longer to wind down, it might take longer.)

I always urge parents not to stop prematurely—it's a common mistake. For example, I received an email from the mother of a five-week-old who wrote: "Once Kent enters stage three, his eyes pop open and he wakes up. The only way we've been able to get him to go to sleep is by patting him on the back and 'shh-shh.' I don't know how to get Kent to learn to pass through stage three on his own. At the beginning he is not crying but when we leave him to do it on his own, he will eventually start crying." Well, luv, Kent isn't ready to do it on his own, but the shush-pat method is a sleep tool that will eventually teach him how.

Take the time, and say to yourself, "I'm going to be there to see it through." You'll know your baby is in a deep sleep when his eyes stop moving side to side under his lids, his breathing slows and becomes more shallow, and his body completely relaxes, as if he's melting into the mattress. If you spend the full twenty minutes (or longer, depending on your baby), then you can get that Y time for yourself, the Y in E.A.S.Y. You won't have to keep going back in and out, in and out, which is more frustrating than just staying there. Also, by staying with your baby, you observe your child as he goes through the stages, which teaches you more about him and adds another baby-whispering skill to your parenting repertoire.

Variable #3: Accidental Parenting

In the Introduction to this book, I stressed the importance of P.C. parenting, which stands for patience and consciousness. *Accidental parenting* is the opposite of P.C. parenting. You grab at the most convenient solution—a quick fix—because you don't have the patience to see through a long-term solution. You also might feel guilty, as if your baby's sleep disturbance means that you're a bad parent. In response, you take an action or start a practice in desperation and without thinking it through, because you don't have the skills or knowledge to do it any other way. Let's face it, luv, babies don't come with a manual.

Prop dependency. A "prop" is any object or action outside of the baby's control that a parent employs to get a child to sleep. They are one of the central themes of accidental parenting. When I ask parents what they do to get their child to sleep, I include questions such as, **Do you routinely hold, rock, walk, or bounce your baby to sleep? Breast-feed or give her a bottle to calm her down? Allow her to fall asleep on your chest, in a swing, or a car seat? Take her into your bed when she's upset?** If you answer "yes" to any of the above, you're using a prop, and I promise it will come back to haunt you. Rocking, walking, car rides are motion props. You become a human prop when you give the breast to aid sleep, lay the baby on your stomach, hold her in the crook of your arm, or take her into your bed and allow her to fall asleep with you.

Often, prop dependency starts out as a desperate measure. The baby is overtired and crying at 3 A.M., so Dad walks the floor with her. Magically, the little one quiets down and falls asleep. Even if you employ a

---

Tip-Off #3

These complaints often indicate that **accidental parenting** is at least in part responsible for your baby's sleep problem:

My baby won't sleep unless I . . . rock her, feed her, lay her on my chest, etc.

My baby seems tired, but the minute I start to put her down, she cries.

My baby wakes up at the same time every night.

When my baby wakes at night, I feed her but she rarely takes much.

I can't get my baby to nap for more than a half hour or 45 minutes.

My baby wakes up at 5 A.M. to start her day.

My baby refuses to sleep in her own crib.

My baby wakes when the pacifier drops out of her mouth.

Props vs. Comfort Items

A prop is *not* the same as a comfort item—it depends on who is in control, parent or baby. A prop is something *the parent* chooses and controls. A comfort item, like a blankie or a favorite stuffed toy, is something *the child* adopts. Props are often given within the first weeks of birth; babies don't adopt comfort items until 6 months or older.

Pacifiers can go either way: If the child always wakes when it falls out and needs a parent to put it back in, it's a prop. If the child stays asleep without it or can pop it back in on his own, it's a comfort item.

prop a few nights in a row, it will quickly get to the point where she can't settle down or drift off to sleep without it. A month or so later, even though walking the floor feels old to Dad, and perhaps really annoys him, he now *has* to keep it up, because, as he explains it, "She won't go to sleep without it."

I had one little boy, Xavier, who was a happy, healthy baby in every respect, except that he thought the living room couch was his bed. His parents had gotten into the habit of rocking and walking him to sleep or just holding him. When he finally passed out, they put him down on the sofa, fearing that if they walked too far, or lowered him into his crib, he'd wake up. And wake he did, several times a night. That's because when he woke up, he had no idea where he was—remember, he started out in Mum or Dad's arms. He also had no idea how to send himself back to sleep. By the time I met him, he was fourteen weeks old, and Mum and Dad hadn't had a decent night's sleep for over a hundred days! Nor did they have a life. They were afraid of running the dishwasher or washing machine at night, couldn't have friends over, and of course had no time for themselves as a couple.

Sometimes parents offer a prop out of their own needs. A mum who enjoys cuddling her baby or breast-feeding doesn't see the harm in giving her cranky newborn what she sees as "extra attention" to help him settle down. Now I'm all for holding, comforting, and loving your baby, but you have to be careful of what you're doing, when you're doing it, and what you're inadvertently "telling" your baby. The problem is when Dad paces the floor with his baby and Mum breast-feeds hers to sleep, both babies get the message, "Oh, this is how I get to sleep." If you start employing a prop with a newborn, he'll quickly get used to it. And by the time he's three or four months old, if you don't keep up whatever prop you've gotten him used to, he'll cry to bring you back into his room to replace it.

A PLAN: Before it's too late, think through the practices you adopt. Will you want to be pacing or nursing when your baby is five months old? Eleven months old? Two? Will you want to take him into your bed in the middle of the night until *he* decides he doesn't need it any more? Better to

---

Spotlight in the Trenches

Even a Pacifier Can Become a Prop . . .

. . . if you're attached to the other end of it! The mother of a 7-week-old wrote to me, "I try to put Heather down when I see the 'sleep signals' and after I have calmed her down, like your book says. However, it seems that as soon as I put her down or as soon as the pacifier comes out, she wakes up crying . . . and she doesn't want the pacifier back. So instead of letting her cry it out, I pick her up and console her, check to make sure nothing's wrong, and then put her back down. Then she cries again . . . it's a pattern that we'll repeat for hours. Especially at nap time. What do I do? Should I let Heather cry it out? Or is that cruel, like your book says."

When a baby can find and use a pacifier without a parent's help, it's a comfort item. But in Heather's case, it's a prop. The tip-off phrase is ". . . it's a pattern that we'll repeat for hours." It's not that Heather consciously thinks, *Great, all I have to do is spit out the pacifier, Mum will come running, and I'll get a cuddle.* Rather, Heather's mum has unintentionally conditioned her to expect the pacifier and holding in order for her to go back to sleep. Indeed, research has shown that *at birth* babies, when presented with predictable patterns on a television screen, begin to have expectations of what they'll see next. In this case, Mum has provided not only visual but tactile stimulation as well, and Heather is anticipating what will happen next. I recommended that she stop using the pacifier altogether. She had to stick with the Four S ritual, spending a bit of extra time with Heather, waiting until she dropped off to sleep.

---

avoid the props now than take them away later on, which is much harder.

If you've already fallen into the trap of using a prop, the good news is that bad habits fade quickly in these early months. Instead of relying on your prop, do the Four S ritual (pages 182–186). Include the shush-pat if your baby needs extra calming. It may take three days, six days, even longer than a week, but if you're consistent, you can wean him from the bad habit *you* created.

The perils of rushing in. A baby's sleep pattern, whether she wakes frequently and/or at the same time every night, often gives me important clues about where parents inadvertently go wrong. If your child wakes quite frequently, I need to find out, **How many times does she wake up during the night?** A newborn on a good routine should wake no more than two times a night. If your baby is waking up every hour, or even every two hours, and we've ruled out hunger and pain, there's a good chance that *you* are doing something that makes nighttime appealing to her. Especially as your baby passes the six-week mark, her brain development is more advanced, and she starts to make associations. So if you've dealt with her night waking in a particular way—for example, taken her into your bed—she's going to expect that and be rather vocal when you don't.

Don't get me wrong. Your baby isn't consciously trying to manipulate you—not yet, anyway (more on manipulation in chapter 7). But it's now, during the early months, when accidental parenting starts. When parents say, "She won't let me . . ." or "She refuses . . . ," it usually means that they've lost control of the situation and are following the baby instead of guiding her. Another key question, then, is, **What do you *do* with her when she wakes up in the middle of the night or when she wakes up early from a nap? Do you rush in? Do you play with her? Take her into your bed?**

By now you know that I don't believe in allowing a baby to cry. However, sometimes parents don't realize that stirring is not the same as waking. If you answered "yes" to any of the above, you might be going into your child's room prematurely and actually disturbing her sleep, or cutting it short. Left to her own, she might fall back to sleep and her "too short naps" would extend or her "frequent night wakings" would diminish or disappear altogether. It's the same with early morning wake-ups. Where parents make a mistake is rushing in and saying, "Good morning. I missed you all night." It's 5 A.M.!

A PLAN: Listen, respond to cries, but don't rush in and rescue. Every baby makes little infant noises when they start to come out of a deep sleep; get to know what your baby sounds like. I call it "banguage," and it sounds like they're talking to themselves. It's *not* the same as crying, and they often drift back to sleep. If you hear your baby in the middle of the night or during an afternoon nap, don't rush in. And when she wakes at 5 or 5:30, and you know (because we assume you're on a good routine and you're monitoring her daytime feeds) that she's hungry, just feed her, swaddle her, and then put her right back down at 5:30. Use the shush-pat if necessary. You don't give her wakey-wakey time. When you finally do go in later in the morning, watch your tone. Don't act as if this poor little thing has been abandoned by you. Rather say, "Look at you, just lying there having a good time by yourself. What a good job!"

Habitual waking. Just as adults tend to get into waking habits, so do babies. The difference is, we look at the clock and groan, "Oh, God, it's four-thirty A.M.—just like last night," and then we roll over and go back to sleep. Some babies do that, but others cry out, and their parents come running. When they do, they inadvertently reinforce the habit. To find out if a baby is in a habitual pattern, I ask, **Does she wake up at the same time every night?** If so, and if she wakes up more than two days in a row at that time, recognize that there's a pattern developing. Chances are, you're going into your baby's room and employing some kind of prop. Let's say you rock her or give her your breast. That might put her to sleep, but it's a short-term fix, a Band-Aid. What you need is a solution.

A PLAN: Nine times out of ten a child who wakes habitually doesn't need more food (unless she's going through a growth spurt; see pages 115–119 and 197). Instead, reswaddle, if necessary, give her a pacifier to calm her, and comfort her with the shush-pat. (Note: Unless a baby is pacifier-dependent—see box, page 189—I recommend pacifiers for babies under three months old because most don't become dependent on them; see page 199.) Keep stimulation to a minimum. No rocking or jostling. Don't change her unless her diaper is soiled or soaking wet. Do the Four S routine and stay with her until she's settled into a deep sleep. You also need to take steps to *break* the waking habit. So, let's say you've ruled out other causes such as pain or discomfort. You've also eliminated hunger by both upping her food during the day and tanking her up at night (see also the section on hunger, pages 195–200). This is what I call my "wake-to-sleep" technique: Instead of lying there waiting for her to wake up, set your clock an hour earlier than her habitual waking time and *you wake her* (see sidebar this page). She probably won't wake up completely, but her little eyes may dart back and forth under her lids, she'll murmur and move a bit, just as an adult would if you interrupted his deep sleep. Do this for three nights in a row.

I can just hear your response: "You must be out of your mind!" I realize that wake-to-sleep is a shockingly counterintuitive suggestion, but it

---

> ## Wake to Sleep? Tracy, You've Got to Be Kidding
>
> Parents are often shocked when I suggest the wake-to-sleep strategy for habitual night waking. Set your clock an hour earlier than your baby usually wakes and go into his room. Jostle him gently, rub his belly a bit, and stick a pacifier in his mouth—all of which will help stir him to semi-consciousness. Then, leave. He'll fall back to sleep. This gives *you* the control, rather than your sitting around hoping that your baby's habit will magically go away. (It won't.) By waking him an hour early, you'll disrupt his pattern.

does work! Sometimes, in fact, it only takes one night to break the habit, but I recommend that you keep it up for three nights nonetheless. If it doesn't work, you have to reevaluate whether her habitual waking is due to another cause. If you've ruled everything else out, do this wake-to-sleep technique for at least another three days.

Breaking the bonds of trust. So many parents who come to me with sleep problems have tried this method or that. Inconsistency is a form of accidental parenting. It's not fair to keep changing the rules on your baby. I refer to my sleep strategies as "sensible sleep"—a middle-of-the-road philosophy that respects both the needs of the baby and the needs of the parents. It's not flashy or extreme; it just requires consistency. Other baby experts advocate more extreme sleep measures, with co-sleeping at one end of the continuum and the delayed-response method, sometimes known as "Ferberizing" or "controlled crying" (whereby the baby is allowed to cry for increasingly longer periods) at the other. Each approach has its merits, of course, and you can find armies of parents who swear by one or the other. If one of them has worked for you, fine. I suspect, however, that if you're reading this chapter, your baby is still having sleep difficulties. And if you started out with your baby in your bed or in your room and then swung to the other extreme, you might also be dealing with a breach of trust.

When a parent tells me that her baby "doesn't like to go to sleep" or "hates his crib," I always include the question, **Where has he been sleeping? A bassinet? A crib? Is his crib in his own room, in a room shared by a sibling, or in your room?** When a child is resistant to the crib, it is almost always a case of the parent not starting as they meant to go on. I then ask a series of questions: **Did you subscribe to the idea of the "family bed" when your baby was born?** If you answer "yes," my hunch is that you didn't really think the philosophy through in practical terms, nor did you determine at what point you'd move him out of your bed and into his own bassinet or crib. If he's been in his own bed, and you're now taking him into your bed because it's more convenient in the middle of the night, you've definitely set up a pattern of accidental parenting.

I'm not an advocate of either extreme. I don't believe that co-sleeping allows a child to develop the skills of independent sleep (nor you to have an adult relationship for that matter), whereas when we allow a child to cry alone, it can break the bond of trust between parent and child. Rather,

I believe it's crucial to teach a child to sleep in her own bed, be it bassinet or crib, and encourage her to go to sleep on her own from Day One.

If you're doing a family bed and it works for you (and your mate), and your child sleeps well, by all means carry on. There are parents who are happy with it—Mum and Dad have made the decision to do co-sleeping, and they work as a team. I rarely hear from such parents because they don't have a sleep problem. But some parents try co-sleeping because they've heard somewhere that if they don't share their bed, their baby won't bond with them. (In my opinion, attachment is a matter of caring and tuning in, twenty-four hours a day. If you don't sleep with your baby, know that she will still be attached to you.) Others take babies into their bed out of their own neediness. Or they hear about the practice, decide it's appealing, but they don't think it through or consider whether it's right for their lifestyle. Often, one partner is more committed to the idea and talks the other into it. For any number of reasons, it doesn't work for them.

The parents then swing to the opposite extreme, banishing the baby to a crib down the hall, at which point the little one has no self-soothing skills. Of course, the baby reacts to the change. He screams his little head off, as if to say, *Hey, where am I? What happened to those warm bodies?* The parents are confused, too, because they don't know how to begin to soothe their baby.

With these types of scenarios I have to ask, **Have you ever left him to cry it out?** I don't believe in allowing infants to cry alone, not even for five minutes. Your baby doesn't know where you have gone or why he's suddenly abandoned. To use another analogy, it's as if you have a boyfriend, you set a date, and he doesn't show up for two nights in a row. You wouldn't trust his word. Trust is the foundation on which any relationship is built. My hair stands on end when parents tell me they've allowed a baby to cry for an hour, two hours. Some infants get so upset and cry long and hard enough that they vomit. Others simply expend energy, become even more overstimulated, and eventually get hungry as well, leaving both of you confused and exhausted. Many babies who've been left to cry it out become chronically bad sleepers from that point on, putting up a battle whenever it's time for sleep, even becoming fearful of their own beds. Meanwhile, the daytime routine is turned totally upside down—there's no semblance of structure in the baby's day. He's exhausted, out of sorts, falls asleep while he's eating, and gets neither good feeds nor a good sleep.

If you've tried one extreme and then swung to the other side, and now your baby is miserable and mistrustful and still not sleeping, you have to go back to Square One. Make sure you've got a good daily routine, and use the Four S wind-down ritual (pages 181–186). But please, please, please stick with it. There will be days and nights when things don't go as planned, and it may take three days, a week, or a month to change a pattern. But if you follow my suggestions and are consistent, they *will* work.

Of course, the picture is more complicated if you've left your baby to cry it out, and she's now fearful about being abandoned. So you first have to build back the trust. Intervene and attend to her needs as soon as she makes a squeak. In other words, you've got to be more tuned in and more attentive to her needs than ever. Ironically, babies who've experienced a breach of trust are often harder to console. First you leave her, now you're there—and she's confused. She's so used to crying that even as you start to be more responsive, she might be inconsolable when you try to calm her.

A PLAN: Be prepared to take several weeks to build back the trust, even if your baby is only three or four months old. (You'll find additional strategies for older babies and toddlers in the next two chapters, but the following can be used up to eight months.) Take slow, steady steps to show her that you're there—for good. Each step might take three days to a week until she trusts you enough to feel comfortable in her crib, and the whole process could take three weeks to a month. (With a very frightened and distrustful baby, I've even resorted to getting into the crib *with* her! See "Sleepless Since Birth," page 240.)

Keep a careful eye out for her sleep signals. At the first sign of sleepiness, begin the Four S wind-down ritual, including the shush-pat. Swaddle her and sit cross-legged with her on the floor with your back against the wall or a couch. When she is calm, instead of trying to put her into her crib, lay her on a thick, firm standard-size sleeping pillow that sits on your knees. Be there with her, continue the patting and shushing until you see her fall into a deep sleep. Wait at least twenty minutes more and then gently unfold your legs and let the pillow slide to the floor. Sit next to the pillow, so that you'll be right there when she wakes up. Meditate, read, listen to a book on tape with headphones, or take a snooze yourself by lying next to her. You must stay with her all night. This is a sacrifice you have to make to regain your baby's trust.

The second week, do the same routine but start with the pillow on the floor in front of you, not on your lap, and when she's ready, put her

---

Spotlight in the Trenches

Curing Crib Phobia

I recently worked with Dale, the mother of a 6-week-old who had misread her baby's cues. She was certain that little Efram's nighttime cries were a sleep problem. Desperate for some sleep herself, she tried the controlled-crying method, which only intensified the problem. After 2 nights of crying it out, Efram was petrified of his crib. He was also underweight, which Dale had assumed was anxiety. But I asked her to do a yield and it turned out that it was a hunger issue—Dale wasn't making enough milk. I worked with her to increase her milk production (see box, page 98), but also told her that she had to counter Efram's fear and the loss of trust. Dale had to devote over a month to this process, as she moved Efram from sleeping on a cushion on her lap to sleeping in his own crib (see "A Plan," page 194), but by then Efram was a plumper, happier little boy.

---

down on it. Again, stay by her side. The third week, sit in a chair with her, and put the cushion in the crib. When you lay her down on it, place your hand on her back, so she knows you're still there. For three days, stand by her side until she's in a deep sleep. On the fourth day, remove your hand but stay by the crib while she's sleeping. Three days later, leave the room when she's in a deep sleep, but if she cries go back in *immediately*. Finally, the fourth week you should be able to lay her down on her mattress, instead of the pillow. If not, use the pillow for another week and try again.

If it sounds tedious and a bit hard on you, it is. But if you don't take steps now to cure crib phobia, it will only get worse, and you'll probably have a clingy child on your hands for the next several years. Better to restore her faith in you *now*.

Tip-Off #4

These complaints often indicate that **hunger** is at least in part responsible for your baby's sleep problem:

My baby wakes up crying several times a night and has a full feed.

My baby doesn't sleep more than three or four hours at night.

My baby was sleeping five or six hours every night but suddenly started waking.

Variable #4: Hunger

When infants wake up in the middle of the night, it's often because of hunger. But that doesn't mean we can't do anything about it.

Tanking up. Whether your child wakes every hour or at least twice a night, I would ask you, **How often is he feeding in the day?** My goal is to find out whether his day feeds are enough to see him through the night. With the exception of premature babies (see sidebars on pages 27 and 179), feeds should be every three hours before the age of four months. If you're feeding less frequently, he is probably not getting enough food to sustain him and is waking at night to make up for the lost calories.

Newborns can't hold much food in their little tummies, so they wake every three to four hours even during the night. This can be a very trying time for parents, but it goes with the territory. As your child grows, the goal is extend the time between nighttime feeds to five or even six hours by first getting rid of the 2 A.M. feed. If you are concerned about night waking, especially if your child is six weeks or older—typically, old enough to miss one feed—I would ask, **What time does he wake up after his last evening feed?** If he's still waking at 1 or 2, he doesn't have enough calories to sustain him.

A PLAN: To encourage longer sleep at this point, make sure you feed your baby every three hours during the day. In addition, you put a little more food in their tummies *before* bed by "tanking up" (see pages 93–95), which includes cluster feeding (giving extra feeds in the evening) and a dream feed (a ten or eleven o'clock feed during which you try *not* to wake the baby).

Knowing—and responding to—the signs of hunger. You must always feed a hungry baby. One common problem, though, is that parents, especially in the first few weeks, tend to interpret every cry as hunger. That's why I went into great detail about cries and body language in my first book. Crying might indicate hunger or pain caused by gas, reflux, or colic. Your crying baby could also be overtired, or too hot or cold. (See the crying questions on pages 24 and 109.) This is why it's so important to learn your baby's cues. **What does he sound and look like when he's crying?** You'll know his little tummy is empty (even before that first wail) if you pay close attention, because you'll see him lick his lips first and then start to root. His tongue will come out, and he'll turn his head like a baby bird looking for food. Although he's too young at this point to bring his fist to his mouth and chew or suck on it, he might reach for what I call the "feeding triangle"—which has the nose as its tip and the mouth as its bottom. He'll flail his arms and try to hit the feeding triangle but of course he can't actually zero in on it. If you don't give him a bottle or breast in response to his body language, he'll emit a vocal cue. You'll hear a kind of cough-like sound in the back of his throat and finally, the first cry, which is short to begin with and then a steady waa, waa, waa rhythm.

Of course, if your baby wakes up in the middle of the night crying, you don't have the benefit of the visual cues. But if you listen carefully, with a little practice you'll hear the difference in his cries. If you're unsure, try a pacifier first (if you have mixed feelings about pacifiers, read my thoughts on them, later in this chapter, pages 199–200). If that soothes him, put him back into bed, swaddled. If he rejects the pacifier, you know that it's hunger or pain.

Does she wake at different times every night? As I explained earlier, erratic waking almost always indicates hunger. If you're not sure about the pattern, keep track for a few nights. But you also have to consider other questions:

Is he steadily gaining weight? This is a concern of mine with babies after six weeks, especially if Mum is breast-feeding for the first time. It often takes as long as the first six weeks for breast milk to be established. Lack of weight gain could be a sign that the baby is not getting enough to eat, either because Mum's milk supply is still insufficient or because he's having trouble suckling.

A PLAN: If your baby is not gaining weight steadily, consult your pediatrician. You can also do a yield to rule out inadequate milk supply (see page 104). If your baby is bobbing on and off the breast, it could mean you have a slow let-down. If so, you need to "prime" your breasts to get the milk flowing: Use a breast pump and extract milk for two minutes before you actually put your baby on your breast. If your baby is having trouble sucking, get a lactation consultation to make sure he's latched on properly (page 102) or doesn't have some sort of anatomical problem that prevents proper sucking.

Growth spurts. You might have had no difficulties in the feeding department. You might have had your baby on a great routine. Still, at around six weeks, twelve weeks, and at various intervals thereafter, your baby will probably go through growth spurts. His appetite will increase for a few days, and even if he's been sleeping five or six hours at a stretch, he'll suddenly start waking during the night for a feed. I get tons of calls from parents of two-, three-, or four-month-old children: "We had an angel baby and now we have a devil. He's waking up two times a night and downing both breasts. We can't seem to fill him up." I ask, **Has he ever slept a five- or six-hour stretch at night?** Invariably, when parents tell me that their baby *was* sleeping well and suddenly started waking up, I know it's a growth spurt. Here's an example:

> Damian is 12 weeks old. I started putting him down for naps in his crib two weeks ago. For the most part, he goes down easily and sleeps for 1 or 1½ hours. One week ago today, we started putting him down for the night in his crib. He goes down without crying but he wakes in the middle of the night anywhere from 2 to 3 hours all night long. I swaddle him and give him a paci when he goes down. He whimpers in the middle of the night and I go in and he's unswaddled and his paci is out. I put the paci in and he goes back to sleep. While he's asleep I reswaddle him, hoping this is the last time he will wake up. But this is a nonstop cycle. He will cry if I don't go to him. I don't know what to do!!! Please help me!!

This is a classic example of a so-called sleep problem that is actually a food problem. But because this mum is concentrating on the fact that she just moved her baby into a crib, she doesn't seem have considered hunger. The tip-off is that Damian is waking every two to three hours, which sounds like a feeding schedule. To be sure, I'd ask all the hunger-related questions, including whether Mum is breast-feeding—perhaps her milk is not sufficient to sustain Damian. In any case, my suggestion would be to try upping Damian's food during the day.

This is the point when a lot parents first get into trouble. Because they haven't recognized a growth spurt or they don't know what to do about it, they start feeding the baby at night, instead of upping his calories *during the day*. And when they start feeding at night, they set up a pattern of accidental parenting.

A PLAN: It's a matter of conscious parenting. Notice what your baby is consuming during the day and at night. If you're formula-feeding, and he's draining his bottle at each feed, give him more. So let's say he's having five four-ounce feeds a day, and you see that he's waking in the middle of the night and taking another four ounces. That means he needs four more ounces during the day. But you don't add another feed. You add an ounce to each of the five bottles.

If you're breast-feeding, it's a little more complicated, because you have to send a message to your body to manufacture more milk. So, for three days, you have to take steps to increase your milk production. You can do this in one of two ways:

A. Pump one hour after each feed. Even though you'll only get an ounce or two, put that extra bit of breast milk into a bottle and use it to "top off" your baby at her next feed. Do this for three days, and by the third day, your body will be producing the extra amount that your baby needs.

B. At each feed, have your baby empty one breast, and then put her on the other breast. When she's emptied the second breast, switch back to the first. Even though it will feel empty to you, the body always produces milk in response to a baby's suckling (which is how wet-nursing works). Let her suckle for a few minutes on the first breast and then a few minutes on the second breast. Feeds will take longer with this method but it, too, will induce your body to boost your milk production.

Using a pacifier. When parents tell me, "My baby wants to feed all night," I always suspect that they're confusing hunger cues with a baby's instinctual need to suck. To find out, I ask, **Does your baby have a pacifier?** Some people suggest using a pacifier only if a baby needs a bit of extra comforting, but I'm all for them at this age. A pacifier helps to calm babies down. Very few babies become pacifier-dependent (see box, page 189), and in those cases I suggest that parents discontinue their use. However, in my experience, most babies suckle themselves to sleep and, once they're off to Dreamland, the pacifier falls out, and they continue to sleep peacefully. Using a pacifier when a baby wakes up early from a nap or during the middle of the night is also a good way to test whether your baby is actually hungry or just needs to suck.

Parents are sometimes shocked and resistant: "I don't want my kid walking around the mall with a pacifier in her mouth," one mum objected. I heartily agreed with her. I would never *start* a baby four months or older on a pacifier if she hasn't ever had one. But her "kid" was two weeks old—walking around the mall was a long way off. Although I advise parents to start weaning babies off their pacifier by around three or four months, or later (especially if you confine pacifier use to the crib), babies under that age *need* the extra suckling time. They can't yet find their own fingers, so suckling is their only form of self-soothing.

Parents who resist using a pacifier in these early months often get into a very bad pattern. When a baby is only allowed to suck on the bottle or breast, she either doesn't feed efficiently or is fed too often. The tip-off to me of the former is that the mum will call and say, "I can't get the baby off my breast—she takes an hour to feed." The baby does that loose jaw sucking thing that means she's using the time not to eat but to just suckle. Similarly, when a baby is trying to fall asleep and comfort herself, she instinctively starts to suck. She *seems* hungry but is actually just settling down to sleep. Misreading the cues, Mum offers the bottle or breast. That calms the little one but she doesn't eat much because she wasn't really hungry—she just needed to suck. Both are examples of how accidental parenting starts. The baby who is allowed to feed for an hour becomes a snacker. And the one who is suckled to sleep repeatedly becomes a baby who depends on breast or bottle to fall asleep.

Admittedly, some babies resist a pacifier at first, as this email exemplifies:

> My five-week-old infant, Lili, is an extremely alert baby. She nurses, has wake time, and then when it is time for a nap, I can't get her to go down unless I nurse her again for a few minutes. Lili will not accept a pacifier and I have tried everything to get her into sleepy mode and it seems that my breast is the only thing that works. Can you help me?

I can assure you, if that mum keeps giving Lili her breast (a particularly common form of accidental parenting), she'll regret it in a few months, maybe earlier. Remember that it takes, on average, twenty minutes for any baby to fall asleep, perhaps even longer for an extremely alert baby.

A PLAN: Mum needs to keep trying the pacifier during Lili's waking hours, and she should also try different types, starting with ones that resemble her own nipples Also, if she just shoves a pacifier into Lili's mouth, without placing it properly, her little one will most likely reject it. Putting it on her tongue will make the baby's tongue go flat, and she won't grasp it with her lips. Instead, she has to position the paci so that it hits the roof of Lili's mouth. Mum must be persistent—she has to do it until Lili takes it.

Variable #5: Overstimulation

An overstimulated or overtired baby can't fall asleep, tends to sleep fitfully when he does, and often can't stay asleep either. Therefore, one of the most critical keys to aiding a baby's sleep is to start your wind-down ritual as soon as you see his first yawn or first jerky movement (see Variable #2; page 181, about the sleep window).

Nap problems. Daytime sleep patterns tell me a lot about whether overstimulation or overtiredness play a role in nighttime sleep problems. **Have his naps during the day gotten shorter, or have they always been less than forty minutes?** If your baby always took short naps, that might just be his biorhythm. If his naps are short, he's not cranky during the day, and he's sleeping well at night, then there's nothing to fix. But if his napping pattern has changed, it often means he's overstimulated during the day. In turn, he's probably not getting a good night's rest either. Remember that good sleep begets good sleep. Unlike adults who become exhausted and pass out when they're tired—and are able to catch up on their sleep—babies get *more* revved up with less sleep. (Which is why you don't keep a baby up later in hopes that he will sleep better or stay asleep longer.)

This is a typical email: "I have a three-month-old, and every time I put him in the crib for a nap he either cries right away or wakes up within ten or twenty minutes. Do you have any suggestions?" Some babies, around eight to sixteen weeks, might start taking twenty- to forty-minute power naps. If the baby seems even-tempered in his waking hours and sleeps well at night, short naps might be all that he needs. (Sorry, Mum, I know you were looking forward to longer naps!) But if a child is out of sorts after a nap and his nighttime sleep is fitful or interrupted, his short naps are obviously a problem. Chances are he's overstimulated, and as he drops into a deep sleep after twenty or more minutes, that jolt of the body wakes him up. Often, parents accidentally reinforce the pattern by going in to the child at once and cuddling him instead of letting him fall back to sleep on his own.

> ## Tip-Off #5
>
> These complaints often indicate that **overstimulation** is at least in part responsible for your baby's sleep problem:
>
> *My baby doesn't settle down to sleep easily.*
>
> *My baby wakes frequently or sleeps fitfully, often crying at night.*
>
> *My baby fights taking his afternoon nap.*
>
> *My baby falls asleep but then suddenly jolts himself awake a few minutes later.*
>
> *My baby resists going down for a nap, and when he does, he won't nap for more than a half hour or 40 minutes.*
>
> *We just started a new play group, and my baby's started waking up in the night.*

A PLAN: Look at what you're doing during the day, and especially in the afternoon. Try not to have too much company or do too many errands. And don't involve her in stimulating activities before bed or nap times—too-bright colors or even too much kitchy-koo can rev up an infant. Most important, take more time with your wind-down ritual (pages 181–186), including the shush-pat. And remember that overstimulated babies often take twice as long to settle down. They don't drift into sleep—they jolt into sleep, and sometimes that sudden start wakes them up. Stay with her until you see that she's in a deep sleep. (More on nap problems in older babies on pages 249–252.)

Missing the window. I've also found that parents sometimes *ignore* their baby's sleep cues. **Do you frequently keep your baby up because you think he will sleep longer?** This is one of the most destructive sleep myths. The reality is that if you keep him up past his sleep window and allow him to get into the overtired zone, he not only won't stay asleep longer, he'll have a restless sleep and perhaps even wake prematurely.

A PLAN: Stick to your routine. Observe your baby's cues. Both of you will be a lot happier if his naps are consistent. Once in a while it's okay to veer from your routine, but some children are easily thrown. Know who your child is. If he's a Touchy, Grumpy, or Spirited baby, I would say that it's never a good idea to depart from your routine.

Do you keep your baby up for company, or so that you and/or Dad can see him after work? I understand how hard it is for working parents to be separated from their baby during the day. But it's really selfish to ask an infant to conform to an adult's work schedule. A baby needs to sleep. If you keep your baby up later, chances are your time with him won't be particularly enjoyable, because your baby will be overtired and out of sorts. If you or Dad want to spend more time with the baby, come home earlier or carve out other times to be with him. Many working

---

Start Now

Build in Quiet Time

Parents nowadays are eager to make their children smarter, to make sure they know their colors and have watched every educational kid video on the market. No wonder children are overstimulated. The antidote for our fast-paced culture is to build in quiet time for your infant. Encourage low-key activities during the day—staring at a mobile, cuddling with a person or a soft stuffed animal for a while. While you're at it, give her quiet time in her crib. Let her see that it's a nice place for quiet play, not just a place to sleep. It will pay off in the months ahead as your baby starts to become more mobile (see sidebar, page 238).

mothers rise a little earlier to do the morning ritual. Dads often take over the dream feed. But whatever you do, don't deprive your child of sleep.

Developmental disturbances. Overstimulation is often caused by physical development. The baby's growing body actually works against peaceful sleep. **Has your baby recently made physical advances— turning her head, finding her fingers, rolling over?** Often parents complain, "I put my baby down in the center of the crib, and a few hours later, he's crying. When I go in, he's all scrunched up in the corner. Could he have hit his head?" Yes, he could. Or they'll say, "My baby was sleeping fine until she started to roll over." What happens is that the parents put the baby down on her side, and even if they swaddle her she manages to wriggle out and roll from side to back. The problem is, she can't roll back to her original position, and that might wake her and frustrate her. Also, because babies are totally uncoordinated at this age, they can easily disturb themselves when they flail their little arms and legs. They wriggle a hand out of the swaddle, pull their ears and their hair, poke themselves in the eyes—and wonder who's doing it to them. Their little fingers absently scratch the sheet, and the noise can wake them up. They also start to realize that they can make little noises that both entertain and disturb them.

A PLAN: Seeing your baby master her body is exciting. You can't, and wouldn't want to, stop development. But there will be periods when physical development definitely stands in the way of sleep. Let's say rolling over is a frequent problem. Use a wedge or rolled-up towels on either side of your baby's body to keep him stable. During the day, you also could start teaching him to roll back the other way, but that might take two months! Obviously, some of these changes you just have to ride out. Others are solved by swaddling.

Increased activities. As the day wears on, babies get more and more tired, just from regular activities, like being changed, taking in their immediate environment, hearing the dog bark and the doorbell ring and the vacuum cleaner hum. By three or four o'clock, they're already tired. Now add to that the kind of activities available to mothers nowadays. That's a lot for a little being to handle. **How much stimulation does your baby get during the day? Have you introduced more activities? If so, does she tend to have sleep disturbances on that particular day?** Overstimulation is often a cause of babies' sleep problems ("We just started a new play group"). If a child seems to love a particular Mummy and Me group or a music class, you may decide that a day's poor sleep is worth it. But if an activity disturbs your child's sleep more than that one day, you probably should reevaluate it. For Touchy babies, who are hypersensitive to stimulation, baby yoga and baby this and that may not be a good idea. Wait a few months and try again. A mother recently told me, "My baby cried through group." That's a sign right there.

A PLAN: If too much activity seems to affect your baby's sleep, don't go out after two and three in afternoon. Now that's not always possible, I realize. You may have an older child you have to pick up at 3:30. If so, you might either make other arrangements, or accept that the baby might fall asleep in the car on the way there and back and might not get as good a nap as she would in her own bed. Given the circumstances, you can't avoid that. You could leave her asleep in the car seat and consider that nap time. Or, if she's cranky in the car—some babies don't like to sleep in their car seats—you have to calm her down at home and try to at least get her to take a forty-five-minute catnap in the late afternoon before dinner. It won't ruin her sleep. In fact, she'll sleep better for it.

Tip-Off #6

These complaints often indicate that **discomfort** is at least in part responsible for your baby's sleep problem:

My baby doesn't settle down to sleep easily.

My baby wakes up frequently at night.

My baby falls asleep but then wakes up within a few minutes.

My baby only falls asleep in an upright position, like the swing or car seat.

My baby seems tired, but the minute I start to put her down, she cries.

Variable #6: Discomfort

It's obvious: Babies cry when they're hungry and overtired, but they also cry when they're in pain, uncomfortable (too hot or cold), or sick. The question is, which is it?

Looking for signs of discomfort. As I've said repeatedly, a structured routine enables you to make a better-educated guess about the cause of your child's crying. But you also have to use your powers of observation. **What does he sound and look like when he's crying?** If your baby grimaces, if his body gets rigid, if he pulls his legs up or flails wildly in his sleep or when trying to get to sleep, any and all of these signs might be indications of pain. A pain cry is more shrill and high pitched than hunger. Also, there are different kinds of pain cries. For instance, the look and sound of a gas cry is different from reflux—as are the strategies you employ to make your baby more receptive to sleep (see pages 109–115).

The important thing to remember is that at this age babies don't usually cry because of accidental parenting—it's because they *need* something. It's true that a baby who cries the moment you put him down could be one who's had some accidental parenting. He's now used to his parents' carrying him, and that's what he thinks going to sleep involves. But it also could be reflux if your baby cries when you try to put him down. In a horizontal position, the stomach acid comes up and burns his esophagus. **Does he only fall asleep in his car seat, infant seat, or swing?** As I explained on page 112, one of the red flags of reflux is the baby who only sleeps in an upright position. The trouble is, they get used to an upright position and can't sleep any other way.

A PLAN: If you suspect that some type of intestinal pain is keeping your baby up or waking her, reread pages 109–115, which will help you differentiate between gas, colic, and reflux, and give you suggestions for managing each condition (also see "The Vicious Cycle of Reflux" at the end of this chapter, page 215). Rather than encouraging swing addiction, or having to drive around or put her car seat in her crib, take steps to make her more comfortable in her own bed. Elevate the bed and any other surfaces you lay her on, like the changing table. Also, fold a receiving blanket in thirds, and wrap it around your baby's waist, like a cummerbund, and then use another blanket to swaddle her. The cummerbund's gentle pressure can ease the pain in a far safer way than putting your baby to sleep on her stomach, which parents of reflux babies are often tempted to do.

Constipation. Like old people who sit around and watch TV, young babies have limited mobility so they tend to get constipated, which can disturb their sleep. **How many poops a day does she make?** If you answer, "My baby hasn't had a poop for three days," I also have to ask, **Is she formula-fed or breast-fed?** because "normal" is different in formula-fed and breast-fed babies. If a formula-fed baby goes for three days, she might be constipated. The problem doesn't happen as often with breast-fed babies, who poop almost after every feed and then all of a sudden they don't poop for three or four days. That's normal. All the breast milk has been absorbed, gone into the system to form fat cells. If a breast-fed baby cries for no other apparent reason, is bringing his knees up to his chest, and seems to be uncomfortable, he may be constipated, too. He might also have a distended tummy, eat less, and/or have deeper yellow and more pungent urine, which might indicate that he's a bit dehydrated.

A PLAN: If your baby is formula-fed, make sure she gets at least four extra ounces of water a day or water mixed with prune juice (one ounce of prune to three of water). Give her an ounce at a time, one hour after each feed. (Also be sure that you're mixing the right amount of water with the formula, as I explained in the sidebar on page 97.) It can also help to bicycle her legs.

With breast-fed babies, use the same remedy. However, you might want to wait a week to see if he's really constipated. If you're really concerned, see your pediatrician, who can assess whether any other problems exist.

Wet discomfort. Before twelve weeks, most infants don't cry from being wet, especially if they're in disposable diapers that wick the moisture away from them. However, some infants—particularly Grumpy and Touchy types—are particularly sensitive even at a young age and will wake up if they feel wet.

A PLAN: Change her, reswaddle, and calm her, and then put her back down. Use lots of diaper cream, especially at night, as a barrier against her urine burning her skin.

Thermal discomfort. Before twelve weeks it's up to parents to regulate a baby's temperature. He will show signs of being too cold, hot, or clammy. **Do you feel his body when he wakes up—is he sweaty or clammy or cold?** The room may be too hot or too cold, especially when going from summer to winter. Feel his extremities. Put your hand over his nose and forehead. If it's cold, he's cold. **Is he very wet when he wakes up or soaked through?** Urine goes cold, and that can make his entire body cold. On the other hand, some babies overheat, even in winter. In the summer, some babies also get clammy hands, feet, and head. They ball up their fists and curl their toes under.

A PLAN: Raise or lower the temperature of your baby's room. If he's cold, swaddle him in a second blanket or a warmer one, and comfort him. Put an extra pair of socks under his sleeper. If he kicks out of his swaddle, and this is a regular occurrence, you might invest in one of those fleece sleepers which stay nice and warm all night.

If your baby is warm or clammy, never place his crib under or near an air conditioning vent. Depending on how hot it is outside, you might even want to use a fan in front of an open window, which will bring air inside but not blow directly on the baby. (Insect bites are worse to deal with than heat. So make sure there's a screen in the window.) Don't use an undershirt under his sleeper. Use a lighter receiving blanket. If that doesn't work, you might have to resort to what we did with baby Frank, who was so naturally hot that he sweated through his pj's every night. We had to swaddle him naked with only his diaper on.

Using the Six Variables: What Comes First?

As I said earlier, the six variables are not in any particular order. Also, many represent overlapping issues. For example, when parents don't have a routine, they often lack a consistent bedtime ritual as well. Where a baby is overstimulated or overtired, I usually suspect that some degree of accidental parenting is at work, too. Indeed, more often than not, sleep disturbances are caused by at least two if not three or four of the variables—at which point parents ask, "So what do I tackle *first*?"

Here are five common-sense guidelines to go by:

1. *No matter what other variables are at work and what other steps you have to take, keep or establish your routine and a consistent wind-down ritual.* In virtually every instance of a child having problems settling down or staying asleep, I recommend doing the Four S ritual and staying with the child until he's in a deep sleep.

2. *Make changes in the day before you tackle nighttime issues.* None of us are at our best in the middle of the night. Besides, making changes in the day often solves nighttime problems without your having to *do* anything extra.

3. *Deal with the most urgent issue first.* Use your common sense. If, for example, you realize that your baby is waking because your milk supply is insufficient or because she's going through a growth spurt, your first priority is to give her more food. If your baby is in pain, no technique will work until her discomfort is relieved.

4. *Be a "P.C." parent.* Dealing with sleep difficulties requires patience and consciousness. You need patience to effect change. Expect each step to take *at least* three days, or longer if somehow the bond of trust between you and your baby has been broken. You need consciousness to hone your awareness, of your baby's sleep signs and of his reactions to this new regime.

5. *Expect some regression.* Parents will call and say, "He was doing beautifully and now he's suddenly waking up at four A.M. again." This is very common (especially with little boys). Go back to Square One and start all over again. But please, please, please, don't change the rules on your child. Once you commit to trying any of the strategies I suggest, stay with them and, if necessary, repeat them.

To help you see how these guidelines affect my thinking, I'm going to share a series of real-life cases with you. They are taken from emails I've received (I've changed names and some details). If you've read through this chapter thus far (instead of starting at the end like I do sometimes!), you should be able to spot the telling phrases in each email and to problem-solve right alongside me.

How Much Sleep Help Is Too Much?

Remember that in the early months we're *teaching* babies to go to sleep. Particularly if you've tried other methods, it can take weeks, even a month, to change a pattern or calm a baby who's become fearful. Sometimes parents get confused and wonder, as Hailey's mother does, "when our job ends and her job begins."

> We have read your book and loved it, especially after being dissatisfied with other methods recommending "crying it out." Our nine-week-old baby girl, Hailey, is now able to take naps, thanks to your insights—something she never did consistently before—and is sleeping between 6 to 7 hours a night, which you can imagine is a Godsend.
>
> Sometimes Hailey goes right to sleep. However, more often than not, she fusses a little and flails her arms and legs. This flailing keeps her awake or will even wake her up when she has just fallen asleep. To help her along during these more difficult times, we often swaddle her from the waist down (or fully if she is overtired or overstimulated), and we stay with her, "shushing" her rhythmically, and patting her belly. This will usually lull her to sleep. We are concerned that we are becoming a tool for her to fall asleep during her naps. At night, she seems to have no problem going to sleep.

When should we stop trying to help Hailey sleep? If she isn't crying, but still wide awake and fighting sleep, should we just walk away? What do we do when she starts crying again? It is hard to tell when our job ends and her job begins.

When a young baby needs help, we give it. Rather than worry about "spoiling" her, we keep the focus on reading her cues and meeting her needs. We also need to hang in there. In this case, the parents are *not* doing too much—in fact, they *need* to stay with Hailey to help her fall asleep. I suspect that trying "cry it out" methods has compromised this baby's trust. Hailey is not sure her parents will be there for her. Also, if she "fusses a lit-tle and flails her arms and legs," she's overtired and perhaps overstimu-lated. Mum may be doing too many stimulating activities before her nap time, and perhaps not taking the time to transition from activity to sleep with a proper sleep ritual. I'd suggest *always* swaddling her, and not just the bottom half of her body. (Remember that babies under three months don't realize that their arms are part of them. When they're tired, they're more likely to flail about, and those waving appendages disturb them!) Hailey sounds like a baby who needs to feel safe and needs extra calming down. Unless her parents stick with it now, taking the extra time during the day and before bed, they'll regret it in the months to come.

How Parents' Needs Can Overshadow the Baby's

Sometimes parents' self-interest stands in the way of seeing the real issues. They seem to forget they have *a baby* who needs to be taught how to sleep and, even after learning the skills of self-soothing, won't sleep twelve hours at night. In many of these cases, the so-called problem is more about satisfying the parents' needs or their desire to fit the child into their lifestyle without much inconvenience on their part. Consider the following from a mother about to go back to work who is trying to rush the baby along to meet *her* schedule.

My son Sandor is 11 weeks old and I have just started trying your method. It's been about four days and I don't know what to do about two things: 1. He gets tired around 8 or 9 at night and I'm scared if I put him in his crib he will sleep and then wake me in the middle of the night. He is typically giving me anywhere from 5–7 hours at night. He gave me 7 hours one night and then the next night 9. Then he reverted to his 4 A.M. wake-up again. So do I put him down for the night at 8 or see if he just naps? Very scary. 2. Then there is the fact that he does wake me up around 4–4:30. Do I use the pacifier and try to put him back to sleep and if he doesn't, do I feed him? Will this establish a habit of eating in the middle of the night? Also, how long do I try to get him to go back to sleep with the pacifier if that's the way for me to go? I go back to work full-time in 10 days and am petrified that he will keep me up at night draining both of us.

Whew! I got exhausted myself reading that email. Sandor's mother is obviously very disturbed and distressed. But she says that at eleven weeks little Sandor slept for seven and nine hours at a time. Sounds pretty good in my book. I know mums that would kill for a baby like that!

This mother's major concern is the fact that her son has "reverted" to waking at 4 A.M. and disturbing *her* sleep. I suspect he's going through a growth spurt. He had already gotten to the point of sleeping long stretches, which tells me his tummy is big enough to hold an amount of food that could sustain him for seven hours. To confirm my hunch, I would need to know more about what's happening in the day—how much Sandor is eating, whether he's fed by formula or by breast. I suspect that he's waking out of hunger. (While habitual waking is usually the result of accidental parenting, there are exceptions, especially when other hunger clues are present.) If he's hungry, she has to feed him and then up his calories during the day. If she starts feeding Sandor during the night instead, it will establish a habit and then she'll really have a problem on her hands.

But there's even more to this email than meets the eye, and if she's ever going to have peace of mind at work, Sandor's mother has to step back and look at the whole picture. For one thing, it's clear to me that her son has no routine. Otherwise, he wouldn't be staying up as late as 8 or 9 P.M. She needs to move his bedtime back to 7 and give him a dream feed at 11 (and most likely continue that dream feed until Sandor starts solid food). But Mum is a bit impatient and unrealistic, too. Sandor is almost three months old, and the older a baby is, the longer it takes to change bad habits. She is upset that she's not seeing any changes after only *four* days. Some babies take longer. (I also don't know what she means by "just started trying your approach"—it certainly doesn't sound like Sandor is on E.A.S.Y.) She needs to stick with one plan and ride it out. As for her return to work, if she's been breast-feeding I would also want to ask whether she's introduced a bottle, and who's going to be looking after the child. She has to start looking at more than her own fatigue.

Improper Intervention: No P.U./P.D. Before Three Months

Some parents who've read about my pick-up/put-down method (P.U./ P.D.; see the next chapter) try it on babies under three months, which is too stimulating for a young baby and therefore rarely works. Besides, as I will explain in the next chapter, P.U./P.D. is meant as a teaching tool to help babies learn how to self-soothe, and before three months, your baby is too young to start. Only the shush-pat is appropriate for calming infants. Typically when parents try P.U./P.D. at a too-young age, accidental parenting and other variables are also at work, and the parents grasp for anything that might help without realizing that their baby isn't developmentally ready:

> I have what by Tracy's definition is mostly an angel baby. Ivan is about four weeks old. About half the time I put him down for his nap he goes down easily for about 10 minutes, putting himself to sleep, then wakes up fussing so much and squirming. He's already turning himself over for a week now—so much that he comes out of his swaddle. He gets so agitated that it takes me an hour and more of picking up/putting down to get him to sleep. Sometimes he fidgets all the way through nap time until the next scheduled feeding. What should I do? He is so good most of the time this is quite disheartening.

First of all, P.U./P.D. can actually make the situation worse because a baby gets overstimulated when you keep picking him up. Also, Mum might not be doing it correctly. She might be picking him up and allowing him to fall asleep in her arms. Then when she puts him down, he startles and wakes. If that's the case, she's also starting a bad pattern of accidental parenting. My suggestion would be for her to go back to basics and spend time doing the Four S wind-down ritual with Ivan. After all, her son goes down easily for his nap, then he squirms. It tells me that during the ten-minute period his mother describes, he goes through the first stages of sleep but then she leaves the room. She needs to take an extra ten minutes *with* him, to make sure he's fast asleep. If she stands by the crib, pats him when his little eyes pop open again, and also shields his eyes with her hand to block out visual stimulation, I guarantee he'll go back to sleep and stay asleep. But each time the cycle is interrupted, she has to start over again. If she doesn't spend the time now, he won't be an Angel baby for long!

First Things First

As I explained at the outset of this chapter, many sleep problems have multiple causes. Naturally, parents are desperate. Some realize they've gone wrong along the way; others don't. Regardless, we need to figure out what to do first. The following, from Maureen, is one for the books, as they say:

> Dylan has been a fussy sleeper for all 7 weeks of his life. He started out with days and nights reversed. He has disliked sleeping in his bassinet from the start and this has gotten worse over time. He has cried for more than an hour in there and even when I try the pick him up, put him down method, it didn't work. He fights sleep regularly, startles himself awake after 5, 10, 15 minutes, if and when he does fall asleep, and then can't put himself back to sleep. He wants to be held and cuddled most of the day and night and usually sleeps well then. Things are getting worse—now he won't even sleep well during a ride in the car or stroller because he startles awake (at least I used to be able to count on this). I love your philosophy and want to give Dylan independence and healthy sleep habits. I've tried many suggestions from your book but they just don't seem to fit Dylan. (I think he is best described by your spirited category.) I need to get Dylan on some sleep schedule but can never count on him taking a nap or staying asleep under any circumstances.

Throughout her email Maureen seems to attribute willfulness to Dylan ("he fights," "he wants," "he dislikes," "can never count on him taking a nap or staying asleep"). She avoids taking responsibility for what *she* has done (or not done) to affect her son's behavior.

Maureen's expectations are also a bit high. She says, "He started out with days and nights reversed." All babies do start on a twenty-four-hour clock, and if parents don't teach them to separate day from night (see pages 177–179), how will they know the difference? She points out that Dylan "can't put himself back to sleep," but, again, as far as I can see no one has taught him how! Instead, they've taught him that sleeping means being held and cuddled.

But the most telling part of Maureen's email is her revelation that Dylan "has cried for more than an hour in there." By leaving Dylan to cry on his own for so long, she has broken the bond of trust. No wonder he's now hard to console. Adding insult to injury, the parents have employed all sorts of props to get Dylan to sleep—holding him, putting him in the stroller, car rides. I'm not surprised things are getting worse. The fact that Dylan regularly "startles himself awake after five, ten, fifteen minutes" tells me that he is also overstimulated.

In other words, from Day One, Dylan hasn't been respected or listened to. His cries are his way of speaking to his parents, but they haven't paid attention or taken any action in response to his "requests." If he cried because he "disliked sleeping in his bassinet from the start," why didn't they consider another alternative? Some babies, especially Spirited and Touchy types, are very sensitive to their environment. Bassinets usually have flimsy two-inch mattresses, and maybe Dylan was uncomfortable. I'd wager that as he gained weight and became even more aware of his surroundings, he became increasingly uncomfortable.

To sum it up, rather than listen and respond to Dylan, his parents have employed one quick fix after another. I suspect that Maureen also tried P.U./P.D. ("I've tried many suggestions from your book"), which is not appropriate for such a young child. So where to start? It's clear that this mother has to commit to a structured routine—waking him every three hours in the day for a feed will deal with the day-for-night issue. But first she has to get him out of the bassinet, which is probably uncomfortable, and, at the same time, begin to build back the trust. She should begin with the cushion method I describe on page 194 and very gradually move him to his crib. His parents have to do the Four S ritual—setting the stage for sleep, swaddling him, sitting with him, and doing the shush-pat—*at every sleep time, not just at night.* And each time, someone has to stay at Dylan's side until he's fast asleep.

Another common sleep scenario that involves multiple variables happens when parents follow the baby, instead of establishing a structured routine. The baby gets confused—she never knows what's coming next. And the parents are less likely to be able to "read" her cues. This has a reverberating effect, causing chaos and confusion in the whole family and giving rise not only to sleep disturbances (yours and the baby's and siblings' if there are any), but also to dramatic and negative changes in a baby's personality, as Joan's email about her six-week-old exemplifies. I'd bet little Ellie probably started out as an Angel baby but is fast becoming a Grumpy type:

> . . . She is feeding well from a bottle and alert and smiling, but I am having difficulty reading her sleep cues. I feel like I spend the greatest part of my day encouraging sleep. It can take 60 minutes of soothing, patting, etc., to get 20 minutes of sleep. This concerns me as she is overtired and grumpy for a large part of her day.
>
> Ellie generally sleeps well overnight and I feel like she has worked out the difference between day and night. She can sleep for a 7- or 6-hour stretch at night and then follow with another long stretch. We have to feed her sometimes only twice from 6–7 P.M. and 6–7 A.M. Why would she only sleep for such short periods during the day? She wakes up grumpy and tired, often crying. I pat and rub her tummy and talk soothingly to her. She seems to go into stage 3 and then drift off on her own but wakes or bounces out of stage 3 and wants to play. As if she's had an hour's rest. What can I do to encourage day sleep?
>
> I have tried implementing E.A.S.Y., but find that she often is sleepy with her feed because she is overtired from a short nap in the previous eat activity sleep cycle. I am being treated for postnatal depression. I had PND with three-year-old Allison as well. Allison's day naps were forty-five minutes and she was a good sleeper at night. With her, too, I spent a lot of time encouraging day sleep. I eventually gave into it. Grateful that she was pretty good to us at night from 4–5 months sleeping 12–15 hrs up until about 18 months. It's now a solid 11–12 hrs. I can't complain. She is dropping her day sleep.

Although Joan says she "tried implementing E.A.S.Y.," she's clearly following her baby instead. She is allowing Ellie to sleep through two feeds, one during each of the two long stretches she describes. A six-week-old baby needs to eat every three hours during the day. It's great that Ellie can last for a six- or seven-hour stretch at night, but she shouldn't be allowed to follow that with "another long stretch" of sleep. Of course she's sleeping for "such short periods during the day." She's just come out of a twelve- or fourteen-hour period of sleep. That's fine for a three-year-old, but Ellie is a baby. Joan, who is obviously having her own emotional problems, might be grateful that her baby is letting her sleep in the morning, but she's also paying the price. Ellie wakes up "grumpy and tired, often crying" because she's hungry.

Ellie's daytime sleep will improve naturally if her mother wakes her for a feed instead of allowing her to sleep through it. In other words, she has to start her on E.A.S.Y., feeding her at 7, 10, 1, 4, 7, and a dream feed at 11. Given Ellie's track record, she'll sleep through until 7 the next morning.

Ellie's mother also has to *look at her baby*. She needs to accept who Ellie is. Interestingly, Joan has important information at her fingertips about her child, but she's just not putting it all together. Ellie is her second child, and if I'm not mistaken, she has many similarities to her older sister Allison, who also took forty-five-minute naps and was a good sleeper at night. Joan says she "eventually gave into" Allison's natural sleep cycles, but she's not doing the same with Ellie. I'll just bet that if she feeds Ellie every three hours during the day, and allows her one good stretch of sleep at night, her mood will improve. As for her day sleep, Ellie, like her older sister, might only need forty-five-minute naps. And Joan will just have to live with that.

The Vicious Cycle of Reflux

I get countless emails from parents who say their babies "never sleep" or are "up constantly." Some have already been diagnosed with reflux, but the parents are still having trouble making their babies comfortable enough to sleep. Others don't realize that their babies are in pain, but certain clues let me know that the baby is not just a "fitful sleeper"—she's in pain. Admittedly, reflux, especially serious cases, wreaks havoc in a household. Often, the routine is totally thrown off kilter as well. In all of these cases, you have to deal with the pain first. Interestingly, even parents who are aware that their child has reflux often don't realize how interrelated all these issues are, as this email from Vanessa, the "desperate mummy of a five-week-old" exemplifies.

> We're working on many of your sleep techniques but are really struggling. As soon as Timothy begins to show signs of being tired we put him in his crib. The first 2 nights that we did this we got 5 straight hours out of him. That was last week and we haven't gotten that since. He seems to get stuck on the 3rd stage. He'll yawn, do the 7 mile stare, and then when he's almost settled, he does the third stage jolt. He goes through the whole process all over again. He'll start crying so we reassure him, he settles down, and then the whole vicious cycle starts again. It's getting exhausting and is taking hours. He is worse during nap time also. We're trying to keep the same routine, but it's becoming frustrating. He also has reflux badly, so if he cries too much, which we try to avoid, he vomits. Please help!! (We also took your test in the book, and Tim falls between a Spirited and Touchy baby.)

First of all, like many parents, Vanessa and her mate are not staying with Tim long enough. This is particularly important with Touchy *and* Spirited babies, and this little guy is a combination of the two. Timothy's parents have to be by his side when that third jolt happens. But they also need to deal with the pain caused by his reflux by elevating all areas where they lay him—the changing table as well as the crib. If they haven't already done so, they should seek the help of their pediatrician or a pediatric gastroenterologist who can prescribe antacid and/or pain medication to relieve Tim's symptoms. When you have a baby in pain, you have to give him some relief *first*, by elevating his mattress to a forty-five-degree angle with a wedge (or *Encyclopedia Britannica*!), using a cummerbund under his swaddle, and medicating his condition (see pages 111–114). All the sleep techniques in the world aren't going to work if you have a baby in pain.

To my dismay, however, many parents see medication as a last resort:

> I'm concerned that prolonged feedings and general gassiness are interfering with ten-week-old Gretchen's sleep time. I've followed all the BW advice for several days and no results (e.g., multiple sequential rounds of pat/shush; crib mattress on incline; frequent burping; minimized visual and aural stimulation). I'm

really not sure what to do next. Should I just keep going as is, or is there something I'm missing? Should I escalate to the pediatrician?? I'm exhausted, thinking perhaps Gretchen is too young to "manipulate," however I very much ascribe to Tracy's "start as you mean to go on" mantra. What I'm seeing is not tenable in the long run for either of us . . .

Gretchen definitely has a digestion problem—probably reflux—because prolonged feedings and general gassiness are typical red flags. The fact that in describing possible alternatives, her mother uses the phrase "escalate to the pediatrician," tells me she doesn't realize that she has to deal with her baby's *pain* first and get that sorted out before doing anything else. If you even suspect a digestive problem, check with your pediatrician *first,* not as a last resort.

In particular with reflux babies, you have be very careful not to comfort your baby past the point that he stops crying. It's a certain set-up for accidental parenting. Though you're at your wit's end, don't employ a prop to quiet and soothe your baby. Granted, certain types of props—a car seat, an infant seat, a parent's chest, or a swing—comfort a reflux baby because they elevate the head. I understand parents' desperate need to relieve their baby's discomfort, but if you use a prop, long after the pain of reflux disappears, the baby will still be dependent on it. Here's a typical example:

> My 9-week-old daughter, Tara, has reflux and has been sleeping in her infant seat since she was a week old. It was the only way that she would sleep if not on my chest because she would spit up so much. Now that Tara is bigger (12 lb. 5 oz.) and on medication, I want her to sleep in her crib. My doctor suggested the Ferber method, but my daughter became hysterical. I know there is no way that I can do that again. I read in your book about "accidental parenting" and I know this is what I have done. How can I get her to sleep on her back and then into her crib? She bucks and screams when I lay her down on her back to sleep. I'm going crazy and so is my husband. Any help would be appreciated.

I'm sure you've guessed that Tara's parents have to get her out of her infant seat and off their chests. They have to elevate the mattress; the forty-five-degree angle will feel similar to Tara's infant seat. Because they tried Ferberizing, they probably also have to spend extra time with her before each sleep period. They will need to stay with her until she's asleep, so as to rebuild Tara's trust (see pages 192–195). But I also use this case to exemplify another important point: If Tara was diagnosed at one week, it's now two months later. She probably has almost doubled her birth weight. The dosage of antacid or pain medication originally prescribed might not be enough to ease Tara's pain *now*. The parents need to check with the doctor to make sure they're giving her the proper amount for her weight.

So how did you do? Were you able to diagnose the above cases, figure out what other questions you might have to ask, and put together various plans of action? Can you now analyze your own situation? I realize that this is a lot of information for you to absorb, but that's the good thing about a book. You can refer to it time and time again. I promise that this knowledge of sleep will see you through the months and years to come. It's the foundation on which all my other observations and techniques are built. And the better you are at assessing problems when your baby is three months old or younger, the better prepared you'll be for the rest of the baby and toddler years, which I cover in the next two chapters.

SIX

PICK UP/PUT DOWN

A Sleep Training Tool—Four Months to a Year

⌄

A Severe Case of Accidental Parenting

When I met James, he was five months old and had never slept in his own crib—not for naps and not at night. He couldn't sleep unless his mum was right next to him, in Mum and Dad's bed. But this was no idyllic family bed situation. James's mum, Jackie, had to put herself to bed at eight o'clock every night and lie down with him every morning and afternoon when James took his naps. And his poor dad, Mike, had to sneak in when he came home from work. "If the upstairs light is on I know he's awake," Mike explained. "If not, I have to creep in like a cat burglar." Jackie and Mike turned themselves inside out for their son and he *still* didn't sleep well. In fact, he woke several times a night, and the only way his mother could get him back to sleep was by breast-feeding him. "I know he's not hungry," Jackie admitted to me when we first met. "He just wakes me up for company."

As with many babies who have sleep difficulties during the first year, the problem originated when James was only a month old. When he seemed to "resist" their efforts to put him to sleep, his parents first took shifts in a rocking chair. He'd fall asleep eventually, but the moment they put James down, his eyes would pop open. In desperation, Mum started to calm him by laying him on her chest. The warmth obviously comforted him. Dead tired herself, she lay down in her own bed with him, and the two of them fell asleep. James never went into his own crib again.

Each time James woke, Jackie would put him on her chest and hope that he'd fall back to sleep. "I did whatever I could to delay the inevitable, feeding him again." But of course, she always ended up giving him an extra feed as well. Naturally, James napped better in the day—he was exhausted from being up all night.

By now you should recognize this as a full-blown case of accidental parenting. I get literally thousands of calls and emails from parents of four-month-olds and beyond who tell me that their baby . . .

. . . still wakes frequently at night

. . . gets them up at an ungodly hour in the morning

. . . never takes a long nap (or as one mum put it, "doesn't do naps")

. . . depends on them to get to sleep

The above, in their many variations, are the most common problems of the first year. If parents don't take steps to change the situation, these types of issues get worse and last well into toddlerhood, if not longer. I picked James's case because it embodies all those problems!

By the time babies are three or four months old, they should be on a consistent routine, sleeping in their own cribs for naps and nighttime. They should also have the skills to settle down to sleep and to put themselves back to sleep when they wake up. And they should be sleeping through the night—that is, for at least a full six-hour stretch. But many babies don't meet that description, not at four months, eight months, a year, or even older. And when their parents contact me, they sound a lot like Jackie and Mike. Desperate for help, they know they've taken a wrong turn somewhere, but they have no idea about how to get back on track.

To determine how to solve a sleep problem, especially with older babies, we have to look at the entire day. Every one of the above issues can be traced back to an inconsistent, nonexistent, or inappropriate routine (for example, a five-month-old who's on a three-hour routine). Of course, some degree of accidental parenting is also involved.

Generally, almost every scenario takes the same predictable course: In the first few months, the baby doesn't sleep well or sleeps erratically. The parents look for a quick fix. They take the child into their own bed or let her fall asleep in the swing or the car; or they use themselves—Mum offers the breast for soothing, Dad paces the floor. It takes only two or three nights for a baby to become dependent on the prop. In every case, the solution involves getting the child back onto a good routine. To establish or tweak a routine with a baby three months and older, I teach parents "pick up/put down"—P.U./P.D.

If your baby is sleeping fine and is on a good routine, you don't need P.U./P.D. But if you're reading this, you probably do. This chapter focuses exclusively on P.U./P.D.: what it is and how the technique is modified for different age groups. I highlight typical sleep issues in the first year and walk you through some real-life cases in each age group to show you how P.U./P.D. comes into play. Near the end of the chapter (pages 249–252), I also include a special section on naps, a problem that cuts across age groups. Finally, because many parents have written to me to tell me that P.U./P.D. doesn't work with *their* child, I look at where mums and dads often go wrong.

What Is P.U./P.D.?

Pick up/put down is the cornerstone of my middle-of-the-road philosophy on sleep. It is both a teaching tool and a problem-solving method. With it, your child is neither dependent on you or some kind of prop for going to sleep, nor is he abandoned. We don't leave the child to figure it out on his own—we stay there for him, so there's no "crying it out."

I use P.U./P.D. on babies from ages three months through a year who have not learned the skills of sleep—sometimes later, in particularly difficult cases or where a child has never had any kind of routine. P.U./P.D. doesn't replace the Four S wind-down ritual (182–186); it's more of a measure of last resort. It is most often needed because of accidental parenting.

If your child is fitful at sleep times, or if you need to use a prop to get him to sleep, it's critical to change these habits before they become deeply entrenched and even worse. When baby Janine was two months old, for example, she would "only sleep in the stroller," according to her mum, who now "can't get her to sleep unless I take her for a ride in the car" (more on Janine on page 224 and a better approach on page 205). Prop addiction, like all kinds of dependencies, only gets worse with time. And that's where P.U./P.D. comes in. I use it to:

- teach prop-dependent babies how to get to sleep on their own, during the day and at night

- establish a routine in older babies or reestablish one when parents have gone off course
- help a baby make a transition from a three-hour to a four-hour routine
- extend too-short naps
- encourage a baby to sleep longer in the morning when early waking is due to something the parents have done, not the baby's natural bio-rhythms

P.U./P.D. is not a magic. It involves lots of hard work (which is why I often suggest that parents coordinate their efforts and take turns; see page 258 and the sidebar, page 174). After all, you're changing the usual way you put your baby to sleep. So, when you lay her down without the prop, she's probably going to cry, because she's used to the old way of going to sleep—with a bottle, a breast, rocking or jiggling or walking—whatever prop you've given her in the past. You're going to get resistance straightaway, because she doesn't comprehend what you're doing. So you go ahead and pick her up, reassuring her that at least *you* know what you're doing. Depending on how old and how physically strong and active your baby is, you will adapt the practice accordingly (you'll find out how to do this in each of the age-specific sections that follow). However, P.U./P.D. is basically this same simple procedure:

When the child cries, you go into his room. You first try to comfort him with words and a gentle hand on his back. Up to six months, you can also do the shush-pat; in older babies, the shush-pat—especially the sound—can actually disrupt sleep, so we just lay a hand on the child's back instead to make our presence felt. If he doesn't stop crying, then pick him up. But put him down the minute he stops crying and not a second later. You are comforting him, not trying to put him back to sleep—that's for him to do on his own. If he cries and arches his back, though, you put him down immediately. Never fight a crying child. But maintain contact by placing a firm hand on his back so that he knows you're there. Stay with him. Intervene with words as well: "It's just sleep time, darling. You're only going to sleep."

Even if he cries the minute he leaves your shoulder or on the way down to his crib, still lay him all the way down on the mattress. If he's crying, pick him up again. The idea behind this is that you're giving him comfort and security and letting him have the emotion. In essence, your behavior says to him, "You can cry, but Mummy/Daddy's right here. I know that you're finding it hard to get back to sleep, but I'm here to help you."

If when you lay him down, he cries, pick him up again. But remember not to fight him if he arches his back. Part of his struggling and squirming is that he's trying to put himself back to sleep. The pushing away and the burrowing down is his little baby way of settling himself. Don't feel guilty, you're not hurting him. And don't take it personally—he's not angry at you. He's just frustrated because he's never learned to go to sleep, and you're there to help and reassure him. Like grown-ups who toss and turn on a sleepless night, all he wants is to get some rest.

On average, P.U./P.D. takes twenty minutes, but it can go on for an hour or more. I'm not sure what my record is but I've had to do it over a hundred times with some babies. Often, parents don't trust the method. They're sure it won't work with *their* baby. They don't see P.U./.P.D. as a *tool.* Mums, in particular, will say if I don't use my breast, what do I have? How can I calm him? You have your voice and the physical intervention. Your voice, believe it or not, is your most powerful tool. By talking to him in a gentle sweet tone, and saying it over and over, if necessary ("You're just going to sleep, darling"), you're letting your child know that you're not going to abandon him. You're just helping him get to sleep. Babies whose parents do P.U./P.D. eventually associate the voice with comforting, and they no longer need picking up. Once they feel safe hearing their parents calming words, that's all it takes to reassure them.

If you do P.U./P.D. correctly—pick him up when he cries and put him down the minute he stops—he will eventually lose steam, and cry less. At first, he might start snuffling, gasp in between whimpers, as he's winding down. In England, we call those short shallow breaths one takes after a good cry "heart sluffs," and they're almost always a sign that sleep is around the corner. Just keep your hand on him. The weight of your hand coupled with verbal reassurance lets him know you're there. You don't tap, you don't shush, and you don't leave the room . . . until you see him drop into a deep sleep (see page 186).

P.U./P.D. is about reassuring and instilling trust. If it takes fifty or one hundred times, or even 150, surely you're prepared to do that in order to teach your baby to sleep and to get your own time back, aren't you, luv? If not, you're reading the wrong book. There are no short, easy solutions.

P.U./P.D. doesn't prevent crying. But it does prevent fear of abandonment, because *you stay with the child and comfort him through his tears.* He's not crying because he hates you, or because you're hurting him. He's crying because you're trying to get him to go to sleep in a different way, and he's frustrated. Children *will* cry when you're changing a habit. But they cry out of frustration, and that's a far different kind of cry than the cry of being left alone, which is a more desperate, fearful, and almost primitive wail, designed to get you into the room immediately.

Take little Janine whom I mentioned earlier, for instance. When her mum no longer used a motion prop, neither the stroller nor the car, to get her to sleep, Janine didn't like it. She cried and cried at first, and really what she was saying was, "What are you doing, Mum? We don't go to sleep this way." But after a few nights of P.U./P.D., she was able to go to sleep without a prop.

To be effective, P.U./P.D. has to be developmentally appropriate. After all, dealing with a four-month-old is different from dealing with an eleven-month-old. It makes sense, then, to adapt P.U./P.D. to fit baby's changing needs and characteristics. In the following four sections—three to four months, four to six, six to eight, and eight months to a year—I give you a quick overview of what babies are like in each age grouping, how the common sleep issues change slightly over time. (Sleep problems after the first year are covered in chapter 7.) Not surprisingly, many of the common issues, such as night waking and abbreviated naps, can persist. I also include the key questions I ask to help me fully understand a particular problem. Of course, I usually ask additional questions about sleep patterns, eating habits, activity, and so on, but I assume that if you've read this far, you have a good sense of how extensively I probe. (As I've urged you in the past, please read through *all* the age groupings. Even if your baby has passed some of the earlier stages, those questions will give you additional information that will help you figure out why your baby is having a sleep problem.) I then explain how to adapt P.U./P.D. for each age group. After each section, I've recounted a case study for that age group to show you how P.U./P.D. is used in different situations and at various stages of development.

Three to Four Months: Tweaking the Routine

You may be surprised that we focus on only one month, rather than having a "three to six months" category. That's because a window opens during babies' fourth month. That's the time when most babies are able to transition from a three- to a four-hour routine (you might want to review the chart in chapter 1, page 34). Where your little one was taking three naps and a catnap at three months, at four months she will take only two naps and a catnap. Where she had five feeds a day (at 7, 10, 1, 4, and 7) plus the dream feed, she will now have four (at 7, 11, 3, and 7) plus the dream feed. And where she was only able to stay up a half hour to forty-five minutes, after a feed, she'll now be able to stay up for a good two hours or more.

The four-month window sometimes coincides with a growth spurt (see pages 115–119 and 197–199). However, unlike earlier growth spurts, this one not only involves giving more food during the day but also *extending* the time between feeds. If that seems strange, just remember that now your baby's tummy is larger; he's also a more efficient eater and can down more at one sitting than he could in his earlier months. He also *needs* more because his activity levels are about to increase, and he can stay up longer. If you don't adjust his routine, or if you haven't had any structure in the day thus far, this is the month when many sleep troubles "mysteriously" develop, troubles that just as mysteriously disappear by establishing or tweaking the routine. Likewise, if you don't realize that your baby is going through a growth spurt and start feeding him when he wakes in the middle of the night, even a baby who already slept through might develop "sudden" sleep problems.

Your baby still has limited physical capabilities at three months, but he's growing by leaps and bounds. He can move his head, arms, and legs. He might be able to roll over, too. He's more alert and tuned in to his environment. If you've gotten to know his cries and body language, you should know the difference between hunger, fatigue, pain, and overstimulation by now. A hungry baby, of course, always needs to be fed. But a tired and/or frustrated baby needs to be taught how to go back to sleep. He might arch his back as he's crying. If he's not swaddled, he also might throw his legs up in the air and slam them down on the mattress when he's frustrated.

Common issues. If a child has no structure in his life, or hasn't made the transition from a three- to a four-hour routine, there's a good chance he will either wake in the middle of the night, take only catnaps, wake up too early—or all of the above. When parents have been following their baby, instead of guiding the child, I get emails like this one, from the mother of a four-month-old:

> Justina has not been on any type of schedule. I am able to get her
> to fall asleep for naps with just a little reassurance from me, but

no matter how relaxing the atmosphere of the nursery, she will not sleep for more than thirty minutes and is still sleepy when she awakes.

In a later part of the email, Mum claims that *Justina* makes it "hard for me to follow the E.A.S.Y. schedule," but it's really her problem, not her child's. She has to take the lead. If, in addition, Justina's parents have used a prop—themselves or motion—to put their baby to sleep, it only makes the problem worse.

Also at this age, just as a baby drifts into a deeper level of sleep, her body goes slack (and her lips), and the pacifier pops out. While many babies stay asleep, some wake when the pacifier falls out. For those babies, the pacifier is a prop (see page 189). This can continue to happen up to around seven months, at which point the baby can replace her pacifier without a parent's help. In the meantime, though, if you keep popping the pacifier back into your baby's mouth, you're reinforcing a common pattern of accidental parenting. Instead, just leave it out and comfort her in other ways. (If you haven't offered a pacifier until now, it's best not to start.)

Key questions. **Have you ever had your baby on a routine?** If not, you'll have to introduce one (see pages 39–46). **Are you trying to keep your baby on a three-hour routine?** If so, you've got to start helping him make the transition to a four-hour one. The process is the same as putting a four-month-old on E.A.S.Y. (which I explain in great detail on page 228). Are his naps getting shorter? This, too, could mean that your baby should be on a four-hour routine. At around four months or so, babies can start to hold their own for at least two hours. It happens earlier for some, later for others, but if they're still eating on a three-hour schedule, too-frequent feeds will cut into nap time (refer to the side-by-side chart of three- and four-hour routines on page 34). Even if they've been napping well up to this point, they then start to take shorter and shorter naps. It usually happens very gradually and many parents only become aware when the naps are down to forty-five minutes or less (see pages 249–252). If you're watching for it, you can see the pattern as it starts. Don't let it get established. Instead, switch to a four-hour routine.

Does he want to eat more often—say, he's due for a feed at 10 A.M. but seems extremely hungry earlier? When he wakes at night does he take a full feed? If so, he's probably going through a growth spurt.

Again, you need to start moving him to a four-hour routine. Resist the temptation to feed him more often. Instead, use the feeding plan I lay out on pages 198–199, which calls for giving him more food at 7 A.M. and, over a period of three or four days, gradually increasing the amounts at each feed—adding ounces to the bottle, or feeding from both sides of breast, which will increase your milk supply. If he doesn't take the extra food, then he's not quite ready, but keep a careful watch on his food intake from now on. By four or four and a half months, he will be able to last four hours between feeds. The exception would be a premie, who is four months old chronologically but, if he arrived six weeks early, is developmentally like a 2½-month-old (see page 146 and the sidebar, page 179).

Does he wake up earlier? At this age, babies don't necessarily cry for food the moment they wake up—like adults, some do and some don't. Many will babble and coo, and if no one goes in to them, they fall back to sleep. Here's where it's important to read your baby's cues. If your baby cries because he's hungry, you have to feed him. But then put him right

---

Early Wake-Ups

Your Baby's or Yours?

I recently met the parent of 8-month-old Oliver, who was taking good 2-hour naps during the day, going to bed at 6, and sleeping through until 5:30. Mum didn't like getting up so early, so she told me, "I've been trying to keep him up later." Oliver, who was normally a cheery chap thriving on a good routine, had suddenly turned sullen in the evenings. Mum wanted to know what to do now, since keeping him up later was clearly not working and this little boy who never resisted bedtime before was having trouble getting to sleep. "Should we try the cry-it-out method?" she asked. Absolutely not. She had to take responsibility for making no problem into a problem. Babies have their own internal clocks. If your baby is getting 11½ hours of sleep—say from 6 P.M. to 5:30 A.M.—that's the proper amount of sleep, especially if he naps well during the day. You could try to extend his bedtime, say to 6:30 or 7—testing it out in 15-minute increments, to make sure he doesn't get overtired. But his body clock might resist, in which case you have to keep the 6 o'clock bedtime. If *you're* tired because you don't like getting up so early, go to sleep earlier!

back to sleep. If he doesn't fall back to sleep, you have to do P.U./P.D. to get him there. As you increase his food intake during the day and move from a three- to four-hour routine, his wake-up time will probably stabilize. But let's say that he doesn't take a full feed. Then you know that he obviously wasn't very hungry, and he's just nursing for comfort. **In the past, have you always gone in to him and given him a feed?** If so, it's a pretty sure bet that he's gotten into a bad habit of waking you up for your breast or a bottle. Instead of giving it, you'd do P.U./P.D.

How to adapt P.U./P.D. With a baby this young, in addition to the basic procedure I described above, when you first go in, you may have to re-swaddle. Do it while he's lying in the crib. If you can't comfort him *in* his crib with reassuring words and a soft, reassuring pat, then pick him up. Hold him until he stops crying, but no more than four or five minutes. Don't keep holding him if he's fighting you, arching his back or pushing away from you. Put him down. Again, try to use the shush-pat to calm him in the crib. If that doesn't work, pick him up again. On average, P.U./P.D. takes around twenty minutes to work at three or four months. Luckily even if your baby has developed a habit in response to your accidental parenting, it's probably not too entrenched. The only exception would be if you've already tried controlled crying and thereby have broken the trust.

Changing Your Four-Month-Old's Day to Solve Sleep Problems at Night

When four-months (or older) babies are kept on a three-hour E.A.S.Y. routine, they have irregular naps and often wake at night. If they don't naturally make the transition, we have to help them along. (If your baby hasn't ever been on a structured routine, refer to pages 39–46, to learn how to introduce E.A.S.Y.)

The following plan, designed specifically for a four-month-old, is given in three-day increments. It works well with most babies, but don't worry if your child takes more time to get to the goal. For instance, the chart (page 230) assumes that a feed takes thirty minutes, but your baby might take forty-five. If your child has already gotten in the habit of forty-minute naps, it might take extra time to get him accustomed to longer spans of daytime sleep. The important thing is to keep moving in the right direction. In the section following this chart, you'll find Lincoln's story, a case study in which we had to help a baby make this transition and used P.U./P.D. to extend his naps.

Days One to Three. Use this time to watch your baby's three-hour routine, how much he eats, how long he sleeps. Typically, three-month-olds eat five meals a day at 7, 10, 1, 4, and 7. At the bottom of page 230 is an "ideal" day, but many babies don't conform. (I only list feeding, activity, and sleep times, leaving out "Y" for simplicity's sake.)

Days Four to Seven. Feed your baby at 7 when he wakes up, extend his morning activity time by fifteen minutes, and for the rest of the day his feeds will be fifteen minutes later—for example, the second feed will be at 10:15, instead of 10, his third at 1:15, instead of 1. He will still have three naps (1½, 1¼, and two hours) plus a thirty- to forty-five-minute catnap, but the span *between* naps will have increased a bit, and will keep increasing as you continue with this plan. In other words, he'll be staying up for increasingly longer stretches. You'll use P.U./P.D. to extend his naps.

Days Eight to Eleven. Continue feeding your baby at 7 when he wakes up, but extend his morning activity time by another fifteen minutes, which will make all his feeds another fifteen minutes later as well—his former 10 A.M. feed is now at 10:30, 1:00 at 1:30, and so on. You will also eliminate his late afternoon catnap for a few days in order to extend the other three naps—approximately 1½ and 1¾ in the morning and two hours in the afternoon. When you cut out the catnap, your child may be very tired in the afternoon. If so, you might need to put him to bed at 6:30 instead of 7:30.

Days Twelve to Fifteen (or longer). Begin now to extend your baby's morning activity time by a *half hour* more, which will make all his subsequent feeds a half hour later as well—his former 10 A.M. feed is at 11, the 1 at 2, and so on. Continue to avoid his late afternoon catnap to allow his other naps to lengthen, approximately to two and 1½ hours in the morning, 1½ hours in the afternoon. These will be the hardest days, but stay with it. Again, if your child is tired because of missing his catnap, put him to bed earlier. If you've been cluster feeding, top him off at 7 before bed.

I can just imagine the letters I'm going to get: "But Tracy, you said you should never feed to sleep." That's true. Feeding-to-sleep—whereby a baby becomes dependent on a bottle or Mum's breast in order to fall asleep—is one of the most common forms of accidental parenting. Babies who feed-to-sleep can't settle any other way, and they also tend to wake frequently at night. There's a big difference, however, between feeding-to-sleep and feeding *at bedtime*, right before sleep and again at the dream feed (when he's not even awake), which helps the baby then stay asleep for a good five- or six-hour stretch. I suggest feed, bath, and bed, but you could also switch the order and do the bath first. It depends on the baby. Some get wound up by a bath, so it's better to do it before the feed; others get drowsy and sometimes even fall asleep at the bedtime feed. You have to figure out which works best with your child. Either way, the seven o'clock feed is not the same as accidental parenting, in which he must feed at *every* sleep period in order to fall asleep.

The Goal. At this point, his morning feeds will be at the proper times—7 and 11. Over the three days or week (or more), you work on adjusting the afternoon mealtimes. Hold off for fifteen to thirty minutes on the two afternoon feeds, which are now at 2:15 (you want to get to 3) and 5 (you want to get to 6 or 7). As you extend his awake time, your baby will probably need his catnap. By continuing on this path, as you'll see in the last column in the chart below, you eventually consolidate the five feeds into four—at 7, 11, 3, and 7, plus the dream feed—and the three daytime sleep periods into two two-hour naps in the morning and early afternoon, plus a catnap in the late afternoon. You also increase his awake time so that your baby is staying up for two hours at a stretch.

Days 1–3	Days 4–7	Days 8–11	Days 12–15	The Goal
E: 7	**E:** 7	**E:** 7	**E:** 7	**E:** 7 feed
A: 7:30	**A:** 7:30	**A:** 7:30	**A:** 7:30	**A:** 7:30
S: 8:30 (1½ hrs.)	**S:** 8:45 (1½ hrs.)	**S:** 9 (1½ hrs.)	**S:** 9 nap (2 hrs.)	**S:** 9 nap (2 hrs.)
E: 10	**E:** 10:15	**E:** 10:30	**E:** 11	**E:** 11
A: 10:30	**A:** 10:45	**A:** 11	**A:** 11:30	**A:** 11:30
S: 11:30 (1½ hrs.)	**S:** 12:15 (1¼ hrs.)	**S:** 12:30 (1¾ hrs.)	**S:** 12:45 (1½ hrs.)	**S:** 1 (2 hrs.)
E: 1	**E:** 1:15	**E:** 1:45	**E:** 2:15	**E:** 3
A: 1:30	**A:** 2	**A:** 2:15	**A:** 2:45	**A:** 3:30
S: 2:30 (1½ hrs.)	**S:** 2:45 (2 hrs.)	**S:** 3 nap (2 hrs.)	**S:** 3:30 nap (1½ hrs.)	**S:** 5 to 6: catnap (½ to ¾ hr.)
E: 4	**E:** 4:15	**E:** 4:30	**E:** 5 feed	**E, A, S:** by 7:30, feed, bath, and to bed
A: 4:30	**A:** 4:45	**A:** 5	**A:** bath	**E:** 11, dream feed
S: catnap (½ to ¾ hr.)	**S:** catnap (½ to ¾ hr.)	**S:** no catnap!	**S:** in bed by 6:30 or 7	
E & A: 7, feed and bath	**E & A:** 7:15, feed and bath	**E, A, S:** by 6:30 or 7, feed, bath, and bedtime	**E:** 11, dream feed	
S: 7:30	**S:** 7:30	**E:** 11, dream feed		
E: 11, dream feed	**E:** 11, dream feed			

Fourth Month Case Study: Getting on a Four-Hour E.A.S.Y. Routine

May came to me because 3½-month-old Lincoln was disrupting the whole family. "He will not fall asleep on his own and will not put himself back to sleep at night," May explained. "If I lay him in his crib awake, he will cry forever—not fussing but screaming. I go to him, because I don't believe in letting him cry it out, but he is hard to soothe. He doesn't seem to want anything, except his bottle. During the day he might nap, but never at the same time or for the same amount of time. Or he might not nap at all. He doesn't sleep through the night. He doesn't wake at the same time every night. He will sleep five or six hours and wakes to eat a six-ounce bottle and falls back to sleep for about two more hours. But sometimes he only takes an ounce or two at a feed—I never know." May was worried because not only were she and her husband sleep-deprived, she was losing patience. "He is the totally opposite of Tamika, who is four, slept through the night from the time she was three months, and always took good naps. I just don't know how to deal with him."

When I asked May how often her son ate, she said every three hours, but it was apparent to me immediately that Lincoln lacked a structured routine. He was clearly going through a growth spurt as well—he woke erratically and downed six ounces after a five- or six-hour stretch of sleep. We needed to deal with the growth spurt at once, by upping Lincoln's food during the day. But we also had to look at the lack of routine in this little boy's life, which was making it difficult for May to read his cues. And there was also some accidental parenting happening as well. Lincoln was used to two different props—his mum and his bottle. We had to get him on E.A.S.Y., which would both deal with his hunger issue and help May tune in to his cries and body language.

Because Lincoln was almost four months old, our goal was to transition Lincoln from a three- to a four-hour routine. We would use P.U./P.D. to do it, but the process, I warned May, could take around two weeks or longer. Because Lincoln was two weeks shy of four months, he might not be able to get through to a full four-hour stretch immediately, so we had to extend the time between feeds gradually, especially because his eating pattern was so erratic. I suggested the plan on pages 229–230, which I've used in hundreds of similar cases: Every three days, I had May move Lincoln's feeds a bit later, first fifteen minutes and then a half hour later. We also added a half hour to activity (A) time. In this way, we could work at consolidating his four daily forty-minute naps into two long naps and one catnap.

While going through this process, it was important for May to keep a log that charted feeds, activity times, naps, and nighttime sleep. Wake-up would always be at 7 A.M., bedtime at 7 or 7:30, and the dream feed at 11. But by adding time to his activity periods, his feed and nap times would change, in fifteen-minute and thirty-minute increments. This situation and when getting a four-month or older baby on E.A.S.Y. for the first time (see pages 39–46) are the *only* times I suggest clock-watching. Especially when parents can't read their baby's cues, keeping close track of the time gives them an idea of what he needs. At this age, parents often keep feeding, because they don't know whether their baby is tired or hungry.

I explained to May that because Lincoln's sleep pattern had been so erratic, we couldn't just cross our fingers and hope that he'd conform to the new routine. We'd have to train him. This is where P.U./P.D. comes in. She would use it to extend Lincoln's naps during the day (when, for example, he slept only forty minutes instead of an hour and a half), to get him back to sleep in the middle of the night, and, if necessary, to extend his morning wake-up as well.

Naturally, Lincoln balked at the new regime. The first day he woke at 7—a good start. May fed him as usual. By 8:30, even though Lincoln yawned and looked a little tired, I suggested that May try to keep him up until 8:45, instead of putting him down for a nap, because we were trying to move him to a four-hour routine. She was successful, but he slept only forty-five minutes, both because he was used to sleeping in short spurts and probably because he was also a bit overtired from being kept up a little longer. You know I always insist on putting a sleepy baby to bed, but this is a special situation because we're trying to adjust Lincoln's inner clock. It's a matter of striking that delicate balance—not keeping them up so long that they're overtired but keeping them awake long enough to extend the activity time a bit. Extending it for fifteen minutes to a half hour is usually doable at around four months.

Because our goal was to eventually extend Lincoln's nap to at least 1½ hours and eventually two, when Lincoln woke at 9:30, I showed May how to do P.U./P.D. to get him to sleep longer. He was having none of it.

She was at it for nearly an hour. Since it was almost his feed time, I told her to stop, and to take him out of the room. She had to keep the activity level very low-key and calm because this was supposed to be Lincoln's sleep time. Needless to say, he was tired and cranky by ten, which was his next feed time. But all the crying made him hungry as well, so he took a good feed. It was a challenge for her to keep him awake until it was time for his next nap at 11:30. But May worked hard to keep him up. She changed his diaper in the middle of the feed, and as soon as she saw him falling asleep, she'd take the bottle out of his mouth and sit him upright. Most children can't sleep in that position, and their little eyes will pop open, like a baby doll's.

By 11:15, Lincoln was really tired. May did the Four S wind-down ritual and tried to put her son down without his bottle. She had to do P.U./P.D. again. Although she picked him up fewer times this go round, he still didn't get to sleep until 12:15. "Don't let him sleep later than one o'clock," I cautioned her. "Remember that you're trying to train his body to sleep on a good schedule."

Skeptical but desperate, May followed my directions and stayed the course. Even in three days she started to see a difference. Although Lincoln had a way to go, he was settling down more quickly for his naps. She continued to follow the plan, and although there were days when he regressed, by the eleventh day, she saw that at least things were progressing: He was taking in more food at each feed, instead of snacking as he had been. Also, the time it took to pick him up and put him down was getting shorter.

May was exhausted herself and couldn't believe how difficult it was. But when she looked at her log she could see little bits of improvement And that encouraged her to keep going. Where Lincoln had been waking up at 2:30 A.M., now on a dream feed, he was waking at 4:30, but she was able to use his pacifier to get another hour out of him. She fed him at 5:30 and although she normally would have gotten him up at that hour, she now used P.U./P.D. to send him back to sleep. It took her forty minutes, but he then slept until seven. Actually, he was still sleeping *at* seven. May was tempted to let him sleep in (and her, too!), but she remembered what I had told her about starting as you mean to go on. If she allowed Lincoln to sleep later than 7, it would throw off his new routine, and undo all of her hard work.

By Day Fourteen, Lincoln's activity periods were longer, and his morning and afternoon naps were lasting at least an hour. He no longer demanded a bottle when she put him down to sleep, and May was able to stop doing P.U./ P.D. Even if he woke, more often than not all she had to do was put her hand on him and he'd settle back to sleep.

Four to Six Months: Dealing with Old Problems

As your baby's physical repertoire expands, mobility can cause sleep disturbances. She's able to do much more with her arms and legs and hands—reach out, hold objects—and her torso is stronger, too. She is starting to get up on her knees and can push herself forward in the bed.

You'll put her down in the middle of the crib and find her scrunched up in a corner hours later. She might try to get up on her knees and lift her torso off the mattress when she's frustrated. When she's tired, her cry will reach three or even four very distinct, escalating crescendos: Each time, the cry will start and get louder and louder and more and more frantic, and then all of a sudden it will reach a peak and start to come down the other side. If you're trying to correct accidental parenting or you've missed her cues and she's gotten overtired, you'll also see a lot of body language: When you hold her, she'll start to arch herself backward, or push down with her feet.

Common issues. Many problems are those we've seen in earlier stages, which haven't been dealt with. If movement wakes her and she hasn't developed the skills to put herself back to sleep, that could cause night waking, too. Sometimes parents are tempted either to introduce solids earlier or to put cereal into her bottle at this point. Contrary to myth, solid food doesn't make babies sleep any better (see sidebar, page 143), and it certainly isn't a remedy for accidental parenting. Sleep is a learned art not the result of a full tummy. If a baby has gotten into the habit of sleeping in short spurts, and no one has taught her how to go back to sleep, too-short naps can be a problem at this point, too.

Key questions. I ask the same as in earlier stages. Because naps are often the biggest issue, I also ask, **Has she always had short naps, or is this something that started recently?** If it's a recent occurrence, I ask about other issues—what's going on in the household, feeds, new people

---

It's a Myth

Later Bedtime Means Later Wake-Up

I'm shocked at the number of parents who call complaining about early wake-ups and whose pediatricians have advised them, "Try to keep him up a little later." But that means he'll be overtired when he finally goes to bed. Babies need to be put to sleep *when they show signs of being tired.* Otherwise, their nighttime sleep will be fitful, and they'll still get up at the same time in the morning.

and activities (also see "A Few Words on Naps," page 249). If things have been pretty stable, I ask, **Does your baby seem cranky and out of sorts after her nap? Does she sleep well at night?** If the baby is fine during the day, and a good sleeper at night, it might just be a case of her bio-rhythm—she doesn't need the longer naps. If she is cranky during the day, we have to do P.U./P.D. to extend her nap times, because she obviously needs more sleep.

How to adapt P.U./P.D. If your baby is burrowing her head into the mattress, turning her head from one side to the other, getting up on her knees, or flopping from side to side, don't pick her up right away. If you do, you'll get kicked in the chest or have your hair pulled. Instead, continue to talk to her in a low, reassuring tone. When you do pick her up, *hold her for only two or three minutes*. Put her down even if she's still crying. Then pick her up again, and follow the same routine. Babies at this age are more likely to put up a physical struggle when you're trying to change a habit, and the most common mistake parents make at this age is that they hold the baby too long (see Sarah's story on pages 236–237). If your baby fights you, don't keep holding her. For instance, she might bury her head forward and down and push away from you with her feet and arms. At that point, say, "Okay, let me lay you down." She probably won't stop crying, because

---

The Mantra Cry

By the time your child is 3 or 4 months old, you should understand her cues—the body language, the different types of cries—and her personality. You should be able to tell the difference between a genuine cry for help and what I call the "mantra cry," an odd burst of a cry which most babies do as they're settling down. *We don't pick up with a mantra cry.* Instead, we hold back to see if the child can settle herself. We *do* pick up with a genuine cry, because it's your baby's way of saying, "I have a need that has to be met."

The success of P.U./P.D. depends, in part, on your knowing the difference between a genuine cry and a manta cry. Each mantra cry is unique to the individual. Get to know what your baby's mantra cry sounds like. You'll see that when she's physically tired, she'll blink and yawn, and her legs and arms might flail if she's overtired. She'll also do a kind of "waa . . . waa . . . waa . . ." sound. Like a mantra that's repeated over and over, the pitch and tone is the same throughout. It does *not* sound the same as a genuine cry, which usually escalates in volume.

she's in fighting mode. Pick her up straightaway. If she again starts to fight with you, put her in the crib. See if she can start to settle herself on her own and perhaps lapse into a mantra cry (see box, page 235). Lay her on her back and hold her little hands and talk to her, "Hey, hey, come on, shhh. You're just going to sleep. Hey, hey, it's okay. I know it's hard."

Parents with babies around the five-month age range often comment, "I've picked the baby up, and she calms down. But then, when I go to put her back down, she starts crying on the way down, before I've even gotten to the mattress. What do I do?" You lay her all the way down, take away the physical contact, and then say, "I'm going to pick you up again." Or else you're teaching her to cry in order to get picked up. So you've got to see it all the way through, laying her down onto the mattress. Then, go ahead and pick her up again.

Four to Six Months Case Study: Holding Too Long

Rona called because she didn't know how to handle five-month-old Sarah, who had been a good sleeper for the first four months of her life. "Whenever she cried, I picked her up," Mum said. "But now she wakes up at midnight and is up for an hour. I keep going in to her. She settles, and then a few minutes later I have to go in again." I asked Rona to recall the *first* time Sarah woke at midnight. "Well, it was so surprising, because it wasn't like her, so the both of us, Ed and me, ran in to see what was wrong. We felt so bad."

I explained that it doesn't take very long for a baby to realize that *when I cry like this Mum or Dad come running* (in this case, Mum *and* Dad). And it doesn't take very long for them to associate going to sleep with being given a prop—Mum or Dad picking Sarah up. Now this may sound strange to you. My method is *pick up*/put down. The problem is, many parents comfort past the baby's needs and the pick-up part is too drawn out. At this age in particular, it is very important not to hold a baby too long.

In this case, though, I've found that whenever a parent says, "she used to . . ." it's a red flag. Typically, something has happened to the child that affected her sleep. So, I asked Rona if there were any other changes in the family, and sure enough there were quite a few. "We moved her from our room into her new room," Rona explained. "The first two nights she slept well but now she wakes up." She paused and suddenly looked at me. "Oh, and I also started working part-time—Mondays through Wednesdays."

That was a lot of change for a five-month-old. But at least both parents were eager to get involved and help solve the problem. We would start on the weekend when everyone was off work. But I also had to find out who would be with Sarah during the days that Rona was away from home. No sleep strategy works unless it is consistently carried out, day and night, weekdays and weekend. Rona's mum was the nanny on her daughter's work days. So, I suggested that Grandma come over, too. Even though Sarah was only waking at night thus far, given the changes in the household, there was a chance that her naps might be disrupted as well. I though it was best to explain the plan to the three of them . . . just in case.

Because Sarah was so accustomed to her mother intervening in the middle of the night, I suggested that Ed be the first to use P.U./P.D. when his daughter woke. He would do it on Friday night and Saturday, and Rona was not to go in to help him. She would be "on duty" the next two nights. "If you think you'll be tempted to go in and help Ed out," I offered, "then it's best for you to leave the house altogether. Have a sleepover at your mum's."

The first night was difficult for Ed, who used to sleep through, or at least lie in bed, when Sarah woke up. Normally, sleep duty was Rona's domain. But he was eager and willing. He had to pick Sarah up over sixty times before she'd settle, but he was also proud that he could finally get her down. The next night when Sarah woke, it took only ten minutes to get her back to sleep. Sunday morning, when I checked in with the couple, Rona admitted that initially she didn't think that Ed could handle P.U./P.D. She was so impressed that she suggested he do another night. As it turned out, Sarah stirred on Sunday night but then put herself back to sleep. Dad never had to go into her room.

For the next three nights, Sarah slept all the way through. However, on Thursday night, she woke again. Because I had warned Rona and Ed that there might be a regression—there almost always is in cases of habitual waking—Rona at least knew what to expect. She went in to Sarah, but only had to do P.U./P.D. three times to get her to settle. Within a few weeks, Sarah's midnight waking was a distant memory.

Six to Eight Months: The Physical Baby

Your baby is much more physically advanced now. She is working toward independent sitting or is already sitting up on her own and may be able to pull herself to a standing position as well. She should be sleeping a good six- or seven-hour stretch through the night sometime by the end of the fourth month, certainly by the time solid food is introduced. Dream feeds stop at around seven to eight months, by which time your baby is drinking between six and eight ounces per feed and getting a fair amount of solid food. It's important not to stop the dream feed abruptly; it can cause sleep problems if you do. So you must gradually increase the calories during the day before taking them away at night (see the box on page 123 for a step-by-step plan for gradually cutting out the dream feed).

Common issues. Increasing physical abilities and motion can disturb a baby's sleep. When she wakes as a normal course of sleeping, she might sit up in bed if she doesn't go back to sleep immediately or even stand up. If she hasn't yet mastered the art of getting down, she'll be frustrated and will call out to you. Depending on how it's dealt with, this could start a bad pattern of accidental parenting. Your child also might experience tummy aches as solid foods are introduced. (That's why you always introduce new foods in the morning; see page 153.) Teething has to be factored into the equation at this age, as well as booster shots. Both can also throw off sleep routines. Some babies begin to experience separation anxiety in the seventh month as well, which tends to affect naps more than nighttime sleep, but it usually happens later (see "Eight Months to a Year," page 242).

Key questions. **Does your baby get up at the same time every night or are his wake-ups random? Does he just wake up once or twice throughout the night? Does he cry? Do you immediately go in to him?** I've already explained that random waking usually means he's going through a growth spurt and/or is not getting enough food during the day to sustain him through the night. The rule of thumb is if they wake you in the night add more food in the day (pages 198–199). Habitual waking, on the other hand, is almost always a sign of accidental parenting (page 191). But the older your baby is, the greater the challenge of changing the habit. If he's just waking up once a night, try my wake-to-sleep technique that I

Making the Crib Fun

If your child has an aversion to her crib, put her in it when it's not time to sleep. Make it into a game. Put lots of fun toys in the crib (remember to take them out at bedtime, though). Put her in and play peekaboo. At first stay in the room with her. Busy yourself, putting clothes away, for example, but talk to her the whole time. As she becomes involved with her toys and begins to see that the crib is quite enjoyable and not a prison, you'll eventually be able to leave the room. Don't overdo it, though—and never leave her to cry.

described in chapter 5 (see sidebar, page 191): Instead of lying there dreading the usual wake-up at 4 A.M., you go in an hour earlier and wake him! If he is waking up *several* times a night, it's not just his body clock jarring him awake, it's also because the minute he stirs, you've been rushing to his side. And if this has gone on for several months, you have to do P.U./P.D. to get him out of the habit. **Do you start the wind-down ritual the moment he gets tired?** By six months, you should know your baby's sleep cues. If he's fussing, and even after you give him a change of scene, he's still fussing, then you know he's tired. **Do you put him down the same way you always did? Was he always like this? What have you done to calm him in the past?** If this is a new occurrence, I ask a series of questions about his entire day—what his routine is like, what he does as activities, what changes have occurred. **Has he cut out a nap?** At this age, babies still need two naps, so he might not be getting enough sleep during the day. **Is he very active, able to move independently by scooting, crawling, pulling himself up to an upright position? What kinds of activities is he doing?** You may need to do calmer activities with him before sleep periods, certainly in the afternoon. **Have you started him on solid foods? What have you added to his diet? Do you introduce new foods only in the morning?** (See page 153.) New foods might be upsetting his tummy.

How to adapt P.U./P.D. Generally when parents say, "He gets more upset when I pick him up," they're talking about a baby who's between six and eight months old, a point at which a child is quite capable of putting up physical resistance. So you want to make this a kind of partnership. Instead of swooping down and picking him up, hold your arms out, and wait until he holds out his. Say, "Come in to [Mummy's/Daddy's] arms. Let me pick you up." The minute you pick him up, put his body into a horizontal cradled position, and say, "It's okay, we're just going to sleep." Don't rock him. Put him down immediately. Don't make eye contact when comforting him—he can't help engaging with you if you do. You may have to help him control his arms and legs. Once he starts

> ## Try This at Home . . . or Not
>
> When a child has been traumatized by her crib or just can't seem to settle without the presence of a warm body, I sometimes climb into the crib (see Kelly's story, page 240), or at least lay the top part of my body down next to her. Don't climb into your child's crib if you weigh more than 150 pounds. And ladies (especially short gals), make sure that you have a stool—otherwise, breasts catch on the bars in transit! Take note: Some kids will push you away if you get into the crib and try to lay your head next to theirs. That's fine. Take the cue and lift your body up. You know that this technique isn't appropriate for *your* baby.

flailing around, he has no skills to calm himself. He needs your help. Most six-month-olds are no longer swaddled, but you could wrap a blanket tightly around everything but one arm. Holding him firmly but gently (maybe putting the weight of your forearms along his body) might help him settle.

Once he starts to calm, what you'll see is some self-soothing. The cry might be more of a "mantra" cry (see box, page 235). Leave him alone, but be a soothing presence. Keep a gentle hand on him but don't shush or pat. At this age, the sound and sensation can keep a baby awake. If he cries again, extend your arms and wait for him to extend his. Continue the reassuring talk. If he raises his arms toward you, pick him up again and do the same thing. When he's settling, you might have to take a step back so he doesn't see you. It depends on the child. Some are less able to fall asleep when you're in plain view—you're too much of a distraction.

Six to Eight Months Case Study: Sleepless Since Birth

"Kelly screams like crazy when it's time to go to bed! Why is she like this??? What is she telling me???" Shannon was at her wit's end about her eight-month-old. Kelly's nighttime behavior had become even more exasperating over the last several months. "I've tried picking her up until she calms down and then putting her back into her crib. But it only makes her more upset when I put her back down." Every evening, Shannon admitted, she had come to dread Kelly's bedtime and most recently, it was happening at nap time as well. "She screams like this every time she falls asleep in her bed, in the car, or in her stroller. I know she's tired because she rubs her eyes and pulls at her ears. I keep her room dark—nothing but a small light. I've tried with and without a night-light, with music and without music. . . . I just don't know what to do anymore." Having read my first book, Shannon added, "I haven't done any accidental parenting. She never falls asleep on me or in my bed. She just loses it."

I might have been at a loss too, except that Shannon gave me several important pieces of information. For one thing, she told me, "This has been going on since she was born." Though Mum *thought* she hadn't done any accidental parenting, it was clear to me that Kelly had come to depend on her mum to rescue her. Picking her up had become a prop. Certainly, it's important to comfort a crying child, but Shannon was holding Kelly *too long*. Although I applauded Shannon for observing her daughter's sleep signs, I suspected that she was waiting too long in that department, too. By the time an eight-month-old rubs her eyes and pulls at her ears, she's pretty tired. Mum has to act earlier.

With older children you have to take small steps to get to your goal. I told Shannon to start teaching Kelly how to settle by using P.U./P.D. first at nap time and then continue the practice at night. She called me the next day, "Tracy, I did everything just like you said, but she was worse, just screaming her little head off. I thought, *This can't be what Tracy has in mind.*"

So we had to go to a Plan B, which is often necessary with an older child who has been in a bad sleep pattern since birth. We're dealing with a deeply ingrained habit. I came to help Shannon the next day. When it was time for Kelly's nap, we did the customary wind-down ritual. Then I laid Kelly on the mattress. She started crying immediately, as her mum predicted she would, so I put the side of her crib all the way down and climbed into the crib *with* her. I put my whole body into the crib. You should have seen the look on her little face as I made my way over the side—and Shannon's surprise as well.

Lying next to Kelly, I put my cheek next to Kelly's. I didn't pick her up. I just used my voice and my presence to calm her. Even after she settled and drifted into a deep sleep, I stayed there. She woke an hour and a half later, and I was still at her side.

Shannon was confused: "Isn't that co-sleeping?" I explained that the end goal is for Kelly to sleep independently, but right now she doesn't have that skill. Also, I sensed she had a fear of her crib. Otherwise, why would she "screech"? It was therefore important for me to be present when she woke up. Furthermore, we didn't take Kelly into an adult's bed. Rather, I stayed with her *in her own bed.*

When I delved deeper and asked Mum a series of questions, Shannon admitted that she had tried the controlled crying method "once or twice" over the last several months but gave it up because "it never worked." Hearing this was like a key turning in the lock. I knew immediately that we were dealing as much with a trust issue as with a bad sleeping pattern. Even though she only tried controlled crying twice, each time Shannon had done a complete 180-degree turn on her daughter. She'd left her to cry it out, and then started to pick her up again. Not realizing it, she had confused her daughter. Worse, Shannon had unwittingly made Kelly suffer by leaving her to cry it out, only to then rescue her from a practice *Shannon* had initiated.

In these kinds of cases, you can't even go to P.U./P.D. until you deal with the trust issue. Once we had this discussion, Shannon saw that, indeed, she *had* done a fair amount of accidental parenting. For Kelly's second nap, I got into the crib *first* and asked Shannon to hand her baby to me. I lay down, and then when Kelly was lying next to me, I climbed out of the crib. Naturally, Kelly started to scream. "Now, now," I said to her in a soft reassuring voice. "We aren't going to leave you. You're just going to sleep." At first Kelly's crying was intense, but it only took fifteen times of stroking her tummy to get her to sleep. Shannon continued to P.U./P.D. that night when Kelly woke up. She realized that cradling Kelly in her arms and putting her down straightaway was very different from picking her up and holding her. I also encouraged her to put Kelly into her crib for increasingly longer periods just to play. "Put toys in there. Make it a fun place during her waking hours. She needs to see that her crib is actually a place nice to be [see sidebar, page 238]. In time, you'll even be able to walk out of the room without your daughter pitching a fit."

After a week's time, Kelly started to like playing in her crib. Her naps and nighttime sleep became more consistent. She still woke every now and then and screamed for her mum, but at least Shannon now knew the proper way of doing P.U./P.D. and was able to get her baby to settle fairly quickly.

Eight Months to a Year: Accidental Parenting at Its Worst

Many babies are cruising, some walking, and all can pull themselves up to a standing position at this point. They often use toys in the crib as missiles when they can't sleep. Emotional life is richer, too—their memories are greater, and they understand cause and effect. Although separation anxiety can happen as early as seven months, at this age, it is usually full blown (see pages 80–84). All kids have it in varying degrees, because they're old enough now to realize that something is missing. They might cry because they miss their dolly or their lovey blanket. So they can also figure out, "Oh, Mum left the room," and wonder, "Is she ever coming back?" You have to start paying attention to what they see on TV now as well, because the images stick in their mind and can disturb sleep.

Common issues. Because your baby has more energy—and is more fun to be with now—you might be tempted to keep him up later. But at around seven or eight months, he'll actually want to go to bed earlier, especially if he's cut out a nap. Although teething, a more active social life, and fears can cause occasional night waking, when the pattern persists, it is almost always due to accidental parenting. Sometimes, of course, the bad habits have been entrenched for months ("Oh, he was never a good sleeper, and now he's teething"). But new ones often develop when parents rush in and rescue their baby in the middle of the night instead of calming him and teaching him how to get back to sleep. Of course, if he's scared, you must comfort him; if teething, you must treat the pain—and in both cases offer a little extra cuddling. But you have to draw the line, too, so that you don't *over*react. He'll pick up on your pity and will very quickly learn how to manipulate you. Sleep issues that result from accidental parenting at this age are often more difficult to unravel than those at earlier ages, because they have several layers of long-term problems (see the case study about Amelia, beginning on page 246).

This also can be an unstable time for the routine, and we see a lot of variations across families. Some days your baby might need a morning nap, on others, she'll skip it all together or skip her afternoon nap. Most babies now take a forty-five-minute nap in the morning, and a longer one in the afternoon. Some will go from two 1½-hour naps to one three-hour nap. If you go with the flow, and remember that it will only last for a few weeks, you're less likely to indulge in accidental parenting than if you panic and try to reach for a Band-Aid solution. (More about naps on pages 249–252.)

Key questions. **How did the night waking happen, and what did you do the first time? Does he wake up at the same time every night?** If you can set a clock by him, it's almost always a bad habit. If erratic, and particularly if he is around the nine-month mark, his waking might be due to another growth spurt. **If this has been happening for several days, have you continued to do the same thing? Do you take him into your bed?** It only takes two or three days to develop a bad habit. **Do you offer him a bottle or breast when he wakes?** If he's chowing down, it could be a growth spurt; if not, it's accidental parenting. **Does this only happen with you or with your partner as well?** Often, one person tells me that it's separation anxiety and the other doesn't agree; sometimes the mother is territorial and thinks she handles the child better than the Dad could. We need to determine who's going to take charge. Clearly, it's best if parents can coordinate their efforts and each take charge every two nights (see page 258 and the sidebar, page 174), but that assumes that both are home at bedtime and that they're on the same wavelength. However, if one parent tends to hold the baby too long, or is haphazard about bedtimes, or relies on a prop to get the baby down, this inconsistency will eventually lead to sleep problems. **Do you try to keep your baby up a little later now that he's older?** If so, by keeping him up, you're breaking into the natural pattern you've established, which could upset his sleep. **Does he have teeth? How is his feeding?** If he has some teeth, they sometimes come in all at once. Some babies teethe very badly and they can be miserable—runny nose, sore bottom, fitful sleep. They often start to refuse food, but then they wake in the night because they're hungry. With others you suddenly see a tooth without symptoms preceding it.

If I suspect fears are disturbing sleep, I also ask, **Has he ever choked on solid food? Has something scared him recently? Has he started a new play group? If so, has anyone started to bully him? What's changed in your household—a new nanny, Mum going back to work, a move to a new house?** Usually something new has been introduced or is happening. **Have you introduced any new things to watch on TV or video?** He's old enough to remember images that might later scare him. **Did you move him from crib to bed?** A lot of people think that by a year it's okay to move babies into a big-kid bed but it's too early in my opinion (more about the big-kid-bed transition on page 272).

How to adapt P.U./P.D. When she cries for you, go into her room, but *wait for her to stand up.* An eight-to-twelve-month-old can often settle a lot more quickly *out* of your arms. So don't pick her all the way up, unless she's very upset. In fact, with most babies over ten months, I just do the P.D. part of the method without picking up (see page 278). If you're of short stature, as I am, have a stool nearby—it will make it easier when you have to pick her up.

While standing at the side of the crib, put your arm underneath her knees, and with your other arm around her back, turn her and lay her back down on the mattress, so she's looking away from you, not at your face. Each time, wait until she stands up all the way before you lay her back down again. Then pick her up and *immediately* lay her straight back down the same way. Reassure her with a firm hand on her back: "It's okay, darling, you're just going to sleep." At this age you start to use your voice even more than at younger ages, because they understand so much. Also start to name her emotions for her, a practice that will continue even after you no longer use P.U./P.D. (more on this in chapter 8). "I'm not leaving you, I know you're [frustrated/scared, overtired]." She'll stand up again, and you may have to repeat the process many times, depending on how much accidental parenting preceded her particular sleep issue. Use the same reassuring words and add, "It's bedtime" or "It's nap time." It's important to introduce those words to her vocabulary if you haven't already done so. Help her view sleep as a good thing.

She'll eventually start to run out of steam. Then, instead of standing, she'll sit up. Each time, lay her back down. Remember that at around eight months, she is starting to have enough memory recall to comprehend that when you leave, you do return. So with P.U./P.D. your being there to comfort her is actually building that trust. It's also a good idea to tell her, at other points during the day, "I'm going to the kitchen—I'll be right back." It shows that you keep your word, and you continue to build on that trust.

If your child hasn't already adopted some kind of security object like a soft blanket or cuddly stuffed animal, this is a good time to begin to introduce one. When she's lying down, put a little blankie or animal into her hands, and say, "Here's your lovey blanket [or name of stuffed animal]" and then repeat the words, "You're just going to sleep."

Frequently, parents of ten-, eleven-, or twelve-month-old babies, who have used P.U./P.D. or some other method, will ask, "My child has learned how to fall asleep on her own, but she cries if I don't stay until she falls completely asleep. So how do I get out of the room?" You certainly want to avoid a hostage situation, which is not much better than pacing the floor with her. When you've done P.U./P.D. to the point of your child's being

---

Using a Blow-up Bed

In certain cases where I employ the P.U./P.D. method, I also bring an inflatable bed into the child's room and set up camp next to her. I might do it for a night, or for a week or longer—it depends on the situation. I've done it as early as three months, but I most often use one with older babies and toddlers when:

. . . a child has never slept on his own

. . . weaning a child who can't sleep at night without suckling Mum's breast

. . . a child has had no consistency and you need to get in there and send her back to sleep the moment she wakes

. . . a child has been left to cry and no longer trusts that his needs will be met.

able to settle fairly quickly, it still may take two or three days (or longer) for you to get out of the room. The first night, after she's settled down, stand by the crib. She will probably bob her head up to see if you're still there. If she is too distracted by your presence, stand first but then squat down to be out of her line of sight if possible. In any case, don't say anything and don't make eye contact. Stay there until you're sure she's in a deep sleep. The next night, do the same thing, but move farther away from the crib. Each successive night, you keep moving back farther toward the door until you're finally out of the room.

If your child suffers from separation anxiety, and starts clinging to you so you can't put her down, at least keep your body in the crib and reassure her, "Okay, I'll say right here." When crying escalates, you pick her up again. Expect the crying to be fairly severe on the first night if you have previously tried a controlled crying method. That's because she *expects* that you're going to leave, and she'll keep checking to see if you're there. In such cases, I bring in a blow-up bed and sleep *in* the child's room at least for the first night. On the second night I take the blow-up bed out, and only do P.U./P.D. Usually, by the third night, we're there (see also pages 279–280).

Eight Months to a Year Case Study: Multiple Problems, One Plan

Patricia contacted me initially by email because she was concerned about eleven-month-old Amelia. I followed up with several phone calls to Patricia and her husband, Dan, together on a speaker phone. I'm using this case because it shows how insidious accidental parenting can be—one bad habit builds on another—and how a temporary setback, like teething, can further complicate a situation. It also shows how the interplay between a couple can sabotage plans designed to correct the situation:

From two to six months, Amelia used to go to sleep and sleep through the night. Ever since she got her first teeth at six months it has been downhill from there. I got into a bad habit of strolling her for naps for months which I finally put an end to. Dan and I also would take her in the bed with us when she wouldn't go back to sleep. However, this does not work anymore because now she won't fall asleep in our bed. Now I rock her to lullaby music for naps and bedtime. And we have our bedtime routine of books, bottle, rocking with music. I don't always give a bath every night. Is that a problem?

I am just starting the P.U./P.D. method. Sometimes it gets her more upset and angry and she will cry harder and harder until finally I can't take it, and I rock her to sleep in my arms again. I am trying to get my husband to understand that we have to teach her to go to bed on her own. Is it too late to teach her at eleven months? I don't know if I should let her have a bottle in the middle of the night at this age. She used to just wake for me to put her pacifier in her mouth and then go right back but now she just won't go back. It is also very difficult because my husband can't stand to hear her cry for more than one minute. He constantly holds her when she is only fussing/not crying. I am trying to educate him as well. Help, I am feeling very unsuccessful at all my efforts.

Over the last many months, little Amelia has been taught that if you just cry hard and long enough, someone will pick you up, hold you, and rock you. You've probably already recognized that telltale phrase, *she used to*. So here we have a baby whose parents have been doing accidental parenting from Day One. Although Patricia said she "put an end" to pushing her in the stroller, she later admitted that she and Dan had almost always had to rock Amelia to sleep, even from the beginning. Then, when Amelia started teething, the parents began to intervene even more. Complicating the situation further, Mum and Dad don't sound like they're on the same page. In this case, it's Dan who seems to have a bad case of what I call the "poor-baby" syndrome, which occurs when parents feel guilty about a child's crying and are willing to turn cartwheels to make the little darling feel better.

I loved this couple, though, because they were so earnest and willing to change their own behavior. They were also quite self-aware. Patricia knew she had never taught Amelia how to sleep. She knew that both of them had done all sorts of accidental parenting. I think she even knew that she was trying to make herself feel better about her own accidental parenting by pointing out what Dan was doing wrong ("He constantly holds her when she is only fussing/not crying"). But Patricia didn't really want to make her husband the scapegoat. In fact, she was relieved when I said, "The first thing we need to establish here is that you two are on the same team. Let's not worry about who did what. Let's come up with a plan."

I told them they had to do P.U./P.D., laying Amelia down the moment she popped up to a standing position. They used to rock her but now they have to show her how to lie in the crib. "She'll be absolutely infuriated," I warned, "and she'll be very, very frustrated. But remind yourselves that crying is her way of saying, 'I don't know how to do this. Can you do it for me?'" I also suggested that Patricia be the one to go into Amelia's room. "Dan, you're a great dad—very involved. But you've already said it's hard for you to see Amelia cry. In this case, it's better if Mum goes in, because it sounds like she might stick with it, whereas you might cave in. It sounds like you're afraid, as many parents are, of abandoning your child or that if you don't respond to every cry, she won't love you."

Dan admitted that I was right. "When Amelia was born, I saw this precious little girl, and I felt I had to protect her from the world somehow. When she cries, I feel like I've failed her." Dan is not alone; many fathers—of little girls in particular—feel the need to shelter them. But Amelia needed teaching now, not rescuing, so I made a pact with Dan. He promised he wouldn't interfere.

After the first night, Patricia called. "I did what you said, and Dan kept his word, too. He was in the other room listening to everything. He never came in. I don't think he slept, though. Is it normal to have to pick her up over a hundred times? Even *I* felt like we were torturing the poor child. I was in there for over an hour."

I congratulated Patricia for staying with the plan, and I reassured her that she was on the right track. "You're just teaching her to go to sleep. But because you've already taught her that she has to cry for a certain period and then you'll pick her up, she is wondering how long she has to cry to get you to do the same thing."

By the third night, everything seemed a little better, because it only took Patricia forty minutes to comfort her daughter. Dan admired his wife's stamina, but Patricia was disappointed. "So much for that three-day magic you talked about in your first book." I explained that in many cases, in fact, we do see a change in three days, but Amelia had a deeply entrenched habit. Patricia had to look at her progress—where she started and the increasingly shorter length of time it took to put Amelia down.

By Day Six, Patricia was jubilant. "It's a miracle," she exclaimed. "Last night it only took me two minutes to put her down. There was a little bit of fussing but she just took her lovey blanket and rolled over and went to sleep. But I still had to reassure her with my voice." She was clearly on the right track. All children need reassurance, I told her. It's very rare that you just pop your baby into the crib and off she goes to Dreamland. I cautioned her to be very careful about maintaining the bedtime routine—read a story, have snuggle time, and then put her down.

Two weeks later, Patricia called. Eight days had passed with Amelia going straight to sleep. The problem now was that Mum and Dad were afraid it wouldn't last. I warned her, "If you stay stuck in that frame of mind, I promise you, Amelia will pick up on it. Try to stay in the moment. Take it for what it is. And know that if she does regress, you at least know what to do. With parenting, we have to take the rough with the smooth. If ninety-nine percent of the time your child is sleeping well and one percent you have to lay her down and talk her through it, that's just the way it is."

Lo and behold, one month later, Patricia checked in again. "I'm proud of myself. Amelia woke up in the middle of the night. We think she's teething but I knew what to do. I gave her some Baby Motrin for the pain, stayed with her, and reassured her. Dan was skeptical, but because we had had so much success with pick up/put down, he didn't fight me on it. It worked, of course. So now I'm ready for whatever comes next."

A Few Words on Naps

Although I touch on nap difficulties in each of the previous sections, the issue of daytime sleep—children not taking naps, taking too short a nap, or napping erratically—cuts across all age groups. Naps are a very important part of the E.A.S.Y. equation, because getting a proper amount of sleep during the day actually improves babies' eating patterns and enables them to go longer stretches at night.

The complaint I hear most often from parents whose babies have nap issues is, "My baby won't nap longer than forty-five minutes." No mystery there really. The human sleep cycle is approximately forty-five minutes long. Some babies only make it through one sleep cycle, and instead of transitioning and going back to sleep, they wake up. (This sometimes happens at night, too.) They may make little baby noises or even let out a few mantra cries (see box, page 235). If a parent then rushes in, they become accustomed to taking these shorter naps.

Too-short naps, or no naps at all, also happen if a baby is overtired when she first goes to sleep (in which case she might not even last the full forty minutes). Sometimes naps are erratic when parents wait too long to put their baby down. When she yawns, rubs her eyes, pulls at her ears, or maybe even scratches her face, her sleep window is already open. Especially with four months and older babies, you have to act immediately. When parents don't read the signs and keep them to the point of their being *over*tired, too-short naps are often the result.

Overstimulation is a common cause of nap disturbance, so it's also important to get your baby *ready* for a nap. You can't just plunk her in bed without a wind-down. I find that while most parents are well aware of the importance of bedtime rituals—the bath, the quiet lullaby before bed, the snuggling—they forget to take similar steps at nap time.

Naps shouldn't be too short or too long; either upsets the routine. Bad nap habits at this age both disrupt a routine and cause routine resistance, because a perennially overtired baby *can't* stay on track. Here's a perfect example from Georgina, a mother in Tennessee:

> I have read your book and believe that the E.A.S.Y. schedule will work for my Dana. Unfortunately, Dana will be four months old in a week and has not been on any type of schedule. I am able to get her to fall asleep for naps with just a little reassurance from me, but no matter how relaxing the atmosphere of the nursery, she will not sleep for more than thirty minutes and is still sleepy when she awakes. This makes it hard for me to follow the E.A.S.Y. schedule because I can't feed her when she wakes since it has been only two hours at the most since I fed her. I would really appreciate your opinion in this matter.

Dana doesn't need more feeds—that's a common error parents make. She needs more daytime sleep in order for E.A.S.Y. to work. Georgina will have to set aside a few days to extend her sleep periods by doing P.U./P.D. At this age, Dana should be napping for at least an hour and a half, twice a day. If she sleeps only a half hour, then for the next hour Georgina has to do P.U./P.D. Then, get Dana up. Her feed will be slow on the first day—

no doubt she'll be tired—but eventually the short-nap habit will be broken, and Dana will be on track. (Georgina also needs to put Dana on a four-hour routine at this point; see pages 39–46.)

Poor napping habits are often part of an overall sleep problem, but we almost always work on naps first, because good daytime sleep leads to good nighttime sleep. To lengthen naps, chart your baby's day for three days. Let's say we're dealing with a baby in the four-to-six-month range. She wakes at 7, and her morning nap is usually around 9. If you've gone through the twenty-minute wind-down stages (page 186), and your baby typically wakes up in forty minutes (at around 10), you have to send her back to sleep. (Six- to eight-month-olds also take a first nap at around 9. Between nine months and a year, the morning nap might be as late as 9:30. Regardless of age, however, the same principles apply to extending naps.)

There are two approaches you might take:

> ## Nap Intervention Guidelines
>
> Knowing when to intervene is often a matter of trusting your judgment and using common sense. Once you're good at reading your baby—hopefully, by four months you are—if you pay attention, there's not so much guesswork involved about naps:
>
> - If your baby wakes up early from a nap *every once in a while* and seems happy, let him be.
> - If he wakes up early but is crying, that usually means he needs more rest. Physically intervene by using P.U./P.D. to help him go back to sleep.
> - If he wakes up early from a nap *2 or 3 days in a row*, watch out. A new pattern may be developing, and you don't want him to get accustomed to 45-minute naps. Nip it in the bud by doing wake-to-sleep or P.U./P.D.

1. *Wake-to-sleep.* Instead of waiting for her to wake, go into her room after thirty minutes, because that's when she first starts to come out of a deep sleep. (Remember that sleep cycles are usually forty minutes.) Before she comes all the way up to consciousness, pat her gently until you see her body relax again. It could take fifteen or twenty minutes of gentle patting. If she starts to cry, though, you'll have to send her back to sleep with P.U./P.D. (See also pages 191–192.)

2. *P.U./P.D.* If your baby is resistant to naps altogether, you can use P.U./P.D. to put her to sleep. Or, if she wakes up forty minutes after you put her down, you can use the method to send her back to sleep. Granted, the first time you try this to remedy either situation, you might spend the entire nap period doing P.U./P.D., and then it's time for the next feed. Now both of you are tired! Because sticking to the

routine is as important as lengthening her nap, you need to feed her and then try to keep her up at least half an hour before putting her down for her next nap—at which point you'll probably have to do P.U./P.D. again because she's overtired.

Parents who are more accustomed to following the baby than a structured routine often get confused when I instruct them about naps. They want to extend their child's nap time, but they tend to forget about maintaining their routine, which is just as important because it's all part of the daily plan. A mum will say, "He gets up at seven, but sometimes he won't eat until eight. Shouldn't I put him down later for his nap then, too?" First of all, you should be giving him his breakfast by 7:15 or 7:30 A.M. at the latest—remember we're on a structured routine here. Either way, though, you should put him down at 9, or at the latest 9:15, because that's when he'll be tired. Then they'll ask, "Aren't I feeding him just before he goes to sleep?" No, after four months old, his feeds no longer take forty-five minutes. In fact, some babies can down a bottle or empty a breast in as little as fifteen minutes. So he can still have a little activity time after eating.

Admittedly, tweaking naps can be a frustrating undertaking. In fact, it takes longer to establish a good nap schedule than it does to solve nighttime sleep problems—typically, a week or two compared to a few days. That's because at night you have a longer time period to work with. During the day, you only have the span of time from when the nap begins to the next feed—usually around ninety minutes. But I promise that on the days that follow, P.U./P.D. will take less and less time, and your baby also will sleep for longer periods each time. That is, unless you give up too soon or fall into any one of the other pitfalls that I discuss in the next section.

The Dirty Dozen: Twelve Reasons P.U./P.D. *Won't* Work

When parents follow my plans, they work. Still, since my first book came out I've gotten thousands of emails about P.U./P.D. Parents hear about P.U./P.D. from friends, read about it on my website, or read my first book (in which the basic philosophy was covered only briefly). Many of their emails are like this one:

I am so confused and desperate. Heidi is one now and I have just begun the P.U./P.D. technique. What do I do when she gets up and sits on her bed? Am I supposed to talk to her during this? Do I Shh . . . shh? Tap her or not? Do I leave the room and come back in (immediately or wait till she cries) or just stand by the crib and do P.U./P.D.?? How do I get rid of the dream feed now? It's at 10:30 P.M. Why does she wake up at 5.30 or 6 A.M.? Anything I can do to change this?? Waiting so eagerly and desperately for your reply. Please, please answer me.

At least "A Desperate Mother," as this mum identifies herself, admits she's confused and doesn't know where to begin. Others' emails go on and on about the baby's problem ("He won't . . ." "She refuses . . ."). Finally, the writer—usually a mother—insists, "I tried P.U./P.D., but it doesn't work with *my* baby." Getting such a slew of emails about the so-called failure of P.U./P.D. encouraged me to look at the hundreds of cases I've handled over the last several years, and to analyze where parents typically go wrong:

1. ***Parents try P.U./P.D. when their baby is too young.*** As I wrote in the previous chapter, P.U./P.D. is not suitable for babies under three months because it can overstimulate them. They can't handle the constant picking up and putting down. Also, they burn up so many calories crying that it gets hard to tell whether they're hungry, overtired, or in pain. Therefore, the method usually fails before three months. Instead, I tell parents to review their sleep time routine, make sure it's consistent, and use the shush-pat to calm their baby rather than a prop.

2. ***Parents don't understand* why *they're doing P.U./P.D.—and therefore do it wrong.*** Where the shush-pat technique is for calming your baby, P.U./P.D. is to teach the skills of self-soothing when the shush-pat isn't enough. I never suggest starting off with P.U./P.D. Instead, try to calm him in his crib. Start with your wind-down ritual: Darken the room, turn on the music, kiss him, and put him down. All of a sudden the crying starts. What do you do? Stop. Don't rush in. Bend down to his ear and go shh . . . shh . . . shh. . . . Cover his eyes to block out visual stimulation. If he's under six months, get a rhythmic pat going on his back. (For babies over six months, the shush-pat distracts but

doesn't calm them; see page 184.) If he's older, just place a hand on his back. If that doesn't calm him, start doing P.U./P.D.

As Sarah's story (pages 236–237) shows, some parents also hold their baby for too long. They comfort past the actual need. You hold three- or four-month-olds at most for four to five minutes, and at older ages, you hold them for progressively shorter times. Some babies will stop crying as soon as you pick them up. And the parent will say, "He stops when I pick him up, but the minute I put him down he starts again." That's a sign to me that she's holding her baby too long. She's creating a new prop: herself!

3. *Parents don't realize that they have to look at—and adjust—their baby's entire day.* You can't solve a sleep problem by just looking at sleep patterns or even by focusing on what's happening right before sleep time. You have to look at what your child is eating and especially at his activities. Almost all babies are at risk of overstimulation nowadays. There are so many gadgets and so much pressure on parents to buy them—the swings, the seats that jiggle, the mobiles that light up and play the Irish jig. It seems like there has to be something going off all the time. But less is more with a baby. The calmer you can keep them, the better they'll be at sleeping, and the more neurological growth they can achieve. Remember that infants can't get out of the way of things hanging over their head. Often during activity time, parents will hear that first fussy cry and think, "Oh, she's bored" and jiggle something in her face. Whenever you hear your child do any kind of first fuss, it's an indication that something's up. The faster you swing into action—that first cry or the first yawn—the greater your chances of getting your child to settle without having to do P.U./P.D.

4. *Parents haven't focused on their baby's cues and cries or how to watch her body language.* P.U./P.D. has to be tailored to *your* child. When I instruct the parents of a four-month-old, for example, I tell them to hold her "at most four to five minutes." But that's *an estimate.* If your baby's breathing gets deeper and her body more relaxed in less time than that, put her down. Otherwise, you risk holding past the need. Also, I tell parents to pick up only in response to a genuine cry, not a mantra cry (see box, page 235). If you don't know the difference, you risk picking her up too often. Sometimes when we've used a lot of

props, we miss the essence. Parents often don't recognize what a frustrated cry sounds like, because they've always fallen back on rocking the baby to sleep or comforting her with a breast. It's not necessarily because the parents aren't attentive. It's just that they get into habits that work for the short term and only realize when it's too late that they've gone down a dark alley, and it isn't quite as easy to find their way back. What we're trying to do is develop habits and teach our children ways to go to sleep that will work for the long term. Admittedly, I do this all the time, so I know babies' facial expressions, the way they throw their arms out, or the way they slam their legs on the mattress. I can immediately tell the difference between a self-soothing mantra cry and one that needs intervening, because I've been in every possible situation. Please, luv, don't beat yourself up if it takes you (who have only one baby to study) a bit longer.

5. *Parents don't realize that as the baby develops they have to adapt P.U./P.D. to make it developmentally appropriate.* P.U./P.D. is not a one-size-fits-all technique. Where you can hold a four-month-old for up to four or five minutes after picking her up and a six-month-old for only two or three, you have to put a nine-month-old down straightaway. Where a four-month-old feels comforted by patting, it disturbs a seven-month-old. (See the previous "How to Adapt P.U./P.D." sections for each age group.)

6. *Parents' own emotions get in the way, especially guilt.* When they comfort their child, parents sometimes have a tone of pity in their voice. It's one of the symptoms of the poor-baby syndrome (see page 247). P.U./P.D. won't work if you sound as if you're feeling sorry for your child.

When a mum comes to me and says, "It's all my fault," I think to myself, *Pardon me, Mum, your guilt is showing.* In some cases, Mum has nothing to do with her baby's sleep problem. Teething, illness, digestive problems, for example, are beyond her control. True enough that with accidental parenting, there is "fault." Parents do get babies into bad habits. Still, guilt helps no one, not the baby and not the parents. So when a parent has been doing something that works against sensible sleep and says, "I did this," my response is simple: "It's good that you recognized it. Now let's move on."

Sometimes mothers will also ask, "Is it because I went back to work, and I don't see him enough in the day?" Usually what that means is that Mum believes her baby has missed her and wants to see her at night, so she lets him stay up longer. Instead, she might have to make a choice about her own schedule, or at least commit to having the nanny get him in bed on time.

When a parent acts guilty, a baby doesn't consciously think, *Great, I've got Mum and Dad right where I want them*, but he will pick up on the emotion and emulate it. A guilty parent is often also confused, hesitant, unable to zero in on a particular strategy and stick with it—all of which can induce fear in a child. *Hey, if my parents don't know what to do with me, where does that leave me? I'm just a baby!* For P.U./P.D. to be successful, parents have to exude an air of confidence. Their body language and tone should tell the child, "Don't worry. I know how frustrated you are, but I'm going to help you get through it."

Parents who feel guilty are more likely to give in (see #12 page 261) because they feel like they're hurting their child or depriving her of love when they use P.U./P.D. I know for a fact that P.U./P.D. works, but you have to see it as a teaching tool, not a punishment or something that could harm your baby or make her feel as if you don't love her. I also sense that guilt is at work when a parent asks, "How many times do I have to do it?" Although that question could also mean the person is a bit lazy or not really committed to doing things differently, it also tells me that he or she puts P.U./P.D. in the category of medicine—painful medicine at that. But it's not. You're doing it to teach her that it's okay to go to sleep in her own bed. P.U./P.D. reassures the child and lets her see that you're helping her develop skills of independent sleep.

7. *The room isn't ready for sleep.* You have to minimize distractions when you do P.U./P.D. It rarely works in broad daylight or with a bright light glaring overhead, or the stereo blaring in the background. Of course, you have to have a chink of light in the room, from a hallway light or a little night-light. You have to be able to see your baby's body language, and also have an uncluttered and visible escape route when you leave the room.

8. *Parents don't take their child's temperament into consideration.* P.U./P.D. has to be tailored to different personality types. By the time you use the method—no earlier than four months—you should have a pretty good

idea of what your baby likes and dislikes, what sets him off, what calms him down. Angel and Textbook babies are relatively easy to put down. Grumpy are often more aggressive—they're the ones who usually arch their backs and push you away when they're frustrated. You'd think the Spirited type would fit that description, but I've found that's not the case. But with Spirited, as well as with Touchy types, be prepared for P.U./P.D. to take a little longer. Both tend to cry a lot and get very frustrated. They're also distracted easily, so you have to figure out whether there's too much light filtering in, cooking smells wafting in the air, sounds in the household, siblings, and then try to get rid of or at least minimize as many of those distractions as you can.

However, the method itself is basically the same, regardless of your baby's temperament. You just have to be prepared to do it a little longer. Also, the quieter the activity time before bed, the better it will go. You can't take a baby straight from the Gymini and put her down. You've got to build in at least fifteen or twenty minutes of wind-down time (see pages 181–186). Darkening the room and blocking out visual stimulation is going to be especially important for Touchy and Spirited babies. Some, especially Touchy types, can't seem to keep their eyes shut. Then they start processing the environment and can't switch off. And that's why you'll get a baby who seems to be crying the world out—and she actually is. She goes to that extreme to "switch off" the world. When she's younger, the patting and the shushing will take the focus from the crying to the physical touch and the audio. And when she's over six months, use only your reassuring words and P.U./P.D., just to the point of comforting her.

9. ***One parent isn't ready.*** P.U./P.D. doesn't work unless both partners are on board. What happens sometimes is that one parent is fed up and instigates a change. Let's say a couple has been up for weeks on end, and Dad finally says, "There must be *something* we can do. He ends up in our bed every night." If the mother isn't quite there—or in fact enjoys cuddling with her baby and thinks she's helping him feel more secure by doing it—she will explain the situation this way: "My husband wants the child to sleep through the night, but it really doesn't affect me."

A similar scenario happens after a visit from the grandparents. Grandma makes a comment, such as, "That child should be sleeping through the night by this time, shouldn't he?" and Mum (who secretly agrees with her but doesn't know how to do it) is embarrassed. She may call for a consultation, but I can hear that she's not ready to take action and change her own behavior. I'll tell her a plan, and she immediately wants to modify it. "But every Thursday and Friday I do such and such, and you're telling me I have to stay home?" Or she'll come back with a series of what ifs: What if I don't mind taking him into bed? What if he cries longer than twenty minutes? What if he throws up because he's so upset? I stop at that point and ask, **How committed are you? What is your life now? Forget your husband and your mother—do *you* think the routine needs to be changed?** I implore parents to be honest. I can give them all the plans in the world, but if they come up with a thousand reasons not to do it and keep insisting it will never work, then guess what? It won't work.

10. *The parents don't coordinate their efforts.* To change a sleep pattern, as I explained in the case of Patricia and Dan (page 246), the parents need a plan that tells them what to *do*. A good solution also anticipates any unforeseen contingencies that might come up—a Plan B. At the same time, parents need to be aware of the pitfalls when *both* of them do P.U./P.D. This email from five-month-old Trina's mum, Ashley, shows how parents can unwittingly sabotage the process and, just as important, why some tend to give up too soon (see #12, page 261):

> After five months of bouncing Trina to sleep, I am in the middle of trying P.U./P.D. The second day was the best. It took twenty minutes of belly patting for her to fall asleep. Now, on the fifth day I am almost ready to give up. This morning she didn't fall asleep at all. When I start to put her to sleep and then my husband comes in to give me a break, she cries hysterically whenever my husband picks her up, and then comes down when I take her. Is that normal? I really want this to work and her to learn how to fall asleep unassisted, but I don't know what I am doing wrong.

This is a very common scenario: Mum gets tired and grumpy, and then Dad has to intervene. But what the parents don't realize that *to the baby,* Dad's coming in is a distraction. Even if Dad steps in and starts doing P.U./P.D. exactly as Mum did, it's the same as starting over. It's a new person, and we all know that babies don't respond the same way with each parent. Also, when both parents are in the room it can be very distracting, especially if the baby is six months or older. Therefore, I usually suggest that each parent commit to taking two nights in a row so that the baby is only dealing with one parent at a time.

In some cases, it's best if Dad actually takes over or at least gets the process going for several nights. I might suggest that if Mum is physically unable to pick up and put the baby down so many times. Or, if she's tried P.U./P.D. in the past and given in, it's best to have Dad do it for at least two or three nights. Some mums know they can't handle it. Take the case of James, whom you met at the very beginning of this chapter. When his mum, Jackie, heard my plan, she admitted, "I don't think I'll be able to get him back to sleep without nursing him. I can't bear the crying." She was a chronic rescuer and had been reluctant to allow Dad to participate much until now. In such cases, I go even further and suggest that Mum leave the house altogether and stay with relatives for a few nights.

Dads are often more efficient at doing P.U./P.D. than mums, but some also fall prey to the poor-baby syndrome (see pages 247–249). But even if guys are ready to tackle a sleep problem, it's not easy for them either, believe me. James's father, Mike, had to just *be* with his son for two nights before we even attempted P.U./P.D., because James wasn't at all used to Mike holding him. So when Mike first tried to comfort him, James became even more upset. He wanted his mummy, because that's all he knew.

When Dad is elected to do the intervention, Mum has to be careful not to try to take over in midstream. I often caution, "Even if that baby reaches out to you, you have to let Dad handle it. If not, you're going to turn him into the bad guy." In the same vein, Dad has to commit to staying the course. He can't, in the midst of his baby's cries, turn to his wife and say, "You do it." The wonderful thing is that even when a father has had minimal participation or has left the problem-solving up to his wife, being successful with P.U./P.D. can change the entire dynamics of a relationship. Mum gains respect for Dad, and he has newfound confidence in his own parenting ability.

11. *Parents have unrealistic expectations.* I can't repeat this too many times: P.U./P.D. is not magic. It doesn't "cure" colic or reflux or ease the pain of teething or make an obstinate baby easier to handle. It's merely a common-sense way of reconditioning your child to sleep longer. She will be very frustrated when you start—expect a lot of

crying—but because you're with her, she won't feel abandoned. As I said before, certain temperaments are more difficult (Touchy, Spirited, Grumpy). With all situations you have to allow time for change and expect a relapse. Bear in mind that you're dealing with an overtired baby who has no routine, and you've used accidental parenting to get her to sleep. Now you have to resort to a more extreme measure to undo those mistakes. Are you putting your baby through anguish and pain? No, but you are going to make her frustrated because you're changing what she's used to. She'll cry and arch her back and flop around like a fish in the bed.

Now I've done this with thousands of babies, and I've seen it take as long as an hour to get a child down—and as many as ninety or even over a hundred times of picking up and putting down. When I get a baby like eleven-month-old Emanuel, who had been waking nearly every 1½ hours for a feed, experience tells me one night isn't going to do it. When Emanuel woke at 10 the first night, I knew that we were lucky to get him down by 11, at which point I said to his parents, "He'll be back up at one." And sure enough he was. The good news was that even though he slept only two hours at a time that night, each time it took fewer P.U./P.D.s to get him back to sleep.

I can make such predictions because of my experience. Following are four of the most common patterns I've observed over the years of doing it with thousands of babies. Your baby might not conform exactly, but this will give you an idea of what to expect:

• If a child goes down reasonably fast with P.U./P.D.—say within twenty minutes to a half hour—you'll probably get a three-hour window out of her at night. So if you start at 7, she'll be up at around 11:30. That first night you'll be doing P.U./P.D. at 11:30 and then again at around 5 or 5:30 A.M.

• If you have a child like Emanuel who is eight months or older and has been waking frequently at night for several months, and you've responded with some form of accidental parenting, you might have to do P.U./P.D. over a hundred times. And when you finally get him down, he's not going to sleep more than two hours the first time around. The only thing I can suggest is to get some shut-eye yourself immediately after he's gone down, and be prepared to do it again and again and again for the first few nights.

- If a child has been taking short naps—anywhere from twenty to forty-five minutes apiece—when you first start to do P.U./P.D., she typically will stay asleep only for twenty minutes more because she's not used to sleeping longer than forty-five minutes. Go back in and do P.U./P.D. until you get her back to sleep, or until her next feed period, whichever comes first. But never allow her to sleep past her feed time.

- If you've done the controlled crying method and left your child to cry it out, P.U./P.D. will take longer (naps *or* nighttime) because your child is fearful. Sometimes you'll have to take steps to rebuild the trust before you can even attempt it. P.U./P.D. does eventually work, and when it does, you might have two or three nights of full sleep and you think you've cracked it. Then, on the third night, he wakes up. At that point, I get a call from you, "Tracy, it doesn't work, because he started waking again." But that only means you have to be consistent and do it again.

12. ***Parents get discouraged—and then don't stick with it.*** When they have a bad night or a bad day, many parents feel as if P.U./P.D. has failed them. It hasn't, but if you quit now it will. You have to stick with it. That's why it's important to write down where you started and chart your progress. Even if your baby sleeps ten minutes longer than he used to, that's progress. When I do consultations, I bring my notebook and tell parents, "This is what your baby was doing a week ago." In order to propel yourself forward, you have to see some movement. Spirited and Touchy and Grumpy can take longer, but don't give up.

When you're trying to teach a baby to sleep, there are no half measures. The worst thing you can do is stop in the middle. You might have to keep going for a while, picking up and putting down. Be prepared to be in there the long haul. Believe me, I recognize that P.U./P.D. is both difficult and trying for a parent, especially mums. So I'm not surprised when . . .

They cave in as early as the first night. When I later ask, **How long did you do it?** they say, "Ten or fifteen minutes, and then I couldn't stand it." Ten minutes won't cut it. For babies with deeply entrenched problems, I've done it for over an hour. Believe me, the second time gets shorter. When I do house visits, and actually *do* P.U./P.D. *with* a client (to deal with either a nighttime problem or too-short naps in the day), mums often admit, "I'd have never lasted twenty minutes with P.U./P.D." If it's at night, they say, "I would have caved in and given him the breast to get him to sleep." If during the day, "I'd have given up, gotten him up from his nap, even though I knew he'd be cranky for the rest of the day." Well, with me at their sides, they have to stick it out. But on their own, many parents don't go the distance.

They try it for a night and stop. If you've been consistent with accidental parenting, you have to be just as consistent with strategies meant to correct the situation. Admittedly, some of my advice seems counterintuitive to many parents—like waking a baby to keep her on a routine. In their hearts, if they don't believe something will work, when they don't get instant results, they immediately try something else. Because they don't stick to any one method, their baby is confused—and P.U./P.D. seems not to work.

They give up after they've had just a little progress. Say they've gone from a twenty- or thirty-minute nap to an hour nap. Mum is happy with the hour, but that's not enough to keep her child on a four-hour routine. Equally important, as he gets older and burns more calories he'll get grumpier, more uncoordinated, and more tired unless he has a 1½-hour nap. Staying the course avoids a return of the problem later on.

They experience initial success but when the problem recurs, as sleep issues often do, they don't go back to P.U./P.D. They try something else instead. If they had stayed with P.U./P.D. it would have taken less time to get back on track because the baby will remember, and each time it will take less intervention to calm him down.

Of course, there are no pat formulas for dealing with sleep problems, but I've personally never had a case in which P.U./P.D. didn't work. In the box on page 263 are some strategies to help you stay the course. Remember that if you are as consistent with the new method as you were with the old, it *will* produce change. But you have to be patient and see it through to the end. It eventually will work.

Keep in mind also that at this point sleep problems are infinitely more manageable than if you let them slide into toddlerhood. In fact, even if your baby hasn't reached his first birthday, it might be a good idea to read the next chapter and see what you're in for if you *don't* resolve your child's sleep problems now. That might be the best incentive of all!

P.U./P.D. Survival Strategies

How NOT to Give Up

As the saying goes, "Don't give up before the miracle." Here are some survival techniques that might help you stay the course.

✓ Think your plan through before starting. P.U./P.D. is very stressful for one parent to do alone. It's darn hard! Especially if you know your own temperament and fear that there's going to be a point where you won't be able to stand it, do *not* attempt this on your own. Do it *with* someone. Even if you don't have a partner, a parent, or a best friend you can team up with (see #10 page 258, and the sidebar, page 174), at least invite someone over for moral support. The person doesn't necessarily have to *do* anything with your child. It will be helpful for you just to have someone there for *you,* allowing you to complain about how hard it is, and reminding you that you're doing this to help your child sleep and to restore calm to your household.

✓ Start P.U./P.D. on a Friday, so that you have the weekend and are more likely to secure the above-mentioned help from Dad or Grandma or a good friend.

✓ Use ear plugs when you're in the room with the child. I don't tell you this to suggest that you should ignore the child, only to deaden the sound of her crying a bit, so it's less likely to grate on your ears.

✓ Don't feel sorry for your child. You're doing P.U./P.D. to help her become an independent sleeper, which is a great gift.

✓ If you're tempted to quit, ask yourself, *What will the situation be if I cave in?* If your child cries for forty minutes and you give up and go back to whatever old habit of soothing you adopted so many months ago, you've made your child have a miserable forty minutes for nothing! You're right back to where you were before you started, she is no better equipped to soothe herself, and you feel like a failure.

SEVEN

"WE'RE STILL NOT GETTING ENOUGH SLEEP"

Sleep Problems after the First Year

An American Crisis

American babies and toddlers aren't getting enough sleep, according to a 2004 poll conducted by the National Sleep Foundation. The results were released just as we were writing this chapter about sleep problems past the first year. Although the poll focused on birth to the teenage years, we concentrated on the data about toddlers (which they define as twelve to thirty-five months). Reading between the lines, it's easy to see how the findings underscore the importance of teaching our children how to go to sleep and stay asleep:

- *Sleep problems are persistent well past infancy.* Babies and parents of babies are hardly the only sleep-deprived humans in our culture. Sixty-three percent of toddlers experience sleep-related problems. Toddler problems include stalling about going to bed (32 percent), resisting bedtime altogether (24 percent), and/or being overtired during the day (24 percent) at least a few days or nights a week. Almost half of toddlers wake at least once a night; 10 percent wake several times, and each time are awake for an average of nearly twenty minutes. Around 10 percent stay up for forty-five minutes or more.

- *Most babies and toddlers go to bed too late.* The average bedtime for infants (birth to eleven months) is 9:11 P.M. and for toddlers 8:55 P.M. Nearly half of toddlers are in bed after 9 P.M. I see this problem frequently among my clients, some of whom keep their toddlers up so that they can spend more time with them after work. Others do it because they've never gotten their children into the habit of a decent bedtime, and now they can't get them to sleep any sooner. I recommend a 7 or 7:30 P.M. bedtime at least until age five, but the poll shows that only around 10 percent of toddlers (or babies for that matter) are in bed that early. And yet in both categories the average wake-up time is a little past 7 A.M. You don't need to be a mathematician to see why children aren't getting enough sleep. (I wouldn't be surprised to find that this is one of the reasons we're seeing so much hyperactivity and aggression in children. A lack of sleep doesn't cause these conditions, but it certainly aggravates them.)

• *Many parents are in denial about their children's sleep habits.* When asked how the number of hours their children are actually getting compares to what the parents think their children *should* be getting, around a third of parents with toddlers said their children were getting less sleep than they should. But when asked, on another question, whether their child gets too little, too much, or the right amount of sleep, the vast majority—85 percent—said that their child gets the right amount of sleep. Also, despite the prevalence of toddler sleep difficulties, only one in ten parents is concerned. (My hunch is that the worried 10 percent are the same who reported that their toddlers stayed awake forty-five minutes or more in the middle of the night!)

The researchers' findings illuminate a common problem I see every day: Parents tend to allow poor sleep habits to persist until they—the parents—are absolutely desperate. Usually, parents call me for help when the woman is about to return to work and is concerned about being able to function the next day on the job, or when a couple's fighting has seriously escalated because the child's constant waking is wreaking havoc on their relationship.

• *Accidental parenting is alive and well among parents of toddlers.* Close to half of all toddlers (43 percent) go to sleep with a parent in the room, and one in four is already asleep when put to bed. In both cases, that means that a parent or other caretaker is literally putting these children to sleep rather than allowing them to fall asleep on their own. While half of parents whose toddlers wake at night allow them to fall back to sleep on their own, the poll shows that 59 percent of parents run to their rescue, 44 percent stay with them until they fall asleep, 13 percent bring them into an adult's bed, and 5 percent allow the child to sleep with them. I suspect those last two figures are even higher. When one online poll conducted by babycenter.com asked, "Will your—or does your—baby sleep in your bed?" over two-thirds of the parents answered "occasionally" (34 percent) or "always" (35 percent). Perhaps the anonymity of an internet poll encouraged parents to answer more honestly.

The good news is that the poll also shows that parents who *teach* their child the skills of independent sleep tend to have children who sleep better: They don't wake too early, they take naps during the day, they go to bed easily and fall asleep without much difficulty, and they are less likely to wake during the night. For example, children who are put to bed awake are more likely to sleep longer than children who are put in bed already asleep (9.9 hours compared to 8.8 hours) and nearly three times *less* likely to wake repeatedly during the night (13 percent versus 37 percent). And when parents say they are rarely or never present in the bedroom when their child falls asleep—a sign that their children are able to go to sleep on their own—they are also more likely to report that their child does not wake during the night.

This was the largest study to date to examine the sleep habits of young children, and while it shows that some children are learning good sleep habits and are able to fall asleep on their own, a whopping 69 percent of young children experience sleep-related problems a few times a week. Not surprisingly, their parents also lose as many as two hundred hours of sleep a year. With so many adults and children deprived of sleep, every member of the family is affected, and relationships are stressed to the max. Parents gets angry at their children; siblings battle; couples fight. Among other causes of this epidemic of sleeplessness and sleep disorders, the report cites the pace of modern society. One of the members of the sleep foundation, Dr. Jodi Mindell, a professor of psychology at St. Joseph's University who specializes in sleep disorders, explains: "All of the pressures of society are not just affecting adults but are filtering down to our children. This is a warning that we need to pay as much attention to the sleeping half of children's lives as the waking half."

I would weigh in with another reason: Many adults aren't *teaching* their children how to sleep. They often don't even realize that sleep is a learned art, and they expect that their baby will eventually learn how to go to sleep on his own. And by the time the child is a toddler, he's in big trouble, and his parents don't know where they went wrong or how to resolve the problem.

In the next two sections below, I summarize the sleep issues in the second year (young toddlers) and the third year (old toddlers). Those might sound like very broad age groups. However, even though there are subtle developmental differences every few months during toddlerhood, those changes don't affect a child's sleep patterns or the kind of intervention I suggest. I then review sleep strategies I introduced earlier, explain how to adapt them for toddlers, and include typical cases that exemplify the various techniques.

Sleep Issues in the Second Year

Developmental changes and a growing sense of independence account for some sleep problems in the second year. So, whenever a parent tells me that nighttime sleep or daytime sleep is "off," I ask, **Is he walking? Is he talking?** Your baby learns to walk at some point past his first birthday. Even late walkers have significant leg strength by now. As I explained in the previous chapter, this newfound physical achievement can affect him when he's resting as well—in particular during the period in which he is taking those first few tentative steps. Some children stand themselves up in the middle of the night while still sleeping and walk around the perimeter of the crib. Then they wake up, don't know how they got there, and don't know how to get down. Also, muscle spasms can wake your child and so can the sensation of falling. Think of how many times your child falls during the day.

I don't recommend allowing young toddlers to watch TV or video presentations, because these media can overstimulate or leave disturbing images in their little heads, which also can upset their sleep. At one year, REM time decreases to about 35 percent, but there is still ample time for dreaming in a young toddler's sleep. Although they can have nightmares, too—replays of fearful moments—they are more likely to have night terrors, which are less about bad dreams and more about physical exertion and stimulation (see the chart on page 271). Toddlers re-create those moments in their sleep.

You also need to consider the rest of the family: **Has he got older siblings who wind him up?** When a toddler starts to walk, it becomes fun for his brother or sister to torment him—all in good fun, of course. But this can really upset a child and also cause him to wake up at night.

Your young toddler is more inquisitive as well as active. "Into everything" is the phrase most often used to describe children between the ages of one and two. Even if she's not talking in full sentences, she is probably chattering more and certainly understands everything you say. You might hear her in the morning babbling to her stuffed animals—that just means she's learned to amuse herself. Unless you run right in, this developmental achievement gives you a few more delicious moments in bed.

When a formerly good sleeper suddenly starts having sleep problems as a young toddler, I also look for clues related to his health or in his environment. **Have you changed the household routine? Is your child teething? Have you started new activities? Has he been sick recently? Have you started a new play group? Have there been changes in the lives of other family members with regard to work, health, availability?** You may have to think back several weeks or months, and look at what happened and what you did in response to it. For example, Ginny contacted me recently because her sixteen-month-old had suddenly started waking at night. When I posed a series of questions, Ginny insisted that there had been no changes. Then, almost as a stray afterthought, she added, "But Ben had a cold five or six weeks ago, and come to think of it, he hasn't slept well ever since." Not surprisingly, when I questioned her further, she told me she had taken Ben into her bed "to soothe him."

Naps get trickier now, too. This is a time when children usually transition from two 1½- or two-hour naps to one long one (see box, page 284). That seems simple enough on paper, but the getting there can be like riding a mechanical bull—lots of ups and downs that threaten to throw you! Your toddler might skip his morning nap for a few days, but then revert to his old pattern for no apparent reason. And unlike younger babies for whom good naps ensure a good night's sleep, when a baby is over a year old, a late nap can disturb nighttime sleep. When a toddler has grown accustomed to napping later in the day, I often suggest moving the nap earlier, and warn parents to get the child up by 3:30. Otherwise, there may not be enough activity time for him to expel his energy and get ready to sleep. That said, there are always exceptions to the rule: If your child has lost sleep in previous days and needs to catch up, if he's sick and needs more sleep than activity time, or if you just sense that on a particular day, it's important for him to have extra sleep, then by all means allow him to sleep a bit later.

The most important developmental leap is the fact that your child now understands cause and effect. You can see it when she operates her toys. Because of this newfound understanding on your child's part, accidental parenting can happen a lot faster. In the past, if you rocked your baby or gave her the breast in order to lull her to sleep, it eventually became a habit in much the same way that Pavlov's dog was conditioned. His master rang the bell every time he presented food and it wasn't long before the dog began to salivate at the sound of a bell. But now, because your child understands cause and effect, accidental parenting is not just pure conditioning. Each lesson you teach (consciously or not) is put into that little computer, and stored for future uploads. If you're not careful at this stage, you will prepare your toddler for the fine art of parental manipulation!

Let's say your fifteen-month-old wakes up suddenly at 3 A.M. It could be because her molars are coming in, or because she's had a bad dream. She could have had a particularly active play group or a very stimulating visit with Grandpa. Or, it could be something even simpler: She's come out of a deep sleep, and a sound or a shaft of light happened to pique her insatiable curiosity. Toddlers are interested in just about everything. So when they wake during their nighttime sleep, they're less likely to settle down.

Especially if this is her first time waking in the night (an unlikely scenario in most families), it's very important that you not *start* accidental parenting. If you rush in, pick her up, and say to yourself, "Just this one time I'll read her a book to calm her down," I guarantee that tomorrow night she'll wake up and want you to read her a book again, and she'll probably up the ante as well, demanding two books, a drink, and an extra cuddle. That's because she's able now to actually make the connection between what she does and what you do. *This is the noise I made. Mum came in and something happened.* By the third night, she has it down cold: *I make this noise, Mum comes in, she reads me a book and then starts rocking me. Then I make the noise again as she is putting me into the crib, and she rocks me some more.* Now you are caught in a huge mousetrap known as the manipulative toddler.

It's not hard to tell when a parent has fallen into this trap. I often ask, **Does he have tantrums during the day?** Once a toddler learns how to manipulate, the behavior colors his whole day. Most little tyrants will demonstrate the same demanding patterns around waking behavior—meals, cooperation when dressing, playing with other children (more on these behavioral issues in the next chapter). Remember, too, that this is the Age of "No!" Toddlers feel powerful when they learn the word and love to use it.

Naturally, when parents have been doing accidental parenting all along, sleep problems like early waking, night waking, erratic naps, and prop dependency are less related to developmental issues than to firmly entrenched bad habits. Two key questions help me determine whether a child has a troubled history when it comes to sleep: **Has your child ever slept through the night?** and **Have you always had trouble putting him to bed?** A "no" to the first question and "yes" to the second tells me I am looking at a child who has never learned to fall asleep on his own and who lacks the skills to put himself back to sleep when he wakes. Then I have to get to the details, find out what kind of props the parent has been using, with a series of questions, among them: **How do you put him down now? Where does he sleep? Are you still breast-feeding? If so, do you use that as a form of putting him to sleep? Do you feel sorry for him when he cries at night? Do you rush in? Do you bring him into your bed? When he was younger, were you able to leave the room before he was fully asleep? How long are his naps in the day and where? Did you ever try the controlled crying method?** All of these kinds of questions also help me gauge the degree of accidental parenting. Some cases are no-brainers, as this all-too-typical email shows:

> My twenty-two-month-old daughter hasn't learned to fall asleep on her own, so I have to sleep with her night after night, and I have a new baby coming. I don't think my husband is helping. I don't think he is saying the right things to her, when she constantly needs to be on top of me every night. Please help!!

Sadly, neither Mum nor Dad know what to do, and this is often the case. When a child has been allowed to sleep wherever and however she wants for nearly two years and still hasn't learned the skills of independent sleep, we're going to have to come in with a very detailed plan—and make sure both parents are on board, not rowing in separate directions, or worse, arguing with each other about where to go. Additionally, if there has been a breach of trust between parent and child, the situation is even more complicated, because the child also doesn't feel safe and confident on her own. Therefore the first intervention must include trust-building (see pages 192 and 279).

Why Do Toddlers Scream in Their Sleep?		
	Nightmare	Night Terror
What is it?	A *psychological* experience that occurs during REM sleep, it is the proverbial "bad" dream, in which the child relives an unpleasant emotion or previous trauma. His mind is active but his body (except for the rapid movement of the eyes) is at rest.	Called a "confusional arousal" in toddlers (a true night terror happens in adolescence and is rare), it, like sleepwalking, is a *physiological* experience. Instead of making the normal transition from deep sleep to REM, the child gets caught between the two stages. His body is active, but his mind is not.
When does it happen?	Usually in the second half of the night, when REM sleep is most concentrated.	Usually in the first 2 to 3 hours of sleep—the first third of the night.
What does it sound and look like?	Child awakes screaming but is conscious when you come to him, or awakes shortly thereafter. He probably will remember the experience—bad dreams can haunt children for years.	Begins with a high-pitched scream. Child's eyes open, his body is rigid and possibly in a cold sweat, and his face might be flushed. He may not recognize you when you come to him and won't remember anything about it later on.
What do you do when it happens?	Comfort and reassure your child, and encourage him to talk about the dream if he remembers the specifics. Don't minimize his fears—the dream is very real *to him*. Soothe him with lots of cuddles, even lie with him for a while, but don't take him into your bed.	Don't wake him; it will only prolong the episode, which typically lasts about 10 minutes (it also could be as short as one minute or as long as 40). This is more upsetting to you than to him, so try to relax yourself and ride it out by offering only verbal reassurance. Protect him from banging into furniture.
How do you prevent future episodes?	Figure out what might be stressful or fear-inducing for your child and avoid daytime encounters with it. Stick to your regular bedtimes and wind-down rituals. If your child is afraid of "monsters," give him a night-light and check under the bed.	Try to keep his routine consistent, and avoid letting your child get overtired. If these episodes occur frequently, or if a tendency toward sleepwalking runs in your family, you might want to talk to your pediatrician or consult a sleep specialist.

Making the Crib-to-Bed Switch

Don't rush into it (try to wait until your child is at least 2), but also, don't wait too long to make this transition if you're expecting another child. Be sure to start the process at least 3 months before the baby is due.

Do talk about the transition and involve your child in the process: "I think it's time we got you a bed like Mummy and Daddy's. Would you like to pick out some new sheets for it?" If she's under 2, consider a bed with removable sides to start with.

Don't change bedtime rules or your routine when you make the switch. It's more important than ever to be consistent.

Do send your child back to bed immediately—and without cuddling—if he manages to get out and comes into your room.

Don't feel guilty for enforcing a stay-in-your-room rule after bedtime and putting up a gate if necessary. If your child is an early riser who once amused himself but now comes into your room early in the morning, get him his own alarm clock or put a light on a timer—when the alarm goes off or the light goes on, he can come out.

Do make her room safe (if you haven't already)—cover outlets, get cords out of the way, put locks on lower drawers, so she can't use them for climbing to high places.

Don't take chances, especially if your child is under 3. Place the bed against the wall; use a mattress only (no box spring), so the bed is closer to the ground; and, at least in the first few months, use a guard rail.

Sleep Issues in the Third Year

Many of the second-year issues continue into the third year, but older toddlers have even greater mental capacity and sensitivity to what's going on around them. They're more affected by changes in the family and in the environment. They're even more curious than their younger counterparts. If you're having company, they think everyone coming through the door is their playmate. They don't want to miss anything. Noise can wake your child where it didn't before.

They are physically more able, too. **Does your toddler climb out of his crib and come into your room?** Some toddlers manage this feat as early as eighteen months but not necessarily on purpose. Before the age of two, your child's head is still out of proportion to her body, and when she leans over the crib side, she could topple over and fall out. But by two she might figure out how to stand on the bumper and actually climb over. And then she comes wandering into your room in the middle of the night. This is an age when parents normally start thinking about getting their child into a bed (see box, page 272). I say put it off as long as possible—at least until age two if not longer—because it somewhat curtails those middle-of-the-night visits. (The only exception is when a child is crib phobic; see pages 280–281.) **What do you do when your child comes into your room in the middle of the night?** If you allow it once or twice in a week, chances are you'll have a problem on your hands.

Because older toddlers are also extremely sensitive to changes in the household, I always ask, **Has life in your family changed?** A new arrival, a death in the family, parents' marital problems and/or divorce, new partners, a new caregiver, more challenging social situations—any of these can throw off an older toddler's sleep, especially if she's never learned to sleep on her own or to self-soothe. This is also the age of increased sociability, and as I stressed earlier, activities affect sleep. **Have you started a new play group or added another type of group, like Gymboree, Mommy and Me, baby yoga, baby aerobics?** Delve deeply and look at specifics, too: **What's actually happening in the play group? What kinds of activities is your child being asked to do? What are the other children like?** Even a child who was once a good sleeper can fall apart in the face of too much stress (a toddler shouldn't be given formal lessons or have a gymnastics "coach," for example) and, in particular, if she's the brunt of teasing or targeting by a pint-size bully (see Alicia's story in the next chapter, pages 313–314).

Sleep problems are now more exhausting than ever for parents. These children have the gift of speech, to ask for a glass of water, a story, just one more cuddle, and to endlessly negotiate and harangue. Many parents tend to lose their tempers with an older toddler whereas at an earlier stage they'd rationalize, "She doesn't understand" or "She can't help it." If it's a deeply entrenched habit, and the parent doesn't respond the way the child expects and wants, she's likely to get angry and shake the crib. She might have tantrums during the day as well. Older toddlers understand quite well that a particular behavior will cause Mum and Dad to come running.

If you have a two- to three-year-old who has a sleep problem, it's always important to look back in history. **Has your child ever slept through the night?** In lots of cases we have to start at Square One. We have to look at emotional history as well. If there's a history of demanding behavior, now the little dictator is probably a full-blown tyrant. It can manifest in many ways: head-banging, pushing, slapping, biting, hair-pulling, kicking, throwing themselves on floor, going rigid when being held. If his parents haven't intervened in the correct manner during waking hours (see pages 324–331), it's worse at night because he's tired.

Parents often mistake older toddlers' manipulation for separation anxiety, which usually starts between seven and nine months and disappears by fifteen to eighteen months, that is, if parents are gentle and reassuring and haven't resorted to some sort of accidental parenting as a solution to their child's fears. Therefore, when the parents of a two-year-old come to me and say, "My child is waking at night because he has separation anxiety," nine times out of ten that's a child who has learned how to manipulate them. The sleep problem is not because the child is fearful—it's because normal separation anxiety has been dealt with by accidental parenting (see pages 80–83 and 187–195).

Make no mistake, however: There are also genuine fears at this age, because comprehension is so much greater. Your child grasps fully what's going on around her: that a new baby is coming, that Mummy and Daddy are angry at each other, that one kid in play group always grabs her toys, that the little fish in *Finding Nemo* was separated from his daddy. Older toddlers are also very impressionable. I recently heard a great story about a child who watched his dad put locks on every first-floor window in their house. Dad explained to his 2½-year-old son that he was doing it "to keep burglars out." That night the boy awoke at 3 A.M., screaming, "Burglars are coming! Burglars are coming!" I had a very similar experience with my older daughter when she was around three. I thought it would be fun for her to watch the movie *ET,* which was popular then. It seemed harmless enough to me, but for months afterward Sara had nightmares, thinking that little ETs were coming through the cat door.

Because parents tend to allow more TV-watching and computer games in the third year, it's not surprising that nightmares go with the territory. It's important to try to screen everything you offer your child and see it through your child's eyes. Are you sure they'll really enjoy watching *Bambi* or *Finding Nemo*? Or might it be disturbing for a little child to see that in both movies the main characters' mothers are killed? Watch what kinds of stories you tell as well and what kinds of books you read, too. Spooky tales and dark images might stay with your child. Most important, if television and computers are a part of your child's day, be sure to build in a wind-down time before bed. Personally, I advise a "no media" rule at the end of the day.

Sleep Strategies for Toddlers

Many of the practices and strategies I've explained throughout this book are applicable to toddler sleep problems, albeit with some modifications. Here are a few important reminders, with real-life examples. To help you look for a particular problem, refer to the problem identification boxes in the margins.

You still need a routine, but you might have to modify it as your child gets older. Lola called about her nineteen-month-old: "Carlos is suddenly cranky during his bedtime routine. And he used to love his bath, but now he gets really upset." After a few questions about what's been going on in Carlos's life, it came out that the family had recently taken a trip to Lola's native Guatemala and also Carlos had started a new music class. I explained to Mum that she had to expect some reverberation. The trip was a departure from the usual routine, and music class meant a whole new level of socializing. Additionally, because Carlos is more active now, his bedtime routine might have to change. Many young toddlers, for example, do better if put to bed at 6 or 6:30. Also, at this age a bath before bedtime can overstimulate some children, in which case Lola would have to either bathe him earlier—say at 4 or 5 before dinner—or do a morning bath and quick sponge before bed at night. Lola protested at first: "But we do the bath at night so Dad can do it." Well, that was her choice, of course. But I was honest. "Fine, but just accept that you're thinking of yourself, not your baby." Luckily, Carlos, a Textbook toddler, was adaptable, and Lola was creative. She suggested that Dad try taking him into the shower in the morning. Carlos loved it, and a new ritual with Dad began.

> "Suddenly cranky during his bedtime routine"

Take pains to make your bedtime ritual consistent, and use it to antici-pate problems. Bedtime routines should of course include time for book-reading and cuddling. In addition, because toddlers' comprehension is so much greater, you might consider adding conversation to the routine, as Julie, the mother of twenty-three-month-old Megan, found out. Julie takes Megan to work with her and admits "our days are often unpre-dictable." I'm reprinting portions of her lengthy web posting here to applaud her resourcefulness and her powers of observation. By knowing who her child is (she says Megan is a Touchy type), tuning in to her, and also sifting through suggestions, she then cobbled together an ideal ritual for her child:

> "Takes a long time to fall asleep; naps are inconsistent"

I wrote a couple of weeks ago about my daughter's sleep issues. I was trying to teach her to fall asleep on her own and she ended up singing, laughing, talking for two hours every night! Her naps went to 40 minutes during the day after being very consistent at 1.5 to 2.5 hours. She wasn't cranky during day—not fussy or cry-ing when put down—just not sleeping . . . Someone suggested that because Megan is on her best behavior all day long, maybe by the end of the day she's done all the adapting that she could and that's why she was having trouble settling at night. I think that was right on the mark . . .

So the first thing I did was institute a consistent routine: two books, a kiss, two short stories in bed, one chorus of "Rock-a-Bye-Baby," and that's it. I also had a suggestion that she might need help processing her day. Never thought of that one! I started out doing this before the books, but it got to be long, so now we talk about different parts of the day as we get ready for bed. By the time jammies are on and we're in the room, we've talked all about the day. The last thing I did was I made her crib into a cozy little nest. I have always noticed that she naps better when we're at work. Her crib in the crib room at work is smaller than the standard size we have at home, and the room itself only 5' x 5'5".

I thought about Tracy's suggestion to recreate a womb-like atmosphere for a Touchy baby, so I tucked a very soft faux suede blanket down around her mattress, which she instantly loved. I also stuck in a section of my sheepskin rug, big enough for about half her crib. I trimmed down the fur so it isn't so long, but still very cozy and smells like mommy. Last, she gets a small (maybe 6" x 6") accent pillow that is faux suede on one side and fleecy on the other. She's also started asking for a blanket rolled up alongside her. Just like I used to do when I bolstered rolled-up towels around her as an infant.

She looks like a little caterpillar in its cocoon, but she loves it! She was really stuffy the other night and I offered to hold her while she fell asleep. After about 5 minutes, she asked for her crib. This is a child who slept in my bed for a year and who has ALWAYS preferred being held to anything else.

Anyway, I'm not sure if this will help anyone else, but I am sure that Megan needed a smaller, safer environment in which to sleep, along with help processing her day and a very predictable bedtime routine to counter a very unpredictable daytime schedule. I know two-year molars are coming, so I hope this helps us through!

Now perhaps Megan's nightly ritual wouldn't suit your baby, but I offer it as an example of how being tuned in to your child helps you design a ritual that really fits.

Also use the bedtime routine to anticipate problems that might arise and deal with them *before* bed instead of later. For example, at twenty-one months, Jason began waking at around 4 A.M. with the excuse, "I'm thirsty." Luckily, Maryann called me after he did this two nights in a row, because she realized that a pattern was beginning to develop. I suggested that she give him a nonspillable sippy cup of water every night to take into his crib with him. "Make it part of his bedtime ritual," I explained. "Just say to him right before the good-night cuddle and kiss, 'And here's your water in case you wake up and get thirsty.'"

In another case, two-year-old Olivia had been having bad dreams. So I suggested that when Dad puts her to sleep he make a big deal about "Googie," the furry little fox Olivia had adopted as her special comfort item. The last thing Dad said before "good night" was "Don't worry, Liv. Googie will be here for you if you need him." Figure out what will work with *your* child. The goal is to plant the idea that your child has the skills to see herself through the night. If incorporating other actions into bedtime rituals helps your child feel safe, like checking under the bed for monsters, by all means add that, too. Going over the day is also a wonderful idea, especially because it helps a child process her fears. Even before

| "Stalls at bedtime; wakes at night" |

| "Having bad dreams" |

your toddler is fully verbal, at least you can talk *to* her about things that happened during the day.

It is especially important to maintain a consistent bedtime ritual when your child makes the transition from crib to big-kid bed (see page 272). You want to take pains to make everything the same—except, of course, the new bed. Interestingly, many children who switch to a big-kid bed never get out of bed once they're tucked in. It's as if they remember the restrictions of their crib. Of course, some do, and they will test their parents to see if this new bed also means new freedoms. By keeping to your routine—sticking to however many stories you once told, the same bedtime, the same good-night rituals—you're sending a message: The bed may be new, but the old rules apply.

When your child cries during a sleep period, don't rush in. It's absolutely critical during toddlerhood to continue a practice (I hope) you started when your baby was a wee thing: Observe before you jump in. If your child doesn't cry, don't go into her room. You might hear her babbling in her crib. If let be, she'll probably fall back to sleep on her own. If she does cry, try to distinguish whether it's her mantra cry or a genuine call for help (see box, page 235). If the former, wait a bit. If the latter, go in but say nothing. Don't talk to her; don't engage at all.

"Cries out at night"

"P.U./P.D." turns into "P.D." Because toddlers are heavier than babies and harder to lift, and because you've lowered the mattress, I don't suggest picking them up—just do the put-down part. In other words, you allow your child to stand (most toddlers are often already on their feet by the time a parent reaches their room), but don't pick him up. Just lay him down. Use the same reassuring words and add, "It's bedtime" or "It's nap time."

Of course this technique will take longer with children who've had a history of accidental parenting. Even if you realize what you've done, expect the *un*doing to take a while. Betsy, for example, wrote to me fully aware of what she'd done wrong with Noah. The subject line of her email read, "Eighteen-month-old rules the roost at sleep time." It is a classic case in that it embodies several familiar themes—a long history of accidental parenting complicated by a toddler's growing physical and mental capacity *and* by illness and hospitalization:

> I've "accidental parented" Noah so that he wants to be rocked as he sleeps. Once he's in bed he can "sometimes" get himself back to sleep. Some nights we hear him barking and talking and then he

goes back to sleep on his own. But other times he wakes up crying. Now if he wakes up it's impossible to get him back in his crib! The minute I move to get up out of the chair, he begins to cry. He does the same thing at nap time. He's been doing this for oh around 18 months. Any suggestions? He weighs 26 pounds and our crib side is a bear to get up and down. He's been sick (got out of the hospital for dehydration four days ago), but the doctor gave him a clean bill of health today. I found Tracy's books while he was in the hospital. I wish I had found her first one 17 months ago!!!

> "Wants to be rocked to sleep; can't get back to sleep on his own"

This is obviously an old problem, which has never been resolved and then further complicated by toddler issues. Interestingly, Betsy claims that Noah has "been doing this" for eighteen months. But really, she and her hubby have *taught* him: *When I cry, they come running, and they rock me.* Now that Noah is twenty-six pounds, that prospect doesn't sit so well with Mum or Dad. (I will credit them, however, for not taking Noah into their bed.) By now, their accidental parenting is not just a matter of conditioning; Noah is consciously manipulating them. So here we need a two-part plan: Put Noah into his crib without rocking, and if he starts to cry, use P.D. They should stay in the room to show him that they're physically there for him, but they shouldn't talk to him. Under no circumstances should they pick Noah up, not only because he's too heavy and it would be difficult to do, but also because that's part of the accidental parenting pattern that they have set up. They should say comforting words: "It's okay, Noah, you're only going to sleep." At this stage, he understands everything. In fact, even though this has been going on for eighteen months, Betsy might be surprised if she is really firm in her resolve.

If it's necessary to reestablish trust, stay with your child on a blow-up bed—even before you do the P.D. method. I can't say this often enough: A baby who has been traumatized by abandonment often has more severe sleep problems at this age, and solutions take longer. Your child *expects* that you're going to leave, and he'll keep checking to see if you're there. With some tough cases I've handled, where the child has developed a serious case of crib phobia, he screams his head off. You put him down, but you can't leave. In such cases, I bring in a blow-up bed and sleep *in* the child's room at least for the first night. Put the bed next to the crib to start. If this is a recent sleep problem, you might be able to take the bed out after the first night. Often by the third night, you're there. But if it's a

> "Won't let me leave the room"

very long-term problem, I suggest moving the blow-up progressively farther from the crib (and closer to the door) every three nights.

Each case is a little different. Sometimes I also do a transition step with a chair. That is, once I get the blow-up bed out of the room, I sit in a chair positioned next to the crib as the child is falling asleep. I leave the room when he's sleeping. The next few nights, I move the chair farther and father away. (For a detailed real-life example, see Elliott's story, beginning on page 281.)

If your toddler hasn't ever slept in his crib, skip the crib and start making the transition to big-kid bed. If your child has had chronic sleep problems, and you're just starting the process of teaching independent sleep at fifteen, eighteen, or even twenty-four months, and up to now your child has slept in your bed, there isn't much point in putting him straight into the crib. At that point, you start the process of transitioning him to his own bed, not a crib (see page 272). During the day, take him shopping for the bed, or at least for the bedding. Let him pick out something with his favorite characters or design. Allow him to help you make the bed that afternoon. You will start by sleeping in his room with him on the first night. He's on his new big-boy bed, and you're on a blow-up mattress on the floor next to him. Then you gradually move your blow-up out, and sit in a chair for a few nights until he's asleep. Eventually, he'll be sleeping in his own bed. If he comes into your room in the middle of the night, gently, and without any conversation, put him back into his bed. If it's a chronic problem, buy a gate and stress that he has to stay in *his* bed. Take him into yours even once, and you'll double the size of the problem, I promise. With very tough cases, I suggest that parents make a game out of it, and reward the child whenever he stays in his room (see Adam's story, pages 289–292).

Ultimately, parents do what they have to do to get a child into his own bed. One case that comes to mind is Luke, a two-year-old who not only slept in his parents' bed, he also wouldn't go to sleep unless he was holding on to Mum or Dad's ear. His mother realized that the only place he seemed to fall asleep independently was the sofa in the den. So they decided to move that sofa into his bedroom, where a brand-new big-boy bed awaited him. Luke refused the bed but willingly slept on the sofa for the next two years, because that's what he knew, and that's what made him feel safe.

I've found that parents sometimes don't connect the dots when their child is suddenly "terrified of his crib," as eighteen-month-old Saman-

| "Gets out of bed in the middle of the night" |

tha's mother described her daughter's problem. Leslie, Sam's mum, swore that her daughter had been "sleeping through the night" until the past two months. "She'll fall asleep anywhere else, but as soon as we lay her in her crib, she wakes up hysterical and proceeds to cough and throw up." Hearing the words "terror" and "screaming" are telltale signals. I suspected immediately that Samantha's parents had tried controlled crying. Even worse, they'd done it on more than one occasion. "Yes, we've tried crying it out and some nights that works, but not all nights," Leslie said, oblivious to how she had contributed to Samantha's problem. That baby has been traumatized, and at eighteen months it's harder to rebuild trust. She sees the crib bars as a barrier between her and her mum, and the crib itself is like jail. Instead of trying to get her *back* into her crib, Samantha's parents have to help her make the transition to a big-girl bed.

"Terrified of her crib"

Always go **to** *your child—don't allow her to climb into your bed.* When she pays a call, take her right back to her own room. Be firm during the daytime as well. Make it a house rule that your toddler has to knock on your door. I have millions of questions from parents who are in a fix because they think structure and rules will damage their child. Codswallop, I say! As children get older, you *have* to teach them to knock on doors. Model this yourself when you go into her room. It's about respect and boundaries. And if she does burst in, simply say, "No, you may not come into Mummy's room without knocking."

If you're dealing with crib phobia, and you need to reestablish the trust, you might have to stay in her room with her on a blow-up bed for a few days, but you don't *stay* there forever. Using a blow-up bed is just a transitional strategy to make the child feel safe.

Of course, in most cases, a child's middle-of-the-night visits don't come out of left field. Rather, they're the result of a long history of accidental parenting. The child's presence just *feels* more intrusive once he's a toddler. I've also found that parents sometimes delude themselves about their child's sleep patterns. For example, when I received this email from Sandra, I knew it wasn't the whole story:

Elliott does not sleep by himself at night. We literally have to lay down with him on his queen size mattress, which is on the floor. He seems to wake every couple of hours and gets mad and comes in and gets us to crawl back in bed with him. HELP! I want my husband and I to get a break from this kid! We can't lock his room

"Comes into my room in the middle of the night"

because he has a room with sliding doors and can open them up. Truthfully, I don't know how much of the crying we could listen to because he was colicky for four months and cried around the clock. How do we get out of this cycle and get him to sleep alone? He is a light sleeper and has always been, we need help!

It would appear that Sandra and her husband are following my suggestion not to allow their eighteen-month-old toddler to sleep with them. But they also haven't done much to promote Elliott's *independence* during the night. By now you should have picked up several clues from this mother's email and have a few questions for her as well. First of all, why is Elliott on a queen mattress on the floor? I bet someone used to sleep with him. Maybe only Mum did, and now Dad wants her back in their bed. In any case, the parents started this habit.

This is a case in which I wouldn't suggest a blow-up bed, because they've already been sleeping in his room. Instead of sleeping *with* him or even lying next to him on a separate bed, they should go right to the chair phase. At bedtime, they should bring in a chair and explain, "Mummy [or Daddy—whoever is less likely to cave in!] will stay here until you fall asleep." After three days, before going into Elliott's room to start the bedtime ritual, they should move the chair a foot closer to the sliding doors, so that Elliott doesn't see them doing it. Every three nights, the chair gets closer to the door. And each night whoever sits with Elliott reassures him, "I'm still sitting in the chair." When they're ready to move it, they'll tell him, "Tonight we're going to take out the chair, but I'll stay here until you're asleep." They'll keep that promise, standing a few feet away from him without engaging. Once the chair is out the door, he hopefully will be able settle down on his own. If not, when he tries to get out of bed or wakes up later in the evening, they have to take him right back to his room, lay him down, and say, "I know you're upset, but you're just going to sleep." They should then stand there, again at a distance, saying "I'm right here." But the parents have to be careful not to make eye contact, get into conversation, or in any way allow Elliott to manipulate them. Eventually, they should take away the words, just do P.D. and lay him back in the bed. They have to make a commitment. As for keeping Elliott in his room, they shouldn't be locking his room anyway. But they can get a child's gate, so he can't get to them.

If your child was a "bad sleeper" as a baby, it's important to analyze and

respect your child's history, but don't let fear dominate your actions today.
Read between the lines of Sandra's email (page 281); pay particular attention to these words: "Truthfully, I don't know how much of the crying we
could listen to because he was colicky for four months and cried around
the clock." It's obvious to me, probably because I've dealt with so many
mothers of colicky babies, that Sandra is still recovering from Elliott's
first four months. It's as if she's always waiting for the other shoe to drop.
I sense, too, that his early history carried on with his having many fitful
nights, because Mum and Dad didn't know how to teach Elliott the art of
sleep. They've just written off his behavior to being "a light sleeper." Now
he's eighteen months, and they're petrified: Will this go on forever? Such
anxiety about the past can sabotage any solutions we might come up with
in the present. Guilt, anger, and worry are counterproductive. That's why
I always remind parents, "That was then—this is now. We can't erase the
past, but we can undo the damage . . . if you hang in there."

> "Afraid this will go on forever"

Use my wake-to-sleep technique to extend sleep times. Wake-to-sleep
(see "Habitual Waking" and the sidebar on page 191) works well with
toddlers, too. I often suggest it to parents who are dealing with either
early morning wake-ups or habitual waking in the middle of the night. In
some cases, in fact, wake-to-sleep is the first step of a plan. For example,
Karen, mother of seventeen-month-old Mac and four-week-old Brock,
wanted to know how she could help Mac go from two naps to one. But
when she told me that Mac was also up at six every morning, I knew we
had to deal with that problem first. Otherwise, he wouldn't have the
stamina to last until noon or 1 P.M., and he'd be too overtired to take a
good long nap. So the first thing we had to work on was getting him to
sleep later. Then, we could *gradually* move up his morning nap (see next
section). I suggested that Karen go into Mac's room an hour earlier and
wake him at 5 A.M. "No problem," she answered immediately, which surprised me because most parents look at me cross-eyed when I make that
suggestion. She then added, "I'm up at that hour anyway with the baby." I
told Karen to change Mac's diaper and put him right back to bed,
explaining, "It's too early to start our day. Let's go back to sleep." I knew
that Mac probably wouldn't wake up fully. He'd go back to sleep, maybe
even a bit crankily, but it would at least get him out of the early morning
wake-up habit. The goal was to get him to stay asleep until 7 A.M. so he'd
have more energy in the morning.

> "Wakes up too early; gets tired by midmorning"

Make changes gradually. Sometimes parents come up with good plans on their own, but they also move too quickly without giving the child a chance to adjust to the new routine. Cold turkey doesn't usually work well with toddlers, who have good memories. They can anticipate events. Don't expect them to fall in line if you change the routine. For example, before speaking with me, Karen had been trying to cut Mac's morning nap out all together and hoped that her Spirited son would just then take one long nap in the afternoon. Instead, he got overtired, ended up napping in the morning anyway, or falling asleep in the car, and then slept fitfully. Instead of going cold turkey, Karen had to phase out his morning nap in increments.

> "Want to trim
> two naps a day
> into one"

Once Mac started to sleep a bit later in the morning, we could move to the second part of our plan (see box below). Where he usually went down for his morning nap at 9:30, Karen would try to stretch him to ten, or if that was too much, just to 9:45. Then, three days later, she'd again

---

Presto! Two Naps into One

By making the morning nap progressively later, you can eventually make it disappear! The suggested timetable below assumes that your child is at least a year old and normally naps at 9:30 A.M. The times might vary, depending on your child, but the principles of gradual transition remain the same.

Days 1–3: Put him down 15–30 minutes later for his morning nap—9:45 or 10.

Days 4–6: If possible, put him down 30 minutes later, so that he's going down at 10:30. Give him a snack at around 9 or 9:30. He'll sleep for 2 or 2½ hours and have lunch around 1.

Days 7 to however long it takes: Every three days, make the nap later and later. He might have a morning snack at around 10 or 10:30, go down at 11:30, and wake for his lunch at around 2. You might have a few rough afternoons.

The goal: Eventually he'll be able to stay up until noon, have his lunch, play a bit, and then take one deliciously long afternoon nap. He might have some days when he just can't make it without a short morning nap. Go with the flow, but never let him sleep more than an hour.

extend the nap, using the same fifteen- or thirty-minute interval. He could have a morning snack and then wake and have his lunch. It didn't happen quickly. The process took a month or so, and there were several days in which he regressed altogether—waking too early, taking a long morning nap. This was normal, not only because we were trying to change a habit, but also because Mac had just become a big brother, and his little mind was still trying to sort out the new situation.

Be as consistent in the new way as you were in the old. If you've been doing some form of accidental parenting, your child expects you to react a certain way when he's having trouble sending himself off to sleep or when he wakes in the middle of the night. When you do something differently—refuse a feed at 3 A.M., lay him down instead of taking him into your own bed—he *will* resist. I promise you! If you stay at it and project an air of confidence and determination, you'll be amazed at the change. But if you're half-hearted, your child will sense it. He'll up the ante— scream louder, wake more often—and you'll cave in.

Don't get confused between comforting your toddler and "spoiling" him. Toddlerhood is an especially erratic time, and children need their parents' reassurance more than ever. Toddlers generally drop one nap, but it doesn't happen overnight. One day he'll skip a morning nap; the next day he won't be able to make it through the morning. Besides, there's a lot of new stuff happening in the toddler's universe. Though they're growing and becoming more independent, toddlers still need to know that Mum and Dad are there to comfort them when the going gets rough. But I sympathize with parents, because it's sometimes hard to know what kind of behavior is "typical"and what kind of response is too much:

> "We caved in after one night"

Roberto is nearly two, and ever since I can remember, after he has had his daytime nap, he is really irritable and will scream and whine for an hour, and then just suddenly click out of it and be fine. I've tried various different techniques. If I sit by him, he will put his arms up to be held but then fight to be put down again. He will say he is thirsty but then refuse a drink, as though he's not quite sure what to do with himself. I've tried leaving him to wake on his own and ignore it, but that doesn't work either. He lies on his front with his arms and legs tucked under him, and normally sleeps for at least 2–3 hours. If he is woken he is even worse, and if someone comes into the house or makes a noise

> "Is grumpy after napping"

when he's like this he is even worse, too. He is fine when he wakes in the morning. Has anyone ever come across this before? It has gotten to the point where I don't let anyone come round when he's asleep or going to sleep now.

This mother has only one baby to observe, while I've seen thousands. First of all, Roberto sounds like a Grumpy type—they often need extra time to rouse themselves after naps. But regardless of type all humans have different wake-up patterns. In addition, Roberto is a very typical toddler. It is important to comfort him. Comforting your child is different from spoiling. It's a compassionate act to give a child a sense of security. Roberto's mum needs to allow him his time to come back to consciousness after naps, rather than try to force him before he's ready. She could hold him for a little while and say, "You're just waking up. Mummy's here. We'll go downstairs when you're ready." My hunch is that Mum may be rushing him, and that's actually prolonging the process. If she gives him the time he needs, instead of trying to cajole him, Roberto will probably just sit there for a few minutes. Then all of a sudden he'll notice a toy and reach for it. Or he'll just look up at Mum and smile, as if to say, "Oh, I've come 'round now."

If your child is having sleep problems in her second or third year, examine your own agenda—and what you've been doing until now. Although the research cited at the beginning of this chapter shows an epidemic of sleep problems in young children, sleep problems aren't catching. Undoubtedly, the stepped-up pace of our culture is affecting our children. But so are parents' attitudes. Some hate to let go of the baby years, and they comfort excessively and take their child into their own beds out of their needs, not the little one's. So ask yourself, **Are you really ready to allow your child to grow up? To have his or her independence?** This may sound like a silly question when you're talking about two- and three-year-olds. But giving children freedom and teaching independence doesn't start when they're old enough to get a driver's license. You have to carefully plant the seeds now, balancing increasing responsibilities with love and nurturing. Remember, too, that a lack of independence at night carries over into the day. Children who sleep well have less of a tendency to cling, whine, and act out during their waking hours.

Also, parents who have been doing accidental parenting or adopted a particular practice, like the family bed, often have a change of heart when their child becomes a toddler (see Nicholas's story at the end of this chapter, pages 292–294). They may be contemplating a second child or Mum is planning to go back to work, full- or part-time, but they're still up two or three times a night with their toddler. I get tons of emails from parents in both situations. Not surprisingly, Mum and Dad have a greater sense of urgency now to correct sleep issues, especially if they've been taking the child into their bed. This web posting is typical of parents' desperation:

> We have a boy who is 19 months old, and he's always slept with us in our bed. Now we are expecting a second baby, and this needs to change! We are afraid to try some of the methods that are out there like leaving him to cry etc. . . . It's just too heartbreaking . . . Does anyone have a tip?

"Can't get him out of our bed"

With a baby, it's easier to rationalize, "he'll grow out of it" or "he's just going through a phase." Parents are also embarrassed by toddler sleep problems. They dread comments such as, "You mean he's *still* getting you up in the middle of the night?" And, especially if another baby is on the way, or if sleep deprivation is affecting their performance at work, they worry: Will we ever get a good night's sleep? Here's the catch: Just because you need a good night's sleep, it doesn't mean your baby is ready, especially if you haven't taken the appropriate steps to get him there.

Sometimes, parents lie to themselves. I can't tell you how many parents insist that they've "done everything possible," as a mum in my native England, Claudia, puts it in the email below, to help their child develop good sleep habits. Again, we need to read between the lines:

> Hi, my problem is that I feel I have done everything possible to help Edward sleep through the night and self-soothe, and now I have run out of ideas. We have a very good routine with him at bedtime and he goes to sleep on his own without crying 99% of the time. We NEVER cuddle him to sleep, and I have never fed him to sleep either. He does not use a dummy [pacifier], and has a special object "Moo."
>
> He wakes, and always has done at various intervals during the night and cries for us. We usually wait awhile to see if he nods back off, which sometimes he does alone. More often than not, though, he starts getting really agitated, so one of us will go

"Tried everything; still doesn't sleep through the night"

in, we don't talk to him, we check that he is lying down, and that he has Moo. Harry and I give him a small sip of water from his beaker and then leave the room, at which point he will often go back to sleep. This doesn't sound like any big deal, but I work part-time and have prep to do at home in the evenings after he has gone to bed, I find it really hard when my sleep is disturbed at least twice a night, sometimes more and then often I can't get back to sleep again either.

When we try not going in at all, he ends up covered in snot from all the crying, standing up in his cot and too hysterical to comfort himself back to sleep.

Claudia has done a lot of the right things: established a good bedtime routine, avoided the feeding-to-sleep trap, and given her son a security object. But she has also misread some of my advice. Rocking a baby to sleep is not the same as cuddling him. Honestly, this mum sounds a bit on the inflexible side. Claudia also doesn't realize that she has, despite her good intentions, done some accidental parenting: She or Harry give Edward water every time he wakes. That glass of water has become his prop. But the most telling part of this email is the last paragraph: "When we try not going in at all . . ." In other words, on more than one occasion, Mum and Dad have left Edward to cry it out. Of course he's "too hysterical to comfort himself back to sleep." I want to ask her what she does on the one percent of the nights when Edward doesn't go to sleep on his own. I wonder if he's left to cry it out then as well. In any case, I know that Edward's parents haven't been consistent with one method. When he wakes up he not only doesn't know how to send himself back to sleep, he also doesn't know whether or not his parents will go in.

Where do we start? First of all, Claudia and Harry have to rebuild the trust. I would put one of them on a blow-up bed to be there when Edward wakes and to help him go back to sleep. I'd do it for a week at first. It will also give them a chance to see exactly what he's doing when he wakes. Gradually, I'd move the bed out of the room (see pages 279–280). But when Edward cries, they have to go in to him and do P.D. They should wait until he's in a standing position and then immediately lay him down. They also have to get him out of the water habit, by giving him a nonspillable sippy cup that he can find on his own if he's thirsty.

This is one of those cases in which I'd sit Claudia and Harry down and explain that they got Edward this far, and they now have to go the distance with him even if it upsets their own sleep for a week or two. Otherwise, they could be in for several more *years* of disturbed sleep.

I conclude this chapter with two additional detailed case studies. Both involve two-year-olds. Both were quite complicated.

Adam, the Nightmare Toddler

Marlene was crying when she first called about Adam. "It's a nightmare . . . no, *he's* a nightmare," she said of her two-year-old. "He refuses to sleep on his own and wakes up two or three times a night and then wanders. He'll some-times want to climb into bed with us and sometimes just ask for a drink of water." Adam, I learned, by asking more questions, was a Spirited child. "Even though I stick to my guns," Marlene explained, "it's a battle of wits all the time and this makes it very hard for my husband and me to cope. He is so strong-willed and tries to dominate. Like if he's playing, and I want to step out of the room, he goes ballistic, crying and saying, 'No, Ma, don't leave.' Isn't this late for separation anxiety? It's hard to keep our sanity sometimes."

First of all, we were dealing here with a Spirited child who also hap-pened to be smack in the midst of the terrible twos. I knew right off that it wasn't so much a battle of wills as the result of two years of escalating accidental parenting. The parents started out by following Adam instead of guiding him. Marlene told me, "At various times, we've tried to listen to different experts' advice, but nothing worked." I would guess that's because they kept changing the rules on Adam. Now he is manipulating them. Granted some children are innately more tyrannical than others— Spirited children certainly have that potential. But even a Spirited child can learn to cooperate and to follow direction *if it's given correctly* (more about this in the next chapter).

I suspected, too, that among the "expert advice" they listened to, they might have tried controlled crying with Adam. Otherwise why would he, at two, be so insistent on keeping his mum nearby at all times? Marlene readily admitted she had. "But that didn't work either. He just screamed for three hours and threw up." I gulped hearing this. *Three hours of scream-ing.* Though Marlene was interested in "trying to get Adam to behave, do as he is asked, and sleep through the night," this was clearly a case in which the trust had to be rebuilt before any other problems could be examined. Perhaps that three hours of crying in and of itself didn't cause

> "Wakes up and wanders; often wants to climb into our bed"

all of Adam's difficulties, but it certainly was a very significant factor in this equation.

This was a complex case and called for a rather long and involved plan. Clearly, there were serious behavior issues that had to be dealt with in this family. But you can't discipline a sleep-deprived child. We first had to go back to basics and look at the bedtime routine. Adam's parents were to do the usual story and cuddling, but also give him a little tray with a cup of water to take to bed. They'd explain to him that now he didn't have to disturb Mummy or Daddy. He could get his own drink if he woke up and was thirsty.

More important, we had to build up Adam's trust. We put a blow-up bed in his room and, for the first three days, Marlene went to sleep when Adam did. She protested at first, not thrilled with the idea of going to bed for the night at 7:30. I suggested, "If you don't want to actually go to sleep, take a book and flashlight with you, and when he's asleep you can at least read." By the fourth night, after Adam fell asleep, Marlene left. A few hours later, he woke, so she went right in and stayed there 'til morning. The next night he slept through.

During the first week I also explained to Marlene that she also had to be especially attentive to Adam, showing him that he could count on her to be there for him during his waking hours. Luckily, she was able to clear her calendar, so that she didn't feel the pull of other responsibilities. She would say to him, "Let's go into your room and play." Once he was engaged with a toy or activity, she then very casually announced, "I'm going to go to the bathroom." The first day, he protested, but we were ready. I had instructed Marlene to have a timer in her pocket. "Mum's going to come back when the timer goes off," she told him. Two minutes later, relieved in more than one respect, she returned to a tense but smiling Adam.

By the beginning of the second week, when Adam played in his room, Marlene was able to leave for five minutes, each time for a different excuse ("I have to . . . check on our dinner/make a phone call/put the clothes in the dryer"). It was also time to take the blow-up bed out of Adam's room. She didn't make a big deal of it—Dad removed it when Adam was eating dinner. That night they did the usual bedtime ritual but explained, "Tonight we're going to brush teeth, read a book, and then say good-night, just like we always do. And I'm going to sit with you for a while when we turn the lights off. But when the timer goes off I'm going to leave." They only set the timer for three minutes (an eternity to a child), so that Adam wouldn't be just drifting off to sleep and be awakened by the timer when it rang.

Not surprisingly, he tested his parents that first night, crying out the moment Dad shut the door. Dad went straight back in—and set the timer again. "I'll sit with you a few minutes and then I'm going to leave." This happened several other times. Once Adam realized that crying wasn't getting his usual result, he quietly got out of bed and came into the living room. Dad marched him straight back into his room without saying a word. They did this for two hours the first night. The second night, it happened only once.

Marlene and Jack then started using the timer to keep Adam in his room by himself during the day. By now he was more comfortable playing on his own, because Marlene had helped him get used to it. Although what we really wanted was to stop Adam from marching into Mum and Dad's bedroom at 6 A.M., we first had to get Adam used to the notion of staying in his room until it was time to come out. Marlene and Jack made a game out of it at first: "Let's see if you can stay in your room until the timer alarm goes off." When he did it successfully, they gave him a gold star. When he had five gold stars, they took him to a park where he'd never been before as a "reward" for staying in his bedroom.

Finally, they said to their son that he was ready for a "big-boy clock." They made a ritual out of presenting him with his first digital Mickey Mouse clock, showing him how the big "7" came up in the morning and that would tell him it's okay to get out of bed. They showed him how the alarm worked and explained, "When it goes off like this, that means it's time to get up and you can come out of your room." But here's the most important part of this strategy: Although they set Adam's alarm for 7 A.M., they set their own for 6:30. The first morning, they were outside his door when the alarm went off, and they went right in. "What a good job— staying in your own bed until the alarm went off. That definitely deserves a star!" The next morning, they did the same thing. Finally, on the third morning, they waited to see what Adam would do. Sure enough, he didn't come out until the alarm went off, and when he did, they once again lavished him with praise.

Adam did not become magically more cooperative. He was still manipulative and tested his parents over just about everything. Now at least his parents were taking the lead, instead of following their child.

When Adam acted like a tyrant, they didn't throw their hands up in desperation. They took steps to correct it; they formulated a plan. Over the next several months, although Adam sometimes tried to stall at bedtime and still woke up occasionally during the night, he was definitely sleeping—and behaving—*better* than when Marlene initially contacted me. As you will see in the next chapter, it's always an uphill battle to attend to behavioral issues when a child is either overtired or sleep-deprived.

Nicholas, the Eternal (and Nocturnal) Breast-Feeder

"Needs to suckle to sleep; still sleeps in our bed—and a new baby is on the way"

I include Nicholas's story because it reflects an increasingly common phenomenon in my practice: Two-year-old (and sometimes older) children who are not only *still* breast-feeding, but who can't get to sleep unless they do. Annie called me when Nicholas was twenty-three months old. "He just won't go to sleep unless he's on my breast, at night or for naps." I asked why she had waited this long to deal with this problem: "Well, Grant and I have been doing co-sleeping, so it's not really a hassle for me at night. But I just found out that I'm four weeks pregnant. I would really like to get him weaned and sleeping in his own bed before the baby comes."

Annie was in for a long haul, I explained, so she'd better start now. I first asked her, "Are sure you are committed to weaning him? Is your husband willing to help?" Both were keys to the success of this plan. Annie had to wean Nicholas immediately. During the day it would be easier, because she could distract him with some other activity or a snack whenever he wanted her breast. During the night, Dad would have to play a big part. I always use dads, or at least someone other than Mum, in these cases. After all, you don't want to be cruel to the child. If you've been giving him the breast and suddenly you stop, the baby doesn't understand why Mum is withholding. He doesn't expect the breast from Dad.

Another aspect of this situation is that at twenty-three months, it didn't make sense to put Nick into a crib. I suggested that they buy him a big-boy bed and get a gate for his door. There was no quick solution to these problems, I explained. They were looking at two weeks at best. Here's the plan I designed for this family:

Days One to Three. We first needed to get Nicholas out of his parents' bed and transition him from sleeping between them to next to them.

Annie and Grant bought a new big-boy bed for Nick's room. They took the mattress off the bed and positioned it next to their own bed, on Dad's side. The first night Nicholas cried and kept trying to climb into his parents' bed next to Annie. Each time, Dad intervened and put him back on the mattress and did P.D. He screamed bloody murder. Shock and indignation registered on Nick's face, as if to say, *Hey, we've been doing this for two years.*

No one got much sleep that night. So the next night I suggested that Annie sleep in the guest room. At least if Nicholas climbed in, she wouldn't be there. Also, as she was weaning her son cold turkey, she had to take care of herself—wear a tight bra, make sure she was well rested. (If Annie had said she was afraid she'd go in to "rescue" Grant in the middle of the night, I would have suggested that she stay at her parents' or a friend's house.)

The second night, Grant intervened as he did on the first night. No matter how intensely Nicholas cried, he kept doing P.D. I had warned him not to get *on* the bed with Nicky—he could kneel at the side if he had to. He also kept saying, "Mommy's not here. I'll hold your hand, but you have to sleep in your own bed." Grant was a trouper. He stayed the course, and after two or three tantrums, Nicholas finally fell asleep on his own bed for the first time ever. He had even less trouble on the third night, but we weren't out of the woods yet, far from it.

Days Four to Six. On the fourth day, I suggested that Annie and Grant tell Nicholas that as a reward for sleeping on his own mattress, they were going to let him choose his own special set of sheets and pillows *for his room.* He chose his favorite character, Barney, and Mum explained that they were now going to put the mattress in his room on his new big-boy bed with his new sheets.

That night Annie went back to her own bed, and Grant put a blow-up bed in Nick's room, next to his new big-boy bed with the Barney sheets. They put a gate at the door. It wasn't quite back to Square One, but Nicholas was understandably very agitated at bedtime. Dad kept reassuring him that he'd stay with him; otherwise, Nick would have kept getting out of bed. Of course, he kept trying at first. And when Grant went to lay him down, as soon as his feet touched the mattress, he propelled himself upward. I had warned Grant, who kept a firm hold on Nicholas, "Be careful not to turn P.D. into a game." Sometimes at this age if a child has a tantrum and you keep putting him back he thinks, *Oh, this is fun. I stand up and Dad puts me down.* I told Grant not to make eye contact, not to say anything. "By now, it will be enough for you to just use the physical contact," I explained.

Days Seven to Fourteen. On the seventh day, Grant started moving the blow-up bed progressively closer to the door. I explained to Grant, "It could take another week for you to get the blow-up bed out of the room. You have to be firm but consistent. When you're ready, don't try to fool him or sneak around. Tell him, 'Tonight Daddy is going to sleep in his own room.'"

Annie was pretty much out of the equation thus far. In cases where weaning is involved, it's always better to use the father if he's willing. And once Dad starts, he should keep doing the bedtime routine rather than switch back to Mum. After all, for two years, Annie had been breast-feeding Nicholas to sleep and then allowing him to sleep between them. (With single mums or when a father is unwilling to get involved, the woman has to engage someone else to help her for at least three nights until her breasts are no longer an issue; see box, page 126. If not, she's likely to give in and give her child the breast.)

As this story turned out, Nicholas was successfully weaned by the end of the first week. But by the end of the second week, Dad was still in Nicky's room on the blow-up bed. Annie was elated about her new freedom, but Grant was getting very tired of sleeping in his son's room. Jointly, the parents decided that maybe co-sleeping wasn't the problem after all. At least Nicholas was no longer dependent on the breast to get to sleep. "Co-sleeping suits us," Annie said, explaining their decision. "We're going to let Nicholas continue to sleep with us. When the baby comes, I'll put him or her into a bassinet, and we'll take it from there."

I've often seen parents who settle for less than the original goal because they don't want to do the extra work, because they can't imagine that a strategy will actually work, or because they had a genuine change of heart. Maybe all three reasons were at work here. Who are we to judge why parents make a particular decision? In fact, I always say to clients, "If it's working, that's fine—it's *your* family."

EIGHT

TAMING TODDLERS

Teaching Children to Be Emotionally F.I.T.

The Make-'Em-Happy Epidemic

"Courtney has been an Angel child until now," insisted Carol, when she first called me about her two-year-old. "But all of a sudden she started having tantrums when she doesn't get her way. If we don't pick her up or give her a toy that she wants, or if another child is on the swing and Courtney wants her turn, she just has a meltdown. It's really upsetting, and Terry and I don't know what to do. We've given her love, attention, everything a two-year-old could possibly want."

I'm always skeptical when parents insist that a toddler's behavior has come "out of nowhere." Unless there's some kind of family catastrophe or a traumatic event, children's emotional responses don't usually appear without warning. More likely, tantrums start as small emotional outbursts, and as the child grows, if no one does anything to teach her that the behavior is unacceptable, the outbursts grow, too, into full-blown tantrums.

"What do you do when she starts a meltdown?" I asked, hoping to gain some insight into how Carol and Terry handle Courtney's feelings. All children have emotions; it's how parents react to them that matters. "Have you ever said no to her or tried to stop this kind of behavior in the past?"

"No," Carol said, "we never really had to. We've gone out of our way to amuse and entertain her, and to teach her things. We never wanted her to feel as if we've ignored or abandoned her. We've always worked really hard at keeping her from crying. So I guess we've always given her what she wanted. It's worked—she's a really happy child."

A few days later, I met these parents—lovely people, both in their late thirties—at their modest home in the Valley. Carol, a graphic designer, stayed home for Courtney's first year and now works $2\frac{1}{2}$ days a week, and Terry owns a hardware store so he's usually home at a reasonable hour. They try to have a family dinner most weeknights. Listening to these parents talk about Courtney, a long-awaited child who was conceived after several years of trying, it was apparent that both clearly adored their daughter and went out of their way to organize their lives around hers.

Courtney, a curly redhead, adorable and very articulate for her age, was both a happy and charming child. As she led me toward her room, I wondered if this was the same little girl her mother had described. Once inside, I realized that Carol and Terry had, indeed, given their child everything she ever wanted. That little girl had more merchandise in her bedroom than a Toys-R-Us warehouse! Shelves were piled high with every educational and recreational gadget on the market. On one wall, an entire bookshelf was stocked with picture books; on the other, Courtney's own TV and DVD/VCR. She had a video collection that would make a Hollywood mogul envious, especially if he was a Baby Einstein fan!

After I had spent a few minutes alone with Courtney, Carol came in and said, "I'm going to take Tracy into the den now, honey, so that Daddy and I can talk with her." Courtney didn't skip a beat. "No! I want Tracy to play." I reassured her that I'd be back in a few minutes, but she was having none of it, and that's when I got to see Courtney throw herself on the floor and kick wildly. Carol tried talking softly to her and attempted to pick her up, but Courtney was like a little wild animal. I purposely hung back, because it was important for me to see how Mum and Dad, who came running into the room, reacted to their toddler's outburst. Carol was obviously embarrassed and, like many parents, went for the quick fix. "Come on, Courtney. Tracy's not leaving. How about if you come into the den with us, and I'll give you a cookie while we have our tea."

Carol and Terry are like so many parents I've met over the years. Though they have given their child everything, there is one important thing they didn't give her: limits. Making matters worse, their giving was often their response to her emotions. They felt guilty when Courtney was sad or angry, so they lavished toys on her to distract her. And they constantly caved in when Courtney balked even a little, each time reinforcing their toddler's growing ability to manipulate them.

Carol and Terry are victims of what I've come to believe is a "make-'em-happy" epidemic. Older parents and working parents are particularly susceptible, but this is a phenomenon that transcends age, economic status, geography, or culture. In my travels not only throughout the United States but in the rest of the world as well, a vast majority of parents nowadays have trouble disciplining their kids because they seem to think their job is to make their children happy. But no one can possibly be happy all the time—life isn't like that. Parents need to help their children identify and cope with the full range of human emotions they feel. If not, they deprive their child of her right to learn how to soothe herself as well as how to be in the world. She needs to be able to listen to directions, relate to other people, and transition from one activity to another, all of which are skills of emotional fitness.

Thus, we need worry less about making kids happy and more about *training* them to be "emotionally fit." The idea is not to protect children from their feelings but to give them tools to deal with everyday upsets, boredom, disappointment, and challenges as they move through life. We do this by setting limits, helping them understand their own feelings, and showing them how to manage their moods. When you stay in charge, your child can depend on you to say what you mean and mean what you say.

Emotional fitness reinforces the bond between parent and child, because it fills the reservoir of trust that begins to develop from the day a baby comes into the world. This foundation is critical for growing children—after all, you want them to know that they can come to you with their fears, anger, and excitement, and that they can tell you what they feel without your overreacting.

This chapter will help you look at the ingredients of emotional fitness: why it's important to deal with runaway emotions (like Courtney's tantrums) and what to do when a child loses control. We'll look at the importance of being *objective* parents who know how to step back, see their child for who he is and see his behavior clearly, and equally important, know how to keep their own emotions out of the equation, so that they can act on, rather than deny, their children's feelings.

Runaway Emotions: The Risk Factors

Even though your child's emotional portrait changes between ages one and three, one important theme runs through the various developmental stages: the need for parents' guidance and limits. You need to teach your child how to distinguish between actions that are good or bad, right or wrong, and to show her how to understand and manage her emotions. Otherwise, she won't know what to do when she has very strong feelings. Then, particularly when she is faced by a limit or a boundary, she will become frustrated and experience what I call "runaway emotions."

When your child experiences runaway emotions, she doesn't understand what's happening to her, and she's powerless to stop the escalating cycle of feelings. Not surprisingly, children who are prone to runaway emotions often become social outcasts. We all know the kind of child I'm talking about ("We used to invite Bobby for play dates, but he's such a wild kid, we had to stop"). And it's not poor Bobby's fault. No one has taught him how to tame his feelings or to deal with them when they get out of hand. Sure, he might have been a Spirited child to begin with, prone to grand emotional outbursts, but temperament need not be destiny. Runaway emotions can also lead to chronic bullying, which is actually unrestrained emotion and frustration taken out on others.

As the chart on page 299 summarizes, four elements put a child at risk for runaway emotions: *your child's temperament, environmental factors, developmental issues,* and perhaps most important, *your behavior.* These four risk factors obviously work together, although sometimes one is predominant. In the sections following the chart, I look briefly at each element.

Runaway Emotions: The Risk Factors			
Child's Temperament & Emotional/Social Style	Environmental Factors	Developmental Issues	Parents' Behavior
Children are more likely to have runaway emotions when they have a more vulnerable . . .	*Children are more likely to have runaway emotions if . . .*	*Children are more likely to have runaway emotions if they are going through . . .*	*Children are more likely to have runaway emotions when parents . . .*
• temperament (Grumpy, Spirited, Touchy) • emotional/social style (easygoing but unassertive, highly reactive, ultrasensitive)*	• their houses are not properly child-proofed • they don't have a place to let off steam • there have been changes or chaos in the family	• separation anxiety • a period in which they lack expressive language • the twos • teething	• are subjective not objective (see box, page 309) • don't nip undesirable behavior in the bud • are inconsistent • have different standards and argue with each other • don't prepare children for upcoming events that might be stressful

Types of temperament are outlined on pages 54–57 and "emotional/social styles" on pages 300–301.

Children's Emotional/Social Styles

Certain temperaments make children more prone to meltdowns—Touchy, Spirited, and Grumpy toddlers all need an extra bit of attention when it comes to emotional readiness. For example, Geoff (whom you'll meet again on page 305) was a Touchy toddler who always needed extra time to ease into new situations. When his mother rushed him or pushed him to interact with other children before he was ready, he cried inconsolably. In addition to their temperament, which we see literally from birth, children also develop certain emotional/social styles *in relationships:*

The happy camper plays in a group nicely. You can reprimand her about misbehavior and she learns easily. She will share her possessions willingly and even offer her toys to other children. At home she's the type who usually does what you ask—for instance, she puts her toys away without a fuss. This is a child who is often a group leader, but she doesn't seek to be in charge. Other children naturally gravitate to her. You don't have to do anything to optimize this kid's social life; she's a natural in groups and adapts easily to most situations. Not surprisingly, most happy campers are Angel or Textbook types, but some Spirited children, whose parents have channeled their high energy into appropriate activities and interests, also fit this description.

The easygoing but unassertive child sticks to himself. At home, he's placid and doesn't usually cry unnecessarily, unless he hurts himself or is tired. This is the child who watches the interactions of other children carefully. If he has a toy, and another, more aggressive child wants it, he usually gives it up immediately, because he's seen how the other kid acts and he's scared. He is not as fearful as an ultrasensitive child, but you have to watch what kind of situation you put him in. It's good to expose him to other children and new situations, but make sure you sit on the sidelines *with* him. Don't express concern about his being a loner. See it as a sign that he's confident enough to play on his own. You can try to broaden his social life by arranging play dates with another easygoing but unassertive child or even a happy camper with whom he gets along. Many Grumpy tots can be in this category as well as some Angel and Textbook types.

The ultrasensitive child lives up to his label. The least bit of stimulation upsets him emotionally. He is the child who has been carried a lot as a baby and young toddler. He likes to stay close to his parents in new situations. In a group, he's likely to be on his mum's lap, watching but not interacting with the other children. He cries easily. If another child gets too close, grabs a toy, or even if mum gives another child attention, it can set him off. He tends toward whiny behavior, or as we say in Yorkshire, he's very mardy (he seems like he's angry at the world). Some ultrasensitive children are also quick to anger because they're so easily frustrated. It's important for parents to allow this child to take his time, and to take care when introducing new situations. Many Touchy children fall into this category and some Grumpy types as well.

The highly reactive child has lots of energy. This can make her very assertive, even aggressive and impulsive. Though most toddlers think everything is theirs, this child is even more determined. She is very strong, adept, and physical. She realizes very quickly that she can slap or bite or kick or in other ways use force to get what she wants. If you try to force her to share, she might have a screaming meltdown. Others often see her as the group bully. These children need lots of activity to help channel their energy. It's important for her parents to know what sets her off, to be aware of the signs that she's losing control, and to head off a tantrum rather than let it happen. Highly reactive children do well with behavior modification—lots of charts and rewards when they're on good behavior. Typically, Spirited children fall in this category and sometimes Grumpy types as well.

Where temperament is fairly consistent; emotional/social styles evolve as the child grows. An easygoing but unassertive child might eventually "come out of his shell." A highly reactive child could mellow out by the time he goes to preschool. But all of these changes usually happen *with a parent's guidance*. That's why "goodness of fit" between parent and child (see pages 68–71) continues to be important. A parent's nature can either collide with or complement a child's personality. As our children get older, we get to know them better and see them interact in a wider variety of situations. But it's important for us to look in the mirror, too— to know where our own vulnerabilities are, and to realize what buttons our children are likely to push. If we're mature, we can adapt ourselves to act in our child's best interest, which is the essence of an *objective* parent, as I will explain on pages 309–316.

Environmental Factors

Because ages one to three coincide with a burst of understanding and self-awareness, toddlers are particularly sensitive to changes in their environment. Even though adults don't think their two-year-old understands what is going on during, say, a divorce or if there's a death in the family, children are like emotional sponges. They pick up on their parents' feelings; they know when things are different around the house. If you move to a new house, have a baby, change your daily routine (for example, by going back to work), if one parent is home for a week in bed with the flu—these and other departures from the norm will play on your child's emotions.

In a similar vein, if your child starts a new play group, or meets a new child (who happens to be a bully), expect some reverberations—more crying, more aggression, more clinginess. As with adults, there's chemistry between children as young as nine months. If you put certain types together, one of them is likely to have runaway emotions. So if your child repeatedly ends up in a fight, either as the aggressor or the one who's picked on, it isn't working if someone always ends up bleeding. Respect your child's likes and dislikes in people. That goes for family members, too. He might not like Grandpa or an old aunt. Give them time together, but don't push it.

Of course, life throws us curveballs all the time. I'm not about to suggest that we keep kids in plastic bubbles, only that you need to be aware and watch for signs that your child might need a little more guidance, a little more protection, because of what's going on around him.

Also, toddlers need a safe place to let off steam. If your house is not properly child-proofed, and you're constantly running around after your child saying "no" to this and "don't touch" to that, I guarantee you're going to have a frustrated toddler on your hands, just working up toward a meltdown. Leave some of your nonbreakable and less valuable items out, and teach your child that there are certain things that he can only touch with a parent's help. Also, toddlers grow out of their baby toys, and it's important to update their environment and make it more stimulating and more challenging: Get rid of old toys, play more challenging games with your child, and create spaces indoors where he is allowed to roam and to experiment, and outdoors as well, so that he can explore safely without your fearing for his safety. Especially in the dead of winter in cold climates, children (and adults) are likely to get cabin fever unless they're bundled up and taken out into the fresh air to kick a ball, run across a field, make angels in the snow.

Developmental Issues

Certain periods are marked by more emotional upheaval than others (practically all of the toddler years!). Of course, you can't, and wouldn't want to, stop your child's development. But you can keep an eye out for the times when your child is more likely to have a rough time harnessing his feelings.

Separation anxiety. As I discussed earlier, separation anxiety usually begins at around seven months and can last through eighteen months in some children. In some children, it's barely noticeable; in others, parents have to be particularly careful to build up trust (see pages 71–73). If you push a child off your lap when she's not yet ready to join the group, don't be surprised if you have a hysterical toddler on your hands. Instead, give her time. Respect her emotions, and structure small group situations with other gentle children rather than pair her with a highly reactive child.

Lack of vocabulary. If your child is going through a period, as most children do, in which he knows what he wants but doesn't have the words to ask for it, it can be very frustrating for both of you. Say he's pointing to a cabinet and whining. Pick him up and say, "Show me what you want." Say, "Oh, you want a raisin. Can you say 'raisin'?" He may not be able to at this point, but you're helping him develop language, and this is how you start.

Growth spurts and gains in mobility. As you learned in the earlier chapters about eating and sleeping, growth spurts and physical growth, such as learning to crawl or walk, can disrupt your child's sleep. In turn, a child who has less sleep than he needs can become more sensitive, more aggressive, or simply out of sorts the next day. When you know your child has had a fitful sleep the night before, keep it low key for the day. Don't introduce any new challenges when your child isn't at his best.

Teething. Teething can also make a child feel more vulnerable which, in turn, can lead to runaway emotions (see the sidebar, page 158, for teething tips). This is especially true if her parents start to feel sorry for her and forget to set limits on her behavior, excusing everything with, "Oh, she's teething."

The twos. This is the one instance in which parents can rightly say, "It came out of nowhere." It's as if your child changes overnight. One minute he is sweet and compliant, and the next he is negative and demanding. There can be sudden mood swings. He's happy at play and you blink . . . suddenly he's screaming. The twos don't have to be "terrible," though, especially if you start early to foster your child's emotional development. During this rocky developmental stage, you have to be more vigilant than ever to guard against runaway emotions, work even harder to hold the line, and let your child know what he can and cannot do.

Parents' Behavior

Although all of the above elements can put children at risk for runaway emotions, if I had to rank the importance of each of the four risk factors, "parents' behavior" would be at the top of my list. Granted, parents don't *cause* misbehavior any more than they can orchestrate their child's development. However, the way they respond to a particular stage or to an act of defiance, aggression, or a tantrum will either help control that kind of behavior in the future *or* perpetuate it.

Objective versus subjective parenting. In the box on page 309, I sum up the difference between *objective parents,* who are motivated by the child's individual needs, and *subjective parents,* who are motivated by their own emotions and who don't see their child or her behavior through unbiased eyes, which makes it difficult for them to respond appropriately. In fact, by doing nothing or doing the wrong thing, subjective parents inadvertently perpetuate the problem. Let's face it: No one wants their child to hit, to lie, or to hurl her truck into another kid's forehead. But by not intervening we're actually condoning the behavior.

The double standard. You can't have one set of rules for home and one for the real world. But what often happens is that the first time the child does something wrong or undesirable—throw food, act aggressively, have a tantrum—his parents will laugh. They think it's cute or oh so grown up, or they view it as his showing his spirit. What they don't realize is that their laughter is positive reinforcement. Then when they're out of the house, and the child does the same thing, they get embarrassed. But if they let him throw food at home, what do they expect him to do at a restaurant? The child doesn't understand why Mum and Dad laughed one time and not the next, so he does it again, as if to say, *Where's the laugh, guys? You were laughing before.*

When parents disagree—another form of the double standard—it also puts a child at risk for runaway emotions. One may be extremely soft and thinks everything the child does is funny or cool or macho, while the other one is desperately trying to teach manners. For example, Mum is worried because little Charlie is starting to hit the other chaps at Gymboree. She comes home and tells Dad about it, but he makes light of it. "Oh, he's just sticking up for himself, Grace. We don't want him to be a puff, do we?" They also might argue in front of the child, which is never a good idea.

Children will of course behave differently with different adults; that's only natural. But in a household where there's a "no eating in the living room" rule, it's not a good idea for Dad to curl up on the couch and eat chips with his son the minute that Mum leaves the house, especially if he says to the little boy, "Mummy would be mad at us, but let's not tell her we ate in here."

Lack of emotional preparation. Parents can unwittingly set up a child for runaway emotions when they don't take the time to prepare them for stressful circumstances. Through toddlers' eyes—which is the way you must look at each upcoming event—stressful situations include anything from a run-of-the-mill play date to a visit to the pediatrician to a birthday party. For example, a friend of mine offered to host her grandson's second birthday party. I happened to be there earlier in the day and watched as they set up a castle in the backyard and strung what seemed like five hundred helium balloons overhead. To an adult, it was magical, but poor little Geoff, who knew nothing of his parents' plans, was scared out of his wits when they ushered him into the backyard later that afternoon. There was a pirate in full regalia, lots of kids—a few his age and several older—and around thirty adults. Geoff was inconsolable, poor dear. The next day his granny said, "I don't know if kids can be ungrateful at this age, but he spent the whole party in my bedroom with me." Ungrateful? Geoff is two years old, and no one prepared him or even told him he was having a birthday party. What did they expect? It threw the lad into shock. I had to say to Granny, "Honestly, who was the party really for?" She looked at me sheepishly. "I get your point—it was really more for the grown-ups and the older children." (See also "Trust-Busters" on page 74.)

The Anatomy of a Subjective Parent

It really gets to me when parents say, "Johnny refuses to . . ." or "Johnny won't listen . . ." as if they've had nothing to do with their child's actions. As I said at the outset of this chapter, too many parents today are desperately afraid of making their child unhappy, and they let the child climb into the driver's seat. They're worried that if they set limits, their child won't love them. They also may not know how to nip undesirable behavior in the bud. And when they finally attempt to deal with the problem, they are either half-hearted about stopping it or inconsistent. Making matters worse, because they've waited so long to intervene, it's even harder to stop the cycle of misbehavior. And then the parent loses it altogether, so everyone's out of control.

We can't teach emotional fitness if we're not emotionally fit ourselves. And to me the essence of adult emotional fitness is objectivity, the ability to step back and really evaluate a situation, without letting your own emotions color your reaction. I tend not to hear from objective parents. Rather, most of the mums and dads who contact me about behavior problems are subjective parents. They unconsciously act on *their own feelings* rather than act in the best interest of their child. That is not to say that objective parents cut off their own feelings. Quite the opposite, objective parents are very much in touch with their emotions, but they don't let their feelings guide them as subjective parents tend to do.

For example, let's say eighteen-month-old Hector has a meltdown in a shoe store because he sees a huge fishbowl full of lollipops on the counter, and he wants one *now*. The subjective parent immediately starts thinking, *Oh, no. I hope he doesn't make a scene.* She might first try to bargain with Hector ("I'll give you one of your special sugar-free lollipops when we get home"). Chances are, she's had a long and painful history of such bargaining, so her own anger and a fair amount of guilt ("I must have made him like this") rise with each of Hector's demands. When Hector starts to whine and then cry, she gets angrier and takes Hector's behavior personally ("I can't believe he's doing this to me *again*"). Embarrassed to be battling with her child in public, when he drops to the floor and starts pounding his fists on her shoe, she gives in.

When parents are subjective, they react to emotions from within themselves, rather than detaching and responding to what's going on within *the child*. That's because subjective parents tend to see everything that their child does as a reflection of themselves. They have trouble accepting their child's temperament ("He's usually an angel") and often try to talk him out of his feelings ("Come on, now Hector, you don't want that lollipop. It will spoil your appetite"). She's afraid to say what she really means, which is, "No, you can't have that."

Because subjective parents so closely identify with their child, the child's feelings might as well be *their* feelings. They often have trouble dealing with the child's emotions, especially anger and sadness. It might be because they can't deal with strong negative feelings themselves or because the child reminds a parent of himself—or both. Not surprisingly, subjective parents don't have good boundaries; they act more like peers

---

Cop-Out Statements

Subjective parents often make excuses for their child or rationalize his misbehavior. They talk *about* him instead of dealing with the real issue, which does nothing to promote emotional fitness. Even worse, it delays the inevitable: problems in the real world. Cop-out statements are often heard when parents have guests or are out with the child.

"He's just hungry and that's how he gets."

"She's out of sorts today."

"You know he was a premie, and . . ." (an excuse will follow).

"This runs in the family."

"She's been teething."

"He's a beautiful boy and I love him so much, however . . ." (They have to validate that he's a wonderful child, but they really don't accept his personality, and they want him to magically conform to the child of their dreams.)

"She's an angel most of the time."

"His dad works long hours and there's just me here, and I don't want to keep saying no to him."

"He's tired. He didn't get a good night's sleep."

"He's not feeling well."

"I'm not worried—he'll grow out of it."

than parents. In the name of building their child's self-esteem, they reason endlessly, rationalize, and cajole, but rarely say, "I'm the parent, and this is unacceptable."

I suspect subjective parenting when a mum says to me, "He's so good with his father (or Granny) but not with me." That could be because her expectations are higher—they're more a reflection of what she *wants,* not what her toddler is capable of doing. She has to ask herself if she's being realistic. Toddlers are not small adults; they have years to go before they really master impulse control. Or, it could be that Dad *is* actually better at getting their son to behave, because he lets him know what's right and wrong and corrects him when he crosses that line. Mum has to therefore ask herself, "What is my husband (or my mother) doing that I'm not?"

The children of subjective parents become pros at manipulation and emotional blackmail. All children, especially toddlers, test parents' limits, and they know when their parents are inconsistent and have no boundaries themselves. It's not that they're bad; they're just doing what their parents have inadvertently taught them: wrangling, arguing, lobbying for what they want, and when that doesn't work, going for the big tantrum. So, even with something as simple as, "Okay, it's time to put our toys away," subjective parents are in for a battle. "No!" the child shouts. So Mum tries again. "Come on, honey. I'll help you." She starts to put one toy on the shelf; her son doesn't move. "Let's go, dear. I'm not going to do this all by myself." He still doesn't move. Mum looks at the clock and realizes that it's almost time to get dinner started. Dad will be home soon. She silently cleans up the rest of the toys. It was quicker and easier to do it herself—or so she thinks. But in reality she has just taught her child (a) that she doesn't mean what she says; and (b) even if she did, all he has to do is say "no" and whine, and he doesn't have to listen.

Not surprisingly, subjective parents often feel confused, embarrassed, and guilty when their child is out of control. They swing wildly from anger to excessive or undeserved praise. If their own parents were ultra-strict, or if they feel social pressure from other parents to have a "good" child, they're afraid to make their child feel unhappy or unloved. And when their child misbehaves in some way, as all young children do, rather than gather evidence objectively and realize that a negative pattern is developing, they tend to ignore or rationalize the child's behavior (see the box on page 307, "Cop-Out Statements"). A subjective parent will first make excuses for the child, try to reason or placate, and then as the

Subjective vs. Objective Parenting at a Glance	
Subjective parents . . .	Objective parents . . .
. . . identify with the child's emotions.	. . . see the child as a separate being, not a part of them.
. . . react from within—their own emotions get in the way.	. . . base their reaction on the situation.
. . . often feel guilty because what the child does reflects on them.	. . . gather evidence by looking for clues that help explain her behavior (see pages 312–316).
. . . make excuses and rationalize the child's behavior.	. . . teach new emotional skills (problem solving, cause and effect, negotiation, expression of feelings).
. . . don't investigate what happened.	
. . . inadvertently teach that bad behavior is acceptable.	. . . make the child deal with the consequences.
. . . praise the child excessively or when he doesn't really deserve it.	. . . use praise appropriately—that is, to reinforce a job well done and good social skills, like kindness, sharing, and cooperation.

behavior escalates, she goes to the opposite extreme and loses it. She tells herself she lost her temper because her son pushed her too far. But in reality, she's been building up her own private storehouse of resentment, and it eventually had to come pouring out of her like lava from a volcano.

The bottom line is that subjective parents practice a particularly insidious form of accidental parenting. When a subjective parent constantly gives in to his child's demand, it temporarily makes his child feel powerful. It also perpetuates his bad behavior. And, at the same time, by allowing his child to control him, the subjective parent loses his own self-esteem and respect. We get angry not just with our children but with all the people around us. It's a pure lose-lose situation.

Becoming an Objective Parent

If you can see yourself in the above description of a subjective parent, take heart. If you're committed to changing your old ways, it's not that hard to learn how to be an objective parent. Once you get into the habit of being an objective parent, you'll feel more confident about yourself. Even better, your child will sense your confidence and feel safer knowing that you'll be there to help him when he needs it.

To be an objective parent, you of course need to be a P.C. parent: Accept your child's temperament and be conscious of what he's going through at a particular developmental stage. An objective parent knows her child's weaknesses and strengths and is therefore able to prepare for situations ahead of time. She can often head off trouble before it starts. She's also patient enough to see her toddler over the rough spots—she knows that teaching takes time. For example, on my website, the mother of a sixteen-month-old was concerned because her son was very possessive of his toys and was just starting to get into shoving and grabbing at play group. An objective mother—"Isaiah's mommy"—shared this strategy in response:

> I find that I need to be right next to my 16/17-month-old when he's playing with others. For now! He is still learning about sharing and playing alongside others and I need to teach him how. So I sit right with him and "show" him exactly what to do. If he starts to get aggressive, I hold his hand and help him touch nicely, explaining that he needs to be gentle with his friends. If he tries to steal a toy, I hold his hand and explain to him, "No, Billy is using that toy right now. You have the truck. Billy has the ball. You need to wait for the ball." He hates waiting and will try again, but I do exactly the same again, hold his hand and explain, and if he goes for it a third time, I pick him up and move him away. I don't do it as a punishment or a time out, just to distract him and to make sure he does not get away with the undesired behavior.
>
> A lot of it is really prevention and teaching the proper behavior at this stage. They just have to go through this and we have to teach them what we want them to do. For like a year!!! It takes a long time and a lot of patience and reminding. They can't quite control their impulses yet, but a lot of help right now makes it easier later on.

Objective parents like Isaiah's mother understand that it's their responsibility to *teach* good behavior. It doesn't just happen. Of course some children are by nature easier to handle than others, more relaxed in a group situation, better able to handle the stimulation of playing with other children. But these differences notwithstanding, parents are their first teachers. Objective parents don't negotiate or wait for their child to "listen to reason," as a subjective parent might. You can't reason with a toddler, especially one on the verge or, worse, in the midst, of a meltdown. You have to be the grown-up and show that you know best.

Let's go back to the example of Hector in the shoe store demanding a lollipop. An objective parent would firmly tell him, "I know you want that lollipop, but no, you may not have one." She probably also planned ahead (there are temptations everywhere when you have a toddler in tow) and brought snacks, which she then offers as a substitute. When Hector continues to insist, she first ignores him and, when that doesn't work, takes him out of the store ("I know you're upset. When you calm down, we can buy your new shoes"). When he stops crying, she hugs him and congratulates him on handling his feelings ("You did a good job calming yourself").

> ## An Anti-B.R.A.T. Acronym
>
> **B**e honest with a child about his behavior—which includes praising him only when he really deserves it.
>
> **R**easoning doesn't work with most toddlers. Instead, set realistic limits and put them in safe situations where they can explore.
>
> **A**ctions (yours) speak louder than words. Step in before runaway emotions take over. Also, model good behavior yourself.
>
> **T**ake responsibility for both giving respect to your child and changing bad behavior when it occurs!

An objective parent is up-front with her own emotions, but never uses them to shame a child ("You're embarrassing Mummy"). She shares what she feels with her child when it's relevant ("No, you may not hit. That hurts Mummy and makes her sad"). Most important, an objective parent always takes a breath before she acts. If her child is playing with another one, and the two of them start scuffling, she first gathers evidence about what really happened, assesses the situation in an unemotional way, and then acts. Even if her child says, "I hate you, Mummy" (which let's face it, many toddlers will do when they don't get what they want), an objective parent doesn't worry, doesn't feel guilty. She just plods ahead and says to the child, "I'm sorry you feel that way and I can see how angry you are getting but the answer is still 'no.'" And when it's all over, she congratulates her child on managing his feelings.

To be sure, living with a toddler is like being in a minefield: There are countless opportunities for explosions throughout the day, especially at transition times: cleaning up after an activity or getting into the high chair, out of bath, into bed. It's always worse when your child is tired and when there are other children around or if you're in an unfamiliar setting. But no matter what the situation, an objective parent plans ahead, takes control, and uses everything as a teaching moment. You don't do it in an angry way like a policeman, but as a gentle, calm instructor showing the way. (To help, use my "F.I.T." strategy, which I explain on pages 316–320.)

Gathering Evidence

If I were to come up with the three greatest lies parents tell themselves, one would have to be, "She'll grow out of it." Granted, certain behavior goes with the territory—as the chart on page 299 shows, runaway emotions often can be caused by developmental issues. However, if a particular problem, like aggression, goes unchecked, it will continue even when the developmental stage is over.

I recently consulted on a case in England in which eighteen-month-old Max banged his head whenever he felt frustrated. When I met him, his forehead was covered in bruises, and his parents were sick with worry. Not only was Max's behavior terrorizing the entire household, but they were also concerned that the blows might do lasting damage. So, every time Max banged his head, they came running and gave him attention, which reinforced the behavior. As a result, Max became a little tyrant, and whenever he didn't get his way, he emotionally blackmailed his poor parents by banging his head on whatever hard surface was near—wood, concrete, glass. Part of the problem was developmental: Max understood everything but had a very limited vocabulary. He was constantly frustrated because he couldn't tell people what he wanted. Would he "grow out of it"? Sure, but in the meantime, his parents had to stop the tantrums. (I return to Max's story and tell you what we did on pages 330–331.)

Regardless of what other factors are at work—developmental issues, environmental factors, or temperament (Max happened to be a Spirited child as well)—when a child exhibits any form of aggression (hitting, biting, throwing, shoving), frequent tantrums, or any other inappropriate behavior (lying, stealing, cheating), look at *the whole picture* and gather evidence before you act by asking a series of questions: **When did this behavior start? What usually triggers it? What have you done about**

it in the past? Have you let it slide, chalked it off to "a stage," or rationalized that "all children do it"? Is something new happening in her life—the family, her social life—that might be making her more emotionally vulnerable?

I want to be clear on this: Gathering evidence isn't about making a case against your child. It's about looking for clues that explain her behavior so that you'll be able to help her deal with her emotions in a positive and appropriate way. An objective parent gathers evidence almost instinctively, because she constantly is observing her child, her child's behavior, and the context in which certain moods emerge. For example, Dyan, one of my oldest clients, who has since become a good friend, recently called because her 2½-year-old daughter, Alicia, started to have nightmares a few weeks ago and also was refusing to go to a gymnastics class that her mother was sure she loved. It was totally out of character for the child.

From the time she was four weeks old, "Alicia the Angel," as we called her, was a great sleeper, even when her teeth came in. But now she was suddenly waking in the night, crying her little eyes out. I immediately asked what was new in her social life. "I don't honestly know," Dyan answered. "She seemed to love this class the first time we attended—we're about halfway through the sessions. But now when I drop her off and leave her there, she has a fit." That wasn't like Alicia either. She never had a problem in the past being left at an activity, but now she was clearly saying to her mother, "Please don't leave me." Her mother thought it might be some kind of lingering separation anxiety, but Alicia was too old for that. I suggested instead that something might be going on inside her active imagination, and that to find out Mum needed to gather evidence: "Be particularly observant," I suggested. "Pay attention to her when she's playing in her room all by herself."

A few days later, Dyan called back excitedly. She had uncovered a very important piece of evidence when she overheard Alicia talking to her favorite dolly: "Don't worry, Tiffany—I won't let Matthew take you from me. I promise." Dyan recognized the name "Matthew" as one of the boys in Alicia's gymnastics class. She had a talk with the teacher, who told her that Matthew was "a bit of a bully" and on several occasions had targeted Alicia. The teacher had reprimanded Matthew and comforted Alicia, but the incidents obviously made more of an impression than she realized. Suddenly, another new behavior made sense to Dyan in light of this discovery: In the last few weeks, Alicia had been packing a special little backpack for herself. In it she put her favorite doll, Tiffany, assorted knick-knacks, and "Woofy," the tattered stuffed dog she had slept with since she was a baby. Alicia, Dyan realized, was upset if she didn't have her backpack with her at all times. "One time we left the house without it, and I had to turn around when she realized it was missing." That was a good sign, I explained to Dyan. Alicia was resilient and resourceful enough to arm herself with security items.

Using the evidence Dyan had uncovered, the two of us came up with a plan: Since Alicia was already comfortable engaging in conversations with her dolly, Dyan could join the discussion, too. "Let's play gymnastics class with Tiffany?" Dyan suggested as she plopped on the floor next to her daughter. Alicia got right into the game. "What do you do in class, Tiffany?" asked Dyan, knowing full well that Alicia would answer for her. After they discussed the routine in class for a while, Dyan asked the little dolly, "But what about that boy Matthew?"

"We don't like him, Mommy," Alicia answered as herself. "He hits me, and he tries to take Tiffany away. One day he ran with her and threw her at the wall. We don't want to go back there anymore."

Thus Dyan opened the door to Alicia's emotional life. Alicia was clearly afraid of Matthew, but talking about it was the first step in her being able to handle the fear. Dyan promised she'd go to gymnastics class *with* Alicia and that she'd also talk to the teacher and to Matthew's mother. He wouldn't be allowed to hit Alicia or take Tiffany anymore. By gathering the evidence, Dyan could see that Alicia needed to know that her mum was firmly in her corner.

Here's another example, but in the following case, twenty-seven-month-old Julia, an only child, is not being picked on; *she's* the aggressor. Her mother, Miranda, was worried because Julia had been "hitting for no reason." She suspected it was because Julia had been imitating Seth, a slightly older child who lived on their street, one whose personality, as Mum explained, "tends toward bossy and possessive of all toys. When they play, I have to constantly remind Seth to share and give toys back to Julia."

I asked Miranda to tell me a little more about Julia's behavior. "Well, for the last few months, she has been quick to get upset. She shouts 'no' to children as they walk by on the playground. She sometimes seems to strike out for no reason, but she also hits whenever another child tries to take a toy from her. A child accidentally ran into her on the slide a few weeks ago and she promptly shouted 'no' and pushed the smaller child down. It's like her reaction to Seth and all other children has become negative. She doesn't seem to want to play much with other children. And when they're around, she is very aggressive."

Miranda was right in suspecting that Julia's behavior was influenced in part by Seth's aggression. Toddlers definitely copy other kids' behavior, and they test out pushing and hitting to see what results they'll get. But I also knew that there was other evidence that Miranda was overlooking. It seemed like Julia was Spirited in nature. Her highly reactive emotional/social style was evident, too, regardless of who she played with. A few more minutes of discussing what Julia was like as a baby and young toddler, and the new evidence confirmed my suspicions: "Julia has always been a bit quick to get frustrated when playing with her toys," Miranda admitted. "For example, when she's building something and the blocks fall over, she is inclined to get angry and knock all the blocks over, perhaps even throw some of the blocks." Her behavior was consistent in other social situations with children. Even though she had been behaving well at a toddler art and music class, she had recently begun to show aggression there, too, her mother realized the more we talked. "She's okay if they are singing in a circle, or making their own art projects—I guess it's situations where there is limited interaction with the other children, but I notice that she shouted 'no' to a little boy who was putting some supplies back and pushed him down."

Miranda sighed into the phone, assuring me, "We have been quick to calmly tell her she may not hit or push, that it hurts or that yelling no is not nice. We remove her from the situation when she hits and take her to time-out in another room. None of this seems to be making a dent in her behavior. We just can't figure out how to help her manage her emotions, especially when faced with another child. Obviously we are doing something wrong."

I told Miranda not to beat herself up. She just hadn't gathered enough evidence, but now she was beginning to see the truth. Way back, when Seth and Julia came to blows over one of Julia's toys, Miranda was quick to remind Seth to share, but she should have done the same thing with her own daughter. Granted, another child can influence your child, but looking at the evidence, Julia was well on her way to becoming an aggressive child before she started playing with Seth. He may have shown Julia a few tricks, but Miranda still had to intervene when her child acted

---

Scientists Agree: F.I.T. Works

Therapists at the Oregon Social Learning Center taught parents of overly aggressive children to break what they call "the reinforcement loop" by "parenting against type." After an explosive outburst, rather than getting angry or punishing their little terrors as they'd been doing—a common response when a child constantly tests parents' limits— they were to talk to their children and, just as important, listen to them. The study showed that allowing a child to vent her anger and then talk about what caused it in the first place helped prevent future tantrums. The children also became less impulsive and did better in school than aggressive kids whose parents didn't learn the techniques.

---

out. Aggression normally escalates, as it did in this case, and I suspected that the reason the parents had failed so far to change Julia's behavior was that they'd started too late. They needed to teach their daughter how to be emotionally F.I.T.

Teaching Your Child to be Emotionally F.I.T.

Not so long ago, Leah, a mother I had met when her son Alex was just born, called and told me, "Alex can't get it together." She seemed to be blaming Alex—a nineteen-month-old—for jumping on the couch when they were at a friend's house, grabbing things from the other child, and running around "like a new puppy." After asking her a series of questions to gather evidence, I learned that at home Alex was allowed to jump on the couch, that Leah thought it was "cute" when he grabbed things from her purse, and that they often played "chase" in the living room. Alex's behavior was totally understandable, but he couldn't change until Leah took responsibility (see page 319).

Children don't "get it together" unless objective parents patiently teach them how. How do you have patience with an unruly toddler? First of all, you don't wait for things to spin out of control. Second, you have a *plan*. You think about things beforehand. For example, if you're going to a play group, ask yourself, what might go wrong? What is my child's Achilles' heel in a group setting? In the heat of the moment, it's hard to deal with a child's emotions unless you've given it some thought. Especially if you're a subjective parent, your own embarrassment, guilt, and a medley of other feelings can get in the way of proper intervention. Though it might be easier to handle your child's changing moods if you're an objective parent—because you see her clearly and don't tend to get emotional yourself—it's still hard to stay the course in the face of a meltdown. So here's a simple solution: Think "F.I.T."

The acronym F.I.T. stands for:

Feeling (acknowledging emotions)

Intervening

Telling (your child what you expect from him and/or what he might do instead)

In short, F.I.T. is a reminder that when the child feels something, you immediately help her identify the emotion, and then help her do an appropriate behavior. You don't just do F.I.T. when your child is having very intense emotions or is on the verge of an utter meltdown. You practice F.I.T. as a normal part of your child's day. Just as you would take the hand of a child learning to walk so that he can practice, here you will be helping your child practice dealing with his emotions. Research on overly aggressive children has shown that the basic premise works even with very difficult children (see sidebar, page 316).

As the following explanations show, each letter of F.I.T. is important. But each also has its difficulties, so you'll need to watch out for the pitfalls.

Feeling (acknowledging emotions). We need to allow children their feelings, rather than try to talk them out of them or ignore the feelings altogether. We need to help children understand what feelings are. Don't wait for an explosion to happen. Use feeling words when you're doing everyday things ("I feel happy when we go for a walk"), when you're watching the telly together

---

Give (and Get) Respect

Respect is a two-way street. Demand respect for yourself by setting reasonable limits, establishing your boundaries, and expecting the basic courtesies, like "please" and "thank you." But also *give* respect to your child:

Keep your own emotions at bay. Don't overreact, scream, or hit. Remember that you must model emotional competence.

Don't talk about your child's problem in front of your friends. I've seen it time and again in play groups: The mums sit around and talk about all the bad things their children do.

See discipline as a teaching opportunity, not as punishment. Allow your child to experience the consequences of her actions, but make sure that the consequences are developmentally appropriate and in proportion to the "crime."

Praise good behavior. Comments like "good sharing," "good listening," and "you really did a good job calming yourself" help foster your child's emotional intelligence (page 48).

("Barney looks sad because his friends went home"), or when he's playing with another child ("I know it makes you angry when Billy grabs a toy").

If your child has gotten really hyped up, and his emotions have taken over, take him away from the action altogether. Give him a chance to cool down. Just hold him on your lap with his back to you. Suggest that he take a deep breath. If he squirms and refuses to be held, put him down, also with his back to you. Speak his feelings for him ("I can see you're [excited/angry about . . .]"), but set a limit ("but you may not go back and play with Danny until you calm down"). As soon as he's calm, give him a hug and praise him: "That was good calming down."

The pitfall here is that talking about emotions may not be easy. As I've stressed in the earlier sections of this chapter, subjective parents sometimes have trouble handling their own emotions, much less their child's. Perhaps the child's emotions remind them of someone else (or themselves). If so, they're likely to want to suppress those emotions in their child. Knowing your own weaknesses is half the battle. If talking about emotions is hard for you, practice. Arm yourself with a script and role-play in advance with your partner or a friend.

Also, parents are sometimes afraid to call things what they are, especially when a child lies or steals. Believe it or not, toddlers are capable of such "crimes," and the behavior has to be acknowledged; otherwise, it persists. And we really can't blame a child if no one has told him that wasn't okay. Carissa, for example, was adamant about not allowing her three-year-old, Phillip, to have a toy gun. She called me when she found four of them hidden under his bed. Shocked as she was, Carissa realized that her son must have taken the guns from other children. But when she asked where they'd come from, he told her, "Gregory left them there."

Protect Your Child!

I often hear from worried parents that another child has been biting, pushing, hitting, or taking toys away from their child. They are concerned on two counts: how to stop the aggressive child and how to keep their own from learning bad habits.

The answer is simple: Find another play option. Children definitely pick up behaviors from other children. What's worse is that by keeping your child in the aggressive child's company, you're showing yours that the world is not safe. A bullied child loses her self-esteem.

And if you happen to witness the bullying firsthand, by all means, intervene. Never leave your child in harm's way, even if it means disciplining someone else's child. Otherwise, it's like saying to your child, "Too bad, you're on your own."

Carissa went on, "I couldn't call him a liar, could I? I mean he's only three—he doesn't understand what stealing is." Many parents feel that way, but as I explained to Carissa, how else will Phillip learn that it's not okay to lie and steal if not from her unless she actually *names* his behavior? Of course, she also has to do something about it—intervene—but first she has to make Phillip aware that stealing and lying are wrong and also that his behavior has an impact on the other children (see page 320).

Intervening. Actions speak louder than words, especially with toddlers. You have to stop the undesirable behavior, by both naming and physically intervening. For instance, a mum asked me on a call-in show, "How can I calm down my three-year-old boy? He's like a wild dog every time we go out." I told her that my first concern was that she was not setting limits and boundaries. Children may be exuberant by nature—Spirited toddlers and children with highly reactive emotional/social styles certainly are. But when I hear a parent compare her child to a "wild" anything, I'm pretty sure it's not just a matter of temperament. He has never ever been told what's expected of him. Discipline requires gentle but firm boundaries. I explained that when her son acts out or displays a tantrum, she has to let him know this is unacceptable behavior. She must physically turn him around, sit him on the floor, and say, "You may not act so wildly when we go out." She has to take him home if he continues. And next time, think it through beforehand. You might take a shorter outing. In any case, you should always have a Plan B in case the trip becomes too much for him.

Telling (your child what you expect from him and/or what he might do instead). If your child has slapped, bitten, hit, shoved, or grabbed a toy from another child, you have to intervene immediately, but you also have to show him an alternative way of behaving. After I consulted with Leah about Alex's behavior and told her about F.I.T., she promised she would intervene immediately whenever her son acted out. Sure enough, that afternoon Alex grabbed her mirror from her purse. Instead of ignoring him, she took the mirror away from him immediately, addressed his feelings, but set limits at the same time: "I see that you want my mirror, but that's Mummy's mirror, and Mummy doesn't want it to break." Leah became *the parent* again. She took control but also gave him an alternative: "So let's go and find something of yours that you can play with." Notice that Leah didn't try to reason with Alex, or explain in great detail why he shouldn't have the mirror. We don't reason with toddlers. Instead, we offer choices, based on the alternatives that are okay with you. In other words, you don't say, "Would you like a carrot stick or an ice cream pop?" but "Would you like a carrot stick or a box of raisins?"

Remember, too, that toddlers are not too young to understand that there are consequences to their actions. "I'm sorry" is no good if it's just parroted, and the child doesn't actually *do* something for the other person. Whenever I see a toddler whack a kid and then quickly say, "I'm sorry," I know that his parents haven't allowed him to experience consequences. Rather, they've given him the idea that "I'm sorry" conveys some sort of immunity, so in his little mind he thinks, *I can do whatever I want, as long as I say I'm sorry.* In Phillip's case, I suggested that Carissa make him return each gun he stole and apologize to the children. (When a child breaks another child's toy, he should give up one of his own.)

You can also have your child dictate a written apology as part of his attempts at restitution. I recently heard about Wyatt, a 3½-year-old, who was playing "fetch" with a neighbor's dog. The neighbor told the little boy not to throw the tennis ball over the hill because it was dangerous for Rufus (the dog) to go into the brambles. But as soon as the adults were busily engaged in conversation, Wyatt hurled the ball over the hill. The neighbor told Rufus to "stay," and then looked sternly in Wyatt's direction. "Did you understand what I told you about not throwing the ball?" Wyatt answered sheepishly, "Uh huh." The neighbor said, "Well then, I guess you owe Rufus a tennis ball." A few days later, the neighbor found a clumsily wrapped package at her front door. Inside were two tennis balls and a note from Wyatt (who had dictated it to his mum): "I'm sorry I lost Rufus's ball. I won't do it again." Wyatt's mum did a good job of helping her son see that there were consequences to his behavior (the neighbor didn't want him to play with her dog) and guiding her son through an act of restitution.

Emotional and Social Milestones: Adapting F.I.T. to Your Child

In chapter 2, we looked at how your child's growing brain continues to enrich her emotional repertoire (pages 49–53). Here I look at the emotional and social milestones from age one through three. Just as you want to know what's "normal" when it comes to intellectual growth or physical growth, you need to understand your child's capabilities in the emotional arena, so that you have a realistic concept of what she can and cannot understand and do—and what you can and cannot do to help her. For example, if you try to "discipline" an eight- or nine-month-old for using the VCR to "mail" a cracker, your words won't mean much. At her age, she's not shoving the cracker in or pushing the buttons to drive you crazy. Rather, she's experimenting with her newfound dexterity and is fascinated by the lights and sounds. It's also how she plays with her toys, and what tells her that your VCR isn't one of them? If you think she's doing it on purpose, chances are you'll lose patience more quickly. On the other hand, if your child is two and you've never said "no" to her or set limits because you don't realize that she has the capacity to exert some self-control, her behavior will only escalate.

One Year to Eighteen Months. At one year, your toddler will be intensely curious about *everything,* and you need to give her the opportunity to explore, but at the same time, keep her safe. She will try out different feelings, some which will seem aggressive, but the behavior is less a matter of conscious anger at first and more about testing out her newfound physical capabilities. She understands cause and effect. When she hits another child, and that child squeals, it's like a game similar to her pushing a button on one of her toys to make a sound or a bunny pop up. You need to be there to explain that hitting a person is different: "No, we do not hit. That hurts Sally. Be gentle." In other words, even though before the age of fourteen or fifteen months she can't quite understand consequences or exercise self-control, you must do it for her. You're her guide, her conscience.

Your child will also become more verbal, and even if she's not saying that many words, she will understand everything you say, though at times she might consciously ignore you! This is the beginning of "testing" behavior and also the beginning of tantrums. She might cooperate when you say "no" or try to test your limits. And sometimes it's not about limit-testing at all—many children lack a sufficient vocabulary to express their needs and a great deal of "bad" behavior at this age is really frustration. Don't try to negotiate and don't try to reason; stay in charge in a loving way. Try to *prevent* incidents by making the house childproof and by taking her to places where she won't have to behave like an adult, rather than getting into situations in which you have intervene constantly. Especially if your child is very physical—an early walker, a very hyperactive or impulsive child—give her opportunities to climb and run and jump. Remember that if you allow her to use your couch as a trampoline, or to stand up at the dinner table, she will naturally think it's okay to do that at Grandma's house or at a restaurant. So start as you mean to go on. Plan for contingencies. Distraction is a great strategy at this age, so if you know you're going to a house where there are lots of untouchables, bring toys to help divert her attention and energy elsewhere.

Eighteen Months to Two Years. Eighteen months is a pivotal time in brain development. It's around the time when parents find themselves saying, "Wow! He's so grown-up all of a sudden." He learns the words "I" and "me" and "mine" or starts sentences with his own name ("Henry do it"). He refers to himself often, not just because he has language; he actually has a greater sense of self. Accordingly, he's becoming more assertive—everything in the world is "mine," in his view (see the "Eight Rules of Toddler Play," page 323). Also, his developing brain finally allows him to gain a bit of self-control (with help from you, of course). *If* you've been teaching him all along what behavior is acceptable ("No, it is not okay to [hit, bite, slap, shove, grab another child's toy]"), by now he can exercise restraint, but it won't be perfect. You can say, "Wait a minute, and I'll get that toy for you," and he can actually wait. But if you haven't shown him the difference between what kind of behavior is acceptable and what is wrong, he's probably become very good at manipulating you. Start to set limits *now*.

It's still important to plan ahead and to know your child and what his tolerance and capabilities are. Remember, too, that self-control is a skill that continues to develop. Sharing doesn't come easily to some children—it's not a sign that your two-year-old is bad or undeveloped. In fact, when most toddlers want to do an activity or have a turn at something, it's hard for them to wait, resist, give back. But it *is* possible to acknowledge a child's feelings and desires *and* set limits. For example, if a plate of snacks is being passed around at play group and your child grabs more than one cookie, an objective parent doesn't immediately say to herself, *Oh, the other mothers must think I've raised a little glutton. I could just die. Maybe they won't notice that Zack took two cookies.* Instead, she would honor Zack's feelings ("I know you want to take two cookies . . ."). At the same time, she would *also* state the rule (". . . but each of us is just taking one . . .") and enforce it (". . . so please put the second one back"). If Zack says "no—*my cookies*!" and clings to his booty, she would take both cookies away and leave the table, explaining, "We share in this group." Remember that you need to help your child manage whatever emotions are too strong for him to control himself. If you do have to leave because he just can't calm down, don't act as if he's "bad" or as if it's a "punishment." Be compassionate: "We just need to work harder on helping you learn how to control yourself."

Two to Three Years. The legendary terrible twos are upon you now, and they seem to come on overnight with some children. (It's a preview of adolescence!) Hopefully, you haven't waited this long to set limits and to teach your child self-control. Although your child is still working on sharing, restraining himself, and managing his moods, by three it *will* get better if you've been consistent. However, if you haven't been guiding him emotionally, watch out, because negativity and aggression peak at around two. With either scenario, though, because your child has so much more to say and so much more she wants to do—and very definite ideas about how to do everything—it might seem as if her self-control has regressed. If your child has language delays, the frustration level now will be even higher. There may be wild swings of emotion—one minute she's playing happily, the next she's pounding the floor with her fists in a meltdown.

Your behavior is more important than ever, as an emotional role model. Because of the emotional volatility typical of the twos, it's almost impossible to avoid tantrums, especially if your child is tired or out of sorts. Your child also will be more incorrigible when overstimulated. But you can at least structure situations to minimize meltdowns. Don't plan outings when it's nap time; don't do too many high-energy activities in one day; avoid situations that in the past have led to tantrums. Also, if you're having a play group, and your child has had difficulties coping in the past, discuss sharing and aggressive behavior *before* the other children arrive. Ask if there are special toys he might want to put away. Tell him you'll be there if he gets upset. You can even role-play. "Let's pretend that I'm Peter, and I'm using your car. What will you do if you want it?" Children at this age are very good at symbolic play. You can suggest alternatives. "We could use a timer, and when the timer goes off, you get a turn" or "When Peter is playing with

---

The Eight Rules of Toddler Play

I found this little gem on the internet and reprint it here because it seems to sum up the emotional and social life of a toddler. Kudos to the anonymous author, who obviously has a toddler at home.

1. If I like it—it's mine.
2. If it's in my hand—it's mine.
3. If I can take it from you—it's mine.
4. If I had it a little while ago—it's mine.
5. If it's mine it must never appear to be yours in any way, shape, or form!
6. If I am doing or building something—all the pieces are mine.
7. If it looks like mine—it's mine.
8. If I think it's mine—it's mine.

your car, you can use the fire engine." Stress that he must use his words instead of his hands.

Watch television and computer use. The American Academy of Pediatrics advises *no TV under age two,* but I know of very few households in which that guideline is followed. In fact, by two, many children are already avid watchers. At least, beware: A whole rash of studies have shown that screen use definitely revs kids up, especially Spirited children or any child who has a highly reactive emotional/social style (and, as I said in chapter 7, some content can also scare them). Instead, build in lots of outdoor time or active indoor play. This is the age when children can start helping you with housework and cooking. Be sure to give them manageable and safe chores—and be patient. Everything is a learning experience.

Finally, try to catch your child when she is behaving appropriately: cooperating, sharing nicely, or sticking with a task that's hard for her. Identify the accomplishment: "Thanks for helping me." "Good sharing." "Wow, you worked hard and made that tower all by yourself."

Typical Toddler Transgressions

Parents always want specific answers about handling runaway emotions. What do I do if he hits? Has tantrums? Bites? As you should realize having read this far in this book, there are no simple answers. Behavioral problems are always complicated, fueled by one or more of the four risk factors (page 299).

Tantrums. This email from Peggy is representative of the many that I receive about tantrums:

> Kerry, my 2½-year-old daughter, spends most of her time trying to control rather than enjoy normal toddler things. I have tried things from your book as well as others and one thing has always been consistent in my behavior during her tantrums . . . I say to her, "Crying will get you nothing." She has always been a difficult child from day one. She has tantrums over everything. I have taken things of value away from her, used time-outs, left from parks, etc. She is extremely stubborn and headstrong. I am at my wits' end and feel that I don't know how much longer I can cope. I am thinking about putting her in preschool full-time and going back to work but that will just give me some peace during the day

and not really solve the problem. She is fine with everyone else she is left with. I truly believe this issue is with me.

First of all, Peggy doesn't realize that "trying to control" is a normal toddler activity. That said, I'm afraid she is also right that Kerry's tantrums are, at least in part, the result of Mum's accidental parenting. The fact that Peggy has tried so many different strategies tells me she hasn't been consistent, and I'll bet little Kerry is confused. She never knows what to expect from her mum, which may explain why Kerry is "fine with everyone else."

Peggy says that Kerry has been "difficult from day one," and I don't doubt it. That kind of temperament puts her at risk for runaway emotions. But Peggy is clearly a subjective parent. She's blaming her daughter without really looking at the evidence and taking responsibility for her part. Peggy has to look at her daughter's history and, even more important, her reactions in the past when Kerry had a meltdown. What did she do? Also, she has to look at her own attitudes. Perhaps she was shocked when Kerry was born, because she suddenly realized what having a child really means. Maybe she felt guilty for those feelings. Whatever the reason, the evidence points to the fact that she hasn't sets limit for Kerry. Therefore, we first have to turn Mum's behavior around. If she approaches Kerry differently, Kerry *will* change—certainly not overnight, because this is a rather chronic (and sadly, all too typical) power struggle.

Peggy has to start planning ahead when she's out with Kerry. She knows who her child is, and her best shot is to structure situations to avoid a meltdown. Let's say Kerry regularly has tantrums when they're out doing errands. Mum needs to bring along snacks and toys to offer when Kerry makes one of her demands. And if that doesn't work, she should address the feelings ("I can see you're upset") but ignore the behavior. Instead of saying, "Crying will get you nothing," which doesn't mean anything to a young child, Peggy has to be very concrete: "Mummy will stay here with you until you stop crying." She should then not talk to her—just *be* with her. She has to reassure Kerry that she knows what she's doing and she's going to keep her safe ("I'm going to stay with you 'til you calm down"). If Kerry doesn't calm down, Peggy has to remove her from the scene. And when they successfully make their way through a tantrum cycle, she has to praise Kerry for gaining control over her emotions ("Good job calming yourself down").

If Mum starts working *with* Kerry, instead of pulling away from her and resenting her behavior, the tantrums will abate. If I read between the lines, I see a mother who is terribly angry and even ambivalent. Her daughter senses the distance, and is using tantrums to reel Mummy in. Once Kerry starts getting attention for the good things she does, she won't need to demand Mum's attention in such a negative way.

Biting. Biting before a year old often starts by accident during breast-feeding. Most mums will shout "Ouch!" when it happens and instinctively push the baby away, which scares him—and is often enough to stop future biting. There are several other reasons that toddlers bite. By gathering evidence you can usually figure out why your child is biting. Consider this real-life situation from my website:

> My one-year-old, Raoul, is starting to bite. It is worse when he is tired, we try to say NO and put him down but he attacks us and thinks it is a game, we have tried everything and even tapped him on the mouth when we say NO. Has anyone gone through this?

Actually, lots of parents go through the same thing. This mum should be reading her son's tired cues and not let Raoul get to the biting stage. That Raoul's biting is worse when he's tired tells me it's probably a combination of frustration and overstimulation. Because Raoul "thinks it is a game," I also suspect that somewhere in the past, someone laughed at him when he tried to bite. With some children, biting is also a way of getting attention, which might be happening here, too. With others, it's connected with teething. Still others can't yet verbalize so they bite out of the frustration of wanting something and not being able to ask for it.

You can see why it's important for Raoul's parents to gather evidence. Once they consider all the possible reasons for his behavior, they then can take steps, wherever feasible, to eliminate the triggers—make sure he gets enough rest, know what Raoul looks like when he's about to bite, and certainly never laugh at the behavior. Each time he bites, whatever the reason, they must put him down immediately, and tell him the rule and how they feel: "No biting. That hurts." They then should not look at him or engage in any way; just walk away. Biting often makes parents angry, and separating from the child gives them a moment to deal with their own emotions.

I've also seen cases where the biter is defending herself. I received an email from the mother of a two-year-old who was concerned because her daughter was "biting other children when they have her me-me blanket. She has done it twice and when she has done it, she is told NO! and is taken away from the other children. Should we be restricting me-me to naps and bedtime, or is that unfair?" Well, I'd bite, too, if I were that little girl. Her mother shouldn't allow anyone else to have her "me-me blanket" in the first place. She's punishing her daughter without taking into consideration the evidence. It's her special blankie. Why should she share it?

Of course, many cases of biting are about a child losing control. You're trying to wipe her hands after a meal and she gets angry and chomps down on your hand to stop you. The trick there is to recognize the situations that set her off. If staying in the high chair too long gets her frustrated, take her out earlier. Perhaps you can wipe her hands over the sink instead. Often, biters are children who have been bullied, so it's important to look at social interactions, too. Most children will take another's abuse for just so long. Then they'll bite as a form of retaliation.

Some parents make light of biting. I often hear comments like, "What's the big deal? All kids do it." The big deal is that biting can escalate into other forms of aggression (see "Harrison's Story" on page 332). Especially if the biting has been going on for several months, and Mum and Dad have gotten a few nips on the shoulder or on the back of the legs, the child also might feel a sense of power and pick up his parents' nervousness. So when it happens, it's critical for parents to be objective and very business-like, rather than emotional.

Remember that biting also feels good to toddlers. It's a nifty sensation. Sinking their teeth into a warm fleshy stuff is a form of physical play to them! I suggest giving a chronic biter one of those stress balls they sell in sporting goods stores. Call it her "bite ball." Make sure you've got one in your pocket when she comes near you with that look on her face that says, *I'm about to chomp you!* Along similar lines, a mum on the website, whose son likes to bite the backs of her calves while she's cooking, keeps a little pile of teething rings on the counter within easy reach. When she sees her son approaching, she gives one of the rings to him and says, "No biting Mummy, but here, you can bite this." When he chomps down on the teether she notes, "I clap and cheer for him."

Sometimes parents suggest hitting a child on the mouth, as Raoul's parents did, or biting back. They say it works, but I don't believe in meeting any form of aggression with another form of aggression. We are children's role models, and it's confusing for them to see Mummy or Daddy doing the very thing they're not allowed to do.

Hitting and slapping. Hitting and slapping, like biting, often start innocently, as this email from Judy about her nine-month-old, Jake, shows. I use it here also because the mother also wonders about childproofing her house.

> My son Jake has been crawling and pulling himself up for around three weeks. I am wondering how I can teach him not to touch things on the coffee tables, plants, and so on and teach him what "no" means. He also has a habit of slapping faces, not with malicious intent, but still I have to watch him with other children. He is a very happy baby and is not trying to be mean. He just doesn't understand that he should "pat" or caress someone's face and not slap at it. I take his hand and caress so that he knows that is what he should do but he then slaps again. I don't know if he is too young.

Judy is on the right track. Jake is just curious about his world. And although he's got half a year to go before any degree of self-control kicks in, it's not too early to start teaching him right and wrong. When he approaches another child, or the family pet for that matter, she should just say "gentle, gentle" and guide his hand as she's been doing. As I said earlier, young toddlers' first aggressive acts are motivated by curiosity. The child is testing to see if he can get a reaction. So Judy has to tell him, "No, you're hurting Annie. Be gentle." When he does slap, she has to put him down and say, "No, you may not slap."

As for the childproofing issue, it's unrealistic at nine months to expect your toddler to have any self-control. I don't believe in stripping a house of everything—children need to learn to live with possessions and not touch some of them. Take away only the things you don't want to risk or anything that the child could hurt himself on. Walk around with him. Explain, "You can touch it when Mummy's here." Let him hold things and examine them. That often takes the mystery out of the many untouchables in your house. Toddlers get bored quickly. Be sure to give him alternative items that he can touch and manipulate. He'll need to bang, make noises, make parts move, as long as it's not your stereo equipment! Boys especially love to tinker. Judy might invest in a little play hammer and knocking table.

Throwing. Throwing often starts when a child hurls a toy out of the crib or food over the side of the high chair. Instead of just leaving it there, and saying, "Oh, you threw your toy. I guess you want that on the floor," Mum or Dad keep picking it up. Then the child thinks, *Oh, this is a fun game.* Or it can start when a child—boys especially—throws a toy at someone (usually Mum since she's with him most), as this email exemplifies:

> Now here is my problem: My son, Bo, is eighteen months and for the last six months he has been throwing stuff: while playing, while eating, and the worst thing, he throws toys at people. I see he doesn't do it in order to hurt, but he is a strong child, and it hurts. Anyway, it must end. When he throws food, I tell him not to do that. I also can take action—stop his meal, put him down, etc. But the problem with throwing toys is that I have nothing to do except say, "Do not throw toys at Mommy. It hurts me," and take the toy away. But then he finds another toy to throw! I can't take everything . . . It's not like I can take him to another place, because we are at home! And he has a lot of toys, so technically I can't take all of his toys away . . .

This is another mother who's on the right track. Bo is probably throwing because he's discovered a new skill, not because he's out to harm his playmates. All the same, his mother realizes she has to stop Bo's throwing immediately. The problem is that she's not giving him an alternative way to behave. In other words, she needs to *show* him situations in which throwing is usually appropriate and doesn't harm other people. After all, she can't, and wouldn't want to, stop his throwing altogether— he's a boy. (I'm not being sexist here; plenty of little girls like to throw things, too, and many will turn out to be great athletes. It's just that in my experience, throwing is usually more of a *boy's* "problem.") So Mum needs to channel Bo's throwing to an appropriate venue: Get him five balls of different sizes to kick and throw. Take him outside and explain, "This is where we can throw things." If it's the dead of winter, take him to a gym. It's important to go to a drastically different place, so he understands that throwing is not allowed indoors at home (unless you have a large, appropriate play space). Give him praise when he throws the ball.

Since this has been going on for six months—a third of Bo's lifetime—I suspect he's also learned how to make a game of it and has become pretty good at manipulating his mother. She can, and should, do more than just take the toy away. Even though she is at home with him, she can remove him from his room full of toys and take him into a boring room (like the living room) and sit *with* him. (I don't believe in solo timeouts; see sidebar, page 75.) He's eighteen months, so he understands everything and will quickly get that his mum won't tolerate his throwing. (More about throwing food on pages 168–169.)

Head-banging, hair-pulling, nose-picking, slapping oneself, nailbiting. You might be surprised that I've grouped head-banging with the four other behaviors. But all five, as well as other types of ritualistic behaviors that toddlers develop, are methods of self-soothing and, often, a response to frustration. Although in rare cases some of these behaviors could foreshadow a neurological disorder, the benign forms are all surprisingly common, even head-banging, which some estimate occurs in 20 percent of all children. Most of these behaviors are more annoying than dangerous and go away as suddenly as they appeared—that is, if parents don't call attention to them. The problem is that when a child bangs his head, slaps his own face, picks his nose, or bites his fingernails, it is extremely—and understandably—upsetting to parents. The more worried or angry they become, though, the more the child realizes, *oh, this is a great way to get Mum and Dad's attention,* at which point the behavior, which started out as a form of self-soothing, now becomes a way of manipulating his parents. Therefore, it's best to ignore the child, but also make sure that he can't hurt himself.

Such was the case with Max, the eighteen-month-old head-banger, to whom I referred earlier (page 312). He initially started banging his head out of frustration—he lacked sufficient language to express what he wanted. Very quickly, though, his head-banging escalated, because Max realized that it was a surefire way of getting his parents to stop whatever they were doing and run to his rescue. By the time I met him, Max was Ruler of the House. He refused to eat, was a very poor sleeper, and his behavior was off the charts—he was a yeller and a hitter. Max knew he could get away with anything, because all rules and limits were relaxed the minute he started banging his head.

To deal with the safety issue, we brought in a small bean bag chair, and every time he began a head-banging session, we lifted him onto the bean bag. Taking away the element of risk made it easier for Max's parents to let him get through his tantrum without interfering or, worse, battling with him. He fought it at first, kicking even more forcefully when we tried to put him onto the bean bag, but we were consistent. "No, Max, you may not leave your chair until you've calmed down."

It was important not to stop there, however. With all of the above self-soothing behaviors, if parents allow themselves to be manipulated, it's almost always a sign that they're letting their child call the shots. I could see that we also had to correct months of Max's domination over the household. It was as if his parents and older brother were held hostage by his behavior. He ate mostly junk food, refusing to eat what his brother and parents had, and still woke up in the middle of the night demanding his parents' attention. We had to show him that there was a new regime, and he was no longer in charge.

I explained to his parents that whenever he tried to take the reins, they had to show him they wouldn't cave in. On my visit, I demonstrated this when Max, as usual, pushed his lunch away and kept saying over and over, "Cookie . . . cookie . . . cookie." I looked him straight in the eye and said, "No, Max, you can't have a cookie until you've eaten some pasta." This was one determined little boy. Accustomed to ruling the roost, he was in shock—and in tears. "Just one piece of pasta," I kept insisting. (You have to start small, luv—even *one* piece of pasta represented progress!) Finally, *an hour later* he relented. He ate a piece of pasta, and I gave him a cookie in return. We had the same battle of wills when it was time to take a nap. Fortunately, the lunchtime match wore him out a bit, so I only had to do P.U./P.D. a few times. Admittedly, I was not his mother or father, and he knew from my performance at lunch that I wasn't a pushover. By watching me, though, his mum and dad could see that it was possible to get Max to behave.

It sounds incredible, but Max was a different child four days later. His parents kept using the bean bag for tantrums and were very conscientious about holding the line at meals and sleep times. At two, children realize pretty quickly that you're changing the rules—in this case, establishing rules for the first time. Max began going to the bean bag on his own when he was frustrated. Within a few months, his head-banging was a rare occurrence, and the entire family felt a sense of calm because now the parents were in charge, not the toddler.

Spotlight in the Trenches

Harrison's Story: Escalating Aggression

Some kids are definitely harder to discipline than others. Their parents have to be vigilant, patient, consistent—and creative. Lori called because two-year-old Harrison bit her one day, seemingly out of the blue. Lori responded correctly, with a loud, "Ouch, that hurts. No biting." But Harrison was persistent and a little bit sneaky. He'd act like he was about to hug her and then bite her. That's where Lori went wrong. Instead of dealing with it ("I had already told him, 'No biting'"), she pulled him away and dodged his biting. A few days later, one of the play group mothers called to tell her that Harrison had hit another child on the face. Lori started to keep a close eye on him, saying, "No, you may not . . ." whenever he was about to lose it. But then the aggression just took a new form—he started kicking. She was beside herself: "I'm sick of saying 'No' to him. There's no nice time with him anymore. People don't want to come around our house, because he started using toys as weapons to hit other kids."

Harrison's escalating behavior was understandable in that he had several of the elements that put a child at risk for runaway emotions: He was a Spirited child in the midst of his terrible twos, and until now, his mother hadn't been consistent. Now she had to start helping him identify his feelings, laying down the law, and when necessary, removing him from the fray. None of it worked right away. I told Lori she had to be patient and keep it up. But she also had to heap on the praise for good behavior. I suggested that she make a "Good Behavior" chart for Harrison. It had four columns, which divided the day into time slots: Wake-up to before Breakfast, Breakfast to Lunch, Lunch through Afternoon Snack, and Afternoon to Bedtime. The deal was that if he got four stars in a day, Dad would takes him to the park. In the summer, he got to go swimming. It took a few months, but Harrison's aggressive behavior is occasional now.

But What If Something's *Wrong* with My Child . . . and He Can't Help It?

In the last decade, child development researchers have learned a great deal about children's brains and how early experiences can actually change the structure of the brain. With this knowledge a growing battalion of therapists who specialize in speech and language pathology (S.L.P.), family dynamics, and occupational therapy (O.T.) have turned their attention to very young children, the theory being that if we can identify and diagnose problems early on, appropriate intervention can prevent more serious problems from developing once the child is in school. It makes sense, and for many children, early intervention is critical. The problem is, some children are put into therapy because their parents are anxious or because they are looking to someone else to deal with their child's behavior.

A 2004 article in *New York* magazine told of a little boy whose mother began a "yearlong odyssey into a subculture of psychologists and occupational and speech therapists issuing diagnoses littered with terms like *dyspraxia* and *prioceptors* and *sensory integration systems,* and recommending intensive therapy." Manhattan is undoubtedly one of those cities where high-powered parents want their children to follow in their footsteps. However, with the explosive sales of educational toys like Baby Einstein and Leap Frog, it's obvious—and understandable—that parents everywhere want their children to excel. And therapists everywhere are willing to help them. Certainly if a child really has a neurobiological problem, it makes sense to get him the right kind of help early on. But what about borderline children, who just happen to talk a little later, who are clumsier than their peers, and who prefer to play on their own rather than interact with other children? How does a parent know when those first signs of aggression are due to a certifiable language disorder or poor impulse control? Will he "grow out of it" or does he need help now?

There are no easy answers. Certainly, if your child is late reaching the various milestones (especially speech) and/or if there's a family history of attention deficit disorders to learning disabilities—an umbrella term that includes language disorders, dyslexia, autism spectrum disorder, perceptual impairment, mental retardation, cerebral palsy—it's better to seek help early on. Cutting through the jargon is frustrating for parents, especially because not all clinicians use the same terms. Still, parents usually know when their child stands out in some way, especially if she has a behavior problem. The hard part is figuring out why. No two children are alike, so it's best to seek professional help to cut through the confusion.

Most experts say that it's difficult to make a conclusive diagnosis before eighteen months, but a good diagnosis is critical to getting the right kind of help at any age, explains S.L.P. therapist Lyn Hacker: "Language-impaired children who have delayed milestones will act out to communicate because they return to the most primitive element—signs and gestures. Hitting can be an expression of frustration if we're sure that the child's comprehension is intact. But hitting can also be a sign of a learning disability, being asked to do what you are not good at doing, or an attention deficit disorder, in which case the child has difficulty inhibiting responses and low frustration tolerance. For me a 'soft sign' of A.D.D. is the kid who can't take being told 'no' because a child with A.D.D. is an existentialist. He doesn't understand that 'no' is not forever, but for right now. Couple that with lack of patience and he doesn't even hear qualifiers, like 'not now' and 'but.'"

Hacker also acknowledges that many behavior problems *start* with the parents. "If a child has had a comprehensive physical exam, and there's nothing wrong, and the milestones are within normal development, then the next step is to look at the parent-child relationship. Maybe the mother needs to learn what sets the kid off and try to prevent it." But even when a neurological diagnosis is confirmed, parents are critical factors in the equation.

First of all, remember that *you* know your child best. Dr. Smith may be an expert in language problems, but *you* are the expert for your child. You see her twenty-four/seven, and Dr. Smith usually sees her in a clinical setting. Even if a professional pays a house visit, which some do nowadays, he or she can't know your child the way you do. Take the case of little Isabella, whose parents sought help shortly before her second birthday, because, as Felicia, Isabella's mother, explains, "She wasn't really saying much at all. What made it all so hard was that she clearly had so much going on in her head but wasn't able to say anything. That led to a great deal of frustration for her, which manifested itself in pushing and somewhat aggressive behavior."

Felicia says she was proactive because of her own history. "I was a late talker, too. My mother can't recall exactly when I started talking, but it was definitely after two, maybe even closer to three. Also, [the county where I live] offers testing and services for free. They come to your house and are just wonderful, so it makes it hard *not* to take advantage of all that they offer."

When Isabella was tested, Felicia recalls, "She wasn't really delayed enough to qualify—you need to be twenty-five percent delayed. But they factored in her play skills which were several months *ahead* of her age. She was qualified because of the discrepancy between language and play." Often, in fact, it's not so much a child's low scores on a particular test that indicate a problem; rather, the fact that she scores exceptionally high in some areas and low in others. The tester suggested language therapy for Isabella. Now, a little more than a year later, she has the vocabulary of a 3½-year-old. Felicia admits, "I really can't say with any certainty whether the therapy itself helped or if it was just maturity—or both. But we've seen such an improvement."

The preschool where Isabella was enrolled had also suggested additional therapy, because of "low muscle tone" and Isabella's aggressiveness toward other children, but Felicia resisted. This is hard for some parents—the *experts* supposedly know best. This wise mother recalls, "I did some research on my own and couldn't find any evidence of low muscle tone. The school had recommended all sorts of additional therapy that would have cost hundreds, even thousands, of dollars. But my take on it was that she was frustrated because she couldn't talk. To placate the school, I had the county come out again and test her, and they said she was perfectly fine. The school wanted me to get a third opinion, but I kept putting it off. Lo and behold, now that she is talking, her aggressive behavior has stopped. Imagine that!"

Felicia's story illustrates the ideal: a *partnership* between parents and professionals. Clearly, parents shouldn't just leave their child's fate in anyone else's hands, no matter what degrees hang on the wall. They also have to be willing to carry on whatever strategies the therapist suggests and they have to be more vigilant than ever about staying in charge. However, many parents start to feel sorry for their child, or they get exasperated—or both. They're paying all this money for therapy, and their child is still acting out. This email from Geraldine captures this problem:

I have a "textbook" baby who turned into a "spirited" toddler. William is almost 2½ and excessively hits his friends and other kids. He had major issues at birth and has been diagnosed with Sensory Integration Disorder. He has had O.T. therapy, is in speech therapy, and attends preschool five mornings a week. We've seen great improvements with the exception of the hitting. I know many toddlers hit and bite, but it seems I can't go anywhere without him hitting someone—not just a few times either. He will even hit older kids up to eight years old. I have noticed an "alpha male" characteristic about him. He does prefer older friends, too. He doesn't do it much at school, though, which is interesting. Every person I have asked thinks it's because his verbal skills aren't developed yet. I somewhat agree, for his hitting isn't always triggered by aggression or not wanting to share. Sometimes it looks like he uses it to talk to other kids. I have spoken to his therapists, his school, etc. I have tried EVERYTHING. I have been the referee, I have tried to tell the other children to tell him they don't like his hitting or walk away, I have tried to give him verbal options, I have taken him and left the situation, I have taken him away from the situation for a few minutes, I have given time-outs etc., etc. They all tell me not to worry. I am 7½ months pregnant and it exhausts me to constantly tell him no and feel like I don't get across to him. He has no fear and doesn't seem affected by anything I say or do. What can I do to help him?

I feel for Geraldine. Some children are genuinely difficult because of their neurobiological makeup, and in many respects William certainly seems to fit that bill. He is undoubtedly frustrated because he doesn't have verbal communication and can't say what he wants. However, there are hidden clues in this email. Even though Geraldine "tried everything," I suspected that she was not seeing her son clearly. It was hard to believe that he was a Textbook baby—ever—because few of his milestones were on time. Also, Mum had probably not been very consistent as well. Even she admitted, "He doesn't do it much at school . . ." I followed up with a call.

As it turned out, there were signs of William's aggressiveness when he was nine months old—he regularly slapped his mum and repeatedly grabbed things, not just from her but from his playmates. Geraldine chalked it off to his being an "alpha male." By the time William was eighteen months, it was clear that he had delays in speech and that he was easily distracted and impulsive as well. He showed no interest in learning how to dress himself or eat with a spoon. He lacked even a trace of impulse control and had a great deal of difficulty making transitions. Bedtime was always a struggle. Much of his behavior was explained by his diagnosis, but regardless of his sensory integration problems, his aggression had gone unchecked for a while. William knew how to get around his mother. When a charming smile didn't make her give him what he wanted, bullying her always worked.

It was only when he started hitting other kids that Geraldine began

Dealing with a Diagnosed Child

If your child has been diagnosed with a learning disability, an attention deficit disorder, or sensory integration problems, or any other of the possible diagnoses of childhood, it's more important than ever to . . .

Respect her feelings. Even if she's not verbal, help her learn the language of emotions.

Set limits. Let her know what you expect of her.

Structure the day. Stick to your routine so that she knows what's coming.

Be consistent. Don't ignore her jumping on the couch one day and say, "No jumping on the couch" the next.

Know what sets her off and avoid trigger situations. If you know your child gets too revved up at bedtime if she's allowed to run around, plan a quiet activity instead.

Give praise and rewards. It works better than punishment. Catch her while she's behaving well and praise her. Use a gold star system to show her how much she's progressing.

Work together with your partner. Make your child's emotional fitness a priority. Talk about it, plan ahead, and iron out any disagreements—but not in front of your child.

Enlist others. Don't be afraid to talk about your child's problems (when she's out of earshot) and explain how they manifest in everyday situations. Avoid meltdowns by helping family, friends, and caregivers understand what works best with your child.

to take his behavior more seriously. But once he was diagnosed, she also thought that the therapy would take care of everything. This is a common misconception of parents whose children are diagnosed with any type of learning disorder. "William's therapist will undoubtedly help him with his speech, with his motor skills, and even with impulse control, but if you don't consistently establish limits at home," I told his mother, "his aggression will continue."

I warned her that even *I* have trouble managing some children, but from William's progress in therapy, I felt that if she were consistent and always prepared to follow through, she would begin to see a difference.

She needed to leave her own emotions aside, not to pity "poor" William for his problems, but to be firm with him instead *at all times*. Also, she had to be prepared; sometimes as one problem is solved another one crops up. In the meantime, she had to do her best to be in charge. She should take time to prepare William, to rehearse whatever situation he was about to be in, and to tell him ahead of time the consequences of his actions if he didn't obey. It was also important for her to do F.I.T. with William, so that he could learn how to express himself with words or at least appropriate actions. She needed to give him alternatives. That way, she would spend more time preventing his aggression than trying to stop it. Finally, I suggested behavior modification. She started a gold star system similar to what Harrison's mother did (see page 332). In addition, we got Dad more actively involved. William needed an outlet for his "alpha male" side, and instead of just labeling his behavior, his parents needed to give him an appropriate way of expressing it. Dad was a hardworking guy, but he nevertheless committed to coming home earlier two nights during the week just to spend time with William, and they had a standing date on Saturday mornings when they did something active together. William's relationship with his father would be even more important in a few months when his sibling arrived. I also suggested that Geraldine get help from other family members and friends. Not only was William less likely to try his tricks on others, but also she needed a break.

William would probably never become an "easy" child, but within a few weeks, Geraldine saw a noticeable difference. William had fewer fights with her at home, transitions were easier (because she was preparing him and giving him extra time to make them), and even when he started to get upset, Geraldine was able to intervene before her son was totally out of control. "I can see now," Geraldine admitted, "that I was living life in a constant state of tension. Now I am more relaxed, too, and I guess that's rubbing off on him."

To be sure, when we are calm, we're not only better at dealing with our children's emotions, but also they tend to emulate us. The bottom line is that emotional fitness, like charity, begins at home!

NINE

E.E.A.S.Y. DOES IT

The Case for Early Toilet Training

Potty Panic

Although parents are most worried about sleep issues, and eating runs a close second, their anxiety seems to reach new heights when they even *think* about toilet training. When do you start? How do you start? What if my child is resistant? What if she has accidents? The questions are endless. Although parents sometimes fret over the various other physical milestones if they occur later than the books predict (or later than playmates exhibit), they nevertheless take each one in stride, allowing time for mind and muscles to kick in. And yet, those same parents will become very agitated about their child learning to eliminate in the toilet, which is really just another milestone.

The statistics show that in the last sixty years, the age of training children has been significantly postponed—in part, because of the trend toward child-centered child-rearing, in part, because disposable diapers do such a good job that children don't feel uncomfortable when they're wet or soiled. The results of this delay are dramatic: In 1957, studies found that 92 percent of children were toilet trained by eighteen months. Today, that figure has dropped to less than 25 percent, according to the 2004 study conducted by the Children's Hospital of Philadelphia. Only 60 percent of children have achieved mastery of the toilet by three, the study found, and 2 percent remain untrained at four.

Maybe the later training gives parents more time to worry about what might go wrong. Or perhaps their anxiety is one that even parents who trained their kids early felt: Bathroom habits have underlying "moral" implications. In any case, it's clear that modern parents, Americans in particular, have trouble viewing the transition from diapers to toilet seat with the same detachment they allow for sitting or walking or even talking.

I say, "Relax." Teaching your child how to go to the bathroom is really no different from any of the developmental milestones you've managed to get through thus far. And if you view it purely as another milestone, your attitude might change. Think of it this way: You don't expect your child to get up on her feet one day and be ready to run the Boston Marathon. You know that development doesn't just happen—it is a process, not an event. For each milestone, there are signs and steps along the way. For example, long before your child actually takes a step, you watch joyfully as she tries to pull herself up. You realize she's practicing and that soon her legs will become strong enough to support her. Then she starts cruising, holding on to the furniture (or your leg). This is her first experience in propelling her little legs forward. One day, you notice that she is starting to experiment with letting go of her supports. First, she lifts one hand, and then two. She looks at you as if to say, "Look, Ma—no hands!" And you respond with a big smile and verbal praise, proud that she is making progress ("Good job, Sweetie!"). She keeps practicing and eventually she is strong and confident enough to take a first step. Seeing this, you hold out your arms to encourage her, or perhaps you give her your hand to steady her as she takes a few more steps. A week or two later, she refuses to hold your hand altogether, nonverbally letting you know, "I can do it myself." She looks a bit like Frankenstein when she toddles here and there. If she tries to make a turn or lift a toy, she ends up on her rear. But as the months go on, she becomes a totally upright human who cannot only walk but also carry things and jump and even run. When you look back, you realize that she "started to walk" four to six months earlier. Walking, like other developmental milestones, is a sign that your child is further along the road to independence. You can see the joy on your child's face and her sense of freedom, as she can finally negotiate the world on her own. Children love to learn new skills, and we love to watch them.

Developmentally, the same thing happens with elimination. The signs that your child is ready to relieve herself into a toilet instead of her diaper start long before she actually *goes* on the toilet. But we often don't pay attention to the signs, and we don't encourage the independence. Part of the problem is that the baby isn't uncomfortable. Modern disposable diapers do their job so well that she barely feels wet. Add to that the fact that most of us lead such hectic lives, it feels overwhelming and time-consuming to make a commitment to toilet training. "It can wait" is the typical attitude nowadays, and it's reinforced by the experts who tell us that our children need to "mature" before we can even attempt to train them. The problem is, we wait too long.

Starting at Nine Months Can Be E.E.A.S.Y.

Although a small contingent of experts take an extreme position on toilet training (see the box below), the conventional wisdom about toilet training—found in most books and voiced by many pediatricians as well—is that children *can't* be taught to eliminate in the toilet before the age of

---

The Toilet-Training Continuum

Just about every subject in parenting finds advocates on either extreme. As always, both sides make some good points. My own theory comes somewhat in the middle of the two ends of the continuum:

Child-Centered Training. A theory that took root in the early 1960s, suggesting that "later is better," this end of the continuum believes toilet training should be solely up to the child. Parents show by example, look for the signs, and give the child opportunities to use the toilet, but never push. The idea is that when a child is ready, he'll ask to use the toilet. It might not happen until your child is four.

Diaperless Babies. Advocated by those who observe that in America prior to the 1950s, babies were toilet trained much earlier and that in primitive cultures babies go without diapers from birth (an idea supported by some environmentalists as well), the goal is to teach the child to tune in to his elimination needs and sensations—even before he's old enough to sit. When parents read the baby's cues and body language, they hold him over a toilet (or bucket) and make a cuing sound, like "ssss" or say "pee-pee." Thus, the child is conditioned to eliminate with an adult's assistance.

---

two and that some won't achieve success until well into their third year. While it is generally acknowledged that some babies will achieve toilet readiness earlier, just as some are "early" or "late" walkers or talkers, most experts nevertheless advise parents to wait until their child exhibits most, if not all, of the signs of readiness. The belief is that the child has to comprehend what the training is all about and that the child's sphincter muscles have to be fully mature (which begins at around a year).

To some degree, even though in England we trained our children months earlier than Americans do, I myself bought into the conventional wisdom when I initially started working with toddlers. In my first book, in fact, I suggested starting at eighteen months. But today, after working with scores of parents, reading the current research on toilet training, and observing what happens in the rest of the world, I find myself disagreeing with both the conventional wisdom and the extremists.

That is not to say that I don't find positive points at either end of the toilet-training continuum. The child-centered approach honors a child's feelings—a basic precept of baby whispering. However, allowing a child to decide when he's "ready" and to guide himself through toilet training is like giving him a bowl of food on the floor and expecting him to develop table manners. He might, but what are parents for if not to guide their children and socialize them? Moreover, if the child is *starting* the process at two or 2½, that's already "late" in my eyes, because by then children have developed the negativity of the twos; they're less

---

What Scientists Say About Early Toilet Training

Although there's not a lot of scientific evidence about the relationship between the age when toilet training commences and the age of completion, a recent study done at Children's Hospital in Pennsylvania confirmed that while early training sometimes takes longer, the children do complete it at an earlier age. Another study, conducted in 2000 by researchers in Belgium concerned about the "increase in voiding problems among children," was reported in the *British Journal of Urology*. The analysis was based on the responses of 321 different-age parents. Group 1 was composed of parents over 60, Group 2, between 40 and 60, and Group 3, between 20 and 40. In Group 1, most had initiated toilet training by the time their children were 18 months old, half before 12 months. "Most authors are convinced that the development of bladder and bowel control is a maturational process which cannot be accelerated by toilet training," noted Drs. J. J. Wyndaele and E. Bakker, whose findings clearly contradict that theory. Seventy-one percent of the children in Group 1 were clean and dry by 18 months, compared to 17% in Group 3, in which training started after age 2.

interested in pleasing their parents and more determined to do things their way, and the parents easily lose control of the process.

As for the diaperless school—also called "elimination communication"—I can't fault a method that relies heavily on observing the child and giving him cues. I also believe that it's good to give a child opportunities to practice new skills before he is actually able to master them. And I certainly agree that training should start earlier than is usually done in the United States where the average age of completion is between thirty-six and forty-eight months. In the rest of the world, "more than 50 percent are toilet trained at about one year of age," according to a professor of pediatrics at the University of Colorado School of Medicine quoted in the March 2004 issue of *Contemporary Pediatrics,* and 80 percent between twelve and eighteen months, according to advocates of this approach. However, I have trouble with any model that bases its philosophy on a primitive culture. We're living in a modern society. I don't think it's advisable to hold an infant over a bucket or even a toilet seat. Equally important, I believe the child should have some control, some input, and some understanding of the process. Putting him on a toilet before he can sit up on his own is, in my opinion, too early.

Not surprisingly, I come down somewhere in the middle of the two extremes, because I recommend starting toilet training at around nine months or whenever your baby is able to sit steadily and comfortably on his own. Many of the babies whose parents have followed my plan achieve complete daytime control by their first birthday. Some don't, of course, but research shows that even they are usually trained by the time their peers are just starting out.

Because the current conventional wisdom about toilet training is so widespread—powered in part by the disposable diaper industry that profits from late toilet training—many parents ignore their own observations and knowledge of their child. For example, this posting, from the mother of a fifteen-month-old girl, appeared on my website:

For the last two months we have been sitting Jessica on the potty before bath time, because she kept wanting to sit on the big toilet. Most of the time nothing happens, but every now and again she pees. Yay! Just luck and timing I'm sure! But here's the weird thing. Last week, she started to randomly bring me new diapers during the day, flattening them out on the floor and lying on top of them At first I thought it was just funny and dismissed it without another thought, but I could not get Jessie away from it, so finally I decided I might as well just humor her and move on. Sure enough, she had a poopy bum!

This has gone on for six days now and if I ask her, "Do you have a poopy bum?" she says "yes" or "pee-pee," and she is always right. Also, she has never brought me a diaper when she is dry and clean. Is this a sign of potty training readiness—so soon? In a way, that would be great because I am home with her until September. On the other hand, I don't want to push her into something she's not ready for. Any thoughts?

Sadly, Jessica's mother has all the signs right there in front of her, but because of what most books, articles, and internet sites advise about toilet training, she's not paying enough attention to *her child*. The so-called gospel ("Don't start before eighteen months") is reinforced by other mothers. For example, one mum wrote in response, "Yes, I'd say it's a sign, but if it's the only one, I wouldn't really start potty training. She's telling you after the fact and not before. Plus, it's only for poop and not for pee, which is more often. But I'd say she's getting the idea and so hopefully she will figure out *before* she goes."

Figure it out? Jessica is only fifteen months. Would her mother also leave her to "figure out" how to use a spoon, dress herself, or behave with other children? I would hope not. Also, toilet training is not an overnight event. It's a process that starts with a child's awareness, which Jessica clearly has. She is telling her mother *after* the fact, because no one is helping her connect the physical sensations. She needs explanations and examples. Finally, it's absolute poppycock to believe that a child needs to show *all* the signs of readiness in order to initiate training. By her actions, Jessica is just begging for her mum's help. (Although I offer such a checklist on page 345, I make it clear that your child doesn't necessarily need to exhibit *every* sign.)

Although at least half of the children in the world are trained *before* they are one year old, many of you are skeptical, if not shocked, when I suggest starting as early as nine months. So allow me to explain. At nine months, I view the process of elimination as part of a baby's daily routine—a parent's job is to make him conscious of it. Just as there's time for eating, activity, and sleep, you also make time for elimination. Twenty minutes after your baby eats or drinks, you put him on the toilet. In effect, you've got him on an "E.E.A.S.Y." routine—eat, elimination, activity, sleep, and time for you (which admittedly becomes less and less as your child approaches toddlerhood). The two E's in E.E.A.S.Y. are switched when your child gets up in the morning, because then you'll put him on the toilet straightaway, before he eats (see "The Plan" on pages 348–350).

When you start between nine months and a year, naturally your baby doesn't have the control or consciousness of an older child. Hence, toilet training is not about teaching your baby as much as *conditioning* him. By putting him on the toilet seat at times that he normally goes to the bathroom, or when he exhibits signs that he's about to pee or poop (which is usually after he's eaten), you're likely to catch him, perhaps not every time but sometimes. Admittedly, success starts as an orchestrated mistake. He feels the toilet seat, and he learns to release his sphincter muscles. When he does, you cheer him on, just as you did when he started pulling himself upright or cruising. He's at an age where he still wants to please you (which he most assuredly *won't* want to do at around two), and that positive reinforcement will help him realize that the accidental act of elimination is something you value.

By starting early, you're also giving him practice in allowing his sphincter muscles to relax and to release his pee and poop into a receptacle rather than his dia-

Toilet-Training Checklist

The American Academy of Pediatrics offers these guidelines for parents. You will undoubtedly find hundreds of similar checklists in other books and on the internet. View all with caution. Some benchmarks are reached later than others. Observant parents will notice facial expressions and postures that signal that their child is peeing or pooping *long* before he learns to walk or undress himself and way before he actually asks for grown-up underwear. Also, children mature at different rates and have different levels of tolerance for being soiled. Use your common sense and your knowledge of your child. It is *not* necessary for him to have reached all of these in order for you to begin toilet training:

✓ Your child stays dry at least 2 hours at a time during the day or is dry after naps.

✓ Bowel movements become regular and predictable.

✓ Facial expressions, posture, or words reveal that your child is about to urinate or have a bowel movement.

✓ Your child can follow simple instructions.

✓ Your child can walk to and from the bathroom and can help to undress.

✓ Your child seems uncomfortable with soiled diapers and wants to be changed.

✓ Your child asks to use the toilet or potty chair.

✓ Your child asks to wear grown-up underwear.

per. And isn't that what acquiring a skill is all about? Practice, practice, practice! In contrast, when you wait until age two, he's already gotten accustomed to eliminating into a diaper, and he has to not only tune in to his own body signals but be willing to release his waste elsewhere. He's also had no practice. It would be like expecting a child to walk but keeping him in his crib in a sitting position until you thought it was "time" for him to walk. Without those months of trial and error, strengthening his legs, and learning how to coordinate their movement, he wouldn't be very good on his feet, would he?

Below, I explain my plan for starting toilet training between nine and fifteen months, as well as at older ages. And at the end of the chapter, I deal with some of the common problems I encounter.

When will your child be totally diaper-free? There's no way of my predicting that. It will depend on when you start, your commitment and patience, your child's personality and body, and whatever else is going on in your household. I can tell you, however, that if you observe your child carefully, stick with the plan, and treat toilet training as you would any other developmental milestone, it will be a far easier transition for your child than if you panic.

Getting Started: Nine to Fifteen Months

If you initiate toilet training between nine and fifteen months as I suggest, you might see some of the typical signs of readiness (see sidebar, page 345), but you also might not. That's okay. If your child is old enough to sit independently, she's ready to start. Just think of toilet training as one of the many new skills your child needs to learn—drinking from a cup, walking, putting together a puzzle. View the process as an interesting challenge rather than a daunting task. You're her guide.

What you'll need. I prefer the seats that you put on top of the regular toilet to a free-standing potty, because that's one less transition you'll have to make. In this age range, there's rarely resistance to the toilet, because children are so eager to please and to participate. Make sure that the seat has a little foot rest—it will make your child feel safe and also comes in handy if she needs to push out a bowel movement. Most nine-to-fifteen-month-olds don't yet have the coordination to climb up and down without an adult's help, but it's important to invest in a sturdy little step stool, too, because you'll want to encourage her independence. She can use it to get on and off the toilet and to reach the sink for other bathroom rituals, like teeth-brushing and hand-washing.

Get yourself a notebook to record your child's toilet habits (see "Toilet-Training Checklist," on page 345). Stock up on patience while you're at it. Don't start this process when you're extremely busy with a project, about to move, or about to take a vacation, or when either of you is ill. Plan to stick with it for the long haul.

How to prepare. Toilet training at a young age (and older for that matter) starts with careful observation of your baby and her daily routine. If you've embraced my philosophy of care thus far and have tuned in to your child, gotten to know her cries and body language, and responded to the little person she is, by the time she is nine months old, you will have no problem discerning how she acts right before she's about to pee or poop. When she was only a few months old, for example, she probably stopped sucking whenever she had a bowel movement. Babies can't focus on more than two things at once. Keep your eye out now for similar signs. If she's not walking yet, she might get a funny expression on her face. She might grunt or grimace. She might just stop what she's doing in order to concentrate on the process. If she's started walking, she might go into a corner or behind a couch when she poops. She might grab her diaper, try to peek inside it, or reach in to feel what's come out of her. Although these are common signals, your baby might do something completely different. I guarantee if you keep your eyes open, you'll figure out what your child does when she's about to eliminate.

Take notes. Context and routine can also be a guide. Many babies by nine months old have bowel movements at pretty much the same time every day. They often urinate twenty to thirty minutes after taking in liquid. This knowledge, coupled with your observation, should give you a pretty good sense of when and how often during the day your child relieves herself.

Even if you don't think she understands you, comment on her bodily functions in whatever way you talk about these things in your family: "Are you pooping, honey?" Just as important, comment on your own habits: "Mummy has to go to the bathroom." Ideally, you're not too shy to actually *show* your child how you do it. It's always a good idea to have the same sex parent demonstrate, but that's not always possible. Since little boys initially learn to pee while sitting down (and that's how their dads should first show them), seeing Mummy sitting on the toilet is a good example, too. Children learn by imitation, and they desperately want to do what their parents do.

In this way, you're starting to make your baby more conscious of what's happening in her body when she has to pee or poop. It's hard to put the sensations into words, especially because you might feel a full bladder in a different way from your child. One mum I know told her fifteen-month-old, "When you feel your tummy tingle, tell Mummy, because that means you want to go pee pee." I'm afraid she's still waiting. "Tummy tingling" means *nothing* to a child. She has to learn by experience.

The plan. For the first few weeks, place your child on the toilet as soon as she wakes up. Make it part of her morning ritual. You walk into her room, greet her with a big kiss, throw open the shades, and say, "Good morning. How's my girl?" Lift her out of the crib. "Time to go to the toilet." *Do not ask.* Just do it. The way brushing teeth becomes part of her bedtime ritual, going to the bathroom—and hand-washing afterward—should become part of her morning wake-up. Of course, she will have peed during the night, and her diaper will be wet. She may or may not pee again. Leave her on only a few minutes—never more than five. Squat down or sit on a stool, so you're at eye-level. Read a book, sing a song, talk about the day ahead. If she urinates, identify it ("Oh, look, you're peeing like Mummy does, and it's going into the toilet") and greet it with oodles of praise. (This is the only occasion in which I suggest that parents go utterly overboard with praise.) But be sure to comment on the act itself. In other words, don't say, "What a good girl"—rather, "What a good job." Also, show her how to wipe herself. If she doesn't pee, just take her off the toilet, put on a new diaper, and give her breakfast.

> ### Elimination Control
>
> Typically, children gain control over their sphincter muscles in this order:
>
> 1. nighttime bowel control
> 2. daytime bowel control
> 3. daytime bladder control
> 4. nighttime bladder control

If you have a son, he might have an erection. I don't like those penis guards on some of the child-size toilet liners and potties because little boys' parts can get caught on them. They also don't teach the child to hold his penis down and aim into the bowl. At first, you'll have to do it for him. A good way is to tuck his penis between his legs and gently hold his little thighs together. At this age, it's better for you to do the wiping, especially after a poop, but explain it and let your child try it on his own. With little girls, remember to teach them to wipe front to back.

Twenty minutes after he has a drink, put your child on the toilet again and repeat the process. You'll do this for the rest of the day as well, after meals and at times when you think he usually has a bowel movement. Also, children often pee and/or poop right before a bath, or they do it in the tub. If that's on your child's agenda, put him on the toilet before his bath as well. Always use the same words. "Let's go to the toilet. Let's get your diaper off. Here I'll help you up." These are all cue words that will help him associate the bodily functions with the toilet. If you build these little visits into the normal routine of your day—E.E.A.S.Y.—just as you go to the bathroom several times a day, the process will seem quite natural to him. Include hand-washing as part of the ritual.

Go slowly for the first few weeks, but be consistent. Some folks suggest putting children on the toilet only once a day at first, but I think that's confusing. Why—do we use the toilet just at breakfast or just before a bath?

The idea is to put your child in touch with his body and to help him make the connection between elimination and sitting on the toilet. Your baby may not have complete control over his sphincter muscles (see sidebar, page 348) until he's a year or older. But even an immature sphincter muscle sends out a signal that he will recognize. By placing him on the toilet, you're providing him with an opportunity to recognize the sensation and practice control.

Remember that patience I told you you'd need? Your child is not going to be trained in a week or two. But he will quickly begin to make the association and before you know it, he'll think the whole thing is so much fun he'll want to go to the toilet even when you don't suggest it. For example, Shelley, who recently started this plan with one-year-old Tyrone, called after a few weeks, exasperated. "He constantly wants to sit on the toilet, and most of the time he doesn't go. To be honest, Tracy, I'm fed up. I don't act angry of course, but it's a waste of time when Tyrone just sits there."

I told Shelley that she had to keep it up, no matter how frustrating—or boring—it was. "It's trial and error at first, but you're helping him recognize the physical sensations of his body. You can't quit now." Shelley's experience is very common. After all, the toilet is a very exciting experience for a young toddler and far less so for Mum and Dad. The toilet has water in it, a handle that makes the water swirl around—what fun! Actually *doing* something while you're sitting there is far less important to your child than to you. But he will eventually do it, and you will act like he's won the lottery when he's successful. The joy of sharing his accomplishment is really all a baby needs to drive him to succeed. The more supportive you are, the better the results.

As soon as he has been dry for a week during the day—without any accidents—you should switch him to underwear, not disposable pull-ups. I don't like using them because they're too much like disposable diapers, which don't allow a child to *feel* wet. It usually takes a few weeks or months longer for children to get through the night. Assume that it's safe to leave a diaper off at night when he's woken up dry for two weeks.

But What If I Miss That Early Window?

Let's say you've read my suggestions about toilet training, but are still skeptical. Nine months, or even a year, in your opinion, is just too young. Marla, for one, protested when I suggested that she start eleven-month-old Harry straightaway, because he was saying "pee-pee" a lot and also seemed to hate being in a soiled diaper. "But he's such a baby, Tracy," she insisted. "How can I do that to him?" She was determined to wait until Harry was at least eighteen months, or two, or even older. That's her choice—and it might be yours. Just know that the plan will be slightly different and that waiting until a child is two years or older means you will have all the other toddler behaviors to deal with on top of toilet training.

Or perhaps you look back and realize that starting earlier would have been a great idea, but your child is already two (see Sadie's story beginning on page 360). Obviously, dealing with the different ages requires slightly different strategies. But you never have to throw your arms up and wait for your child to take the lead. Following are suggestions for training past fifteen months. And in the last section of this chapter, we look at a range of toilet problems.

Still Cooperative: Sixteen to Twenty-three Months

This is my second favorite time to initiate toilet training because this age child still wants to please his parents. You'll proceed much in the same way as you would with a younger child (see pages 346–350), but the com-

munication will be easier, because your child understands everything now. His bladder is also bigger, so he
won't pee quite as often. Also, he now has more control over his sphincter muscles. The trick is to make
him aware of how and when to exert that control.

What you'll need. The child-size toilet seat as
described on page 346. Even though your child is not
going to spend more than five minutes at a time on the
toilet seat, it's a good idea to get a few books that are
read only in the bathroom, some about toilet training
itself, others that your child just enjoys. Take your
child shopping and let him pick out his new big-kid
underpants. Stress that they're like the kind that
Mummy or Daddy wear. Buy at least eight pair
because there will be accidents.

How to prepare. If you don't already know what
your child looks like before he's about to poop or pee, start paying attention. In older children, the signals are usually more pronounced. Take
note of your child's preelimination behavior. Write it in your notebook.
Also, in the month preceding training, change his diaper more often, so
that he gets to feel what "dry" is—and begins to prefer it over wet. Children this age usually urinate forty minutes after drinking. During the
week before you initiate toilet training, change your child every forty
minutes, or at least check his diaper for wetness, so that you can get a
good idea of his patterns.

Also, use this time to discuss toilet training, making sure that you use
the language of elimination, so as to heighten your child's awareness of
the process ("Ooh, I see you're pooping"). If he tugs on his diaper, say,
"You're wet. Let me change you." It's especially important to model bathroom skills ("Want to come into the bathroom and watch Dad pee?").
Read books and/or watch videos about going to the toilet. Whether your
child is in cloth or disposable diapers, I also suggest showing your child
where poop really belongs by taking him into the bathroom and letting
him see you flush the poop down the toilet.

Some experts suggest placing an inanimate object on a toilet as a way
of demonstrating. But to me putting a doll, an action figure, or a teddy
bear on the toilet makes no sense whatsoever. If it works with your child,

Naked Training?

Lots of books and experts suggest initi-
ating toilet training in the summer so
that you can let your child go naked
or at least bottomless. I don't agree. To
me that's like stripping a child down at
each meal so he doesn't get food on
himself. I think we need to teach children how to behave civilly in the real
world. The only time I believe in naked
toilet-going is right before the bath.

there's no harm in it, of course, but many young children won't be able to make the symbolic leap. Young children learn by human example, role modeling, and demonstration. They want to do what Mum and Dad do. Doesn't it make sense that for them to actually learn how to go to the bathroom you *show* them how it is done?

The plan. As described above, put him on the toilet the moment he wakes up. When you get him dressed, put him into underpants or heavy cotton training pants, *not a diaper*. It's important for him to feel a different sensation on his bottom, and to feel *wet* if he has an accident. As I said earlier, I don't like pull-ups—you might as well keep him in disposable diapers. Then put him on the toilet a half hour after meals or if he has a snack and a drink, as most toddlers do. Again, I must stress: Never say, "Do you want to go to the toilet?" unless you want to hear "No" for an answer. Factor in the reality that at this age children take their play very seriously. When you make these trips to the bathroom, instead of interrupting your child just as he's about to complete a major task such as stacking a brick on top of another, wait until he's done.

Sit with him but never longer than five minutes. Distract him from the process by reading a book, singing a song. Don't pressure him (but you can run the water to bring on a tinkle!). Your child is now quite capable of expressing his likes and dislikes, and particularly if you're starting this process close to age two, you might get some resistance. Success will be an accident at first, but once your child starts making the connection, it becomes a very reinforcing cycle, especially if you really go overboard on the praise. If your child is resistant, he might not be ready. Wait two weeks and try again.

If he has an accident, don't make a big deal of it. Just say, "It's okay. Next time you can do it." Remember to empty bowel movements into the toilet to show where it goes ("This time I'll put it in the toilet for you"). Before the age of two, most children don't think of themselves as "smelly" or "messy," so eliminate such words from your banter. Only an adult's negative response teaches a child that there's something to be ashamed of.

Sippy Cups and Toilet Training

Many parents nowadays encourage children to walk around with a beverage in hand. With the advent of non-spillable sippy cups it's easier than constantly asking, "Are you thirsty." As long as you use water or water with a splash of juice, there's no harm in this practice *except* when toilet training. What goes in must come out! You might want to limit drinks to regular times—after meals, 2 hours between as a snack—so that the liquids at least come out at predictable times.

Avoiding Power Struggles: Two to Three and Beyond

Even though the preparation and plan will be basically the same now, after age two parents often get into power struggles over toilet training because their child is much more independent and capable, and not necessarily interested in pleasing her parents. Your child now has a very distinct personality, likes and dislikes. Some children have a low tolerance for wearing a wet or dirty diaper and will actually ask to be changed. Obviously, they will be easier to train. If your child is generally cooperative and responsive to directions, that bodes well for toilet training, too. But if you're in a perpetual power struggle, you may need to sweeten the pot, so to speak, by creating an incentive system.

Some parents create a toilet chart and dole out gold stars for each successful trip to the bathroom. Others bribe with M&Ms or another small candy that isn't allowed at any other time. Rewards don't work if you just give them for cooperating or sitting on the toilet. The child gets the reward when she produces. I'm all for rewards, but *you* also know your child and what works best. Some kids couldn't care less about rewards; others thrive with incentive systems.

If you are consistent, your child *will* learn to use the toilet. Keep E.E.A.S.Y. in mind and weave bathroom visits into the fabric of your daily routine: "We just had lunch, and you had something to drink, so we go to the toilet, and wash our hands." You can also explain more at this age: Once the child is aware of his own pee and poop signals, you can say, "You just have to hold it in long enough to sit down on the toilet and let go."

Often parents will ask me, "How do you know whether a child is being resistant or just isn't ready?" This email is typical.

My two-year-old puts up a battle every time I want to take her to the toilet. Some friends have told me that she's just not ready, but I also think she's just being a toddler. Should I give it up? If so, when should I try again?

Most children are ready by age two, although resistance goes with the territory, so it can be a dicey time to start. But it's not an insurmountable problem. One of the biggest mistakes I see parents make is that they stop and start and stop and start. This is unadvisable at any age, but particularly at two and beyond. Your child really understands what is happening now, and toilet training can become a great way to manipulate you.

Don't engage in battles over toilet training. However, if your child is resistant, *stop only for a day, two at most.* You'd be surprised; a day does matter. Besides, your child is a lot older now, and if you wait a week or two, he's already a lot older and might be even more resistant. Keep trying. Don't force the issue, but don't give in altogether. Make the experience pleasant, using lots of distraction and rewards. If your child doesn't deposit anything into the toilet, don't praise or reward the effort. Try again in half an hour. If he wets in the meantime, don't make a big deal out of it. Just make sure that you have clean underwear and clothing at the ready. A two-year-old is quite capable of changing his own clothes. If he's wet, it's simply a matter of putting on new bottoms. If he's soiled, have him step into the bathtub fully clothed and tell him to take off his own clothes and wash himself. This isn't a form of punishment—rather, it's a way of his really feeling the consequences. You're not being excessively mean. You're there to assist, but you must put him in charge of the clean-up. Don't lecture or humiliate him in the process. Just make him a partner and show him that he needs to share the responsibility.

For your own information, try to figure out whether it really was an accident, or whether your child was purposely waiting until he got *off* the toilet to relieve himself. If the latter, you know that he's figured out a way to use the toilet as blackmail and that he's looking for attention. The best strategy would be to give him positive attention in other ways—spend more one-on-one time and give him a special job to do *with* you, like sorting socks when you fold the laundry. Give him a little section of your garden to plant, or a pot for the windowsill. As he watches it grow, draw the parallel: "It's growing up, just like you are."

Watch your own temperament and reactions as well. Especially if you've been at it for a while, you're going to be more emotional about this process, and your child will sense your tension. It's a sure formula for a battle.

At this age, be prepared for all the age-appropriate acts of rebellion—kicking, biting, screaming, back arching, and other types of tantrum behavior. Introduce the elements of choice: "Do you want me to go first, or do you want to go on the toilet before me?" or "Would you like me to read this book to you, or would you like to look at it yourself while you sit here?" Your choices, in other words, need to be around the toilet experience, not, "Do you want to watch the telly for half an hour and then go to the toilet?"

Use the same rule of thumb for nighttime training: When your child has woken up dry for two weeks, switch to underpants, or just let him wear his pajama bottoms. Limit the water and other liquids he consumes before bedtime. At this age, although children do have accidents at night, once you see continued dryness during the day, and dry diapers on waking, he's likely to have success at night, too. (Interestingly, very few of the queries I get from parents of toddlers focus on nighttime problems, which tells me that once you get the daytime elimination routine going, night dryness follows quite naturally.)

Many of the problems I see result from too-late toilet training (see "Toilet Troubles" below). If your child is not trained by four—98 percent of all children are trained by then—seek the help of your pediatrician or a pediatric urologist to make sure that physical problems aren't impeding his progress.

Toilet Troubles

Below I've taken a few real-life problems from my website, in-box, and client files. In each case, the first two questions I ask are: **When did you start toilet training?** and **Have you been consistent?** I've found that toilet troubles are caused, at least in part, by parents' lack of follow-through. They start (in my opinion, too late) and then at the first sign of resistance, stop and start again, and they continue to stop and start and before they know it, they're into a battle of wills. You'll see that theme in many of the following cases:

"Shows No Readiness at Twenty-two Months"

My almost 22-month-old son, Carson, started saying "pee-pee" last week. I asked him did he have to go pee-pee or has he already done pee-pee? I didn't really get a response one way or the other. He has not shown any readiness for toilet learning. He could be in a diaper ready to explode from urine and BM and not care. We have a potty in the bathroom for him and right now he uses it to stand on to get at the sink. I don't know if he is saying pee-pee just because it is a new word he knows or if he has figured out what it means. Should I try putting him on the potty when he says pee-pee? He has seen both me and my husband in the bathroom plenty of times and I tell him, "We are going potty." I'm trying to lay some groundwork. Also, when do you start putting your child in pull-ups? He is still in regular diapers. I don't think I need to bother with pull-ups until he is ready for toilet learning.

At his age, Carson understands everything. He might be one of those boys who couldn't care less about sitting in pee and poop, but he is certainly capable of knowing that pee and poop belong in the toilet, especially if he's been observing his parents. I also don't agree that he "hasn't shown any readiness." He very likely knows what "pee-pee" is and what it means. I'd ask, **Have you tried putting him on the toilet at all?** I suspect not. Well, what is Mum waiting for? She has to start a plan and stick to it, putting her son on the toilet forty minutes after he drinks. Also, give him a crate or a little step stool for reaching the sink. Otherwise, how will he understand the true purpose of a toilet? Better yet, get him a small seat to put over the regular toilet. He already knows that's what Mum and Dad use, and then you won't have to make another transition later on. I would remind this mother that toilet training takes lots of patience. She needs to leave less to chance, and take a more active role in getting her son trained.

"Two-and-a-Half-Year-Old Not Trained after a Year of Trying"

Betsy is 2½ years old. We've been working on toilet training since she was about eighteen months old. She's wearing pull-ups now. Some days she refuses to use the toilet at all and screams her objections to it. Yesterday, she sat through dinner with a soaking wet pull-up on and didn't even tell us. When the mood strikes her she'll use the toilet. When we're out she'll ask to use the bathroom but usually it's for something to do. How can I get her toilet trained?

When I hear a case like this, where a child started training at eighteen months and a year later is using the toilet only when "the mood strikes her," especially if it's a girl (they do generally learn faster than boys), I know that the parents have been inconsistent—and, I have to add, lazy. Part of the problem is that disposable diapers let parents off the hook as they remove the guilt once felt about leaving a child in a wet nappy. Hence, we live in a culture in which many parents don't feel motivated to start toilet training in the first place, and then they switch to those darn pull-ups, which aren't much better. With Betsy, I'd tell Mum to immediately take her shopping for some big-girl underwear. Betsy might be a lot less complacent about sitting through a meal in soggy cotton underpants as opposed to pull-ups. If she wets or soils them, she has to change herself.

But I think there's more to this story, too. Because Betsy "screams" when she doesn't want to go to the toilet, I'd ask her mother, **Do you *ask* if she wants to go to the toilet or simply tell her "it's time to go to the toilet"?** With a child this age, it's always more effective to tell her, "It's time to go to the toilet," and give her an incentive, "and when we come back we can play teatime together." I sense here, too, that Mum has gotten frustrated with the process (who wouldn't after a year?). **Does your child have tantrums around other requests that you make?** Perhaps Betsy is temperamentally strong willed. If her mother isn't handling her tantrums well in other contexts, she's certainly not going to have success in the bathroom. At 2½, the child is in control of the elimination process, not the parent. **Have you ever lost your temper or reprimanded your child for soiling herself?** If so, Mum has to take a deep breath and do something about her own behavior. Threats aren't good teaching tools. I would suggest then that Mum take herself out of the equation as much as possible. Instead of her reminding Betsy about the toilet, she could set a timer and explain to Betsy that when the bell rings, it's time to sit on the toilet.

Finally, with a child like Betsy, incentive programs work well. To design an effective one, I'd ask Betsy's mum, **What motivates your child?** Some children love to get stars that eventually add up to a special outing. Others perform for the sake of an after-dinner mint.

"Tried Everything—and Still Not Trained at Three and a Half"

My son, Louis, is 3½. I have tried everything I can think of, but he refuses to be potty trained. He knows how, and when, and he doesn't show signs of being afraid. Sometimes, he goes by himself. Sometimes he goes with encouragement. But most of the time he refuses. I've tried punishment, and quickly gave that up, as it made things worse. I've tried candy, stickers, cars, and toys as rewards. I've tried praise, hugs, and kisses. Nothing so far has motivated him for more than a few days. He only seems to care that he is wet about half the time. If you have any ideas, please tell me.

Louis's mother has many of the same difficulties as Betsy's mother (although the issue has gone on even longer), and I would ask her the same questions (see page 357). But I include her email as well because it's a great example of inconsistency. Whenever someone tells me they've "tried everything" (including punishment, in this case), it usually means that they haven't stayed with one approach long enough to give it a chance to work. What's probably happening in this case is that the moment Louis has an accident, Mum changes the rules.

First, Louis's mother had to choose one method and stick with it no matter what happens. She also has to take control of the process. As it is now, her 3½-year-old son has the reins. He sees her frustration. He knows how to get her to react—to cajole, to reward, to praise—and he's become empowered by it.

Second, she has to put Louis in underpants (she doesn't say, but I'll bet he's in pull-ups). Then she should use the timer method just as I advised Betsy's mother. She has to take care not to schedule trips to the bathroom to coincide with an activity—he's less likely to cooperate if interrupted. She should make him in charge of the dressing and undressing.

A note on "punishing" a child: It never works and often creates really serious problems in the future, such as fear of the toilet and bed-wetting. Moreover, by the time a child is Louis's age, the real world will be punishment enough. At his age, most children are toilet trained. It won't be long before some of Louis's playmates comment on his dirty or wet pants. Mum shouldn't add to his humiliation, or point out that "other children" (good children) use the toilet or that they don't need to wear pull-ups anymore.

"Two Years Old and Suddenly Afraid of the Toilet"

My two-year-old daughter, Kayla, was doing great in the potty department. She was dry for several weeks during the day, and then she suddenly became afraid of the toilet. I don't know what happened. I work three days a week, and we have a wonderful nanny who comes in when I'm at the office. Is this common?

Kayla's mother has to respect her daughter's fear, and also figure out where it came from. When things have been going smoothly, and suddenly a child becomes afraid of the toilet, it's almost always because something happened. **Has she been constipated lately?** If so, and she pushed a little too hard one day, she might now associate that discomfort with the toilet. Just to be sure, I would suggest increasing the fiber in her diet—corn, peas, whole grains, prunes, fruit. Also increase her liquid intake. **What kind of seat do you use?** If it's an add-on seat, maybe Kayla wasn't held properly one day and started slipping through, or perhaps the seat wasn't on securely and shook when Kayla got on or off. If it was a free-standing potty, maybe it tipped. **Do you use a stool underfoot?** Without one, Kayla might have felt insecure.

Because Kayla's mother is not the only one to handle toilet training, I would also ask about the nanny. **Did you take the time to explain your plan—better yet, write it down—and to show your nanny exactly what to do?** If your child is in someone else's care during the day, it's important to make sure that the center or nanny or Grandma knows exactly what you're doing and carries out your toilet-training plan when you're not there. **Did you include information about what you do when Kayla pees or poops in her pants?** It's also important to assess attitudes, especially if your childcare provider is from another country. Some people ridicule children or even smack them when they poop in their pants. Granted, it's sometimes hard to figure out exactly what went on in your absence, but these are all possibilities that you might (tactfully) explore.

When a child is afraid, we have to respect her fears. Mum can ask Kayla, "Can you tell Mummy what you're scared of?" Once she finds out how her daughter's fear started (from Kayla or her other inquiries), Mum has to go back to the basics: Read one or more children's books about using the toilet. Go to the bathroom with Kayla and give her a choice: "Do you want to go before Mummy, or should I do it first?" When you take a child to the bathroom with you, she gets to see that there's nothing threatening about it. If all else fails, Mum could see if Kayla was willing to sit on her lap when she's on the toilet and have Kayla go between her legs. Until her fear diminishes, Mum could act like a human training seat. Kayla is not likely to get dependent on her mother. Two-year-olds want to be "big kids," and as soon as the fear dissipates, Kayla will want to go to the bathroom on her own.

Sometimes children develop a fear of public restrooms. In that case, make sure that your child empties her bladder before leaving home and try to take short excursions while you're in the training phase. If you're doing local errands, arrange to stop at another mum's house en route.

"Got a Good Start and Then Regressed"

> I thought my son Eric was well on his way to being toilet trained, but when we moved to our new house he started putting up a fight every time I wanted him to go to the toilet. What did I do wrong?

How close to your move did you start toilet training? Eric's mum may have a case of bad timing on her hands. It is never advisable to start toilet training too close to a big family change such as a move or a new baby, or when the child himself is in the middle of any kind of transition—for example, teething or just after an illness. **Is anything else new happening at home?** Toilet training can also be interrupted by parents' arguments, a new nanny, or if something else is happening at home or in a play group that's upsetting to the child.

Again, go back to the basics, and start your toilet-training plan from the beginning.

"Missed the Window and Now We're in for a Battle"

> Sadie showed several signs of readiness between seventeen and twenty months, but I put it off because #2 was coming. Sadie was really ready, and actually went on the potty a few times, voluntarily, when #2 was a newborn. But #2 was such an awful handful that I didn't have the mental or physical energy to put into it. So now I have to wait until she decides that she wants to, or get tough and have a traumatic fight with her.

I respect Sadie's mother's honesty and that she knew training too close to a big family change wasn't a good idea. But she also has potty panic, and that's preventing her from seeing her other options. Sadie first started showing signs at seventeen months. Had her mum stuck with it at that point—which was before the second baby arrived—Sadie might have been trained. In any case, that's not what happened. Sadie is now over two, and while it is harder to initiate training at this point, especially with a new baby in the house, there are other solutions besides getting "tough" or having a "traumatic fight" with her daughter.

Sadie is obviously ready to learn and can communicate with her mother. I would suggest that Mum implement my plan: Take a week to just observe Sadie's elimination patterns and to talk about bathroom habits with Sadie. Make a point of taking Sadie to the toilet with her. Also, take Sadie on a shopping expedition for big-girl underpants. When it's time to commence toilet training, Mum will change the baby a few minutes before she thinks her older daughter might need to go on the loo. She will involve Sadie in the process: "Would you like to help Mummy change the baby?" Give Sadie a little step stool so she can get closer and let her hold the diaper, the cream, and feel like a little assistant. Mum also might casually point out to her older child, "You don't need diapers anymore because you know how to go on the toilet like I do. As soon as I change the baby's nappy, let's you and I go to the bathroom together." If she allows Sadie to participate, times her bathroom trips well, and gives her choices ("Do you want to go first, or should Mummy?"), she's much less likely to get into a power struggle with Sadie.

"Three-Year-Old Only Pretends to Go in the Potty and Then Does It in Her Diaper"

> Amy will sit on the potty and pretend to go, but never does. She wears big-girl underpants but when she has to go potty, she announces, "I need a diaper, please," and goes into the diaper. We spoke with our pediatrician about this and he says that obviously Amy CAN go on the potty because she has control enough to wait for a diaper. He said not to push her to go on the potty—that the more we push, the more she will insist on doing it her way. This is hard for us as we also have a seven-year-old who was potty trained very easily. I'm afraid with Amy, her will is stronger than mine.

Another mother on my website suggested giving Amy a diaper but cutting a hole in it, so that she could be wearing the diaper *and* go on the toilet. There are some children who have trouble literally letting go of their bowels. And a hole in the diaper might help in that case. However,

Amy is three years old, a very smart and independent child. The fact that Mum says that Amy's "will is stronger than mine," tells me that toilet drama is not the only battle going on in this household. I would ask, **Are you having power struggles in other arenas?** If so, Amy has found one new way to manipulate her family—not an unusual trick for a younger child. My approach would be to get rid of all the diapers in the house and tell Amy that you're doing it. When she asks for a diaper, remind her, "I can't give you one. We don't have any left. Let's go to the toilet instead." I can understand a pediatrician saying not to push when a child is two, but at three, I'm skeptical. Some children need a little shove, and I suspect that Amy is one of them.

"He Uses His Penis Like a Fire Hose"

Of course he does! It goes with territory. Indeed, toilet training a boy is often a case of "be careful what you wish for—you just might get it." Even training boys to pee sitting down at first doesn't necessarily solve the problem. Once boys get the knack of using their penises, they're especially fond of target practice. One father made the most of it and sped up his son's training in the process, by putting Cheerios in the toilet bowl and telling him to aim at them. If his son missed, he cleaned it up. A mother trained her sons and daughters without a potty or a child-size seat altogether by facing backward on the toilet seat.

"She Wants to Pee Standing Up"

Especially if she's seen Dad or an older brother peeing, you can't blame her. You just have to be patient and explain, this is how girls pee and that's how boys pee. Show her. At worst, let her try, but warn her that if it doesn't end up in the toilet, she'll have to clean it up. Usually the sensation of pee running down her leg is all that it takes to nip this habit in the bud.

"Have Trouble Getting Her *Off* the Potty"

> My daughter showed a huge interest in potty training at 18 months, so we started. Unfortunately, it was wintertime and between getting sick and my having a newborn to care for, we started and stopped a few times and finally stopped. She is now almost 23 months old and we are thinking about starting again. I

realize now that we made a few grave errors initially: starting, stopping, letting her sit on the potty for an hour to read books. My question is, do other children give parents a hard time about getting off the potty after three minutes? I have a feeling that my daughter will again, and I want to be better prepared this time. Previously, she wouldn't want to get off, and it would end up in a battle, which I didn't want associated with potty training, so I would let her sit on the potty for as long as she wanted. Any advice on how to get her off without an argument?

The first thing I'd suggest is a timer. Especially at twenty-three months, you can say, "When the bell rings, we have to check for pee and poop." If there's none in the toilet, say, "That was a good try—we can come back later and try again." But there's a bigger issue here as well. This mother bent over backward to avoid a power struggle—she says, over toilet training. But I'll bet that she's backing down in other arenas as well.

The Real Bottom Line—Pardon the Pun—About Toilet Training

One mum, whose son was not trained at three, told me that her pediatrician eased her anxiety by telling her to look around her. "He asked if I knew any adults who were still in diapers!" He was correct. Most children are trained . . . eventually. Some can actually manage the feat in a few days, because they're ready and their parents are willing to put aside everything and just concentrate on this one important task. Others will take a year or longer. If there are a thousand experts out there (of course there are more), you'll probably find a thousand variations on toilet training that span the continuum from tackling toilet training a few months after birth to waiting until the child decides. Read up on all the methods, and pick and choose a plan that seems suitable for your baby and your lifestyle. Talk to other parents and find out what worked for them. Whatever method you choose, lighten up. Laugh about it. The less anxiety you have, the better chance your child has of succeeding. I close this chapter with a series of tidbits from the real frontline warriors themselves: mothers who are in the process of or have completed toilet training. These are the kind of pearls of wisdom I found in the chat room of my website:

- Do not nag, nag, nag your child about going to the toilet. We never pushed our daughter in any way, but we gave her lots of praise and encouragement for her successes.
- I highly recommend *The Potty Book for Girls/Boys,* which helps get the message across and which we parents find entertaining as well.
- Don't start when you have a big life event coming up—a new baby, going to day care, company, traveling even for a weekend. It throws everything out of whack, and you take three big steps backward each time.
- You can leave them naked if you want, but I just have a feeling that they will pee on your floor and then feel ashamed.
- Remember that your child is an individual, and if you make her feel comfortable and in control of the situation (even though you are secretly controlling it), then you are more likely to get positive results.
- Remember *you* are learning to toilet train as much as your child is learning to be trained. Don't be too hard on yourself if you make a few mistakes along the way.
- It won't go as smoothly in real life as it sounds like it will by reading the books. But then again, did your pregnancy? Your delivery? Breast-feeding?
- Don't stress about getting it done in a certain amount of time. Learning to walk was a process with many false starts, and toilet training is, too.
- Don't tell anyone you are toilet training or they will bug you every day with criticism and "helpful advice." Wait until the process is all done and then make a big announcement about your child's great accomplishment. The exception to this is if you have a wonderfully supportive community like babywhisperer.com where you can share your successes and frustrations and people will respond with encouragement and *actual* help.

TEN

JUST WHEN YOU THINK YOU'VE GOT IT . . . EVERYTHING CHANGES!

Twelve Essential Questions and Twelve Principles of Problem Solving

The Inescapable Law of Parenting

When I was discussing the proposed contents of this book with my co-author, we naturally covered all the hot topics first—establishing a routine, sleeping, eating, behavioral issues—and we wondered how to end the book. Our book was to be about solutions, but how could we possibly predict and summarize every problem parents would encounter?

Jennifer, whose son Henry was around four months old at the time, came to our rescue. Henry, an Angel baby with a bright disposition who quickly adapted to the E.A.S.Y. routine and was sleeping a good five or six hours a night by then, had suddenly started waking at 4 A.M. Once we established that he wasn't hungry, I suggested my wake-to-sleep strategy (see sidebar, page 191). Jen was skeptical at first, but a few nights later, the sound of her dog throwing up woke her at 3 A.M.—coincidentally, an hour before Henry's habitual wake-up. "I was up anyway," Jennifer later explained, "so I figured, why not give it a try?" To Jen's surprise, waking Henry broke the cycle, and he was soon back to his old sleeping pattern. But that's not the point of this story. Knowing that we were struggling to come up with a final chapter, she said, "What about, 'Just When You Think You've Got It . . . Everything Changes'?"

Brilliant! From her own brief experience as a mother, Jen had hit on an inescapable law of parenting: Nothing stays the same for very long. After all, this is the only job on earth in which not only do the requirements keep changing, but so does "the product." Wise and skillful mums and dads have an understanding of child development and are able to pull from their bag of tricks the most effective secrets of baby whispering. But even that doesn't guarantee endlessly smooth sailing. Every parent at some time or another is taken by surprise.

We then sent out emails to parents, asking what situations they'd like to see us include. When we received this response from Erica, we knew for sure that we were on the right track. Not only this book, but *every* book on parenting, should end this way!

☺ *Just when you think your child will go to sleep easily, he figures out that if he makes enough of a fuss, you'll stay with him.*

☺ *Just when you think that your child will eat anything and loves vegetables, she develops a penchant for cookies and discovers that she can express preferences.*

☺ *Just when you think your child has learned to drink successfully from a cup, he discovers the joy of spitting.*

☺ *Just when you think your child really enjoys coloring, she discovers that it doesn't have to be limited to paper—walls, floors, and tabletops all make great surfaces for her art.*

☺ *Just when you think that your child loves reading, he discovers the joys of DVDs and cartoons.*

☺ *Just when you think your toddler has the ol' please/thank you wired, she discovers that it's pretty fun to hold out. . . .*

Any parent reading Erica's list could add to it. After all, parenting is a series of "just when . . ." moments. They're an unavoidable fact of life. A child's growth—anyone's for that matter—is characterized by periods of equilibrium (calm) and periods of disequilibrium (chaos and upset). For parents, the day-to-day journey is like a long hike up a mountain. You expend a great deal of effort climbing a steep portion and finally get to a plateau. Then the land flattens, and for a while you go merrily along your way until you come to another ascent where once again the terrain is much tougher to climb. If you want to get to the top, you have no choice but to keep going.

In these final pages, we look at the everyday journey of parenting and at the rocky ground that seems to rise out of nowhere. It can trip up even the most diligent parent. Because there really is no way of my predicting which particular just-when moments will occur in your family, I offer you some strategies for sorting things out. I then show you how to apply those guidelines in a selection of common just-when scenarios. Some are topics not covered elsewhere. Others have to do with sleep, eating, and behavior—issues I've already covered in great depth, which involve using techniques that, if you've read everything thus far, you've already learned. But here the focus is on looking at the complexity of these problems, the bigger picture.

The Twelve Essential Questions

As I explained in the Introduction, my life in the last few years has taken a turn from being the Baby Whisperer to becoming Ms. Fix It. I believe that there's a Mr. or Ms. Fix It inside every parent—you just need a little guidance. Problem solving means asking the right questions, so that you can figure out the source of a child's upset and the reasons for her new behavior, and then coming up with a plan for changing the situation—or learning how to live with the new circumstances.

"But it came out of nowhere," parents often insist. No, luv. Whenever something unexpected happens, there is almost always a reason. Night-waking, a change in eating habits, surliness, unwillingness to interact with other children or to cooperate—whatever the new behavior or attitude, these things rarely come "out of nowhere."

Because parents tend to feel stymied and overwhelmed at these just-when moments, I've come up with a way of helping you step back and analyze what's been going on in your household, in your life, and with your child: the Twelve Essential Questions. Throughout this book, I've posed scores of questions to help you understand how I tackle a particular issue and to train you to think like I do. But here I've pared it down to what I believe are the key questions—the ones you ask *first* because they reflect the most common reason for sudden changes of behavior. In many just-when situations, several factors—your child's development, something you're doing (or not doing), changes in your daily routine or the family environment—are at work. Sometimes, it's not easy to figure out what's going on or what to handle first. Answering all of these questions, even if you don't think some are relevant, will help you become a better troubleshooter.

The Twelve Essential Questions

1. Is your child approaching a new physical plateau—learning to sit up, walk, talk—or going through a developmental stage that might be contributing to this new behavior?

2. Is this new behavior consistent with your child's personality? If so, can you pinpoint what other factors (developmental, environmental, or parental) might have kicked it up a notch?

3. Has your daily routine changed?

4. Has your child's diet changed?

5. Is your child doing any new activities? If so, are they appropriate for her age and temperament?

6. Have your child's sleep patterns—day or night—changed?

7. Have you been away from home more than usual, taken a trip or family vacation?

8. Has your child been teething, recovering from an accident (even a minor one), or getting over an illness or surgery?

9. Are you, or another adult who is close to your child, ill, exceptionally busy, or going through an emotionally difficult time?

10. What else is going on in your household that might affect your child—parents' arguments, new nanny, new baby, a job change, a move, an illness or death in the family?

11. Have you been accidentally reinforcing the behavior by constantly giving in to it?

12. Have you recently tried a new method of child-rearing because something else "didn't work"?

I suggest that you make a copy of these questions and, at least in the beginning when you're just learning how to problem solve, actually write down the answers. A word of warning: When you answer these questions, you may feel guilty, because some responses point to parental responsibility. Believe me, I don't suggest this exercise because I want you to conclude, "Oh, no, I'm the reason little Johnny has been tearing around our house like a cyclone." Guilt, as I've stressed before, serves no one. Instead of rumination and self-blame, put your mind and your energy toward understanding *why* and then take steps to change the situations. Any problem can be solved by going back to the basics *as long as you know where it came from.*

In the sections below, we look at the questions a little more closely—and at examples of real-life situations in which answering them helped unravel various just-when problems.

Heeding the Force of Development

This first question reflects developmental changes:

1. Is your child approaching a new physical plateau—learning to sit up, walk, talk—or going through a developmental stage that might be contributing to this new behavior?

Developmental changes are, of course, inevitable. No parent escapes them. Nor should you want to stop the course of development. But talk about disequilibrium! Even more amazing is that children often change literally overnight. I remember putting my younger daughter to bed one night as an angel and—I swear—she woke up the next morning as the devil. We thought someone had kidnapped the real Sophie. She was suddenly stubborn, more assertive, and more independent. Ours was certainly not an unusual occurrence. I can't tell you how many emails and calls I get from parents who say they're sure that aliens crept in while they were sleeping and switched their child to a little terror!

The trick with developmental leaps is to take them in stride. When parents are thrown by a new behavior, they sometimes forget to stick to their routine, which is more important than ever during periods of disequilibrium. Making matters worse, they also engage in accidental parenting. As you'll see in "Dorian's Dilemma" (pages 381–385)—a true story about a just-when problem that was triggered not only by development but also several other factors—children naturally test out their new skills on the people closest to them, their parents. When we react, and they realize that they have an impact, it empowers them and reinforces the new behavior.

Sometimes you just have to grit your teeth and wait for the period to pass. It helps to view the new behavior as your child's need to explore the world and to assert himself, as opposed to a personal attack (though it might feel like the latter!). Unless your child is in danger, or the behavior is affecting others, it's often best to ignore the situation. But sometimes developmental changes require you to make an adjustment. For example, if your baby once played nicely on her own and is now becoming more demanding of your time, it could be because her brain has matured enough for her to realize she needs you. It also could be because she's outgrown her old toys. Once a child learns how a toy works and masters it, she's ready for a more challenging task.

Often, parents don't realize that what looks like a behavioral problem is really a developmental leap that requires tweaking the routine or taking action to accommodate the child's new needs and abilities. Remember Jake, whose mother, Judy, was concerned about teaching her son not to touch her valuables and also not to slap (page 328)? Actually, Jake's so-called problems were all about his development. Whenever I hear that a baby is suddenly "getting into everything," I know his parents have to make changes to accommodate his more mature self. I advised Judy to childproof her house, so that mother and son would not be in a constant battle and so that Jake wouldn't feel so frustrated by Mum's endless refrain of "no" and "don't touch." Once she created a safe space in which Jake wouldn't feel free to exercise his toddler muscles, she just had to hang in there, be vigilant about his slapping, and wait for this particular developmental stage to pass. If she had been a less conscious and concerned mother, Jake's aggression might have escalated. And wouldn't that have beeen a shame, because the real source of this just-when problem was that Jake was growing up and becoming more independent.

Knowing Your Own Child

The second question relates to the all-important axiom that I stress throughout this book and in all my talks with parents: *Know your own child.*

2. Is this new behavior consistent with your child's personality? If so, can you pinpoint what factors (developmental, environmental, or parental) might have kicked it up a notch?

A parent will say to me, "Of course I realize that she is her own person, and I have to respect her uniqueness." But true acceptance of temperament is a lot harder than lip service (for more on this, refer to "Why Some Parents Can't See," page 65). As children grow, and especially as they get out into the world and spend time with other kids and in new social settings, parents' good intentions often fall by the wayside.

Take Susan, a high-powered attorney in Houston, whom I first met at one of my book signings in Los Angeles. Susan cut back her working hours when Emma was born so that she could "do more" with her daughter. But Emma was far less social than her lively and talkative mother. Susan had to face the truth about her little girl around Emma's twenty-two-month mark. Though she loved music, Emma hid behind the couch when Susan said, "Today is our first music class." At first, Susan thought it was a game, and that Emma's hiding had nothing to do with music, so she just ignored the behavior. When they got to class and Emma proceeded to have a meltdown, Susan assumed (and told the other mothers), "Emma must not have slept well last night." Finally, when Susan witnessed repeat performances over the next several weeks, she called me.

After answering the Twelve Essential Questions, Susan realized that, indeed, Emma had been sensitive since birth, but Mum had always thought—wished—that her daughter would outgrow it. She continually exposed her daughter to lots of social situations, hoping the activities would help her grow out of her shyness. The more her daughter resisted, the more Susan pushed. "At Gymboree, she kept wanting to climb into my lap, but I wouldn't let her. I kept saying, 'Come on, honey, go play with the other kids.' I mean, that's what we were there for, and how would she learn otherwise?" Emma's so-called sudden resistance was there all along, but Susan wasn't heeding the signs. Now, however, developmental factors brought everything to a head. Emma was almost two, understood more, and was better at asserting herself, so she was letting Susan know, *Hey, Mum, this is too much for me!*

Going back to basics in this case meant that Susan had to factor in Emma's sensitivity in their daily encounters. She needed to give Emma the time to adjust to new situations and to groups of children, rather than push her into the fray. "Should we quit the class altogether?" Susan asked. I told her definitely not. That would teach Emma that when something is scary, hard, or frustrating, you stop trying. Instead, I suggested, she should go back to music class, but reassure Emma that she can stay on Mummy's lap until *she* is ready to play with the instruments and the other kids. If it took weeks, or even until the sessions were over, Mum had to stick with it.

In the meantime, though, Susan could ask the teacher for a list of the songs they sing in class (many groups also sell take-home CDs of the music) and sing with Emma at home. Shy children do best when they know what to expect, and they feel like they can keep up. Mum also might consider borrowing or buying an instrument—a triangle, tambourine, or maracas like they use in class—so that Emma could practice and become more familiar with it. If after a few classes, Emma seems even slightly interested in being part of the group, Susan should get down on the floor with her. "She might never leave your side, but that's okay," I stressed. "I guarantee if you give her the time she needs, she'll eventually venture out on her own."

Watching Out for Routine-Busters

The next several questions address your daily routine and the kinds of events and/or circumstances that might upset it:

3. Has your daily routine changed?

4. Has your child's diet changed?

5. Is your child doing any new activities? If so, are they appropriate for her age and temperament?

6. Have your child's sleep patterns—day or night—changed?

7. Have you been away from home more than usual, taken a trip or family vacation?

8. Has your child been teething, recovering from an accident (even a minor one), or getting over an illness or surgery?

Routine is the cornerstone of stability in your family life. I've devoted many pages of this book to problems that arise when there is no routine, or an erratic one. But there are also times when even the most organized and conscious parents can't help but depart from their routine. Teething, illness, and travel can upset the family applecart, and so can changes in any of the letters of E.A.S.Y.—a new diet (E), activities (A), changes in sleep habits (S), something in your own life (Y). But no matter what disrupts your routine, once you're aware, you can always get back to "normal."

Do whatever it takes to get back to your routine. For example, if sleep patterns have been disrupted, use P.U./P.D. to get your child back on track (see chapter 6). Or perhaps you've gone back to work, and your child now goes to day care or is being cared for in your home by another person. If he's acting up, it might be because the day care provider isn't sticking to your routine. Lay out the plan for her; put it in writing. And make sure that when you're with him, you stick to it, too.

A just-when change also might be a sign that your child's needs are different, that she's more independent and therefore might require a *new* routine—for instance, eat every four hours, instead of three (see box, page 34) or cut out the morning nap (page 284). Don't try to turn back the clock. Let her grow up. If she's making the transition from liquids to solids (see chapter 4), she might experience a tummy ache because a new food didn't agree with her, but that doesn't mean you go back to a liquid diet. Instead, you introduce new foods more slowly. Always, you go back to the basics.

The trickiest routine-busters are those that involve a child's discomfort. When a child is teething, hurt, or ill, the poor-baby syndrome kicks in big time (see page 385 for a detailed example). Suddenly, parents let the child stay up later or, worse, take her into their bed. They don't consider the long-term ramifications and then, a few weeks later, are in a panic: "What happened to our little girl? Her sleep is off, she's not eating well, and cries more often than she used to." Well, luv, that's because the recent change disrupted her routine, you felt sorry for her and stopped setting limits, and now she doesn't know what to expect next. When your child is ailing, by all means give her extra love and attention, take care of her discomfort, but try, as much as possible, to stick to the old routine.

Some routine changes are predictable. You know, for example, that if you're going on a trip, you can expect some reverberations for at least a few days to a week after you come home. Especially a young baby who's been on a two- or three-week vacation and who can't retain the memory of "home" for that long, will wonder, "Where am I *now*?" It's even worse, of course, if you've done some accidental parenting in the meantime. "It was a disaster," recalls Marcia, referring to her homecoming with eighteen-month-old Bethany after a trip to the Bahamas. "The hotel advertised that they had cribs, but when we got there, they gave us one of those flimsy port-a-cribs. It was more like a playpen and Bethany wouldn't sleep in it, so she wound up sleeping with my husband and me."

Marcia had to do several nights of P.U./P.D. after she got home to get Bethany used to her bedtime routine again and to help her relearn the skills of independent sleep. But you can make reentry easier if you *plan ahead.* Whether you're staying with relatives or paying for lodging, call ahead and find out exactly what kind of equipment they have. If it's a pack 'n' play, and your child is not used to sleeping in it, borrow one from a friend and let her take a nap in it before you leave. If your child is too big for a pack 'n' play, ask your host if it's possible to borrow a crib from a neighbor or contact rental companies in the area. When you pack for your trip, bring favorite toys and clothes and reminders of home. When you're on the trip itself, even though you're in an unfamiliar setting, maintain your daily practices—keep meals and bedtimes as close to usual as possible. You'll have fewer adjustments to make when you get home.

Protecting the Family Environment

The next two questions address larger, and often more permanent, changes in the family environment:

9. Are you, or another adult who is close to your child, ill, exceptionally busy, or going through an emotionally difficult time?

10. What else is going on in your household that might affect your child—parents' arguments, new nanny, new baby, a job change, a move, an illness or death in the family?

Children, like sponges, absorb everything around them. Research has shown that even babies soak up their parents' emotional state and other changes in their environment. If you're upset, your child will be, too. If the climate at home is chaotic, he will feel as if he's caught up in a whirlwind. Of course, all adults experience rough times and big changes in their lives—we have our own just-when moments. We can't prevent such transitions in our own lives, but we can at least recognize their impact on younger members of the family.

Bridget, a graphic artist who worked at home, lost her own mother after a horrible bout with bone cancer when Michael, Bridget's son, was three. She had been very close to her mother and the loss was profound. For weeks after her mother had passed, Bridget lay on her bed in the dark, alternating between sobs and rage. "Michael had just started preschool when my mother died," she explained, "so at least he was out of the house for three hours every morning. I tried to pull it together when I had to pick him up. Around the same time, I realized I was pregnant."

Then Bridget got a phone call from Michael's teacher. Michael had been hitting other kids and saying to them, "I'm going to make you dead." When Bridget asked herself the Twelve Essential Questions, she suspected that Michael was reacting to *her* grief. "But," she asked me, "how could it be any different? I need time to grieve, don't I?"

I assured Bridget that of course she did. But she also needed to take Michael's feelings into consideration. He had lost a grandma, too, and although Bridget *thought* she was "pulling it together" by the time she picked him up at school, a three-year-old notices reddened, puffy eyes and, more important, feels her emotions. Michael was not only absorbing Bridget's sadness, he felt as if his mother had disappeared. To deal with Michael's newfound aggression at school, I explained to Bridget, we had to come up with a plan that addressed the family environment.

Bridget started to talk to Michael about her mum, which she hadn't really done up to this point. She admitted to him that she had been very sad lately, because she missed Grandma Rose. She encouraged Michael to express his emotions, too. He said that he missed Granny, too. Bridget knew it was good for the two of them to keep talking about her mother and to remember the happy times. "Maybe we can go to that merry-go-round in the park or to the lake where Granny used to take you to feed the ducks," she suggested. "It might make us feel closer to her."

Perhaps most important, Bridget started taking care of her own emotional needs. She joined a grief group, so that she could talk about her feelings with other adults. As Bridget started feeling better about herself and was able to share her emotions honestly—and age-appropriately— with her son, Michael went back to being his calm, cooperative self, too.

Doing Damage Control for Accidental Parenting

The final two questions relate to accidental parenting:

11. Have you recently tried a new method of child-rearing because something else "didn't work"?

12. Have you been inadvertently reinforcing the behavior by constantly giving in to it?

Accidental parenting occurs when parents are inconsistent and keep changing the "rules" on their child—for example, one night allowing the child to climb into bed with them, the next letting her cry herself to sleep. Or, when faced with a new behavior, parents resort to a quick fix—using a prop to help a child get to sleep, picking her up the moment she cries, without taking a breath to figure out the cause of the problem.

As I've pointed out throughout this book, accidental parenting can be the primary cause of a problem, or in the face of a just-when situation, can cause the problem to linger. Quick fixes never solve anything. It's like putting a Band-Aid on a wound but not giving the patient an antibiotic to get to the root of the illness. The wound might not bleed, and it might even heal. But it's not going to go away completely, because the infection is still in the body. In time, it will probably get worse. The same can be said of just-when problems. Some will disappear as fast as they erupted. But some, misinterpreted or mishandled by parents, usher in the beginning of a more serious problem.

Some parents are not conscious of this process. They keep applying Band-Aids—giving in, cajoling, allowing the child to cross their boundaries—and before they know it, the child won't sleep in his own bed, his behavior is off the charts, and he's controlling the adults in the house with his demands.

Other parents, especially those who've read my first two books, are painfully aware of how accidental parenting starts. They'll say to me, "We knew we shouldn't rock her, but . . ." or "We called because we knew we needed a strategy that we wouldn't regret in the long run." But they either do it anyway ("just for one night"), or they forget their good intentions in the heat of the moment.

Here's an interesting email that illustrates how accidental parenting starts and how complex these just-when problems can become:

> Our 13-month-old, Rebecca, is having difficulty going to sleep at night. It started about a month ago. She and I traveled (cross-country) to my brother's home in California. When we returned, my husband and I agreed that it was time for her to stop using her pacifier. Until then, she had only used it during nap time and at

night, never during the day. She was not happy, but we let her cry and tried to encourage her to soothe herself with her blanket. She then got a cold/flu for approximately two weeks. For three nights, she began putting herself to sleep as she had previously done. But now she is getting her first molar, and we are at our wits' end. She will cry for at least an hour before going to sleep every night. She seems not to know how to put herself to sleep without the pacifier. She doesn't wake during the night at all. Should we continue to let Rebecca figure it out on her own or go into her room to comfort her (but not rock her to sleep)? We need help.

As you may have guessed, these weary parents are dealing with a series of events that disrupted their usual routine—travel, then illness, and just when they thought their daughter was getting back to normal, she started teething. And Rebecca's parents also played a part. They might have spared their daughter (and them) some of these difficulties if they had waited a few weeks before taking away Rebecca's pacifier, instead of doing it when they first got back from California. Children need their usual supports when they reenter after a trip. It helps them get back to their old routine. Rebecca's pacifier wasn't a prop because it wasn't something she depended on her parents to provide—she was old enough to put it back in her mouth when it popped out. Nor was she walking around with it during the day. In other words, there was no urgency to make her give it up at that moment. However, I don't think taking away Rebecca's pacifier *caused* this child to "forget" how to put herself to sleep. Rather, it was the fact that while they were away, Mum probably didn't, or couldn't, stick to her regular bedtime, and other aspects of her routine were most likely disrupted as well.

Then, to make matters worse, Rebecca's parents "let her cry," which sounds to me like they were trying to get her to sleep with a controlled crying method. Here was a child who formerly had good sleep habits, whose routine was disrupted, and they not only took her pacifier away, they changed the rules. Of course, Rebecca would have come down with the flu anyway, but at least it wouldn't have felt like a double whammy.

The plan in this case would involve going back to basics. Rebecca's parents may have to use P.U./P.D. to help her regain her sleep skills, but they should not abandon her in the name of making her more independent. It's important, too, for these parents to realize that there are times when pure and simple soothing is called for. When a child is in pain, is frightened, is off-kilter because of unusual circumstances, she *needs* her parents to be there for her.

Designing a Plan: The Twelve Principles of Problem Solving

When you are faced with a "just-when" situation, take a deep breath. Ask yourself the Twelve Essential Questions, and look at the situation through the eyes of an objective parent (see pages 309–312). Then, consider the Twelve Principles of Problem Solving as you design a plan of action. Most of these guidelines will seem familiar if you've read this book from the beginning. It's not rocket science. Rather, it's a matter of using your common sense and thinking things through.

1. *Identify the root—or roots—of the problem.* Ask yourself the Twelve Essential Questions. If you answer them honestly, you should have a good sense of what is affecting your child at this point in time.

The Twelve Principles of Problem Solving

1. Identify the root—or roots—of the problem.
2. Figure out what to handle first.
3. Go back to basics.
4. Accept what you can't change.
5. Decide whether this solution is good for the long run.
6. Comfort your child when he needs it.
7. Stay in charge.
8. Always go *to* your child rather than bringing him to you.
9. Commit yourself to your plan.
10. Be a P.C. parent.
11. Take care of yourself.
12. Learn from the experience.

---

2. *Figure out what to handle first.* Often, it will be the most pressing issue. For instance, if your child wakes three nights in a row because he's been teething, or from a cold or a gastrointestinal condition, he might be developing a bad sleep habit. But you have to ease the pain first. Likewise, if you've tried a controlled crying method and your child screams suddenly at the sight of her crib, you have to reestablish trust (see pages 192–195) before you deal with the fact that she doesn't know how to send herself off to sleep.

In some cases, it makes sense to handle the easiest issue first, just to get it out of the way. So let's say you've been at your parents' vacation beach home where the whole family converges every summer. Your toddler has been staying up until 9 or 10 P.M. every night, and now, back at home, he expects similar privileges. He has also learned how to be more aggressive from playing with his older cousins, tricks he's now trying out on his play group friends. You need to deal with his behavior of course, but reestablishing an early bedtime is the simpler matter.

3. *Go back to basics.* You know how, in Monopoly, one card tells you "Go directly to jail—do not pass Go." Sometimes parenting is like that. You have to start back at Square One. Once you analyze your problem, you can look at why and how you strayed from your initial plan, and base your new strategy on correcting your course. If you've ignored your child's temperament, tailor your plan to suit her nature. If your routine has gone astray, remember E.A.S.Y. If you've used P.U./P.D. in the past to teach your child how to go to sleep independently, and the sleep problem has mysteriously reappeared a few weeks later, go back to what you know works.

4. *Accept what you can't change.* I'm very fond of the *Serenity Prayer:* "God grant me the serenity to accept the things I cannot change, the courage to change the things I can, and the wisdom to know the difference." A host of just-when situations calls for acceptance. Your child is upset because you've just gone back to working outside your home, and puts up a battle every time you leave . . . but you need the money. You're disappointed that your child is less social than you . . . but that's who your child is. You're tired of being the only one who says "no" to your child, and you've made several attempts to get your

partner more involved . . . but she's a workaholic, and you're at home. Your child has suddenly started head-banging . . . but you've been told by your pediatrician to ignore it. None of these situations are easy to accept—you're going to want to get in there and do something. But sometimes you have to back off, and let time be the fixer.

5. ***Decide whether this solution is good for the long run.*** If you don't start as you mean to go on, you're likely to start accidental parenting. If a solution is more of a Band-Aid than a long-term fix, or if it asks more of you than of your child (for instance, you have to keep running in all night to put a pacifier back in your child's mouth), you might want to reconsider.

6. ***Comfort your child when he needs it.*** In any just-when situation, your child might need an extra bit of love from you. Growth spurts, greater mobility, getting out in the world, teething, a cold—any of these things can throw a child's routine off-kilter. It's important not to slip into accidental parenting, but your child also needs to know that you're there to catch him when he falls (literally!). Comforting is a compassionate act that gives a child a sense of security.

7. ***Stay in charge.*** Even if you haven't quite figured out what to do, don't allow your child to become Ruler of the House. If your child is ailing, it's understandable to feel sad, worried, and bad for her. As I stress above, you offer her that extra bit of comforting. But don't go overboard and give her anything she wants or let her have free rein over the household. You'll certainly regret it, because your family life will be chaotic. Even worse, she might turn out to be the kind of child that other parents and children try to avoid.

8. ***Always go*** to ***your child rather than bringing him to you.*** If he's very ill, and you're worried, bring a blow-up bed into his room (see pages 279–280 and Elliott's story, beginning on page 281). I've also known parents to sleep on the floor next to the crib. Believe me, a few nights of your discomfort is better than weeks, or months, of undoing your child's bad habit.

9. ***Commit yourself to your plan.*** Don't give up if your plan doesn't seem to work right away, or if suddenly your child regresses to the old pattern or behavior. I've seen it time and again: Parents are always tempted to try something new. That not only confuses their child, it rarely works.

10. **Be a P.C. parent.** Patience and consciousness are the keys to seeing a plan through. Especially if you have a several-part plan—let's say you're dealing with a sleep problem *and* an eating issue—do each step slowly. You can't rush the process.

11. **Take care of yourself.** Think of the directions given on airplanes when the flight attendant reviews safety procedures: "If you're traveling with a small child, place the oxygen mask over your face first and then take care of your child." It's the same with everyday parenting. If you can't breathe, how can you care for and guide your child?

12. **Learn from the experience.** Just-when situations often repeat themselves, albeit with a slightly different twist. Make a mental note of the issues that came up and how you dealt with them. Even better, write it all down. You might start to see patterns—for example, that you often get into trouble when you don't fully prepare your child for an upcoming event, or that your child is always out of sorts after a play date. That doesn't mean you stay home all the time. Rather, take steps next time to prepare and thereby minimize the disturbance. Shorten visits with other children; pick more easygoing play partners.

In these final pages, I illustrate how the Twelve Principles of Problem Solving are applied to everyday parenting dilemmas. You'll see that in some just-when situations, only three or four of them come into play. However, the first example, "Dorian's Dilemma," required using almost every one of the principles (which are indicated in italics and highlighted in a little box in the margins). Bear with me, luv: It's a bit long and involved, but this case exemplifies the complexity of so many that I've dealt with—and the reason that parents often don't know where to begin.

Dorian's Dilemma: "Suddenly Rebellious All of the Time"

Although many just-when problems *feel* as if they've come up "overnight," invariably a variety of factors have converged. Dorian's email, sent initially to an online mothers' group, captures this complexity.

> Our 20-month-old son, Andrew, who was always very active and intrepid, seems to have made a really sharp change in these past

few days. Suddenly the only word he uses is "NO!" He wants to do everything by himself, gets really upset if I try to help him, and is totally rebellious all the time. Throwing food on the floor or objects at us is also something new. It's not that he wasn't doing those things before, but he seems more determined and energetic while doing it. He's totally aware that even though we're telling him to stop, he keeps doing it. He challenges us all the time. I'm sending this email because I am scared about my own reaction to it. The other day, I got really angry at him for the first time and felt I was losing my cool. Part of it is because I just learned I am pregnant again, and wondered if that was the reason for all this (I didn't tell my son yet, as I am too early into the pregnancy). I have the feeling these are typical early signs of the "terrible twos" coming up, but I'm puzzled with the change being so sudden, as I thought it was going to happen more gradually. Wondering if any of you went through this kind of process, and how did you manage to keep your cool?

Mum is right: Andrew is approaching a very significant developmental period—the twos. Negativity and obstinance go with the territory (see page 303). And yes, this type of change can definitely happen overnight, just as she describes. In addition, I suspect that Andrew's parents probably have not dealt with their son's temperament. Although Dorian describes Andrew as "always very active and intrepid" and admits, "It's not that he wasn't doing those things before," she may not recognize that this is who Andrew is—and this is what she has to work with. When you have a Spirited child, as Andrew is, it's even more important than ever that his parents stay in control in a very loving, gentle manner But when parents placate, cajole, and ultimately keep giving in to a demanding child, whether they do it in the name of keeping the peace or of making their child happy, it's a form of accidental parenting. Their reaction only reinforces the child's testing behavior, and when the twos come along, he turns into a tornado. If they also laughed at his antics—perhaps because the first time he asserted himself they though it was "cute"—they inadvertently rewarded him. Even if it just happened once, children then give repeat performances, several times a day, hoping to get another laugh. But now no one thinks it's very funny.

> Find the root—or roots—of your problem

Reading between the lines, then, it's clear to me that several factors contribute to Andrew's "new" behavior: his development, his parents' reaction to his temperament, and accidental parenting. Dorian's pregnancy, an impending change in the family environment, is also a factor. Andrew may not know about the baby per se, but he's definitely picking up on his mother's anxiety. Also, *her reaction* to his behavior is definitely heightened because of all the changes in her mind and body that pregnancy ushers in. Hence, a plan to deal with this just-when crisis has to take all those factors into consideration and undo the accidental parenting that's happened until now.

Andrew's behavior is clearly the main event, so it's not hard to figure out where to start. He's out of control, and it's not just because he's about to turn two. I have a hunch that neither Dorian nor her husband have set consistent limits for their son. If that's true, it's going to be harder now to rein Andrew in—but certainly not impossible (and easier than when he's a teenager!). Even though it's very (very) tiring, both parents have to hold the line.

Figure out what to handle first

Andrew's parents need to see themselves as his first teachers, and to view "discipline" not in terms of punishment—rather, as a way of helping him understand what's right and wrong, acceptable and unacceptable. As long as he or anyone around him is not threatened by his acting out, they should not reward him with attention. For instance, if he screams at Dorian, she would say in a quiet voice, "I won't talk to you when you yell like that." But she has to *mean* it—and demonstrate to him that she does by ignoring him until he talks nicely to her. Likewise, if Andrew is in his high chair and starts throwing food, *every time he does it,* his parents have to immediately take him out and say, "No throwing food." Wait a few minutes and try again. When he's back in the high chair, if he does it again, they have to take him out. If Andrew hurls a toy, they have to tell him it's wrong. If he's in the midst of a tantrum, Dorian should gently take him by the hand, sit him down on her lap or in front of her with his back to her, and say, "I'll sit here with you until you calm down." Even if Andrew tries to up the ante by kicking, hitting, and screaming even louder, Dorian can't back down.

Go back to basics

Stay in charge

Until now, Andrew's parents have been using quick fixes to get through the day. They now have to take a long-term perspective. Admittedly, this is hard given Andrew's constant challenges to their authority. Still, they have to push themselves even when they're too tired to disci-

Decide whether this solution is good for the long run

pline, stop themselves when they're so exasperated that it feels easier to give in, and continue to keep their eye on the future, even when it feels as if this just-when situation will never change.

Because Andrew is who he is—his temperament isn't going to change dramatically—his parents have to create an environment suited to their son's nature: Give him lots of opportunities for safe, vigorous activities. Get him outside, running, playing, discharging some of that hyper energy. Make play dates with other active and assertive children. Avoid outings where he's expected to sit still.

Andrew's parents also have to think of ways to anticipate and prevent future incidents. They should learn what his triggers are, what he looks like, and how he acts before he spins out of control. They need to make sure he never gets too hungry and, especially, too tired. He should wind down in the late afternoon, so he's not overtired for bed. Spirited children tend to be at their worst behaviorally when they're overstimulated or overtired (as are parents).

Because at least part of Andrew's misbehavior is designed to get his parents' attention, especially his mother's, Dorian needs to show her son that he can get her attention in positive ways. I'd suggest she look at how much real time she actually spends *with* him, without the phone ringing, the television blaring, or Mum catching up on chores at home. Children sense when we're not really "there." She might actually *schedule* certain times that Andrew knows will be dedicated solely to him. Make a fuss over this being his exclusive Mummy and me time—which will be important when the new baby comes, too. Dorian is a working mum (another factor she can't change), and her time is already stressed to the max, but if she carves out time in the morning or when she gets home from work and really spends time *with* Andrew, he might be a lot less demanding at other times. Both parents should also make an effort to catch Andrew when he's on good behavior and praise him for it. Also praise him for gaining control of his emotions ("Good job calming down, Andrew").

If Mum and Dad are really consistent, Andrew will definitely get the message—sooner or later—that his parents say what they mean and then do what they say. Dorian and her husband have to steel themselves against setbacks. Some days Andrew will be more cooperative, and on others it will seem as if he's taken a giant step backward. That's to be expected.

Accept what you
can't change

Learn from the
experience

Comfort your child
when he needs it

Commit yourself to
your plan

Mum and Dad have to watch their own behavior, too, especially Dorian, who admits that this just-when situation has almost pushed her over the edge. I'm not surprised that she's having trouble being patient with her son. She has a lot on her plate: full-time work, a toddler, and a new baby on the way. Still, she needs to keep these developmental ups and downs in perspective. If she remembers who her son is and tailors her strategies to maximize his strengths and play down his weaknesses, by age three most of his negativity and aggression will diminish. She needs to be more conscious, too. With Spirited children, clear signs usually precede an eruption—the child starts talking louder or yelling, becomes more frenzied or angry, starts grabbing things. She needs to catch him before runaway emotions get the best of him and he becomes physically more aggressive (see also pages 324–332). By observing Andrew carefully, distracting him, and giving him choices that *she* approves of, Dorian might even be able to, as they say, head off trouble at the pass.

Be a P.C. parent

Finally, Dorian has to look at herself. What with her raging hormones and her concern about Andrew, it's not surprising that she would "lose her cool." The problem is, her anger will make Andrew even more difficult; you don't meet force with force if you want things to calm down. Dorian has to give as much weight to the "Y" in E.A.S.Y. as she does the other letters. Get her hubby, her parents, and her friends to give her a daily break. Even a few minutes just for herself will enable her to get a second wind and be more careful about how she responds to Andrew. Otherwise, she will set up a very negative pattern with him, a constant battle of wills.

Take care of yourself

Post-Recovery Blues: "We Can't Get Back to Normal"

When a child is ailing or something bad happens to him, and he has to be nursed through recovery, parents often find it hard to regain their footing. Illness, surgery, and accidents are often the most trying kinds of just-when situations. You understandably feel for your child and want to comfort him. You're worried that he'll never recover, even if it's just teething, which every child goes through. All the same, the challenge is to walk that fine line between taking care of him and not allowing yourself to fall prey to the "poor-baby" syndrome, which almost always leads to accidental parenting.

And then, once the crisis is over, not only are you stuck with new behaviors and bad habits, you also don't know how to reestablish your routine and "get back to the way it was," as Linda, the mother of ten-month-old Stuart, put it when she asked for my help.

I met Linda and her husband, George, a lovely couple from Yorkshire, on a recent trip home. Linda explained that when Stuart started to teethe he was around eight months old. Like many children who teethe, he had a runny nose, loose stools, was generally miserable during the day, and woke repeatedly at night. Linda walked and rocked him to sleep every night. By the time his first tooth popped in a few weeks later, Stuart was so used to being walked and rocked that every time either parent tried to lay him in his crib, Stuart would clutch on for dear life. She started making excuses for Stuart's clinginess. "He's not himself" or "It's his teeth coming in." Meanwhile, she was becoming a prisoner in her own home.

Because Stuart suddenly seemed fearful of his crib, but only at night, Linda assumed his problem was night terrors. I asked, "What did you do when he first started teething?" Linda didn't miss a beat: "Oh, the poor little thing. At first, I didn't even realize it was his teeth. I thought it was a cold. I figured he was so cranky and out of sorts because he wasn't getting enough sleep. But then he was so upset it seemed like he was terrified of something."

I knew immediately that Linda had the poor-baby syndrome (see page 247). She felt horrid that she hadn't recognized Stuart's teething earlier. In her mind, she was a "bad mother." Although some ten-month-olds have bad dreams, I was pretty sure that this was a case of tough teething—some children have it rougher than others—and a guilty mother. For his part, George was fed up with his wife pacing up and down outside their son's room every night. "We can't have an evening together," he complained, "because even when Stuart is asleep, she's got an ear to the door, worrying that he'll wake up."

It wasn't hard to decide what to do first in this case: relieve Stuart's pain. I told his parents to get him Baby Motrin and to apply a teething cream, like Orajel, to numb his gums. Once he was more comfortable, we could get his sleep patterns back on track. Getting back to the basics, I suggested P.U./P.D., and stressed that George should handle it. When a mother has the poor-baby syndrome, I almost always prefer to take her out of the equation and let the father at least start the P.U./P.D. process.

It gives Mum a rest, makes Dad feel like he's got an important role (which he does), and we don't risk Mum caving in because she feels sorry for the little lad.

George followed my directions for doing P.U./P.D. to the letter, and although the first night was hell—Stuart was up every two hours—Dad stayed with it. "I couldn't believe how great he was," said an amazed Linda the next day, admitting that she would have given up the first time Stuart grabbed her. "George was exhausted but beaming." Watching her husband that night and the next (I always suggest that couples alternate every two nights when using P.U./P.D. to deal with a sleep issue; see pages 258–259) enabled Linda to have the courage to see P.U./P.D. through. Within a week, Stuart slept through the night.

Like many mums in cases like this, Linda asked me, "Will I have to go through this *again* when he gets his next tooth?" I told her that she might, but she ought to learn from the experience, because if Stuart is ever sick or has a childhood injury, she's likely to face the same dilemma. "If you resort to the old prop," I warned, "you'll be right back where you started."

Sudden Fears: "She's Afraid of the Tub"

Maya called because eleven-month-old Jade mysteriously started balking when it was time for a bath. "She used to love the water," Maya insisted, "ever since she was a baby. Now she screams when I put her in, and she absolutely won't sit down." This is a common, though not very serious, problem. Still, it's upsetting to many parents, which is why I include it here.

When a child suddenly becomes afraid of the tub, nine times out of ten, it's because something scared her. She slipped under the water, soap got in her eyes, she touched a hot faucet. She'll need time to trust again. Don't wash her hair for a few nights, so that soap isn't an issue. (Babies and young toddlers don't really get very dirty!) If she slipped under, that's terrifying. Try taking a bath *with* her to make her feel more secure. If she is unwilling to get into the tub even with you, give her sponge baths for a few weeks.

If it didn't happen on your watch, talk to others who bathe her. It could be that the tub itself feels big to a little girl, or she hears echoes of her own voice, which can be scary to a small child. If that's the case, you'd see her babbling and then suddenly stop, her eyes widening, as if to say, *What's that?*

Finally, it also could be because your child is overtired by the time she gets into the tub, which could cause fearfulness or intensify it. As children get older, more interactive with their toys and people, the bathtub experience turns into what one mother on my website referred to as "the bathtub party"—a wild orgy of splashing in the tub and soaking whoever is giving the bath. Some children can handle this level of activity, but for others, the bathtub party is too stimulating. If that's the case, it might be wise to change her routine, giving her a bath when she's less exhausted (see Carlos's story, page 275).

If you can't determine why your child is frightened, go back to the basics. Reintroduce her to the tub slowly, and keep it low key. Give her new bath toys to entice her (not necessarily toys you buy, but colorful cups and pitchers). If she's really frightened, start with a free-standing infant tub, and allow her to stand outside it and splash while you sponge her off. Tell her, "This is where I washed you when you were a baby." Let her sit in the tub if she wants. When she's more comfortable in the bathroom, run a bath in the big tub but fill it with only a few inches of water. Allow her to stand in it. Never force a child to sit down in the tub if she's frightened. It may take several months, but she will get over it.

Stranger Anxiety: "The Baby-Sitter Couldn't Console Him"

Vera called in a tizzy recently. I'd known her since nine-month-old Sean was a baby. "Tracy, I'm afraid he's changing," she said. "I've never seen him act like this."

"Like what?" I asked, wondering what prompted Vera's call. Sean was a very mellow chap. We were able to get him onto a good routine straightaway, and though his mum called every now and then to report his progress, she rarely had any questions or concerns.

"Last night we went out to dinner and left Sean with a sitter—something we've done many times before without incident. When we were halfway through the meal, my cell phone rang. The sitter, a sweet and very capable woman whom I had met at a friend's house, called to say that Sean had woken up. She tried to coax him back to sleep, using the words I had suggested: 'It's okay, Sean, just go back to sleep.' But, she said, he took one look at her and started screaming louder than before. Nothing she did calmed him down—not rocking, not reading a book, not even turning on the television. We ended up coming home after the shrimp cocktail. Luckily we were only a few minutes away, but he was in a frenzy when we got there. He practically leaped into my arms, and it took no time for me to calm him down.

"Poor Mrs. Grey. She said she'd never had a child take such a disliking to her in all the years she'd been dealing with babies and toddlers. What was going on, Tracy? I realize that she was a new sitter, but it's not the first time we've used someone new. Do you think Sean is developing separation anxiety?"

Her theory was reasonable. Many babies develop separation anxiety at this age (see pages 80–83). However, when we went over the Twelve Essential Questions, it was clear that this was an isolated incident. Sean wasn't clinging to his mother. He could play on his own for forty-five minutes or longer. And he was fine when Vera left the house to do grocery shopping and he stayed behind with Alice, the cleaning woman who had worked in the house long before he was born and now sometimes baby-sat as well. Then I remembered that this was the first time Mrs. Grey sat for Vera. "Had Sean spent a little time with Mrs. Grey before you went out?" I asked.

"No, how could he?" Vera asked, not seeing what I was getting at. "We put Sean to bed at seven as usual. When Mrs. Grey arrived, we showed her around. I told her what to do if Sean woke up. I figured, though, that he probably would sleep straight through."

But of course, Sean *did* wake up. Just when you think your child is going to sleep while you're out for the evening, he doesn't! Making matters worse—and causing his panic—he woke up to a stranger's face. Perhaps a bad dream woke him initially (a possibility at nine months), or the movement of his legs disturbed his sleep (he was just starting to cruise). Whatever it was, he did not expect to see Mrs. Grey when he opened his eyes.

"But he's never done that in the past," Vera protested. "We don't have a steady sitter, so he's had to get used to a string of different faces." I explained to Vera that her little boy was growing up. When he was younger, almost all adult faces (except hers) were pretty much interchangeable. Waking up to a new face didn't cause Sean to panic in his earlier months, because his baby brain didn't register the new person as "a stranger." But after eight or nine months, the neurological circuitry starts to mature. The same development that's responsible for separation anxiety also gives children a fear of unfamiliar people. Even if Mrs. Grey smiled and cuddled Sean, she was still a stranger, so he was frightened.

The moral of this story is threefold: One, eliminate "never" from your vocabulary. How many times have parents eaten their words after saying, "He *never* wakes up" or "She *never* has a meltdown when we're in public."

Two, put yourself in your child's booties, and imagine a situation from his point of view. Vera should have introduced Mrs. Grey to Sean earlier, perhaps had her baby-sit one afternoon or even just come over for a short play visit, so that Sean could develop a relationship with her. That way, he wouldn't have been taken by surprise.

Three, learn about your child's developmental stages. I don't believe in measuring your child's progress against a chart, but it's a good idea to have a general sense of his mental and emotional capabilities. Babies and toddlers almost always grasp more than their parents realize. Parents so often have the attitude that their child is "just a baby"—he won't remember . . . he doesn't understand . . . he can't tell the difference. And they're usually dead wrong.

The Alignment of the Planets

So you've gone through all the questions and the strategies in this book, and you still can't figure out why your baby has suddenly decided that it's playtime at 4 A.M. every night or why your toddler stopped liking oatmeal after a year of it being his favorite food. Well, luv, I've tried to address all the problems you've told me about in person, over the phone, and via email. I've highlighted all the questions I'd ask in order to come up with a plan of action. And I've given you all of the secret strategies stored in my underground vault. If you're still at a loss, you might as well blame the alignment of the planets. Perhaps Mercury is in retrograde. To be sure, with all we do and all we know, sometimes there's simply no reason why yesterday's excellent solution is useless in the face of today's dilemma. Besides, if you just wait it out, I guarantee that a new, more pressing issue soon will be staring you in the face!

INDEX